HAITI, NICARAGUA,
SHANGHAI, PEARL HARBOR, PELELIU,
GUADALCANAL, KOREA.

THE FABULOUS GENERAL CHESTY

"He shouted battle orders in a bellow that rattled the halls of Montezuma. He stalked about under enemy fire as though he were daring anyone to hit him. He had an abiding love for the enlisted man who did the killing and the dying, and a sneering hatred for the staff officer who did the sitting and the meddling. He thrived on combat until he became a legend to his troops . . . a born leader who went off to battle with his green eyes gleaming malevolently, a stubby pipe clenched in his crooked mouth and a copy of Caesar's *Gallic Wars* tucked into his duffel bag."

—*Time*

MARINE!

THE ACTION-PACKED SAGA OF THE MOST DECORATED
HERO IN THE HISTORY OF THE U.S. MARINES.

MARINE!

The Life of Lt. Gen. Lewis B. (Chesty) Puller, USMC (Ret.)

By Burke Davis

BANTAM BOOKS · LONDON · TORONTO · NEW YORK

MARINE! THE LIFE OF CHESTY PULLER

*A Bantam Book / published by arrangement with
Little, Brown and Company, Inc.*

PRINTING HISTORY

Little, Brown edition published February 1962
2nd printing ... February 1962
3rd printing .... May 1962
Serialized in MARINE CORPS GAZETTE
Bantam edition / July 1964

2nd printing .... *August 1964*	*5th printing* ... *January 1973*
3rd printing .... *August 1968*	*6th printing* .. *February 1973*
4th printing .... *August 1970*	*7th printing* .. *December 1977*

ISBN 0-553-11420-4

Published simultaneously in the United States and Canada

PRINTED IN THE UNITED STATES OF AMERICA

ACKNOWLEDGMENTS

THE AUTHOR ACKNOWLEDGES with gratitude the following, who did so much to make this book possible:

Henry Adams, San Diego, Calif.; Thomas H. Barry, Evanston, Ill.; Miss Lucille Bland, West Point, Va.; John A. Blazer, Madison, Tenn.; Mr. & Mrs. Jan Bodey, Paramount, Calif.; Mrs. Rose Altizer Bray, West Point, Va.; Ralph M. Briggs, Jr., Griffin, Ga.; W. R. Broaddus, Martinsville, Va.; Maj. Charles H. Brush, Jr., USMC, Quantico, Va.; Leon Brusiloff, Chevy Chase, Md.; Adm. Arleigh Burke, USN, Ret.; Maj. George Chambers, USMC, Camp Lejeune, N.C.; Col. Parker R. Colmer, Industrial College of the Armed Forces, Washington, D.C.; Col. David F. Condon, Military Court of Appeals, Washington, D.C.; Zach D. Cox, Mount Olive, N.C.; Sgt. Robert Cornely, USMC, Quantico, Va.; Lt. Gen. E. A. Craig, USMC, Ret., El Cajon, Calif.; PFC Paul Curtis, USMC, Camp Lejeune, N.C.

Maj. Lew Devine, USMC, Quantico, Va.; Robert Dutro, Yorktown, Va.; William Evans, Richmond, Va.; Maj. Don Ezell, USMC, Quantico, Va.; David Feild, Georgetown, S.C.; John deSparre, King William Courthouse, Va.; William Ferrigno, Winter Park, Fla.; Maj. Joseph Fisher, Sgt. Carl Fulgenzi, and Col. Regan Fuller, all of USMC, Washington, D.C.; Ambassador James Gavin, Paris, France.

Peter Hackes, National Broadcasting Company, Washington, D.C.; James M. Hayes, Jr., Winston-Salem, N.C.; Henry Heming, New York City; William B. Hopkins, Roanoke, Va.; Peter Hoyt, Fort Worth, Texas; Col. C. W. Kelly, Jr., USMC, Camp Lejeune, N.C.; Sgt. Mike Kolomy, USMC, Philadelphia, Pa.; Col. Edmund H. Lang, U.S. Army Corps of Engineers, Vicksburg, Miss.; Col. William Lee, USMC, Ret., Quantico, Va.; E. E. Linsert, Alexandria, Va.; Capt. John B. Lippard, USMC, Camp Lejeune, N.C.; W/O William E. Lisenby, USMC, Jacksonville, Fla.; Maj. Gen. Homer Litzenberg, USMC, Ret., Washington, D.C.; John Loomis, Arroyo Grande, Calif.; Maj. Gen. Frank E. Lowe, USA, Ret., Harrison, Me.; O. T. Lussier, Pasadena, Calif.

George McMillan, Aiken, S.C.; Miss Helen Mahar, Pictorial Branch, Headquarters, USMC; John V. Mather, Belmont, New South Wales, Australia; Maj. Gen. Armistead D. Mead, USA, Washington, D.C.; Brig. Gen. John C. Miller, Jr., Quantico, Va.; Col. W. M. Miller, head, and Lynn Montross, of Historical Branch, USMC, Washington, D.C.; Rear Adm. Leo W. Nilon, USN, Ret., Washington, D.C.; Sgt. Maj. R. L. Norrish, USMC, Ret., Brooklyn, N.Y.; Sgt. Harvey Owens, USMC, Quantico, Va.

Sgt. William Pennington, USMC, Greensboro, N.C.; Sgt. Robert Pratt, USMC, Camp Lejeune, N.C.; Dr. Thomas G. Pullen, Jr., Baltimore, Md.; Maj. W. C. Reeves, USMC, Ret., Jacksonville, N.C.; Gen. Matthew B. Ridgway, USA, Ret., Pittsburgh, Pa.; Louise Rowe, librarian, Camp Lejeune, N.C.; Mrs. R. A. Rowland, Los Angeles, Calif.; Richard Rowland, Downey, Calif.; Harold L. Ryan, Westfield, N.J.

Margaret Sanborn, Mill Valley, Calif.; Maj. David Schwulst, curator, Marine Corps Museum, Quantico, Va.; Lt. Col. Frank W. Sheppard, USMC, Ret., Hemet, Calif.; H. W. Shoemaker, Troutdale, Ore.; W/O E. W. Smith, USMC, Camp Lejeune, N.C.; Eugene F. Smith, Philadelphia, Pa.; Gen. Oliver P. Smith, USMC, Ret., Los Altos Hills, Calif.; Brig. Gen. F. A. Stevens, USMC, Ret., Melrose, Mass.; Maj. Ray Stiles, USMC, Quantico, Va.; Maj. James Treadwell, USMC, Camp Lejeune, N.C.; Richard Tregaskis, Santa Monica, Calif.

Gen. A. H. Turnage, USMC, Ret., Alexandria, Va.; Gen. A. A. Vandegrift, USMC, Ret., Delray Beach, Fla., Diggory Venn, Boston, Mass.; Col. John M. Virden, USAF, Ret., Chevy Chase, Md.; Brig. Gen. Lewis Walt, USMC, Washington, D.C.; Wilcomb E. Washburn, Smithsonian Institution, Washington, D.C.; Adm. O. D. Waters, USN, Ret.; Gerald White, Geneva, N.Y.; W. B. Winterberg, Washington, D.C.; Percy Wood, The Chicago *Tribune*, Chicago, Ill.; Maj. Lyle Worster, USMC, Quantico, Va.; Maj. Robert Wray, USMC, Washington, D.C.; Maj. Gen. E. K. Wright, USA, Ret., Pebble Beach, Calif.

AUTHOR'S NOTE

GENERAL PULLER'S story seems to me one of the great narratives of our military history, as well as one of the most instructive. Surely no modern American general, even in retirement, has been so candid in his criticism of our military posture, policy, aims and equipment.

This book is as much a memoir as a biography, for it rests largely on a long series of interviews with General Puller and a lengthy study of his official record—buttressed by recollections of hundreds of others who have known him from childhood to the end of his military career, most of whom were interviewed by me.

General Puller's prodigious memory is often relied upon, and in matters large and small his point of view is taken; controversial points are not examined from every side, and thus this does not pretend to be an objective history of the many campaigns in which he fought.

Marine Corps Headquarters made this task easier by providing access to the Puller files—probably the most voluminous in the Corps records—and to other official papers and photographs. Mrs. John W. Thomason, of Huntsville, Texas, kindly granted permission to use a letter by her late husband.

The book was proposed by Charles R. Sanders, Jr., of Raleigh, N.C., a veteran of the Korean War, to whom I am deeply grateful. I also owe special debts of gratitude to the Puller family, including Miss Pattie Leigh Puller of Richmond, Va., and also to Generals J. P. Berkeley and E. W. Snedeker of the Marine Corps, to Dr. Edward L. Smith of Twentynine Palms, Calif., to Sgt. Orville Jones of the 3rd Marine Division, Okinawa, and to Gerald White, Geneva, N.Y.

In addition to those listed in the Acknowledgments, I must express my appreciation to my editor, John A. S. Cushman, to Carlisle H. Humelsine, Donald J. Gonzales, Mrs. Virginia Roseberg and Miss Roberta Smith of Colonial Williamsburg in Virginia, and to my wife and children.

Burke Davis
Coke-Garrett House
Williamsburg, Va.

CONTENTS

THERE was a snowstorm in the morning. It screened Chinese foxholes on hills above the perimeter and muffled artillery fire from the road to the pass, where the First Marine Division was fighting its way to the south.

It was December 8, 1950, on the frozen plateau of Koto-ri in the North Korean mountains. The troops were the First Marine Regiment, rear guard in one of the tragedies of American military history.

A funeral was in progress.

The thermometer by the commander's tent stood at 25° below zero at dawn, when the first men tried to dig graves; their picks were useless in the iron-hard earth. Dynamite crews set off blasts, but the earth heaved up in enormous black blocks of ice. The commander halted them.

More than a hundred bodies waited in a row of tents, stiffly frozen, stacked like cordwood. "They'll stay like that until the spring thaw," the commander said, "but we can't leave them to the wild dogs. Blast out those potato cellars."

When the holes had been opened the officer called in a battalion of tanks for the burial, for there was no other way. The beams of the headlights were lost in the swirling snow and the roaring of the motors was carried away in the wind as the tanks made the graves. Back and forth, crunching icy blocks of earth upon the frozen bodies, the tanks buried the dead.

The commander was Colonel Lewis Burwell Puller, fifty-two years old, thirty-two years a U. S. Marine. He was in the process of winning his fifth Navy Cross—the nation's

second highest military award; no other Marine had won
so many.

He was not a large man, but his slight, spare frame was
erect to the limit of its five feet ten inches; the great thrust
of his chest was obvious beneath the bulky uniform. The
face was seamed and brown, as roughhewn as a totem
pole. Beneath an ancient cap the almond-shaped eyes glint-
ed green. The Colonel gripped a short pipe in his teeth as
if he were on the point of gulping it down. His voice carried
over the wind and down the rows of shuddering canvas like
a Navy bullhorn. Among themselves, he was known to the
men of the Corps only as Chesty Puller.

The Commandant of the Marine Corps had lately spoken
of Colonel Puller: "He's about the only man in the Corps
who really loves to fight. I'll go further: He's the only man in
any of our services who loves fighting."

For two weeks Puller had commanded the rear of the First
Marine Division, cut off in the Chosin Reservoir region by
hundreds of thousands of Chinese Communist troops. The
Colonel was visiting a hospital tent where a priest admin-
istered last rites to Marine wounded when a messenger came:

"Sir, do you know they've cut us off? We're entirely surrounded."

"Those poor bastards," Puller said. "They've got us
right where we want 'em. We can shoot in every direction
now."

There had been last-minute reinforcements, a battalion of
U. S. Army troops which fought its way through the enemy
with heavy losses. Its colonel reported to Puller for orders.

"Take your position along those hills and have your men dig
in."

"Yes, sir. Now, where is my line of retreat?"

Puller's voice became slow and hard: "I'm glad you asked
me that. Now I know where you stand. Wait one minute."
He took a field telephone and called his tank commander.
The Army officer listened to the Marine order:

"I've got a new outfit," Puller said. He gave its position
in detail. "If they start to pull back from that line, even one
foot, I want you to open fire on them." He hung up the
telephone and turned to the Army officer:

"Does that answer your question?"

The last plane flew out in the afternoon through a momentary gap in the clouds; it carried nineteen wounded through the falling snow, the last of twenty-five hundred who had been flown to safety. The rear guard prepared to join the withdrawal.

Puller countermanded part of his orders from his superiors. "Abandon vehicles, they say, and destroy supplies! To hell with all that. Don't leave a thing that will roll or we can carry. Take every scrap you can. We'll take out more trucks than we brought, thanks to the Army. Can you imagine—going off and leaving 'em with the keys still in the locks?"

The Colonel sought his jeep driver, Sergeant Orville Jones. "Load up with the rest of the dead and wounded. But look 'em over close. Make sure they're Marines before you take 'em."

Jones began his work. He lashed the body of a young tank commander to the front bumper; other bodies went across the top. Wounded men crawled inside until the small vehicle could hold no more. The sergeant nosed his way into the stream of traffic on the slippery road to the pass.

Puller left on foot at 3 P.M., when only the reconnaissance company remained behind to face a last barrage of Chinese mortar shells. The Colonel walked to the pass. Three hours later when Sergeant Jones removed the commander's boots he found that the feet were beginning to freeze. The felt pads of the boots ripped with the sound of tearing cloth. Jones put Puller into the heated jeep, but within a few minutes the Colonel was walking again, rotating with other officers and men. He walked most of the way down the long miles to safety.

He stopped often to herd men together by squads, platoons and companies: "You're the First Marine Division—and don't you forget it. We're the greatest military outfit that ever walked on this earth. Not all the Communists in hell can stop you. We'll go down to the sea at our own pace and nothing is going to get in our way. If it does, we'll blow hell out of it."

When he found men of his own regiment he growled more deeply: "You're the finest regiment in the finest division in history. We're not retreating! We've about-faced to get at more of those bastards. Be proud you're First Marines."

The column made slow progress down the road, which snaked its way along the flanks of hills. It halted for stalled vehicles or Communist attacks, but until daylight faded, planes flew cover overhead, and when the enemy was visible they bombed and strafed the hillsides. At Funichilin Pass, the crest of the road, engineers had dropped into place a steel bridge frame, its 2500-pound sections delivered by parachute. The tanks barely scraped across, and the column moved on. When the rear guard had passed, the bridge was blown.

Marines estimated that at least a hundred thousand of the miserable Korean civilians crowded the road in the rear, huddled, pressing as near as they dared, held back only by warning shots. Puller's final instructions to the commander of the last unit had been almost savage:

"Don't let those civilians press in on you. The crowd is full of Chinese troops. Whatever happens, shoot to kill if they come close. Don't be misled by their innocent look—those devils will push women and children ahead of them, and if they get among the tanks we may lose the whole end of the column."

Puller was not content until the young lieutenant repeated the order to him: "Keep the road clear if we have to kill 'em all."

The Colonel's last glimpse of the rear was the pathetic refugee pack, half-frozen in its rags, dark unblinking eyes turned upon the last of the retreating Marines on the icy downhill road.

As he plodded around a bend the Colonel heard singing. Artillery fire interrupted and snow still pelted, but he made out the chanting of the Marine Hymn. There were popular songs, too, some of them as old as World War II. Puller passed the chorus, some Headquarters Company boys from the Northeastern states. One of them was Corporal Robert Pratt of Springfield, Massachusetts:

"All of us were singing at the tops of our voices. We had no idea the Old Man was anywhere around, until he bobbed up in the rear, the way he usually did. We were singing 'Carry Me Back to Old Virginny' when he passed us—none of us knew he was from Virginia. He grinned and waved at us and we howled a little louder, over the wind and the guns. The snow was beginning to peter out. He looked pleased with us, as if he thought we'd make it down the mountains okay."

A mile or so down the slope Puller got grim news: The tanks at the rear had been attacked. Chinese soldiers, pushing civilians ahead of them, had come from the crowd with hidden weapons, offering to surrender. The brave young lieutenant, wary but nervous, had gone to meet them. There had been fighting in the road, and a few grenades under tank treads had done the rest. There were casualties, but now the column inched on without half a dozen of its tanks.

The Colonel shouted to the next file: "All right, Marines! Remember who you are. Nobody ever fought with a better outfit. We're going to get on the beach, and get on some warm ships and eat hot food and get showers. Then we'll fight somewhere again. You're the First Marine Division!"

He walked the last miles to the trucks which waited far below. When he came to the port of Hungnam, under the guns of a waiting American fleet, the high command knew that the rear of the Division was safe.

Lewis Puller was one of the rarest of Marines, a onetime private who rose to become a lieutenant general. From a boyhood haunted by tales of his Confederate ancestors, his life had been one long preparation for war. He had lived through more than a hundred combats in the banana wars of Haiti and Nicaragua to win a grim nickname: *El Tigre*. He had been accused of paying bounty for the ears of native bandits.

He had commanded Horse Marines in Peking in the early 'thirties, and in Shanghai, on the eve of World War II, he had driven a superior force of Japanese troops from the American quarter at gun-point. He had been trained for battle as an infantryman, cavalryman, artilleryman, aviator and shipboard officer. He had led the first championship Marine drill team and had been famous as student and instructor in military schools.

In the first Allied offensive of World War II, at Guadalcanal, he had with one half-strength battalion saved Henderson Field by standing off a Japanese division. On that island his men had won two Medals of Honor, twenty-eight Navy Crosses and Silver Stars—and two hundred sixty-four Purple Hearts. He had been chosen by General George C. Marshall to tour American Army camps, to shatter the myth of Japanese invincibility and to bolster shaky morale in the United States.

At Cape Gloucester on New Britain he had taken over two confused and stalled battalions under fire and led them to swift victory. And at Peleliu he had suffered record casualties in defeating the Japanese in one of the most terrible of Marine battles.

Six years later he had been called from peacetime obscurity to lead ashore the assault at Inchon, where the tide began to turn in Korea.

At home in the village of Saluda, Virginia, Puller had a tangled mass of decorations in a cigar box, more than any other man in Corps history had won for valor in combat. Four of them were Navy Crosses. In the end there were to be over fifty in all, medals, ribbons, stars and palms covering the years since Parris Island during World War I.

His name was legend wherever Marines met in barracks and barrooms to swap tales, for no Marine had approached his twenty-seven years of foreign service or long exposure in combat, and no officer had become such a hero to men in the ranks. When Marines had talked of Lou Diamond or Gimlet Eye Butler or Bigfoot Brown or Pappy Boyington, there were always dozens of stories to be told about Chesty Puller. Incredibly, most of the tales were true.

In the recruit depot at San Diego, California, there were Marine drill sergeants who taught their men traditions of the Corps by assembling them for a final song before Taps. They sang to the tune of "Good Night, Ladies":

> Good night, Chesty! Good night, Chesty!
> Good night, Chesty—wherever you may be!
> After you the Corps will roll, Corps will roll,
>   Corps will rooooooll,
> After you the Corps will roll—on to victoreee!

FIRST LESSONS

LEWIS BURWELL PULLER was born June 26, 1898, into a small boy's paradise, the village of West Point, Virginia, where the Pamunkey and Mattaponi Rivers form the broad York. The waters were full of fish, crab and oysters and the woodlands teemed with game.

West Point was a carnival town in summer. Excursion trains from Richmond bore thousands to Beach Park, a few yards from the Puller home, where they swarmed the barrooms and gambling halls on the piers, rode the carousel and roller coaster, watched trained bears or spent noisy evenings in the skating rink and dance hall.

The village population was under a thousand and the Pullers were among its first families, a matter of some importance to Virginians. Lewis was the oldest son of Matthew M. Puller, a wholesale grocery salesman who spent most of his time on the road, in buggy or train. A grandfather, John W. Puller, had been killed with Jeb Stuart in a cavalry fight at Kellys Ford in the Civil War—a gallant death of which Lewis was often told.

The first Lewis Burwell, born in Bedfordshire in 1621, had come to Virginia as sergeant major of a county military company to establish a notable line which included many members of the colony's House of Burgesses. In contrast, there was also Lewis Burwell Williams of Orange, Virginia, a kinsman who had been expelled from Princeton in 1821 for taking part in a riot. The family preserved one document from this man, an order to a British merchant for one barrel of whisky, twelve decks of playing cards and one English Prayer Book.

7

There were many other noted relatives: Patrick Henry, Philip Ludwell, Robert Carter, John Grimes of the Governor's Council. One cousin, Page McCarthy, a Confederate captain, had fought the last legal duel in Virginia, killing his man over the reputation of a Richmond belle.

Lewis Puller's great-uncle, Robert Williams, a West Point graduate, deserted the South in the Civil War to command a Federal division at Gettysburg which fought against three of his brothers. The Virginia branch of the family never afterwards spoke to him, though he came to new renown by marrying the widow of Stephen A. Douglas.

Lewis Puller had another cousin who would become a famous soldier: George S. Patton.

When Lewis was less than two years old, he won a Beautiful Baby Contest in his village, and when a Richmond photographer chucked him under the chin in quest of a smile, he got for his pains a belligerent scowl which was to change little in a lifetime.

He was quieter than most boys, with a level, openly curious gaze; he kept his own counsel. At the age of four or five he broke an arm in a fall and when he visited the doctor some weeks later for removal of the cast, the physician shook his head, explained that the bones were crooked —and snapped them anew without warning. The boy grimaced but uttered no sound.

Lewis learned to read early and devoured books on war and warriors that might have been beyond his youthful grasp but for his impassioned interest in military life. He read G. A. Henty's adventure novels with a relish he seemed to lose in the schoolroom.

Matthew Puller died in 1908 after a long battle with cancer, cheerful to the end. He was an erect, gray-eyed and handsome man of medium height, a sporty dresser who liked Prince Alberts and bought custom-made shoes from the city, and carried a cane. He had little formal education; he had been raised on a farm by one of his father's cavalrymen after the Civil War. He drove himself to reading and was celebrated as a conversationalist, as well as a good man in a card game, like certain of his forebears.

Lewis and his younger brother Sam were not allowed to go to the funeral, but when their mother and two sisters returned from the cemetery, the family's life was immediately changed. Mrs. Puller called the household into the parlor, where she dismissed the Negro servants—a groom, a maid and a nurse—explaining that she could no longer afford them. She asked the groom to sell the two horses and buggy and carriage.

Lewis began trapping that winter, without explaining the enterprise to his mother. He left the house before daylight each morning to visit traps he had buried in the half-frozen runways of muskrats in the river marshes. He sold the hides for fifteen cents each, and the carcasses for five cents to poorer families in the town. Much of the money went into the family treasury, but there was also a small fund for ammunition.

He was hardly more than twelve when he killed his first wild turkey, quite by mistake and out of season. Alarmed, he stayed in the woods until nightfall, then took the bird to the home of a Negro woman, who reassured him: "Mr. Lewis, don't you bother your head about it. I'll pick him and dress him up nice and take him to your mama tomorrow, and she'll be pleased as punch." But Mrs. Puller was not pleased and the next day gave Lewis a tongue-lashing he long remembered. The small, wiry, reserved woman directed her family with uncompromising discipline, but never whipped the children.

One of Lewis's hunting companions was Dick Broaddus, a year or so older, the son of the president of the local telephone company. Lewis often tossed pebbles against the third-floor bedroom window of young Broaddus, and before daylight they rode with a Negro companion, one George, in the telephone company's buggy to the woods. George taught Lewis: "When a rabbit runs away from you, don't try to shoot down on him, or you'll sight too high or too low and miss him. Go right down with him. Kneel down and you'll get him every time."

Before leaves fell, Lewis and Dick hunted squirrels alone, but after the frosts, when trees were bare, they used dogs and learned to approach the blind sides of the trees where the squirrels hid. Lewis learned both accuracy and frugality, for he bought his own ammunition. He seldom spoke on these trips until noon, when they sat on a log for a sandwich; he often talked of his dream of going to Virginia Military Institute and becoming a soldier. From his reading, his family's traditions, his love of hunting, fishing, and horseback riding, he was drawn to a military life and V.M.I.

Fifty years later, at the end of a fighting career, he would look back to these days in the open: "I learned more in the woods, hunting and stalking, about the actual art of war than I ever learned in any school of any kind. Those days in the woods as a kid saved my life many a time in combat."

The Confederacy was still very much alive in the Tidewater Virginia of Puller's boyhood. Once every week a buggy halted before the Puller home and a stout, graying man with an imperial bearing climbed out and moved up the walk with a basket on either arm. He was Captain Robert E. Lee, Jr., son of the revered Confederate general, now reduced to selling eggs and vegetables to support his family. Mrs. Puller unfailingly bought food from him.

Lewis's favorite Confederate was the mayor of West Point, Sergeant Willis Eastwood, who had ridden with his grandfather and the gray cavalry. Eastwood often told the boys of the death of their grandfather:

"You know your granddaddy was elected colonel of infantry in the county, but he wouldn't have it—he gave it up to be captain in the horse troop. Everybody wanted to ride in that war. We carried shotguns and squirrel rifles and any kind of pistol we had. They had spears, some of 'em— lances, we called 'em, but they were just bayonets stuck on poles. I remember riding into Richmond with the troop, going to join Jeb Stuart, and we were so proud that it killed us to hear the little boys on the sidewalks yell at us: 'Dog catchers!'

"The place they killed your granddaddy was Kellys Ford, up on the Rappahannock, and it was on the thirteenth of March in eighteen sixty-three. Just the night before he told me no Minié ball had been made that could kill him. But the Yankees came pouring across the river when we weren't looking and caught us with our britches down. Jeb Stuart was late getting out there and we lost plenty of fine boys. One of them was Major John Pelham, the gunner. You know all about him.

"Well, your granddaddy, the Major, was riding for the Yankee cannon, just behind General Rosser, when the General yelled without turning around. He said, 'For God's sake, Puller, help me rally the men!' And your granddaddy could hardly speak, but he said: 'General, I think I'm killed.'

"The General turned and saw that it was true. Your granddaddy fell off his horse, dead, and nobody knows to this day how he stayed in the saddle with that wound so long. Cannon fire. It just tore his middle right out of him, all his lights and everything. What kind of a man do you think it took to ride, hurt as bad as that? I'm proud to remember that I was his sergeant major."

The rest of the story was often told at home:

Lewis's grandmother had hung on her parlor wall the sword and spurs of her husband, but a few months after his death a raiding party of Federal soldiers, glimpsing these mementos, burned her house under an order to destroy Confederate munitions. The widow walked the ten miles to Gloucester Courthouse in a sleet storm, dragging four-year-old Matthew Puller with one hand and carrying his two-year-old brother. Within a few days she was dead of pneumonia.

Lewis's mother invariably ended the story with a moral: "Boys, you must be proud of the Confederacy, but it's a mighty good thing that the United States won that war, as terrible as it was. We couldn't live, except as one people."

There were pictures of great Confederates in the Puller home—Lee and Jackson in particular. But there were older heroes, too, from Caesar to Gustavus Adolphus. When his mother first read to him of Genghis Khan, Lewis was so smitten that on his next trip to Richmond he bought a book about the Mongol conqueror from his ammunition hoard. There too he saw his first parade of Confederate veterans, with the still erect figure of General John B. Gordon at the head of shuffling thousands of aging men in gray. The city had been turned over to them and many were so far gone in drink that they toppled from windows or lay in the streets while their compatriots marched before cheering crowds.

Young Lewis had an almost clinical interest in these war veterans, and once asked Sergeant Eastwood: "But how did we lose the war, when there were so many of them left alive? Why didn't we fight until everybody was dead? I wouldn't have given up."

Eastwood gave him a long look. "Boy, you're John Puller's grandson, I can see that. Flesh and blood. It's neck or nothing with you Pullers."

Lewis got into few fist fights, for he demonstrated that he would fight to the finish, whatever the odds. One day when Sam Puller picked a fight with an older friend, Dave Feild, Lewis stood by and watched Feild pound his brother into submission, but when larger boys waylaid friends, Lewis organized a neighborhood gang and took revenge. After Mr. Puller's death Lewis built a boxing ring in the empty stables of the barn and a dozen or more boys fought there in afternoons after school.

Lewis was not quite fifteen when, as the head of the family, he gave away his elder sister Emily in marriage. In the next summer he worked in the new pulp mill in town, an average of twelve hours a day at fifteen cents an hour. He became a merchant on his own initiative. He bought steamed crabs from a nearby packing house and stood among Negro hucksters at the gates of Beach Park, selling crabs for twenty-five cents a dozen. The money went to his mother.

Mrs. Puller managed well on a limited income; she insisted upon the best education within her means for the four children, occasionally with vehemence. Once when the West Point school proposed the dropping of Latin from the curriculum, she organized a parental posse and had the subject retained. Lewis was grateful, but not for considerations of pure scholarship. His efforts at translating Caesar made him impatient for the true message of the soldier-author, and when he bought a "pony" in Richmond, he was so fascinated by the narrative of war that he devoured it in one night. It opened a new world for him and began a lifelong career of serious military reading.

When Lewis was a junior in high school, West Point formed its first football team, though only two of the players had so much as seen a game. The 140-pound Lewis became fullback and manager. The team was equipped in spite of handicaps. The local harness maker split horse collars to make shoulder and knee pads; shoes were Boy Scout models on which the cobbler fixed leather cleats. They played three games in 1916

Thomas G. Pullen, a college senior in Williamsburg, saw the first game, played against William and Mary Academy. Pullen organized a cheering section for the bedraggled and outmanned West Point team. It was a game he never forgot: "There was only one West Point player who could do anything at all. He was the fullback, with a chest like a pouter pigeon and a sort of bullet-shaped head. He was a little taller than most of his team and seemed to be about sixteen. The amazing thing was that he fought on and on, despite the hopelessness of the contest. It was possibly the most one-sided football game I ever saw.

"The West Point fullback ran up and down the line patting his mates on the back, kicking them, hollering and encouraging, and on the few times that his team got the ball, he made some gains."

In the next meeting of these teams three weeks later, West Point fought its way to a tie. In the final game, played against Gloucester, West Point won 48-0 and Lewis scored five touchdowns.

He was captain of the track team that spring, its champion high jumper, and ran well in the 100, 220, and 440-yard dashes—but once had to be helped off the field when he tried to run the half-mile as well. He won a number of blue ribbons in meets at county fairs in the region.

Lewis became catcher on the school baseball team, and though he was a good one, he had a longing to pitch. His coach finally put him on the mound against Gloucester one afternoon, and he gave up twelve runs before he was retired.

Once, when Lewis hit safely and dashed for second base, he was painfully spiked by the opposing player, but made the bag and stood there. The second baseman stepped a few feet away, the ball in his glove. "You son of a bitch," he said.

Lewis lunged toward him angrily—and when he did, the infielder tagged him out and the inning was over.

Puller was also captain of the school basketball team.

The young athlete was not a star student and had little interest in English or mathematics, but never neglected his own reading. One day when he misbehaved in school his teacher, Rose Althizer, challenged Lewis: "Young man, get your books and go home. I can stand no more of you today."

"You mean all of 'em?"

"I certainly do." She was astonished to see him pull more than two dozen books from his small desk and stagger out with a double armful—none of them textbooks.

During the 1916 troubles on the Mexican border, when U.S. troops were ordered out, Lewis went to Richmond with older boys and, after an unsuccessful effort to enlist in the Richmond Blues, came home hopefully with a form for his mother to sign which would permit him to join the Army, though under age. She refused.

In the last week of high school in 1917, the senior class played hooky one day on the theory (which proved to be correct) that the principal would not dare expel them all. Lewis was the leader of this prank, and when they returned from a swim and a six-mile hike to the river, he helped to bring back a dozen or more bullfrogs in paper bags. Lewis and Dave Feild tossed the frogs into a schoolroom window, and were rewarded by screams and other sounds of pandemonium.

Lewis worked in the pulp mill that summer as an electrician's helper for twenty cents an hour. Time dragged for him, for he had been enrolled at Virginia Military Institute and his mind was full of it. By careful management his mother was able to afford the tuition, and Lewis's dream came true.

In early September, 1917, Lewis left his mother and Sam in West Point and boarded the train for Lexington. He was impressed by the first assembly of cadets on the day of his arrival, when the Superintendent said: "This is the last time I will ever speak to all of you young men."

Lewis and his three roommates were puzzled until the next morning, when, as old hands expected, seven boys were found to have deserted during the night. Secret hazers had been at work in violation of state anti-hazing laws. Lewis was lucky, for no upper classman gave him so much as a shaking in the "Rat" treatment.

The four roommates kept their room clean and their clothing in order. Lewis had no leave in his ten months in the school and was on the campus except from 2 until 5 P.M. on Saturdays and Sundays; the only respite was an occasional luncheon visit with the family of his kinsman Colonel George A. Derbyshire, who was Commandant of Cadets. There were no holidays at Thanksgiving or Christmas.

Classroom work was hard and without frills. Classes met from 8 A.M., until 4 P.M., and within five minutes the cadets were on formal guard mount or close order drill and parade. Battalion inspection was held each Saturday. He went out for football and baseball, but made neither team.

The spirit of the Confederacy was strong in Lexington. One of the old men who had fought as a cadet in the Civil War battle of New Market was alive and Lewis saw him often. The statue of Stonewall Jackson overlooking the parade ground was a constant reminder of the great professor of the old school. Two or three times during the year the cadets marched to the cemetery where Jackson was buried. Lewis also visited the tomb of Robert E. Lee on the Washington and Lee University campus across town.

Just before the end of the school year the bars went down

and upper classmen fell upon the first-year "Rats" with brooms. Lewis had his share of beatings from all comers. He was surprised to discover that he could contract the muscles of his buttocks so as to make the punishment nearly painless and he was among the champions the next day, when empurpled bottoms were displayed as badges of honor in the dormitory shower rooms.

Lewis was promoted to Cadet Corporal at the end of the year. Academically, he stood 177th among 233 cadets. His subject standings in his class: Mathematics, 200th; English, 149th; German, 138th; History, 102nd; and, most significantly, Military Science, 89th. He had no demerits for the year, an almost unheard-of record.

His chief disappointment was that they were soldiers without arms, for the rifles were taken by the Army as the war in Europe wore on, and ammunition had been too scarce for target practice. Lewis was impressed by the stern workings of the honor system, and developed a lifelong love for V.M.I. and the town, but felt he had learned little of warfare.

In the last days his cousin, Colonel Derbyshire, called Lewis in for a serious talk.

"I hope you're coming back next year, Lewis."

"No, sir. I'm going to enlist in the Marines."

"Why?"

"Well, I'm not old enough to get a commission in the Army, and I can get one in the Marines right away. I don't want the war to end without me. I'm going with the rifles. If they need them, they need me, too."

"Lewis, I want you to promise me that you'll come back and get as much education as you can, when it's over."

"I hope I can, sir."

"All right, son. I know you've been disappointed with V.M.I. in some ways, but I don't know what you expected. We can give you only the background to be an officer. Not even West Point can do any more. We'll get you as far as second lieutenant, and it's up to you to build on that. Good luck."

On June 27, the day after his twentieth birthday, Lewis took the train to Richmond and enlisted in the Marine Corps, bound for boot camp at Parris Island, South Carolina.

II

THE FLEDGLING

LEWIS was the only man to board the train at Richmond, but four or five hundred Marine recruits from the North kept the cars lively all night and the next day, until they reached a remote siding in the South Carolina low country at Yemassee.

A tugboat and barge bore them to Parris Island, where they were herded into the quarantine station, a few rows of tents in the sand dunes. There they surrendered their civilian clothing and were issued utilities, pajamas, cots and blankets.

Six days later Puller marched with others from quarantine to the supply depot, where he drew his uniforms and equipment, shouldered his sea-bag and marched to their new camp by the maneuver grounds. That night they were issued rifles, Springfield 1903's. They spent hours cleaning and oiling the weapons. By daylight the next morning they were through breakfast, had tried on their uniforms, policed their camp, and were on the parade ground. They formed companies.

The Drill Instructor of Puller's company was a towering Paris-born Dane, Corporal John DeSparre, an athlete who spoke six languages and a student of history who had walked the battlefields of Schleswig-Holstein in his youth with his father. DeSparre soon noticed the soldierly Lewis Puller and marched around to face him.

"What's your name?"

"Private Puller, sir."

"Repeat."

Lewis growled it again, with such spirit that DeSparre thought he must be one of the hardened veterans of the

Philippine fighting. Within three days DeSparre decided that Puller was the natural leader of the company and gave him a platoon to handle.

Lewis took it off like a veteran and on the first afternoon had his men going passably through squad movements, a process usually requiring two or three days. Within a week Puller had the platoon on his own. DeSparre expressed his amazement to his sergeant: "I know he looks like he ought to be in three-cornered pants, but by God, he's a Marine. He looks as if he must sleep at attention. You know I always have to tell 'em to look mean and nasty out there marching, but I never had to tell him. He's a natural. And he never makes the same mistake twice. He's already made the company Number One for parades, and he did it by himself."

"A perfect D.I.," the sergeant said. "We can use him. Drive him. They're pushing us to get 'em ready for overseas in a couple weeks."

Once a week there was a sunset parade and on Saturday morning the Commanding General's inspection, under the eye of General Jack Myers, a Medal of Honor man from the Siege of Peking who seemed to Lewis the ideal of the officer. He could not fail to see, however, that the camp was actually run by two brothers by the name of Broadstrum, a major and a veteran gunnery sergeant who had become a warrant officer. They helped shape Puller's opinion that former enlisted men as officers were superior to graduates of academies or colleges.

The training at recruit camp went on for two months, followed by two weeks on the rifle range, where an instructor stood over every recruit with a swagger stick. When they missed, the sticks rapped hard on their heads. Puller got no raps. "I don't know where," DeSparre told his sergeant, "but he learned it somewhere. He knows how."

DeSparre examined Puller on military history and beat a retreat: "Hell, he gives me an inferiority complex. I've read some, but that kid knows von Clausewitz backwards—and guys I never heard of, by the dozen. He's some kid. This stuff is like a religion with him. He takes in all this stuff about the Huns and their atrocities. He hates 'em like sin."

The noncoms admired Puller's work on the bayonet field, where big signs read: ADVANCE TO KILL! DeSparre set Lewis against bigger men, but Puller was too fast for them, and invariably bested his opponents.

Puller was among the five per cent of the class chosen for

noncommissioned officers' school and went into Drill Instructors' training under Captain Jimmy Wayt, a spectacularly profane and ungrammatical old Marine who taught minor tactics and steeped the recruits in the duties of guard troops, squad leaders and sergeants.

Lewis met a fellow Virginian, Tom Pullen, the cheerleader who had yelled for him at the William and Mary football game long ago; they went into Drill Instructors' school together, but both mourned the departure of their old companies to France, where they were to be used as replacements.

For two months the class went through intensive drills in the bayonet, rifle, boxing, judo and infantry drill. One October evening they were told that they were shipping for Europe and Puller and Pullen went with their group to the mainland and entrained for Quantico. The two Virginia boys used their first hours of liberty in months by walking about the little Marine town, staring at civilians and into store windows, then went into a restaurant where, after solemn deliberation, each ordered a dollar's worth of ham and eggs.

Despite the obvious waning of the war in Europe there was uncertainty and the battalion remained on the base, training in trench warfare in the miles of ditches in a section dubbed Château-Thierry. One day the men were told that their orders had come, and they were packed to leave for Hoboken, New Jersey, to ship out for France. The move was postponed for several days, until Armistice Day canceled the orders.

The replacement battalion was then reinforced by other troops and sent to San Domingo to help put down the rebellion there, but Puller was once more sidetracked from combat. He was detached and sent to the third Officers' Training School. He told Tom Pullen: "I'm going to stay in the Corps, one way or another. I'm qualified for it. I don't know about civilian life."

The winter was unusually bad and the students spent much of it in the wet, snow-filled pits of Château-Thierry, learning the details of trench fighting. Lewis already began to suspect that General Pershing's real contribution in Europe was to get the Germans out of the trenches and return to open warfare after four years of senseless slaughter. Puller looked at the Virginia trenches with an eye to how they might be flanked and their occupants defeated. His instructors found that when called upon in class he had ideas of his own, expressed them belligerently, and could not be influenced by rank or position. There were several gifted instructors: Captain William Rupertus, who would become a Marine general; Eric Johnston, the future movie czar; Dr. Frank Graham, a future university president and United Nations official; and Francis Parkman, who became head of the National Council of Independent Schools.

Puller graduated in June, ranking 128th in his class, with a final average of 2.91. He became a Second Lieutenant on June 4. Two weeks later, when he had finished machine gun school, the end of the war brought a huge cut in the Marine Corps. On June 16 Puller was discharged with hundreds of others of his rank, and he was at loose ends. He had been a Marine officer for two weeks.

He went to West Point for a few days and then with a friend, ex-Lieutenant Lawrence R. Muth, he went north to enlist in a Polish-American army then being raised in Long Island, bound for Europe to help liberate the Poles. They stopped in Washington and quite by accident met Captain Rupertus at Marine Headquarters.

"What are you boys doing?"

When they explained the plight of Poland and their plan to enlist Rupertus countered: "If I were you, I'd go down to Haiti. You'll get commissions in the constabulary down there. They need men, and there's plenty of fighting. You'd see action and have some fun."

Puller and Muth went into a hallway and discussed the matter briefly, and though Puller still yearned for the battlefields of Poland, they agreed to sign for the *Gendarmerie d'Haiti*.

Lewis had a few more days at home, then found himself in Charleston, South Carolina, with Muth, boarding a transport for Haiti. He was barely twenty-one years old.

III

BAPTISM OF BLOOD

THE stench of the tropics welcomed the young Marines to Port-au-Prince when the ship entered the harbor, a sour-sweet breath from mountain forests which also bore the taint of decay from the waterfront. Beyond the red-roofed city the hills rose incredibly green. It was mid-July, 1919.

Puller and Muth got a brisk greeting from Captain Donald Kelly at the barracks: "Report at 4:30 in the morning, equipped for battalion drill. You might like a few beers in the hotel, but beware that rum."

The two took rooms at the hotel, where they met the town's chief of police, a Captain Conn, an old Marine sergeant who seemed impressed by Puller's request for help in learning the Haitian language, Creole.

"You learn just ten words a day, and you'll soon be squawking like a native. It's a bastard French-African. They speak it, but never write it. I'll give you some common words and a few phrases, just as they sound, and you can start tonight." Puller listed these in a pocket notebook, and in the roar of the bar began his acquaintance with the new language.

Haiti was the strife-torn western tip of the island shared with the Dominican Republic; revolutions had been shaking the government since 1914, after almost a century of freedom from France. Since 1916, at the request of the Haitian government, Marines had policed the country amid violence which had taken nearly 2000 lives, almost all Haitian.

General Smedley Butler had created the *Gendarmerie d'Haiti* with a shrewd disregard for precedent. The senior

officers were U. S. Marine officers, whose brief tours of two
years created a supply of field-trained commanders. But he
chose Marine enlisted men to act as junior officers of his
constabulary and allowed them to stay as long as they
wished, on the theory that they became more valuable as
they learned the language and customs of the people. In
practice it was these Marine enlisted men who operated the
force. Under them were many native soldiers, most of them
veterans of the old Haitian army—and from this pool were
drawn many second lieutenants, sergeants and corporals.

In 1919 the rebels were the Cacos, fierce jungle-wise Negro
tribesmen who roamed the hill country, pillaging settlements
and sometimes sweeping into the cities; even the capital,
Port-au-Prince, was not safe from their raids. Atrocities were
common. The war was five years old when Lewis Puller arrived for his first taste of combat, and it still raged furiously.

Puller and Muth were roused by a Haitian maid at 3:30 the
next morning with a pot of alarmingly black coffee, a French
roll and a jigger of rum. At sunrise they reported for battalion drill. As he fell in Lewis saw a striking soldier: Sergeant Major Napoleon Lyautey, a quadroon who stood well
over six feet, a lean, powerful figure of about 190 pounds,
a man of remarkable poise. His high, thin nose gave him an
aristocratic expression; his pale brown scalp was as bald as
an egg. Lyautey had been a general in the old Haitian army.
Puller thought he must have the blood of one of Napoleon's
generals in his veins.

Captain Kelly drilled the battalion for four hours in the
stifling heat. Orders were in English, perhaps the only English these native soldiers understood. It was the most perfect close order drill Puller had seen; V.M.I.'s young cadets
and the Parris Island Marines were amateurs by comparison.

The Haitian noncoms were armed with hardwood sticks
two and a half feet long and an inch or less in diameter. At
the least sign of inattention the culprit was cracked on the
head, and men stepped warily to avoid these sticks, or
cocomakaks, for they were like bars of steel. When the battalion marched off the field to its barracks, Puller saw six or
seven bodies on the ground and hurried to his company
commander, who replied harshly: "Mister, do you think I'm
blind? They'll soon be back. It happens every day. Just a
touch of the heat."

Around the barracks a line of Haitian women squatted

against a wall. When the battalion was dismissed every native soldier stripped naked and the women charged into the open, surrounding them. They brought changes of clothing for the troops and bundled up the sodden garments the men dropped to the ground. While the change was made the women laughed, watching their men and merrily pointing out the variety of exposed charms. They soon disappeared with the soiled clothing. Puller thought it the most efficient laundry service ever devised.

His first foray into enemy country came without warning. The following night at dinner Captain Kelly gave him a casual order:

"A noncom will pick you up at 3:00 A.M. tomorrow on horseback. You will take a pack train to Mirebalais and Los Cohobos. You will carry ammunition and shoes, with an escort of twenty-five mounted men and a sergeant."

Before he went to bed Puller consulted older officers as to the location of the inland towns. When he faced his men in the morning he found that none spoke English, not even the sergeant. He counted the cases of ammunition and bags of shoes, the horses, men and pack saddles, and with gestures and barked orders in English, put them in motion.

The first stop was Mirebalais, a town forty miles away, by roads through bandit-infested country. Puller determined that he would not spend the night in the open, for his head was full of tales of ambush in the Philippine campaigns. While they were hurrying along the trail his sergeant often came to him to complain, gesturing wildly, but Puller could not understand him.

About 4:00 P.M., without warning, Lewis stumbled into the first fight of his career—and proved his instinct for combat. The pack train was ambling around a wooded bend between hills which were littered with stones and cactus, when it met an oncoming Caco band of about a hundred, equally surprised, and in the same formation. Puller spurred his horse and yelled: "Charge! Attack! Vite! (Hurry!)"

The column charged, horses, pack mules and all, and in the thunder and dust and fierce yells the Cacos broke for the hills, firing a few stray rounds as they went. They were gone so quickly that Puller doubted his senses for a moment, but he had shot one of them, a small black barefoot soldier from whose body he took a sword so fine that he could touch its point to the hilt.

Puller's only casualties were superficial bullet wounds to five of his horses and mules.

By driving the column to its limit the Lieutenant reached Mirebalais by 9:00 P.M., and turned over to the *Gendarmerie* officer half of his cargo. Puller asked the officer, a Lieutenant Weedor, to find out the cause of his sergeant's day-long tirade. Weedor spoke to the Haitian and laughed: "He's trying to tell you to slow down. That you can't march the troops at your speed. He says you've been at double time almost entirely since 4:00 A.M., and you're wearing out men and animals."

"Tell the sergeant that I appreciate his efforts, but before anything else is done, he will see to the animals, have them rubbed down, cooled out, and fed. After an hour, they will be watered. At 4:00 A.M. we clear for Los Cohobos. The column will be in line."

The sergeant shouted in outrage.

"Tell that black devil to obey orders and create no more trouble. Tell him to leave the poorer animals here under one guard, and load the rest in the morning."

He went to battalion headquarters with Weedor, where he reported to Major E. A. Ostermann, the commander.

"Congratulations, Puller."

"For what, sir?"

"You've been blooded, man—and come through it."

"I hadn't thought of it. We didn't lose a man, and only a few animals hit. Nothing bad."

At 4:00 in the morning they were on the trail again and soon covered the sixteen miles to Los Cohobos. The sergeant came near mutiny when Puller told him that they would return at noon, but there was worse to come. They reached Mirebalais in the late afternoon and Lewis ordered departure for Port-au-Prince at 4:00 A.M. He considered arresting the raging sergeant.

During the stop at Mirebalais, Puller saw a Haitian soldier report from a raid deep in Caco country. The soldier, Private Cermontoute, reached into his saddle bags and drew out two heads—black, grinning masks already beginning to shrink, lips drawn back over gleaming teeth. He held them high for the Marines to see, immensely proud.

Late the next afternoon when the patrol reached Port-au-Prince an automobile rolled beside Puller and the Department commander, Colonel Walter N. Hill, leaned out.

"Why didn't you go to Los Cohobos?"

"I did, sir."

"I've been sending trains there for a year, and you're the first ever got there and back in three days. You've got a permanent job, running trains. How are your animals?"

"All right, sir, so far as I know. A few flesh wounds."

"They'd better be all right. I'll be down to inspect them at 8:00 A.M. tomorrow."

Puller seemed preoccupied when he turned over the mounts to Lieutenant Richards at the corral. "The Old Man's going to eat me alive about those sore backs. I told him they were okay, and he's inspecting in the morning."

"Puller, I'm an old Seventh Cavalry man, and the best damn vet the Army ever had."

"Biggest liar, too."

"All right. Wait and see. Before the Colonel gets here in the morning, I'll cure every one of those sore backs."

"I'll give you ten dollars if you do."

Before 8:00 in the morning Lewis and Richards were awaiting Colonel Hill at the corral.

"You owe me ten bucks, old man. There's not a sore back in the lot."

Puller walked down the line. "These aren't mine, horses or mules, either."

"The Colonel won't ever know it."

"If he's any kind of horseman he will."

"Just hand me the ten. You're safe. He won't know one end from the other."

Puller paid and when he saw the expression of wonder on the Colonel's face as he inspected the animals, he knew that the money was well spent.

Within a few days Puller was back on the trail, driving his mule train to mountain outposts. Lewis tried to join a small striking force, Mobile Company A, newly formed to clean out Caco bands in the Mirebalais-Los Cohobos area. The company was full, but in less than a week its commander went to a hospital and Colonel Hill summoned Puller to take his place.

The next morning Lewis took his company of 100 by rail to the hill town of Croix de Bouquet. His officers were the newly commissioned native lieutenants, Lyautey and Brunot, and his first sergeant was one Clairmont, a tiny black man who exercised perfect control over his troops. In the ranks was also Private Cermontoute, the head-hunter, whom

Puller had pried from Weedor's command by promising to make the young native a corporal, though he could neither read nor write.

More than a hundred native women awaited the company at Croix de Bouquet, ready to follow and support it. Sergeant Clairmont detailed his woman to act as cook and laundress for Puller. The column marched over the mountain to Mirebalais.

They had only two days of training before plunging into the wild country and Puller spent much of it on the rifle range, where he saw each man fire twenty-five rounds—the first of his efforts to teach every man who served with him to become a sharpshooter. He also broke up the squads into two four-man firing teams, anticipating Marine Corps policy by twenty years.

With the aid of Lyautey and Brunot he drilled the men for short fights against the enemy in ambush. He used his bugler, who would march with him on the trail, to sound "plays," in the manner of a football coach. One bugle blast, and the column faced left; two blasts, to the right; three blasts, and the two leading platoons deployed into line.

The soldiers were taught to seek cover, to prepare foxholes when possible and to fire only when they saw the enemy. Each man carried a grenade and there were a rifle grenade launcher and a Lewis machine gun with every fire team. They had a breakfast of rice, beans and coffee; there was no midday meal. They marched fifty minutes of each hour, much of it at double time, and Puller soon found that he had no more need of the ten-minute rest periods than his mountain-trained soldiers.

A few hours out of town on their first patrol, when he saw men slyly removing their leggings, Puller ordered all of them removed, since they were tight and uncomfortable and slowed the troops. He noted that the men now resembled Confederate infantry, with trousers tucked into socks.

The column soon halted and when Puller moved up he saw a camp follower giving birth to a baby. A group of women calmly attended her at the trail-side. Puller was alarmed, but Lyautey assured him: "It happens much with our people. The column may move. The women will see to her, and she will soon be marching with us."

At reveille the next morning a proud, grinning soldier, Private François, brought his wife and a greasy baby boy to be admired. The child was covered with gun oil in the absence of other lubricants and gave off a martial aroma as he suckled. The woman walked with the column all day.

Lyautey and Brunot made a new proposal: "Captain, we are wasting time with so much daylight marching. We must move by night if we wish to catch the Cacos in camp. We will be ambushed by day, if they are many—or, if they are few, they will hide."

"Fine. We start tonight."

The column pushed on. It was the dry season, and the trail led along the heights. On the second night of the march Puller saw fires on a ridge below them. A man whispered: "Cacos."

Puller reached into his pack and put on a pair of old basketball shoes he had drawn from the athletic officer, and the others took off their shoes. With Lyautey and two sergeants, Lewis moved down the trail toward the enemy camp. Brunot remained in command of the company.

Drums were loud in the camp, which was on a ridge amid open fields, and the small party crept to within a few yards; the Cacos were having a celebration over some victory. The scouts climbed back to the company and Puller prepared to attack at dawn. He placed the men in line on one side of the ridge and sent crews with three of the machine guns to the left, where they covered the enemy rear from one flank. "They will run after the first firing," he told Lyautey, "and they'll run right into our field of fire." The brown man grinned his approval.

The volley cracked in the first moments of daylight and there was complete surprise. The fight ended quickly. Puller found seventeen bodies on the ridge, lying among some old farm buildings and crude lean-tos. Most of the casualties were in the rear where the machine guns had covered the open. At least a hundred machetes were lying on the field.

When the troops occupied the grove the place was alive with gamecocks, staked on short lines, 203 of them in all. The men fell upon them excitedly. They brought out blackened five-gallon tins once used for kerosene and gasoline, and soon had them boiling with water and rice. A cockfight tournament began.

The birds fought in the Haitian fashion, with their natural spurs honed as sharp as razors. Men squatted in a ring about them as fearless cocks were thrown into the ring one pair after another. As one went down a new one took his place. The victim's neck was wrung without ceremony, quick hands plucked and dressed him, his body was cut up and he went into the pot. A tantalizing aroma filled the grove. Puller found the soup from the tins delicious, though its only ingredients were chicken, rice and salt.

The company spent the day fighting cocks and eating chicken and rice and sleeping. At nightfall they were off again, carrying the dozen surviving roosters. When they went back into Mirebalais, the cocks earned them small fortunes in the cockpits of the town. Lyautey told Puller: "A marvelous system for weeding out the boys from the men. Victory or the cooking pot. It is like this in combat, Captain."

On the trail soon afterward, the Captain had a lesson in the stern discipline of the Haitian troops. A soldier near the end of the column began to straggle, a shining black man whose body shook with rolls of fat. He sat at the side of the trail moaning that he was exhausted. Lyautey barked orders and the yelping culprit was trussed with a lariat tied to the saddle of a pack mule, and was dragged at a lively pace along the trail.

The body thumped and tumbled for several hundred yards, until the screams had subsided to groans of desperation. Lyautey then relented and the bleeding man staggered to his feet. To Puller's astonishment he straggled no more and made his way with the column until the next halt, when he fell as if he had been poleaxed.

"It seems cruel, Captain?" Lyautey asked. "Without it, the patrol must fail, for if one man falls, others will fall out. They will indulge their weakness, and we cannot allow this. Do not forget that we are fifty miles from base, Captain—and that if we had left this man alone on the trail for one hour, our tender friends the Cacos would have cut him into ribbons."

Puller was convinced, but when he looked at the blood-crusted skin of the sleeping soldier, Lyautey smiled. "Within a week, Captain, he will be a new man. We are not so savage as we seem."

Lyautey also taught Puller the value of living off the country. In the twilight Lewis saw the preparation of a feast that seemed a miracle. They had bought a steer from a native farm as the column passed; Lyautey had urged generosity, so that the farmer would remain friendly.

"How much?"

"Three dollars."

"For that big steer?"

"It is enough. More than enough. He will not soon again see so much money."

The troops were expert butchers: one man hit the steer on the head with an axe and as the animal sank to its knees another opened its throat with the slash of a knife; as the blood gushed still another tossed a lariat over a tree limb, hitched it to a back leg of the steer and a pack mule dragged the carcass until it dangled in the air.

A soldier slit the hide from tail to hoof, wrapped another lariat around folds of the skin, and as the body rose higher in the air, the hide was peeled from the body by a second mule. In half an hour or less the animal had been cleaned, cut into pieces and dressed, and beef was browning on skewers over dozens of fires. Men shaved off strips with their knives while the meat ran red. They ate for two hours or more.

The hide went onto a pack saddle, and the steer's head, bones and scraps were tossed into a Dutch oven dug into the ground. These were cooked until daylight, when the soldiers ate once more, devouring the last morsels of meat, and gnawing at large bones. When they took up the day's march their bellies thrust out as if they were pregnant.

"They will march three days on such food with nothing more to eat, Captain," Lyautey said—but there was an emergency ration for the future. Each man carried in loops over his belt two-foot strips of beef, each about an inch square. These strips were salted down each night—though Puller thought the sweat of their bodies sufficient to cure it properly. The meat lasted for weeks in this way. But few steers were to be found; day after day the fighting ration of the patrol was beans, rice and coffee.

At mid-morning, a few days later, the head of the patrol reached the banks of La Chival River, in the remote country near the San Domingan border. The men halted, under orders, until Puller came up. The river was about seventy-five yards wide.

From the opposite shore a native in Domingan dress rode out on a magnificent horse, a big buckskin with white mane and tail who splashed through the shallows under perfect control, though without bridle or saddle.

"A wonderful horse," Puller said. "I'd surely like to have him."

Brunot muttered in Creole and a rifle cracked. Puller saw one of his men pull his rifle bolt and eject a cartridge. The beautiful horse stood in the river, looking nervously about. His rider floated downstream in a stain of blood.

The stunned Puller turned to Brunot: "Did you order that man shot?"

"Hell, sir. You said you wanted the horse. Anything the Captain says is our command. We have discipline here, sir." The men seemed unmoved by the cold-blooded killing.

"My God! Catch the horse, get the men over the river—and see if you can find that man's family."

Lewis never again expressed himself idly before these soldiers. His search for the family of this victim was futile, but the horse was his mount for years in Haiti, a strong young stallion which never failed him.

Company A had waded the stream without opposition, but as they mounted a ridge beyond, a rifle fired, and there was a terrifying shriek of a bullet overhead. Puller ducked.

Lieutenant Lyautey was at his side: "Captain Puller, officers do not flinch under fire. They stand. The men take note of this thing. It is of first importance."

"I'm all right. What makes those damned things sing like that?"

"I will show you, sir, when we have driven the enemy."

When the company gained the crest and the ambush had been cleared, Lyautey brought Puller a Caco rifle, a single-shot French .45, a Grau. He exhibited some remarkable ammunition.

"They have little to fight with, sir, and so they make it of what they can. There is little enough lead, and so they cut telephone wire, and stick these bits of copper into the shell, using a little lead to hold them. It is this that makes such devil's screams. At first, it frightens the men."

"It rattled me. I never heard such a sound."

"Captain, you never hear the bullet that hits you. It is one of the few blessings of battle."

During the rest on the ridge a man handed Puller half a pineapple. Lewis began to eat it, but tossed it aside when he saw that it was bloodstained. On closer inspection he found the hillside was sprinkled with the blood of the Caco bandits, though no bodies remained.

"They carry off every body, and every wounded man,"

Lyautey said. "And when they catch our wounded . . . well, Captain, if you see one, you will never forget. The Cacos believe that every man who dies must go before the gods—and they use their knives to see that when our men go, they are beyond recognition. They slash the face to ribbons, and tear the body apart. You will see."

Puller was learning valuable lessons from the Haitian, and made it a point to be near him when the patrol halted for a rest. Every day or two, a soldier was detailed to shave Lyautey's head, scraping the hair to the gleaming skull, and even at these times the big man tutored Puller:

"Captain, it is a matter of life or death for officers and noncommissioned officers to have respect from the men—and something more. Adulation. They must obey orders to the letter, without question, though they die for it. It is the only way to handle men in combat. If you lose control, you lose lives. It is so simple as that."

About three weeks later, when he was off patrol, Puller attended the christening of the child born on the trail, and stood as his godfather. He was surprised to hear the priest call the name: "Leftenant Puller François." It was the first of scores of namesakes in his long career. Lewis gave the priest five dollars and asked that a candle be burned for the child. "It will be done, Captain, and candles will be burned for you, and prayers said. Bless you, sir."

Lieutenant Lyautey was soon taken from Puller, to duty at the palace of President Dartiguenave in the capital. There was an able replacement, a Lieutenant Calixe, who helped to further the education of the Captain in the patrols which followed in rapid succession.

The teaching of Lyautey saved the Capain's life more than once, notably on a patrol near the village of Saut d'Eau, where he had a brush with death.

A priest in this place told Puller of one Dominique Georges, a bloodthirsty Caco leader who had wrought much damage in the region and was now in camp about fifteen miles away. Puller told Brunot to pass the word that they would leave for Mirebalais the next morning, and to see that it got public attention. At ten o'clock the following morning the patrol took the dusty trail, followed by pack mules dragging a number of bushes Puller had cut. He took with him every native they met on the trail, and when they had gone several miles, turned his troops off the main road, the civilians still under guard, and sent the pack mules into Mirebalais.

The patrol went no more than a mile from the trail, put out sentries, and slept until dark. At dusk, Puller had the men leave heavy gear with a guard, and in light marching order headed for the Caco camp. They marched for hours until, about 2:00 A.M., a rainstorm burst upon them. Brunot said that the enemy must be near, and the march slowed, the column in single file, without lights or sound, in the darkness and rain.

Cermontoute led the way, followed by Brunot, Puller and two firing teams, then the massed machine guns and the rest of the company, under Lieutenant Calixe. After an hour the rain stopped and the moon appeared. As they rounded a bend the vanguard saw half a dozen glowing logs at the trail-side, now smoking and steaming.

"This was to light the trail for sentries, Captain," Brunot said.

Puller walked past the logs, and saw a native with a rifle at ready on a high bank above the road. There was a challenge: *"Qui vous?"*

Cermontoute gave a quick reply: "Caco," and the three leaders moved ahead into a clearing. Puller saw a few huts and many lean-tos, with several fires still burning before them. A burly man rose from a hammock in the largest of the huts, where there was a light, and shouted: "Who passes?" The sentry by the trail called reassurance: "Cacos." Puller, Cermontoute and Brunot lay flat in the grass, and Puller held the big man in his rifle sights until he turned back to his hammock—he later regretted that he did not fire, for this was the bandit leader, Georges.

Puller sent Brunot back for the rest of the company, with orders to flank the camp: "And don't mind us. When the shooting starts, we'll be flat. Hurry!" Brunot was only a few yards away when a bandit came from a hut with a rifle, walking straight toward the invaders. Puller put a restraining hand on Cermontoute, hoping that the man would pass by them, but he came on. When he was but a step away he halted: "Who are you?" His rifle was at the ready. Puller shot him, and as the man fell the company charged up and Cacos poured from the shanties. There was a fury of firing, during which Puller took two quick, vain shots at Georges.

It was over within a few minutes, and the estimated 150 to 200 Cacos fled, leaving a few casualties behind. Puller found Georges' rifle, a new Grau with his initials burnt in the stock, and twenty-seven other rifles in the lean-tos. The company had no casualties, and left with the several dozen fighting cocks they had come to expect as loot in raiding a camp. Puller made a brief, matter-of-fact report of the affair to headquarters, but tales of his bravery under fire were told for months in the barracks.

One day when Lewis led his patrol to a supply dump in the field, he met Louis Cukela, one of the legendary characters of the Corps, a dark, barrel-shaped man who spoke rapidly in broken English, a Serbian cook who had won the Medal of Honor in the World War.

In his tent that night, Puller got the benefit of a Cukela explosion: "We fight this war like damn fools, Puller. They scatter us like peas. All over Haiti. Cukela patrol one pea. You one pea. They put us in a few posts, and damned if we can leave the tents to find the enemy. This is not war. This outpost waiting drives me mad. If they want to fight, they must bring all together, and send us out to find Cacos and end this thing."

Puller listened to Cukela for hours, and remembered that night: "I learned one of the great lessons of warfare from him—concentration of force. It was familiar to me from having read Caesar and Napoleon, but no one put it like Cukela, and he was one of the first critics of American warfare I had met. We still have not learned the lesson of military concentration in America and I can't see why. It's plain in every worthwhile textbook."

In the months afterward Cukela went with Puller on many patrols, adding his machine gun company to Company A. One night the combined force set out just after dark, marched all night without incident, and was halted at dawn by the commander, who ordered all hands to sleep until late afternoon. Cukela raged: "No real man can sleep in the day. I will hunt the enemy."

He asked Puller to go scouting with him, but Puller declined, saying that he would obey orders. Cukela borrowed a BAR—Browning Automatic Rifle—got permission to stalk Cacos until dark, and disappeared. He was back at twilight and marched with the patrol all night without a sign of fatigue. Puller and his friends were amazed to see Cukela keep up this pace for a week—and though some scoffed that he merely left camp to sleep away the days, there were few doubters.

Puller got an indelible memory of Cukela on the trail one day when the Serb broke the silence of the march with a roar, halted, and hammered on his huge chest, shouting: "Me! The Great Cukela! Greatest chef in Milwaukee—a goddam second lootenant in the Marine Corps! Helling about in these goddam bushes!"

He ceased as abruptly as he had begun and walked on without another word.

Puller's military reading bore fruit in the jungle fighting; he conducted experiments with the aid of Brunot and Calixe. He told the lieutenants: "In the Boer War, the English found that they killed few enemies when they lay on high ground, and the Boers were low. They always shot overhead. Men usually fire too high on such ground."

The natives saw the point, and Puller went to work on the problem. He had special rifle sights made in a railroad machine shop, with a tip twice as high as regulation. The men used these sights on patrol. When the company went to the rifle range, Puller acted as armorer, inserting the normal sights before the men went to the targets, a simple change which increased confidence and accuracy.

He was also troubled over the inability of men to shoot well in the dark, for they often fired into the ground or high in the air. His remedy was a wooden stake, varying with the height of each man, tied to the stacking swivel of his rifle with rawhide. When the marksmen lay prone they rested the barrels on the stakes, quickly ready to fire parallel to the ground, rather than high or low.

The Captain was less successful in other attempts. When he asked the chief of constabulary for shepherd dogs to use on the trail, for example, he got no reply—but he was told unofficially that dogs were taboo, since the French had used them to hunt runaway slaves in Haiti.

During his months at Mirebalais, Puller was once called into conference between brigade officers and Major Roy Geiger, chief of Marine aviation, who had come on an inspection tour. Lewis was asked for his opinion of the progress of the fighting.

"We could do more with the planes."

"How?"

"They should be out in the country where the trouble is, and not on the field at Port-au-Prince. You could scatter little fields all over Haiti, and keep planes there."

"But we have no strips," Geiger said.

"We have about a thousand prisoners here," Puller said. "In most places you need only to cut the grass. Except in the rainy season, you'd have no trouble."

"We'll try it," Geiger said.

Within a few weeks the little planes, most of them World War Jennies, were using isolated landing fields in the Caco country, and one operated from Puller's strip near Mirebalais within three days. He made some of the first flights.

Buck Weaver, a Marine pilot, flew him for a couple of weeks but they were limited to study of the terrain, for though there was a store of 22-pound bombs there were no bomb racks. A succeeding pilot, a Lieutenant Sanderson, declined Puller's offer to toss bombs overboard from the rear cockpit, and devised a release mechanism by fastening a canvas mail sack under the fuselage with a sash cord sewn to either end. When Puller spotted a Caco camp below, Sanderson loosed the end of the rope tied in his cockpit, and the bomb fell. Puller flew dozens of such missions, but the damage to the enemy was unknown, though Lewis claimed that the crude bombsight had uncanny accuracy. These, so far as Puller knew, were the pioneer flights of close air support in the Marine Corps.

General John A. Lejeune, Commandant of the Corps, had come to Haiti on inspection, and Lewis was anxious to see the hero of the fighting in France, the only Marine who had commanded a division in the AEF. He met him on the porch of the mess hall in Mirebalais, where Lejeune was talking with the district commander, Colonel Thomas Clinton, and other officers. Lejeune won Puller's heart.

A Marine patrol filed past, just in from the hills, and the officers turned to watch: a sturdy band of men moving with the easy gait of jungle fighters, returning from a march that had obviously been long and hard. They were unshaven and ill-kempt.

"I'm afraid the men are a little ragged and out of uniform, sir," Clinton said. "I'm trying to improve them."

"Colonel, I'm a field soldier," Lejeune said. "I don't give a damn what men look like in the field. Only one thing interests me—and that's ending this war. Don't waste your time shining them up for jungle work. Our only objective is success, and I demand that."

Early in 1920 after only eight months of combat experience, Lewis Puller was promoted to command the subdistrict of Port-à-Piment in a remote corner of southern Haiti. He was almost constantly on patrol. In April he was felled by malaria.

He was so weak one morning, with a throbbing head and aching body, that he could not leave his bed. He took large doses of quinine, and on the advice of his first sergeant tried rum as often as he could stomach it. In the fifth day of his fever he lost consciousness.

Lewis opened his eyes to see a stranger leaning over him, a Negro doctor. He turned and saw the round, benign face of the French priest who was the only other white man in the subdistrict.

"You have a bad fever," the priest said, "but you will be better now."

"I have given you quinine intravenously," the doctor said, "and now I must give you more." He held a huge hypodermic.

"My God! You must be a veterinarian."

"The malaria does not easily surrender. You need have no fear. I am trained in France for many years. You will be better now."

Puller walked the following day, and within a week was back at his duties. His first sergeant brought him a bill for two gallons of rum used in the cure.

"You black devil. You poured it between my teeth when I passed out—or you had big parties in the barracks."

The grinning sergeant folded the money away. "The Captain is not the best of patients. Many doctors, many treatments."

A few days afterward Puller rode over the mountain trail to Aux Cayes, for his monthly report to his district commander, who greeted him with a smile and a handshake and chanted, as if from an official document:

"For valor in action, in the outpost region of Trou d'Eau, with fine disregard for his own life . . .

"Captain Puller, I have the honor to inform you that you are to report to Port-au-Prince for the purpose of being awarded the Medaille Militaire of the Republic of Haiti."

There was a brief round of drinks in celebration, and

Puller soon left for headquarters. He was decorated in a ceremony at Port-au-Prince on April 17, the first of his awards for gallantry in action, and after two days' leave was back in his subdistrict, hard at work.

He wrote Tom Pullen, back in the States:

> You may rest assured I was relieved when I found that I had been ordered in to Port-au-Prince to be decorated for killing Cacos, and not to be court-martialed for the same. It's funny as hell to me; every once in a while some misguided fool up in the States, who knows nothing of the trouble here, sets up a howl over a few black bandits being knocked off.
>
> Well, someone has to be the goat, and it is generally a *Gendarmerie* officer. . . .
>
> You don't want to come down here, Pullen. Stay in the States and make something of yourself. It's a dog's life here. . . . Unless I get into the Marine Corps, I have a pretty rotten-looking future ahead of me.

The next month, May, 1920, the Caco campaign came to an end with the slaying of the two chieftains, Charlemagne Peralta and Benoit Baterville, by patrols led by Captains Herman Hanneken and Cy Perkins. An armistice was declared and the tribesmen poured into the cities by the hundreds to give up their arms and make peace. Every soldier who brought in his weapon was given new clothing and ten dollars.

Puller was in Mirebalais in these days, intent upon studying the enemy. He talked with literally hundreds of the bandits, hearing their versions of combats in which he had fought—and searching always for word of the killing of his friend, Lawrence Muth, who had been the victim of a Caco ambush in the last week of the fighting. He had written Tom Pullen of the reports of Muth's death:

> In the fight with the Cacos a few weeks back Muth got his. The Marines and Gendarmes left him when they retreated (damn them). I surely hope he was dead when the black men got to him.
>
> The next day, a large force hiked over to the scene. There wasn't a piece of flesh or bone as large as my hand. His head is stuck up on the end of a pole somewhere now, out in the hills. . . .

Puller picked up Muth's trail from a minor Caco chief, one

Charlieuse, who was in the crowded town. Puller talked with him in his improved Creole, and the arrogant native warrior told of Muth's end without reservation:

"They walked into our trap, and it was beautiful. Your Leftenant Muth, he was the first. He fell, but he was not dead, and when we drove the enemy away, we made talk with our gods.

"We were four chiefs, to make the sacrifice. As always, we took off the head from the Leftenant, and cut up his body."

Puller sickened as Charlieuse told of the obscene atrocities committed on Muth's corpse.

"Then we opened the chest," Charlieuse said, "and took out the heart. It was very large. And we ate of it, each of the four chiefs, to partake of the courage of your Leftenant Muth. It was a glorious day."

Puller controlled himself, and on orders from the commander took Charlieuse to the prison. Lewis taunted the Negro the two blocks to the guardhouse in an effort to sting him into a dash for freedom, but Charlieuse was too shrewd for that. Shortly afterward, however, the chief was killed in an attempt to escape his guards.

Lewis soon got a new post, as commander of the district of St. Marc, where he was military governor of a territory of hundreds of square miles of rugged country, with authority over courts, police and civil affairs for 105,000 people. He had never been so busy, for he was endlessly besieged by the problems of those who came to the little town.

He was ordered to build barracks for his outposts, though he had no experience and almost no money for the purpose. Headquarters sent just enough cement for the floors and sheet iron for roofs—the rest was up to the commander. Puller responded with vigor, and for months he drove trains of prisoners through the jungle in a style that reminded him of the building of the pyramids.

"I may go to hell for this," he told a visiting officer, "but I've got to finish, like it or not."

There were no pack animals, so the half-naked swarms of Haitian prisoners carried logs from distant forests to hew into beams. They stumbled under baskets of limestone they had dug from quarries, then pounded into powder. On the barracks sites they burned this to produce a rich yellow whitewash. For months the men quarried stone, cut it into rough blocks, and bore it under Puller's watchful eye.

Dozens of them broke down under the burdens, and were useless for the work. A few of them died.

But in the hills the twenty barracks rose under the hands of masons and carpenters found by Puller in the prison pens. The small shelters were fourteen by thirty feet, with stone walls two feet thick, pierced with loopholes. Each had an office for a three-man outpost, a jail and sleeping quarters. Puller was forced to fashion bars for the cell windows from the barrels of captured rifles.

The Captain directed each outpost to raise vegetables and supplement the daily ration of ten cents per man, and somehow, despite handicaps, his little military empire prospered.

Lewis did not go unnoticed by his superiors, and early in 1921 he was recommended for a permanent commission in the Marine Corps—where his rank was now that of sergeant. He took examinations, but failed the section on trigonometry, as did ninety per cent of his class; someone had reversed the traditional order that the trig books could be used on the examinations, and Lewis found himself at a loss.

A few months later, Puller had malaria once more. This time he was in no doubt as to his plight, and when he felt the fever, went to the brigade hospital and asked a doctor for intravenous injections of quinine.

"We'd never do that, Captain. It might well be fatal."

"I had 'em before, and they cured me."

"Some foreign doctors practice it, but it's strictly against our orders."

Puller went to a civilian doctor in Port-au-Prince, took the injections, and recovered within a week.

Lewis was again recommended for commission, the papers endorsed by virtually every officer in the command, and in February, 1924, after months of review of Creole, French and mathematics while he served as adjutant to Colonel A. A. Vandegrift in Port-au-Prince, he again became a Second Lieutenant, U. S. Marine Corps; but this time he was a regular.

"I may not have much else to go on," he told a friend, "but I have some perseverance."

He was soon ordered to Marine Barracks, Portsmouth, Virginia, Navy Yard, and embarked with eleven other new second lieutenants.

It was not until years later that Puller realized the full richness of his Haitian experience, and the value of its lessons in soldiering and hand-to-hand combat—he had fought forty actions. He had not only been blooded; the guerrilla combat had been almost continuous, most of it introduced by ambush on the trail. Puller had stood up well under this strain, and had come to trust his own physical prowess and ability to lead men under fire. He had discovered that native troops could become superb soldiers. He had developed his instinctive talent for using terrain in battle, and learned the lessons of jungle fighting. He had become strongly prejudiced against barracks and headquarters soldiers. Despite his youth, he was one of the most seasoned combat officers in the Corps.

IV

NEW SKILLS

THE corporal on sentry duty at the liberty gate, Portsmouth Navy Yard, was Homer Litzenberg, a future Marine general. He checked throngs of passing sailors, out for the evening, and when traffic slowed, retired to his kiosk. A young lieutenant approached—Lewis B. Puller, the officer of the day.

Puller entered the tiny building and struck up a conversation, and there was one moment Litzenberg never forgot: "Puller hooked his elbows over our little shelf, looked down at the new bars on his shoulders and said, 'Well, I've got 'em, now. All I need is a war.'"

At Portsmouth Lewis served as post adjutant under the commander, General Carter Berkeley, as post exchange officer and then as instructor in the Sea School, preparing men for boarding ships and standing guard duty there. Within a few months, in February, 1925, he was sent to Basic School in Philadelphia, where he was outstanding in a small class of eleven men. Instruction in fundamental military skills was not enough for Puller, and during his six months in Philadelphia he took correspondence courses in bookkeeping, accounting and auditing through the Marine Corps Institute.

The earnest young jungle fighter was impervious to practical jokes by his schoolmates, and their efforts soon ceased. Once when a companion, Russ Jordahl, cut up rubber bands and put them into his tobacco pouch, Puller continued to puff at his stubby pipe without a sign of distress. The pranksters concluded that he did not notice the fumes of burning rubber, or was determined to give them no satisfaction.

In July of that year Puller was tossed headlong into the mysteries of artillery, assigned to the Tenth Regiment at Quantico. He confessed to his new commander an almost total ignorance of the big guns. The captain waved airily.

"I'll give you a first lesson." He sketched a triangle, turned to answer a telephone and left the drawing incomplete. When he returned to Puller he said: "Lieutenant, I have permission to begin my leave now. The battalion will begin thirty days of training to prepare for the interservice firing at Camp Meade next month." The commander picked up his cap and halted at the door: "By the way, you'll have to fire a battery problem next Wednesday. God help you." He disappeared.

Puller conferred with his first sergeant, who told him that other junior officers would be of no help, but that the enlisted men and noncommissioned officers were experts.

Lewis spent the noon hour in a gun shed, sweating under the direction of one Bernoski, a gunnery sergeant, who interpreted the sheets of the battalion schedule for the next month, day by day, and then put him to work: "Here are the textbook references you will need, sir. You can study those every night, and keep ahead of the men. And now, if the Lieutenant pleases, I can show him the insides of the 75."

Puller tore down and reassembled the big gun for five hours, learning the parts and nomenclature, reciting them until he was intimate with the secrets of the weapon and its shells. He spent the weekend studying for Monday's firing, and when the battery began blasting, felt somewhat at home. On Wednesday he fired for a critical audience which included the post commander, General Kelly Cole; Colonel Moses, the regimental commander; and Major Freddie Erskine, the battalion commander.

The artillery of the time used the No. 2 gun of a battery as a base, with the three others firing parallel to it. The base gun was corrected after three rounds if necessary, and other guns adjusted to conform. Sergeant Bernoski gave Puller final advice: "Sir, just leave it all to us. Good gunners are supposed to be right on target. General Cole and the Colonel will be watching. Their eyesight ain't too good, sir.

"Now, after the third shot, no matter where we're hitting, if you'll just crack loose right away with a salvo from the whole battery, turn and salute the officers and yell like hell, 'Sir, I'm right on target!' then we'll get away with it. They'll never know the difference."

The battery followed instructions, and in the roar of the

guns Puller went through Bernoski's paces. The senior officers were pleased. To Lewis, it was evidence that the Corps was in fact operated by its senior noncoms and that too few officers knew the basic details of their trade.

Puller's next assignment was more to his liking. His old Parris Island instructor, Captain Jimmy Wayt, now at Quantico, chose Lewis to handle the Marine drill detachment. For years, Army, Navy and Coast Guard teams had outshone the Marines in the national drill competition held in Boston's Mechanics Hall. The Marines had never won, despite their reputation as crack marching units.

Puller took over with vigor. Private Bob Norrish, a company clerk drafted for the detachment, shared the astonishment of his mates: "The Lieutenant told us the first day that we would bring home the cup, or die trying, and from the cold eye he gave us, we believed it. We found we weren't mistaken. He took out the silent drill manual and started us from scratch. He drove us day after day until we figured we'd never live to see Boston. When he was through with us, we literally thought as if we had one head, instead of eighty. Yet somehow, though he was as hard as nails, he could be friendly with us like no officer we'd ever seen. We gave him all we had."

The team entrained for New York, where it faced a crisis in a subway station, the first most of the men had seen. Four or five trains whirled past before Puller contrived to get the whole crew aboard: "Sergeants, each of you take a door, and hold it until the men are aboard. I'll count 'em as they come on. If we lose one here, we'll never find him." The scheme worked.

The Boston drill competition was an all-Marine show. One sergeant remembered: "Puller won that cup all by himself. He didn't look like flesh and blood, he stepped out so smartly and proud and soldierly that it was like watching a mechanical man. He just carried them on his back, and it was hard to keep your eyes off him to watch the ranks."

The Marines wore rosin on their soles for safe, silent footing, and went through the maze of their drill soundlessly, except for the clatter of their weapons. When it was over and the victory had been announced, Puller handed Norrish a dollar bill: "Send Captain Wayt a wire. Just say, 'The cup is ours. Puller.'"

The Governor of Massachusetts presented the cup to Puller, and the men left to stage a brief celebration in downtown Boston. The only casualty was a man who fell from the back of a camel, in a moment of hilarity when the Marines met a circus parade. A number of congratulatory telegrams went into Puller's record, one of which praised him as "an inspiring drill officer."

Back at Quantico, Puller was thrilled by a message from General Lejeune:

> The Major General Commandant is highly gratified over the winning of the cup. . . . The winning of this trophy, which for the past two years has been won by the Army, is a most praiseworthy achievement. You are heartily commended for your excellent leadership . . . and congratulated upon your well-deserved success.

A few weeks afterward Puller was whisked off to his next duty—assigned as a flying cadet at Pensacola, Florida, a chance for which he had been pleading since his first flights in the improvised Jenny bomber in Haiti.

In five months at Pensacola he found that his talents for combat were by no means those required to handle the seaplanes in which he trained. He fell behind in ground school work, where he was considered "average," and though he was "satisfactory" in his five-hour flight test, his instructor noted that he landed "hot" and made sweeping turns. He finally flew in his tenth hour of instruction, but failed two solo tests.

A board advised, after hearing his instructors, that Puller was not "suitable aviator material" and recommended his detachment. Lewis stoutly filed a reply:

> I have nothing to say except that I think I can fly. They said I could not fly a kite until my tenth hour. I could not land until the tenth hour; up to that time, my time was wasted, but I believe I can fly all right now. My ground school work is behind, I know, but I can correct that on examination. When most of the other students were going to school I was in the Marine Corps at that age.

He added that he had been given considerate treatment—and left Pensacola disappointed, but convinced that aviation and ground warfare had an intimate relation and that all infantry field commanders should know the uses of close air support.

The Puller-Pensacola affair went on for some time. In September, 1928, three years after Lewis had left flying school, a medical board in Washington, in answer to his plea for one more chance, found him "physically fit to fly, but not temperamentally adapted for aviation training." Admiral E. J. King declined to give him a waiver, and the aerial phase of Puller's career was over.

In his last days at Pensacola, Puller requested a return to Haiti, citing his experience—but insisting on foreign duty of some kind. His orders sent him to the Marine Barracks at Pearl Harbor.

In the spring of 1926 he had a few days' leave and went home to West Point. He found the town changed; most of his friends had gone. Lewis had never had a sweetheart, despite some high school flirtations, and he now found that the girls he had known were married, and most of them had moved away.

He went to a dance one night in the village of Urbanna, on the Rappahannock, and discovered that the freckle-faced daughter of his family's friend Judge Evans had been transformed. She was now a ravishing brunette of about seventeen, the belle of the ball, and evidently little impressed by the returning war hero. Lewis was dazzled by Virginia Evans' smile; so, apparently, were most of the young men in the ballroom.

He danced with her three times with fumbling attempts at conversation. During the next dance he made up his mind; his manner became assured. "Will you marry me?" She laughed. "Heavens, no! How can I do that, when I haven't even finished school?"

"You will."

He spent the night in the stag line, watching, and dancing with her. She noticed that he danced with no other girl.

After that meeting he did not see her again for almost eleven years, but he never lifted the long-range siege. She was on her way back to school at St. Mary's, in Raleigh, North Carolina, when he departed for Hawaii—he sent her orchids, three of them, in a day when they were so rare that the florist made them into separate corsages; he had spent ten dollars on this display. She wrote him an ecstatic letter, and weeks later had his terse reply: "Marry me, and I'll buy you three dozen orchids, every month of your life."

He sailed for San Francisco on the *President Coolidge,* and arrived in Hawaii in late July, 1926.

He found some 20,000 Army troops on the beautiful islands and a little complement of 620 Marines on guard duty. The chief defenses, Puller noted, were a chain of small Coast Artillery forts. Lewis quickly made himself known.

One day he reported to Lieutenant Albans, the adjutant in the office of the commander, Colonel Newton Hall, and the door was closed behind him. Albans took a heavy book from a vault:

"These are the plans for the defense of the Hawaiian Islands. Familiarize yourself with them. You must read 'em and certify to me that you understand."

"I'll read them now."

"No hurry. At your convenience."

"Just show me the parts that apply to the Marines, and let me read that now. Who knows what might happen?"

The plans designated the Marine detachment as a machine gun battalion, ready to act in an emergency. Puller soon went to his platoon sergeant and asked to see the machine guns.

"Sir, I've been here a year, and I've seen no machine guns."

Puller went to his company commander.

"Captain Curtis, I've read the defense plans, but I can find no guns. Where do you keep 'em?"

"Don't try to start anything, Puller. The Quartermaster has 'em."

Captain Harry Gamble, the Quartermaster, assured Puller that the guns were stored, and in order, but when Lewis persisted and found a clerk, Dickie, he was shown an account book: "Look for yourself. We have guns and tripods, but no water cans, no hoses—not a single stool, and no belts or asbestos gloves, not even a loading machine, for the ammunition."

"Hell, we couldn't fire a shot."

"You tell somebody else, Lieutenant. I've known it all along."

When Lewis went back to Colonel Hall with the problem the commander said:

"I had no idea this was going on, Puller. I'll take immediate steps."

The equipment came from the states some months later; in the interim Puller took four guns and tripods and drilled his platoon in nomenclature and function of machine guns, and was soon teaching his entire company. When the equipment arrived Puller became battalion machine gun officer and instructed all men in gunnery. He also served as rifle range officer.

Puller retained the memory for years: "It was no surprise to me when the Japs caught us asleep at Pearl Harbor. I readily understood the situation. I've been through there many times since, and served there later—and I'll bet we're in the same condition now, more or less. Our trouble is that common sense has gone out the window, and we make generals today on the basis of their ability to write a damned letter. Those kinds of men can't get us ready for war."

Lewis held firm discipline in his company, and some men were probably resentful until they learned that he spared himself less than he did others.

He was ruthless with violators of safety precautions where firearms were involved, and every time a man shot a weapon on the base without good reason, the fine was automatically twenty dollars. One day, on inspection, Puller saw a .45 in the guardhouse, picked it up, released the clip and pulled the slide and trigger. The gun fired unexpectedly, and a bullet furrowed the ceiling. Though he had taken all precautions except a look into the firing chamber, Puller fined himself $100, which he gave to the guards to buy beer for a liberty party.

Lewis also improved his skills in Hawaii. He considered himself a good shot, had for five years been rated an Expert Rifleman, and was thus nettled when a veteran sergeant suggested that he teach him to shoot.

"I know how to shoot, Sergeant."

"I can give you enough pointers in two weeks to raise your score twenty points."

Puller became the sergeant's pupil, shooting when targets became vacant during the training, and shot an average of two bandoleers daily. He improved rapidly, and brought his record score from 306 to 326, of a possible 350. During all these years he qualified as expert with both rifle and pistol, and when a rifle team was sent from Pearl Harbor to a competition in San Diego in 1928, Puller was a member.

While he was in California he bombarded Headquarters with pleas to send him to Nicaragua, where war had broken out and the Marines were trying to put down a native bandit uprising. He reminded the Corps once more of his service in Haiti—and added that if he could not be given duty in Nicaragua, he wanted to go to China, where the Third Marine Brigade was posted. In November, after six months of effort, the orders came through: He was to proceed to Nicaragua at once. He took the transport *Château-Thierry* from San Francisco, and landed at the western port of Corinto, Nicaragua, in early December.

V

THE JUNGLES AGAIN

NICARAGUA was even more rugged than Haiti, a green, rolling country of jungle and plains, dominated by towering highlands upon which were tumbled mountain masses. For many years revolutions had torn the land, despite the presence of U. S. Marines, and now a bitter new war had called them back after a year's absence. In the north lay an unconquered Indian empire whose people did not recognize the central government, and there, where he moved back and forth across the border of Honduras, was the rebel chief, Augusto César Sandino.

Sandino led a guerrilla army of thousands against the government of President Moncada, whom he had once served as an officer, and the country was being wasted anew by raids and atrocities. The Marines and the native force which they led, the *Guardia Nacional,* struggled against odds. It was this fighting that had drawn Lewis Puller so far across the globe.

When he reported to General E. R. Beadle, commander of the *Guardia,* Lewis was dismayed to learn that he must serve as adjutant for a month and a half, while Beadle's man was on leave. Afterward, the general promised, things would change: "I'll give you a company up in the Segovias, in the north. I understand you like to mix it up."

In his post in the capital, Managua, Puller found himself assigned to trifling duties. He was still spoiling for action, and often pleaded with Captain Eddie Craig of his battalion to send him out on patrol when things were quiet at headquarters. Then, when he was assigned to take over a patrol of the First Mobile Battalion in the Jinotega area of central

Nicaragua, a newly arrived major from the States appeared without a billet, and was given the job. Lewis was assigned as quartermaster of the battalion.

He hid his disappointment in hard work. His first coup was the overturning of the scandal-ridden system of the native chiefs, the *jefes politicos* and *alcaldes*, who were renting barracks buildings to the *Guardia*, despite the fact that these were public property. Puller saved a thousand dollars the first month by exposing this fraud, and in the next weeks began building barracks in the outlying districts like those he had put up in Haiti. He then reformed the hauling contracts of bullcart concerns, which were charging twenty-five dollars per cartload for the forty-mile round trip from Jinotega to Matagalpa. When Puller pointed out that this was more than the cost of a cart and a pair of oxen, he was allowed to buy transport for the *Guardia*.

There was a daily ration of fifteen cents per man, and Puller stretched accounts, buying like a miserly native. Cattle on the hoof were under three dollars a head, coffee was three cents a pound, beans a cent and a half, rice five cents, brown sugar two cents, and bread loaves or tortillas a penny each. He sent gangs of prisoners to gather mangoes and papayas from government lands to supplement the ration, and insisted upon bananas, too, despite the disdain of natives, who spoke of them as "pig food."

In March, 1929, after a few months of such work, Puller won a commendation from Beadle "for services in helping to organize the *Guardia* beyond the call of duty." Soon after, in May, Lewis took examinations for the rank of First Lieutenant in the Marine Corps, and in October got his commission. Beadle again promised him a chance at action in the hills, but there was a fresh disappointment.

Just as he was about to lead a company northward, Beadle snatched him away and called him into his office:

"Puller, I want you to go to Corinto and see what you can do. They've wounded Lieutenant Stevens—like a fool he rode a horse into a street mob, and they shot him with his own pistol. Go take command and restore order. The method is up to you."

Lewis boarded the train with a suitcase containing a Thompson submachine gun and ammunition, and when he arrived and found Corinto quiet, and had talked with his tiny garrison force, took the suitcase to the waterfront.

Within sight of a hostile crowd of longshoremen who had

formed the troublesome mob, Puller opened the bag, took out the weapon, and with a few bursts sank several cans in the water some yards away. He then put away the gun, and with the aid of a few *Guardia* arrested half a dozen ringleaders of the mob. Within a few days he had convictions in the courts, but the man credited with the actual shooting of Stevens had fled the country. There was a final conquest in the port city.

The native boss was a fire-eating brigand who had been appointed as the local *jefe politico*. Puller invaded his office, accompanied by a sergeant, and in brief words told the terrorist that he had come to restore order, and that troublemakers would fare badly. He ended quietly: "You will be held responsible for any further disorder. With your life."

As he talked, he saw a partially open drawer in the desk before the chief, and the butt of a revolver. The boss looked as if he wanted to snatch the pistol.

"Go ahead," Puller said. "Use it if you can. We'll settle this once and for all. You'd better be fast."

The chief glanced at Puller's old hand-made holster, worn from so many months on the trails in Haiti, and hesitated. He closed the drawer slowly with his knee and placed empty hands on the desk. Puller walked out without a backward glance, and when they had left, the sergeant erupted in a torrent of praise. The story of the Lieutenant's bravery swept through the city.

Lewis remained in Corinto for several weeks, brushing up on his Bull Cart Spanish with the aid of natives, a correspondence school, and his new-found friend Chris, a Dane who operated a barroom. Puller's major accomplishment in this time was the design of a small hotel for Chris—built almost entirely of old beer bottles and concrete, a low, Spanish-styled structure of rambling wings and patios which the Dane pronounced an artistic triumph.

General David McDougal, Puller's old chief in Haiti, had now arrived to take over the *Guardia*, and things quickly improved. One of McDougal's first acts was to promote Puller to captain in the *Guardia*, and to send him into the hills as commander of Company M.

They were forty miles from the base at Jinotega, deep in Indian country, when the enemy struck from ambush. Puller's patrol of about thirty men was in single file along a wooded trail when, from a long ridge to their left, there was a hail of fire from rifles and automatic weapons, punctuated by unfamiliar heavier explosions. Puller called for one blast from his bugler, and the men took cover.

There was brief firing, as Lewis led a flanking movement and turned the half-seen bandits from their position, but the action had been vicious. The *Guardia* had three wounded, and they found nine bandit bodies on the ridge. The camp had been occupied for several days, the trap waiting.

Puller learned the cause of the heavy explosions of this attack: dynamite bombs, crude bags of rawhide, sewn around sticks of dynamite when fresh, and allowed to harden until they were like iron. The interior was packed with fragments of stone and iron, to act as shrapnel; Puller found them effective only with direct hits, for the fragments flew up or down, and did not cover wide areas.

There was one miraculous escape for Puller in these days of ambush:

He was leading the company, unaware that bandits were in the area, when a rifle went off almost in his ear. He folded his feet beneath him and dropped to the ground, drawing his pistol and turning his head as he did so. A native, no more than five yards away, was ejecting a shell from his rifle, preparing to shoot again. Puller fired three times before he fell, and missed.

It was a moment he remembered vividly: "When I fell to the ground some sanity returned. I knew that the man was almost reloaded, and that I'd better hit him this time, or it was curtains for me. I knew he wouldn't miss twice."

Puller killed his man with the next shot of the .45.

Lewis also saw the first land mines of his career on this expedition—bags of rawhide much like the dynamite bombs, buried in loose earth and staked out on a wire, to be set off by this trigger when an unwary *Guardia* stumbled into it. Puller took one of the mines to headquarters for study.

Puller's career as a guerrilla fighter now opened in earnest. In February, 1930, he was ordered to clear bandits from the area of San Antonio, Le Virgen and Guapinol, and took out a patrol of twenty-eight men and two junior officers. A few days out of Jinotega, about mid-morning, as they marched north of San Antonio, they met another ambush. Puller was in front, with Lieutenant Marcos commanding the center and Lieutenant Rittman the rear. Under orders, men in front and rear sections were walking eight yards apart, and those in the main column five yards apart. This tactic saved them when a Lewis machine gun opened upon the head of the file and rifles fired at the rest.

The troops fell flat on the hillside and returned fire, some of them firing rifle grenades. When the Lewis gun stopped, Puller ordered a charge, and the bandits scattered in the direction of a nearby mountain. There were no *Guardia* casualties.

On the following day, after camping within 2000 yards of a bandit hideout which was screened by dense forest, the patrol found the camp of Pedro Altamirano, one of Sandino's generals. The skirmish was slight, for there were but six bandits in the camp. Altamirano was wounded, and before his death told Puller that the camp had been used for two years —and that Sandino and other officers had fled as the patrol approached. A rebel captain, Sabar Manzanares, was killed outright.

When he returned to base, Puller and the troops got a commendation from General McDougal for these actions—and the young captain also got a replacement, one Bill Lee, who had earlier served three years in Nicaragua, and had been pleading for a chance to return. Lee was a tall, muscular athlete from Haverhill, Massachusetts, who had been sixteen years in the Corps and was conditioned by years of playing fullback on the team of a coal-burning battleship and by boxing and pulling an oar on a crew.

Puller unhesitatingly chose him to help direct Company M, and Lee found Lewis an ideal commander: "He never really gave me orders. He just told me what Headquarters wanted, asked me if I knew the country, and to get up the men we needed. He was a common-sense officer, and you always knew where you stood with him. When he was displeased about something I'd done, he never chewed me out, as so many inexperienced officers would have done. He would say, 'If I'd been doing that, I'd have done it this way,' and that would be the end of it. We got on like brothers. Most important of all, he was not green when he first came to Nicaragua. Haiti had taught him jungle fighting, and he took to the new country like a native."

Their first skirmish together was on June 6, at Los Cedros, when the patrol was ambushed by the *jefes* Marcial Rivera and Ascensión Rodrigues. Lee was walking at the point, in front, and with his eight men dropped and began returning fire against the enemy, who were on a wooded slope above the trail. The two officers worked with an unspoken mutual understanding. Puller took about half the patrol and without so much as a signal to Lee moved for high ground on the bandit flank, under fire. When he was about 150 yards from Lee, Lewis opened fire with all his men, caught the enemy between them, and forced a flight.

They counted seven bandit dead, including the two chiefs, and captured two rifles, sharp-bladed cutachas, detonators and dynamite bombs. The *Guardia* had no losses. Puller and Lee agreed on the cause of their continuing miraculous escapes in ambush: "The Indians were brave, and intelligent, and laid perfect traps, but they were excitable, and not accustomed to the weapons. They usually fired high. If we'd been in their shoes, we'd have wiped out any passing patrol."

Company M fought again at Moncotal on July 22 and at Guapinol three days later, and for a brief time the territory seemed free of bandits. But in August, when they were told of a boy bandit leading a fast-moving gang of horse thieves through the country, Puller and Lee set out again, with the company on foot. The invaders were reported to be from Honduras, all well mounted, but Puller reasoned that determined marchers could overtake them.

The bandits were forced to rest their animals every third day, and during that day the hurrying patrol gained ground. It was the rainy season, when roads and trails were more tiring to horses than to men—and there was mud here, in contrast to the solid footing in the Haitian jungles. Within less than a week Puller and Lee and their forty men caught up with the 150 Hondurans, at a place called Malacate.

A few hours before they found their quarry a woman in a native hut described the chief of the invaders for Puller: "Why, he's so young. Just a boy. He's even younger than you."

The bandits were waiting on a hill which lay at right angles to the trail, and opened fire on the head of Puller's company. Lewis led the column past the point without hesitation, and when he was out of range, turned and struck the flank at a run. Lee remembered it: "We were so strung out when we hit them, from running into the camp at top speed, that most of them got away." They killed two bandits, captured about eighty horses and mules, numerous saddles, and four tons of stolen corn. For months civilians came to Jinotega to claim animals and saddles stolen by the raiders.

This action ended a campaign so effectively that General McDougal recommended Puller for a Navy Cross, citing the five fights against superior numbers without loss to himself, the nine known enemy dead and numerous but uncounted wounded, and the impressive loot of munitions, animals, food, and captured military dispatches.

The recommendation ended:

> Thus by his intelligent and forceful leadership without thought of his own personal safety, by great physical exertion, and by suffering many hardships, he surmounted all obstacles and dealt five successive and severe blows against organized banditry in the Republic of Nicaragua.

President Moncada, an old soldier himself, followed suit by awarding Lewis a high decoration of the country, the Presidential Order of Merit, citing his nine engagements against Sandino forces around Jinotega within a year:

> The activities of this company under the known direction of Captain Puller contributed greatly to the clearing of bandits from many parts of the central area, facilitating thus for the inhabitants the gathering of their crops of coffee and other grain. The activities and operations of Captain Puller, his valor and his personality, assisted in gaining the sympathies of the honorable inhabitants of the country and greatly strengthening the goodwill and the feeling of confidence in the *Guardia Nacional.*

Captain E. E. Linsert, intelligence officer of the Marine Brigade, seldom saw Lewis Puller in Nicaragua, but in his wide reading of native newspapers saw plentiful signs. There was unanimous praise in the press for the fearless young Marine who seemed to thrive on the most deadly bandit attacks, and Linsert made these stories part of his intelligence reports. Puller was becoming a public relations asset in the campaign.

Linsert saw that there were a few jealous detractors: "Now and then the New York *Times* got some of these stories from Nicaraguan papers, and Puller's name became widely known. A few officers around headquarters, who thought of themselves as Clausewitz types, muttered criticisms of Puller, and said he was a publicity hound. I knew that the opposite was true—and that Lewis spent virtually his whole life in this period on the trail, deep in enemy country, while our staff officer friends sat on their duffs in the cities, far removed from the warfare."

Linsert's reaction was supported by Puller's reports of combats, which were so terse as to vex even the most businesslike senior officers.

On March 31, 1931, a disastrous earthquake struck the new capital, Managua, killing more than 1000 of its 120,000 people. Puller was in Jinotega when the news came, and he immediately volunteered to go to the stricken city; he left in an automobile about noon of the same day, riding with the *jefe politico* of Jinotega.

The road was barely passable, and they spent the night on the way. Near dawn, as they approached the city, driving through mobs of refugees, Puller smelled the stench of the dead. He was put in charge of a detail of troops and civilians, recovering and burying bodies. They worked among still-burning and charring buildings; outside the city, great fissures had split open the earth. He buried hundreds that afternoon and the next day, and for the next several days, as the men found bodies so badly burned as to be beyond burying, Lewis carried out grim orders: Burn them with fuel oil where they lie. There were hundreds more of these victims.

Puller had briefly commandel the penitentiary in Managua some years earlier, and was stunned by what he now saw of that building; for its great twenty-five-foot-high walls of quarried stone, with blocks of three and a half by two feet, were so badly tumbled that no two adjacent stones were in place.

On the third day of the work in the city a Red Cross man flew in from San Francisco, bringing a check for $10,000 to the Nicaraguan government for food and medicines. Puller worked in the distribution of these supplies.

Fires continued to break out in the ruins, and the new chief of constabulary, General Calvin B. Matthews, banned civilian cooking in the city. The Marines served the first meal to survivors the next morning, but no more than 11,000 of the original population remained. Puller thought this was prophetic: "Those people went away from their city as far as they could, to the oceans, and Honduras and Costa Rica. It will be the same, some day, when cities of the United States are bombed. When I left Nicaragua for good, two years later, the people of Managua still had not returned." American Red Cross Headquarters sent Puller a commendation for his work in the stricken city.

It was a busy spring for Puller. On one final outing in the far north, he penetrated more deeply into enemy country than any Marine patrol had gone.

They were more than a hundred miles from Jinotega, Company M marching over open country on high ground beside the swift Cua River. Puller and Lee were not far apart when they saw, almost at the same instant, a native dugout canoe speed around a bend to their rear, bearing two men. One of these men fired, wildly. There was also a burst of rifle fire from across the river—another attempt at ambush.

Puller reacted as usual. He ran at top speed toward the river bank, straight for the canoe, pulling his pistol as he went. He fired in motion, and one of the canoeists fell across the gunwale. The patrol killed the other Indian, and when men splashed across the river, they found that the band had fled.

Lee thought Puller's action a climax of the fighting in Nicaragua: "It was the greatest field shot I ever saw. He shot that bird from fifteen to twenty-five yards away from that canoe, going at full speed, and the canoe moving, too. He drilled him right in the ear, so perfectly that we looked over the body for several minutes before finding the wound. He had shot him precisely in the opening of the ear. I don't think such shooting was accidental."

The patrol picked up two rifles and cutachas from the victims, scouted a nearby camp with accommodations for about five hundred men, and Puller made sketches of it in case of a return to the area. They found here some surprising bandit ammunition—the newest type available, 1927 cartridges from the Frankford Arsenal, more effective than the older ammunition used by Marines themselves. This caused a sensation at Headquarters, and launched a search for traitors and smugglers back in the States.

Generals Julian Smith and C. B. Matthews both endorsed Puller's application for duty at the Army Infantry School at Fort Benning, Georgia, about this time. General Smith wrote: "Lieutenant Puller is an officer of the highest type, and will represent the Marine Corps creditably in any Army school." Informally Smith told a reporter: "He was probably the bravest man I ever knew. His was a cool courage, not one of desperation. About the only way to contact the enemy there was to let them ambush him. He would go anywhere without support, knowing that if he got in a jam he had to get himself out. He never hesitated; he invited that kind of work."

General Matthews commended Lewis to Washington as "especially the type who should be given opportunity for education he seeks."

But when word of Puller's coming departure reached the Nicaraguan people a group of about thirty prominent residents of Jinotega wrote General Smith in protest:

> . . . Captain Puller was one of the few officers of the *Guardia Nacional* that worked brilliantly on the task of pacifying this area, where for a long time he revealed himself as the strong and efficient man for this kind of campaign, carried out among all kinds of danger, in an untamed and wild tropical wilderness.
>
> For the above reasons we, the undersigned merchants, farmers and neighbors of this city request that Captain Puller be brought back to Jinotega, as we consider him an important factor in the guarantee for the interests of our community and one of the best officers due to his long experience in dealing with our difficult situation while fighting to obtain peace in Nicaragua. We hope that, in interpreting our petition, you convey to General C. B. Matthews, *Jefe Director* of the *Guardia Nacional,* our wishes in this matter, which will result in Captain Puller being ordered back to duty in this locality.

But in the late summer, Lewis was back in the States, ready for more formal schooling, after three years in the Central American jungles.

In Saluda, Virginia Evans quickly divined that he was in the country, for she got an enormous box of red rosebuds. She was puzzled about the label on the box: "Funeral flowers," until she learned of the admonition from Lewis to a Richmond florist, who was confused or frightened: "I want rosebuds, and if they're not buds, there's going to be a funeral."

There was a brief visit at home, and a stop at Camp Peary, Virginia, where his young brother Sam, a second lieutenant in the Marine Corps, was stationed. An old sergeant major who asked Lewis if he could do anything for Sam was told: "I wish you'd give the first sergeant some leave, and give

Sam the paper work to do. It's the quickest way for him to learn the ropes."

Lewis was soon on his way southward to Columbus, Georgia, home of Fort Benning.

VI

THE STUDENT WHO SPOKE HIS MIND

PULLER landed in one of the crack classes of the Army's Infantry School. This year the classrooms were full of talented men of all services—four of them Marines—and a number of foreign officers.

The assistant commandant was a famous officer of the World War, newly returned from duty in China, Lieutenant Colonel George C. Marshall. Half a dozen other stars-to-be of the second World War were on hand: Major Omar N. Bradley, Major Joseph W. Stilwell, Lieutenant Lightning Joe Collins, Walter Bedell Smith, John R. Hodges and Charles Willoughby.

Puller made himself known from the moment he reported to Fort Benning, September 11, 1931. When he went to the supply officer for uniforms and equipment he was given a bronze holder and one hundred cards imprinted with his name, for display on his uniform—and was asked to pay $1.80 for them. The young Marine roared: "Hell, no! What's the sense of wearing your name around? Anybody worth his salt will know the name of every man in his outfit in a couple of days. I'll never pay for such foolishness."

"Very well, sir," the soldier said, but the next day Puller learned that the supplyman had reported him, and he was called to Colonel Marshall's office. The Colonel was polite, but firm, and Puller thereafter wore the name tag. As old V.M.I men, they had a brief exchange:

"You're a V.M.I alumnus too, Lieutenant?"

"Not really, sir. I spent just one year there."

"Well, if you ever matriculated, you're a V.M.I man, all right. Great place."

"The finest military school in America, sir," Puller said.

Marshall called Lewis into his office several times, evidently to get acquainted with the unorthodox young jungle fighter whose name constantly bobbed up in the reports of instructors, and in whom Marine Corps Headquarters had such an interest.

"Why do Marines always win the national rifle and pistol matches?" Marshall once asked Puller.

"We have more men to pick from."

"Why is that? The Army has fifty thousand men, and you have about eighteen thousand."

"Yes, sir, but all of our men are trained to shoot—and we pick from all of them, and you don't. The Marines stage matches in every area, in the Atlantic and Pacific fleets, in Latin America, and on both coasts, and the winners always move up to the next stage, to the finals at Quantico. After our team is picked, it trains a month for the nationals."

"Couldn't the Army do the same?"

"I don't know, sir. But I do know that your orders this year are that a team will be picked from the troops here at Benning, just a handful. You can't train a winning team like that."

Puller was impressed by Marshall, but was not abashed in his presence, and the colonel seemed to find the Marine's response refreshing. In one of their talks he surprised Puller:

"The Marine Corps is better than the Army. Why?"

"A smaller organization, of picked men. Elite troops."

"What do you mean, picked men?"

"We have a high proportion of re-enlisted men, and have room for few recruits. We keep standards high, mental and physical. Your recruiting sergeants ask us to send them those we reject.

"Most of all, we really train recruits, in the two great centers at San Diego and Parris Island. Your people don't really ground men in basic soldiering."

"Perhaps the Army is too big for that."

"Size wouldn't matter, Colonel, if they wanted to train 'em. You should have more of your people take a look at our boot camps."

"This method of Marine recruiting on an occupational basis, for professional soldiering, strikes me as unfair. Some day I hope to change it. It isn't democratic, doesn't give other services a chance."

Puller was stunned. "Any young man should have the right to choose his service, sir," he said.

About a month after he arrived Puller was asked by Marine Corps Headquarters for a full report on his experiences with the Thompson submachine gun under field conditions, and sent in an enthusiastic report on the weapon's value on patrol.

Perhaps prodded by this communication, he asked Headquarters to keep him in mind, when the school ended the following spring. He asked for future assignment to Nicaragua, China, or sea duty with the Asiatic fleet, in that order.

In December, in the first report period, Puller posted an average score in bayonet drill; a fellow Marine, Lieutenant Gerald Thomas, finished ten places ahead of him. But in marksmanship, with the automatic pistol, he ranked as expert, with a score of 91.13 of 100 points. As a rifleman, he fired 335 of a possible 350, and stood sixteenth in the class of officers. He also ranked as expert with the machine gun, in which he stood high in the top third of the class, with a score of 340.

Puller found that his instructors, who conducted their classes with skill, had been picked from the ranks of schoolteachers and lawyers, and that combat was not a factor. He often found these men at a loss when they were pressed with unexpected questions about field conditions, and that their knowledge was confined to that gained from books. Over a friendly glass, Puller often heard these officers admit that they did not know the answers he was constantly seeking. In truth, it seemed that little had been written about his favorite topic—limited, small-scale, combat.

Lewis drew the attention of Army Lieutenant E. K. Wright, a future general, on the first day, when Puller's "practical and sensible" answers to questions boomed through the room. When Lewis began, other students soon relaxed, knowing that they would not be called upon to handle that question. His replies often included stories of his jungle fighting in Haiti and Nicaragua.

The officers began a game when Puller spoke, in mockery of his bellowing voice. They shouted: "Louder! Louder!" And as Chesty complied, there was bedlam. One instructor tired of this and announced:

"Unless this clamor comes to an end I will have to deprive Lieutenant Puller of the courtesy he deserves when he is asked a question."

Puller yelled from the rear of the room: "Louder, sir, louder!" The laughter of the class brought the session to an end.

Puller sometimes came into open disagreement with instructors. One lecturer told the students that volume of fire in the field was more important than accuracy. That brought Puller to his feet:

"You must have forgotten what happened in the American Revolution," he said. "We won that war with accurate fire, when the enemy had all the volume. It won at Kings Mountain and Saratoga, and every other battle we won. And real shooting almost whipped the mass-firing Federal army in the Civil War. It's still like that, anywhere I've seen men shooting it out. You don't hurt 'em if you don't hit 'em."

There was applause from the class.

The Benning staff asked the Marine officers to provide someone to speak on Nicaragua, since it was fresh in the minds of students and faculty, and the war still raged. Senior Marines were Captains Oliver P. Smith and Gilder Jackson, both to become general officers, but when they were approached, they recommended Puller, who had survived forty bandit skirmishes in Haiti, and dozens in Nicaragua.

But when the combined classes met to hear the Marine Lieutenant speak of his experiences, they were amazed to hear him spiel entertainingly of the lives and customs of the Nicaraguans, including an amusing character sketch of President Moncada, and to speak of geography and climate, plant and animal life—but not a word about the fighting. For some reason, school authorities had forbidden him to speak about his combat experiences, perhaps because they suspected that his pungent observations might reach the public, and precipitate new crises. It was not the last time he would be muzzled in this fashion.

Oliver Smith later recalled that Puller spoke long and well, and that when he ran out of Nicaraguan material, he switched blithely to the Pacific, and expounded on "The Yellow Peril" which threatened America. The Army School had never heard its like.

As Smith left the room an Army officer asked him: "How

many men like that do you have in the Marine Corps?"

Smith smiled. "Just the one," he said. "Just the one."

Omar Bradley discovered something of this during a field exercise. As Puller recalled it:

"One morning my section had a map problem, and we rode out to the area on horseback, left the mounts with horse-holders, and walked through the problem. We walked about eight miles through woods, mapping defensive positions, and then waited for the horseholders on the other side of the woods. We had a long wait, and Major Bradley suggested that we wait in a field of sedge, where the sun would keep us warm. While we were there he began kidding me:

" 'Mr. Puller, while we're here, explain just why the Marine Corps sends its officers to this great Army school.'

"I said, 'Major, I've been here four months, and I still don't understand why the Commandant sends us.'

"Several students sniggered, but Major Bradley was vexed, and kept it up. 'This school is on the division level. You Marines never command more than a platoon. I don't see why you come.'

"I asked him if he'd heard of the Second Army Division, and he said he had. I reminded him that it did most of its fighting in Europe under General Lejeune, a Marine, and he said he knew that.

"The students were laughing by then, but the Major kept pressing me, and I finally said, 'Major, I'll tell you something Lord Nelson is supposed to have said—that before a British naval officer can aspire to high command, he must first know the duties of a seaman. So I say that Marine officers are fit for high command because they not only know the duties of a platoon leader, but have commanded platoons in combat. It doesn't happen in every service.'

"The students all laughed, Major Bradley laid off me, and we soon got back on the horses and left."

Puller also tangled with authority on the rifle range, where he watched an exhibition between two Army teams—first one of ordinary marksmen, and then one of allegedly superior expert riflemen. While students watched, the platoon leaders estimated and announced the range of targets, and the teams fired in turn. The students marched to the targets and counted hits—and a senior officer announced happily: "Look, gentlemen, the experts came out second best!" He looked at Puller. "You Marines waste time and powder trying to make every man an expert rifleman. This test should open your eyes to your error."

Puller had been watching the shooting through his field glasses. "Not at all," he said. "You missed the point because you didn't see where the shots were hitting. All this proves is that the platoon leader of the expert riflemen overestimated his range by about two hundred fifty yards. I could see the impact of the bullets, and though the experts were firing high, their shots were much more accurate in pattern—closer together—than the others. The winning team had the range, and won on points, but their fire was much more scattered. They weren't holding properly."

On weekends, when most students scattered to their homes, or visited in nearby Georgia and Alabama towns, Puller rode or walked the vast pine-clad reservation, until he thought that he must know every inch of the rolling terrain.

These explorations paid dividends in the final field exercise of the school year, when two battalions of the Army's 24th Infantry Regiment were used by student officers in mock warfare. Oliver Smith commanded the Red aggressor forces, which were battling a superior band of Blue defenders. Puller fought under Smith, and was in command of a mule-drawn machine gun outfit which moved in carts, supported by an infantry detachment under Army Lieutenant Armistead D. Mead, who was also to become a general in later life. The young officers had two tanks at their disposal.

Near the end of the day, Smith was ordered to make a daylight withdrawal, hotly pursued by the Blue forces. This was under way across a rough country of timbered ridges when Puller and Mead were brought to bay.

Puller laid a cunning ambush, with his machine guns in line along a hillside, facing across the open to a companion ridge some 1000 yards away. He placed the tanks to his right, with remarkable orders: "When the enemy comes up, and we begin firing, make all the noise you can, go fast for the rear of that ridge over there, turn left, and scatter horseflesh as far as you can."

The "enemy" appeared, and behaved just as Puller expected. It was a horse cavalry regiment, and when machine guns began firing their blanks, the riders dismounted and sent their horses to the rear, with one holder to every four horses—these to stand in line at the bottom of the ridge. The dismounted riders on the ridge, meanwhile, returned Puller's fire. They were soon driven from cover, for when the tanks churned into the woods, with furious clanking, frightened horses ran away from their hapless holders and galloped in all directions. There were shouts of rage over this tactic. Down the hill plunged the regimental commander, a full colonel, an old horseman in the Army tradition. Puller would never forget the sight:

"He looked like Buffalo Bill, with flowing white mustaches and beard, and long hair down over his neckerchief. He was afoot, since he'd lost his mount, and he roared at us that he was ruined. By God, I think he was right. I guess that helped bring the horse cavalry to an end."

As the colonel stormed toward them Lieutenant Mead stepped out to complete the war game victory. "You're my prisoner, Colonel," he said.

"Out of my way, you young whippersnapper, before I ride you down!" Puller and Mead collapsed in laughter as the cavalry struggled to recapture some of their animals—many of which were to roam the country for days. A nearby umpire of the exercise ruled one cavalry squadron out of action entirely, and the other out for several hours.

The old colonel complained bitterly that Puller's guns had opened at such close range as to strike the legs of horses with wadding from the blank cartridges, a violation of principles of fair play and humane warfare. But Puller had learned in the jungles the necessity of point-blank fire for effective ambush.

As night drew on, the cavalrymen, with many mounts missing, continued to press Puller and Mead, and at about 9:00 P.M. some horsemen rode upon the young officers, crying for their surrender. Mead prepared to give up, under rules of the exercise, but Puller blazed angrily: "If this is the way you fight in the buggering Army, I'm leaving." He shouted orders to his sergeants and the machine guns bounced away in the mule carts before anyone could stop them. They were driven mercilessly through swamps thought to be impassable, until 2:00 A.M., when Captain Oliver Smith was astonished to see Puller report to his rear position, proudly delivering mules and guns intact.

Puller's final grades in the officers' school, posted in June: Excellent: mechanism and marksmanship of the rifle, the automatic rifle, musketry, combat practice, rifle, machine gun and howitzer companies, animal management and transportation, equitation, tactics to include the battalion.

Superior: instructional methods.

Satisfactory: the pistol, three-inch mortar, grenade, bayonet training, military sketching, map reading, training, infantry signal communication, and supply.

Curiously enough, the lone "unsatisfactory" was on the machine gun, with which he had distinguished himself in past combats, and would use with such deadly effect in the future. Puller took some solace in an old memory: Stonewall Jackson's lowest mark at West Point had been in infantry tactics, a field in which he made a world-wide reputation.

There was little doubt as to the next duty for Lewis, for in addition to his own insistence that he be returned to Nicaragua, there was an urgent appeal to the Commandant of the Corps from General Matthews, who said Lewis had made himself so valuable that the civilian population of Nicaragua was devoted to him. He added: "His services for the remainder of this year during the critical election period and the process of turning over the *Guardia* organization to the Nicaraguan officers will be of inestimable value."

Lewis left Benning with many new friends in all services— but most important, carried away a distrust of over-schooling military men: "The trouble with this school business is that we've taken it too far, and we sit around in classrooms and will the conditions of battle. Of course in actual battle, you can't will anything, not a damn thing, because the enemy will do what you don't want him to do, or expect him to do, almost every time. Then, when results of actual warfare are studied back in the schools, the staff officers and planners, most of whom have never seen battles, wonder what went wrong with their neat plans.

"You just simply cannot learn warfare in a schoolroom, or anywhere else except in combat. And you'll never know whether you're a fighting man until you're under fire."

Puller boarded a train for New Orleans the day after graduation, and sailed to Nicaragua on a fruit steamer, traveling alone. When he caught the first whiff of land as the ship neared dock in Corinto he realized that he was homesick for the jungle fighting. He was three weeks away from his second Navy Cross.

VII

RETURN OF THE TIGER

LEWIS had a singular welcome to the second phase of his warfare in Nicaragua on the front page of a Managua newspaper:

A ULTIMA HORA
Los Marinos traen al "Tigre de las Segovias" para combatir a Sandino. . . .

He translated rather hesitantly:

BULLETIN
Marines Bring The Tiger of Segovia To Fight Sandino. Late yesterday afternoon, Captain L. B. Puller, The Tiger of Segovia, arrived at Managua by air. It had been brought to his attention that the situation in Segovia had grown worse. He will be sent to Kisalaya where the bandits of Sandino are spreading terror.

There was more to be heard in the market place, where native women provided Puller with the best of his intelligence: Sandino had a price of five thousand pesos on the head of *El Tigre*—and a new atrocity tale was being circulated about Puller, to the effect that he was paying bounty to his men for collecting the ears of Sandino's men, and that soldiers on patrol carried the grisly mementoes in strings on their belts.

Lewis flung himself into the work of Company M once more—but as if he feared that the fighting might soon come to an end, he asked Marine Corps Headquarters that he be sent, upon withdrawal of Marines from Nicaragua, to a foreign post, with preferences in this order: 1. Haiti. 2. Fourth Regiment, Shanghai. 3. Marine Detachment, U. S. Legation, Peking. 4. Sea duty.

With that on record, he took Sandino's trail once more.

In the second week of September, 1932, Puller and his old companion Bill Lee learned of a new bandit supply trail in the hills north of Jinotega. The word was brought by a native who had come down from Metagalpa, in excitement, to speak with *El Tigre:*

"It is the old Incan trail, Señor. Sandino's men bring down ammunition, maybe all the way from Mexico. But you must not go there, Señor. If you take fifty men with you, they will kill you, with four hundred men and plenty of machine guns."

Puller and Lee fitted the company for a long campaign and marched north. They found the trail four days out and hurried along it, destroying several bandit camps as they went. They burned a dozen camp sites within eighteen miles; the next day, covering sixteen miles, they destroyed nine more camps. But despite the fresh signs of the enemy, not a man had been spotted.

On September 26, near the remote settlement of Agua Carta, the column of forty men and eighteen pack mules ran into trouble. Near noon, as they passed along a swale, two rifle shots sounded from cover—the usual signal for an ambush; but when nothing developed, the column pushed ahead. Within six hundred yards the vanguard came to a shallow stream, some thirty yards wide. Lee halted and studied the wooded ground beyond. Puller came by at a trot, one soldier in front of him and the bugler, Rodriques, at his heels.

"Let's go, Bill. What're you waiting for?"

Lewis splashed through the stream with the two natives, with the column after him. No more than a hundred and fifty yards from the bank the man in front shouted: "Look out, Captain! They are here!"

Puller went down on one knee, and as he did so glimpsed a machine gun directly ahead. He recalled the moment with remorse thirty years afterward: "I wasn't as good a man as that Indian ahead of me. He saved my life by yelling, and I could have saved Rodriques, but I just dropped. When I looked behind me I saw a sheet of blood; those machine gun bullets had stitched the bugler's body, every two inches, running from the groin up to the head. They literally cut him to pieces."

Lewis flattened on the ground. The machine gun fell silent, but rifle fire was now constant from both sides of the trail. The machine gun coughed again, and a burst of fire kicked dirt by Puller's right shoulder. He realized that the next burst would hit him, and dove for the base of a large swamp oak; the machine gun tore at the bole of the tree, but the Captain miraculously escaped the point-blank fire.

Puller shouted for his men to deploy into line and get their machine gun into action, but for a few moments could not move, for each time he raised his head, he drew machine gun fire. When his men began to return rifle fire Lewis lunged to his feet and ran rearward, calling to his men to avoid panic: "I'm going to get the machine gun!"

He found Lee lying in the trail, his head and shoulders covered with blood, with the top of his skull evidently knocked in. A nearby *Guardia* called that Lee was dead. Lewis pulled the body off the trail by a foot, under fire from the brush, and led men of the patrol to the high ground on right and left. Within a few minutes he saw that Lee was recovered, and had the machine gun firing; they soon held the ridge beside the trail on either side, and the bandits were in flight.

Puller set up a perimeter defense and began tending his wounded. He found that Lee had a creased skull—a miraculous escape, but the wound looked dangerous. Men buried Rodriques, their only dead man, and Lewis had stretchers improvised from clothing and poles, giving orders to the bearers: "We will take these men back, eight men to a stretcher, so that no one will be worn out. No stretcher is to be put to the ground without orders from me. Any man who drops a stretcher will be shot."

They marched until darkness fell. One of the wounded died in the night and was buried. Lee's head wound was becoming infected, but despite this and other wounds the big man joined the march at dawn. They had left sixteen bandit bodies and many enemy wounded behind, but Company M had never before been so badly hurt. There was more to come.

On September 30, as they neared their base, the company was twice ambushed. Near San Antonio a party of about eighty bandits fired from a brushy hillside, but caused no casualties, and fled when they were charged.

In the afternoon, at Paso Real, there was a more serious threat. Lee, who left the trail to enter a native house, in search of food, found two women huddled together, speechless with fear. He could not persuade them to talk, but was certain that bandits were near, and sent a sergeant forward to Puller with a warning: "Tell him to watch sharp at the stream crossing down the hill."

The column halted on a slope and Lee went up to confer with Puller. "Captain," he said, "if we get past this spot we'll be all right. They're going to be down there, waiting for us, and it's a wicked place."

"Let's give it a try," Puller said, and the file moved down the hill behind him. He was now the only vanguard, since the unwounded *Guardia* were all serving as stretcher bearers, and it was one long train of the wounded. The trail dropped between two steep ridges to the bank of a small stream, then turned right and followed the brook. Yet another hill rose on the far side of the stream.

The attack came when the column had wound around the curve, with Puller in front, beyond sight of Lee. There was a shower of the noisy dynamite bombs, and raking machine gun fire from two directions. Once more, Puller escaped without a wound, and directed the disciplined *Guardia* in returning fire; the men placed the wounded along the edge of the trail and fought their way out. Gradually, as the troops crawled forward, fire lessened from the hilltops, the machine guns of the enemy were stilled, and the bandit band retreated downstream.

The patrol halted in the place for a time, for Lee was weaker, though he insisted he could walk. Puller sent a runner to the base, and on the next morning a plane picked up Lee at the air strip a few miles outside Jinotega.

Company M ended a ten-day march of more than 150 miles, having fought four engagements and killed at least thirty bandits, besides wounding and killing an undetermined number of others. From this patrol Puller got a star in lieu of a second Navy Cross, and Lee a second star for his Cross. Lee soon returned from the Managua hospital, and within a few days led a patrol of his own against the enemy.

Lewis did not get so much as a scratch in the Nicaraguan fighting, and only once was he forced to slow his pace. One day, near the village of Los Cochives, the patrol climbed abruptly above the tropical growth to a high, chilly altitude, and Puller was felled by a puzzling respiratory ailment. His lungs began to fill and he gasped for breath. He could no longer walk.

Lee halted the column and their skilled Navy Medical Corpsman, Tom Lynch, went to work. He sent men to a native hut for unrendered hog fat, heated this over a fire, and smeared hot grease on Puller's chest. He tore uniform shirts into strips and wrapped the patient from shoulders to waist. Within an hour or two Lewis was breathing more easily, and by morning was well enough to walk. It seemed a miracle, but the native troops took the cure as a matter of course.

A more serious affair was now developing at headquarters in Jinotega, where a new battalion commander had arrived from the States. He was vigorous but inexperienced, and issued to Puller a series of naïve and wasteful orders.

One day when Company M was at the village of Corinto Finca, some fifteen miles from Jinotega, a runner brought Puller an order from the new major: A bandit force was reported in a hill town some thirty miles south of Company M's position. Puller would march to this town and destroy the enemy.

The order was mandatory, and Lewis put the men on the trail; he used an old hunter's device from his childhood, and cut directly across the circle in which he expected his quarry to move. He had gone but a few miles when he learned from natives that the bandits had departed the town, and were circling to Puller's left on a wide arc. Company M was immediately turned, and at a crossing of the Tuma River, Puller found that he was only one day behind the bandits.

Puller followed for several days, until he caught the rebels on a hill in open country, attacked and overran their camp, and killed or captured those who did not flee. He killed about fifty wounded animals on the scene, and went back to headquarters with a train of eighty-two captured horses and mules with pack saddles. The new commander watched the victorious patrol pass with its spoils, then questioned Puller:

"Why did you disobey my orders? You should have gone directly south as I told you."

"If I'd done that, you'd never have got these animals, and I'd never have seen the bandits. They'd still be tearing up the countryside. I always carry out orders implicitly, and if I had not found the enemy, I would have marched south before coming back in. Since we were successful, it seems to me it didn't matter whether I carried out the letter of the order."

The Major studied Puller's face, hesitated, and nodded in dismissal.

Throughout the latter half of 1932 Company M was on unceasing patrol, averaging eighteen to twenty miles daily on the mountain trails, stretching it some days to as much as forty miles. There was no communication with Jinotega. In the rainy season, when bandits emerged from the hills to gather supplies, Puller was constantly on call, and for months the company seldom escaped wet blankets and clothing.

Puller and Lee and their troops marched more than ten thousand miles in the Nicaraguan fighting, always on foot, for they early discovered that horsemen drew fire in every skirmish, and so they walked, without the mark of an officer on their uniforms. They also found that horses in numbers slowed progress, since there was little forage in the wild country for a fast-moving force. They could sustain pack mules by chopping down trees when they camped, and allowing the animals to browse on the foliage, but horses required grass.

The Company built a reputation as the most aggressive in the *Guardia,* a fact which was not lost on Puller's commanders. One day Lewis went into headquarters at Jinotega and found General McDougal and his staff officers bending over a large map lying on an improvised table, discussing the possibility of catching a bandit force.

McDougal looked up as Puller entered: "There's the man who can tell us. Puller, how fast will our patrols have to move to catch these devils?"

"Forty miles a day. The enemy will make twenty, easily, and you've got to be much faster to overtake him."

McDougal grunted in disgust, kicked over the table, balled up a marching schedule in his hands and flung it against the wall. "Let's go to Pio's, Puller." The captain and the general repaired to the only oasis in town where cold beer was served and discussed the problems of conquering an enemy who moved at twice the speed of the average *Guardia* patrol.

Near the end of the year, largely because of the victories of Company M, the bandit menace had been so reduced that the Marines could safely make their planned evacuation. For months, Nicaraguan officers had been trained to take over their own forces, and a new president had been duly elected—Juan Batista Sacasa. In theory, the revolution was over.

On January 1, 1933, outgoing President Moncada planned the crowning ceremony of his regime, the driving of a golden spike to complete his new railroad line from León to El Sauce, a branch line which had been under construction for years, but was not yet a model of its kind. Two great bridges, one of them 900 feet and the other 1700 feet, were to be built of steel, but the beams had not arrived from Sweden, and the rails now spanned the gorges on temporary trestles of green pine trunks, fastened with spikes.

On Christmas Eve, 1932, Puller was in the bar of the Managua officers' club when Colonel Leroy P. Hunt, the intelligence officer, came searching for him through the crowd: "I've got something hot. But it's strictly on a volunteer basis."

"Count me in."

"You'd better hear it first, Lewis. The way we get it from the grapevine, Sandino has sworn that Moncada will not live to drive that last spike at El Sauce. All we know is that a band of two hundred fifty horse thieves has crossed the Honduranian border, headed south. They may be only the usual gang, but the President suspects they've come to tear up his railroad, and the General wants a patrol."

"How big a patrol?"

"About eighty men and half a dozen officers."

"I'll get 'em."

"Fine. Have them ready at 8:00 A.M., day after tomorrow."

They boarded their train at León, a box car, a gondola, an engine and a passenger car, and chugged off over the narrow-gauge rails on the eighty-mile route toward El Sauce, the box car in front. The rails were held by few spikes; the box car fell between them several times, and there were halts to jack it up and onto the tracks. Puller went back to the engine when they approached the bridges, held his pistol on the engineer, and forced him to creep across. The structure shivered and swayed under the weight, and men peered anxiously below them into a hundred-foot gorge until they were safely over.

As they neared the end of the line, Lewis rode in the coach; the lookout atop the box car was manned by Bill Lee and Lieutenant Stevens, Progress was slow, for gangs of workmen pounded furiously on the tracks before them, driving spikes. About 4:30 P.M., as the train labored up an incline, Lee saw two men on the tracks ahead. Stevens shouted to workmen below: "Are those men in your gang?"

A machine gun burst answered. Lee shouted below for a BAR, and the weapon was handed up to him; it jammed after one round and he leapt to the ground, banged the weapon with a stone and somehow slipped the jammed firing pin into place. He opened fire.

Bandits on horseback circled the train, firing from covered positions on the necks of their mounts. Puller became aware of the attack when bullets stitched the window pane at his side and showered him with glass. He plunged from the car to the right of the tracks with Lieutenants Bunn and Hays and about half the patrol behind him. The car had halted on a trestle over a dry steam bed. A skirmish line of bandits fired from cover in the train's front, and across the track where Lee had taken another party, more of the ambush lay behind a hedgerow. Still the horses circled wildly, and guns blazed away. The box car was already being splintered. "I'll bet this is the first Indian attack on a train in fifty years," Puller said.

Dynamite bombs pocked the ground nearby. Puller ran across the open, firing his pistol. The patrol followed. Two men fell and Tom Lynch jumped from the train to carry them to safety, an act which won him a Navy Cross.

Puller, Bunn and Hays put the men into a skirmish line, but were pinned down by fire from bandits hiding on an old Indian mound. Puller sent two runners to find Lee and report on conditions across the track. They did not return. Puller darted over the tracks under fire and found Lee preparing to charge.

Puller returned to lead his own men to the attack and though the bandits still shifted to his right in front of him, extending their flank, he finally drove them. Lieutenant Bunn grabbed a BAR from a native soldier and blazed into the open, shooting with such accuracy that the enemy ceased fire and began to flee. On Puller's recommendation, he, too, won the Navy Cross. The *Guardia* charged, and when the flank was turned, Lee and Puller struck the bandit center; most of the enemy escaped, but sixty-three horses were captured.

Bandit casualties were thirty-two dead; the *Guardia* had three dead and three wounded in this fight of an hour and ten minutes, one of the most severe actions of the Marine occupation. Puller lost no time in putting the men to work, burying the dead, cleaning up, and preparing to move into El Sauce.

Several excited men ran to him from a nearby railroad camp, stark naked, to explain that they had been stripped by the bandits, and were lined up for possible execution when the train had arrived. There was a report that the leaders of the bandit force, Benavides and Umanzor, were killed or wounded.

When Lewis tried to move the train there was a delay—the engineer could not be found until, after a long search, he was discovered in the water tender, standing neck-deep in the water, still trembling with fear. The patrol soon chuffed up the hill into El Sauce, and the final threat to the inauguration of the new rail line was removed.

Moncada and a party of dignitaries arrived three days later in a special train, and the President had the cars halted in the precise spot where the action had been fought. For two hours or more he insisted upon being led over the field, while Puller and Lee explained the battle. Captain Linsert, as officer representing Marine headquarters, noticed that Moncada seemed somewhat disappointed at what he saw, and questioned Puller:

"Where are all the bodies—and the dead animals? It doesn't look much like a battlefield. He wants to see some gore."

"I spent the better part of two days cleaning up," Puller said. "I dragged the animal carcasses down the hill for burial, and even had them level up the torn earth."

Moncada made an impressive ceremony of the final moments on this field. He was standing among Nicaraguan officers and political leaders and the few Americans when he shouted as if in inspiration:

"Captain Puller, you deserve promotion for this gallant action. I hereby promote you, Major in the *Guardia Nacional de Nicaragua.*"

As Lewis looked in astonishment, Moncada turned to another officer, unpinned a star from his shoulders, and fastened it upon Puller's uniform.

"There," the President said. "Congratulations, Major Puller. Our friend will have to wait to get another star."

Moncada then elevated Bill Lee to Captain, Bunn to First Lieutenant, and awarded the Cross of Valor to every *Guardia* officer who had fought in the place.

The story was soon made known back in the States, first by the New York *Times,* whose dispatch was labeled "By Tropical Radio to the New York *Times.*" In Saluda, Virginia, it came to the notice of Virginia Evans, whose mother interrupted a family bridge game to hear a radio announcer describe the little battle, and report Puller's decoration.

On schedule, on January 2, 1933, the Marines began leaving Nicaragua. Puller had a physical examination just before entraining, and the Navy doctor who looked him over, admiring the lean physique developed on the mountain trails, told Lewis: "Captain, you're in absolutely perfect shape. Nicaragua has been good for you. It would take thirty years of steady dissipation to break down your body as it is today."

Puller left Managua for Corinto as "the most decorated Marine in Nicaragua," still uncertain as to his future duty.

On the train a general spotted Puller: "I'm going to Washington by plane. Anything I can do for you?"

"Yes, sir. I've put in for China duty. Please try to get me sent there."

When Puller's ship arrived in San Diego ten days later, an airmail letter from Headquarters informed him that he would ship for the Orient in February.

VIII

A CHANGED MAN

IN FEBRUARY, 1933, Lewis was introduced to military society in Peking at the U. S. Legation: His commander pinned on his chest the star for the Navy Cross he had won in Nicaragua.

Less than a month later he took over the Horse Marines, the colorful symbol of American influence in North China, a fifty-man detachment of skilled riders mounted on fine Manchurian ponies. His boyhood riding had prepared him well; he was from the start one of the finest horsemen in the detachment.

One of his first lessons came from a close inspection of Japanese infantry in training; he began to understand the threat which was gnawing away at the Northern Chinese provinces in the bitter war to which Americans had paid so little attention.

Puller drove out with a friend to visit the Ming Tombs, some twenty miles away, and met a battalion of Japanese troops which had marched from the city. Puller retained a memory of the scene:

"It was freezing weather in March and our own Marines were indoors in the city. The Japanese were hung with belts such as we carried, with bayonets, but also had heavy marching gear with full ammunition belts—and on top of each pack was a bundle of firewood, for that barren country was picked clean of all fuel, even to the grass roots. When they passed us the uniforms of these soldiers were saturated with sweat.

"They formed ranks and had setting-up exercises to cool off, then paired off and for fifteen minutes massaged each other, especially on chests, legs and neck. They then stacked arms, got half an hour to cook rice and bean powder and take a look at the Ming Tombs, then fell in and marched back for Peking in that cutting wind.

"We ate a picnic lunch in our car, looked over the tombs and the immense statues of more than a hundred kings, then drove back. We entered Peking about 6:00 P.M.—and found the Japanese troops ahead of us at the gates. When I realized that this was their daily routine, I knew that they would be terrible adversaries in war."

Lewis discovered that the 600-man U. S. Marine battalion held only one field exercise each week—and this was called off in extreme heat or cold or a dust storm—but that the Japanese did not cancel their training marches for any reason.

He put his Horse Marines through their paces daily, excluding Saturdays and Sundays, leading them on long cross-country rides with small dust storms boiling in their wake. He rode into areas where the Japanese were training, in an effort to observe details of their tactical work.

There was also a weekly sunset parade for the American colony of the ancient city—about 3000 strong—followed by the Colonel's reception. A battalion of infantry and the cavalry detachment put on this show, the Horse Marines finishing it by passing at a walk, trot and finally a gallop, with sabers flashing.

Another bonus in his twenty-one-month stay for Puller was a glimpse of the Chinese Army. His commander sent him about fifteen miles north of the city to observe the Chinese troops as they passed southward from Manchuria, much of which had been ceded to Japan. Puller went on horseback with two Marines.

The Chinese poured past Puller's roadside post for three days, a horde which seemed endless. They were well dressed in utility uniforms of the field green color Americans were to adopt many years later. Lewis was surprised to see that thousands of them were no more than fourteen or fifteen years old, and that about half the army was made up of boys in their teens. There was nothing of the mob about these troops, discipline was perfect. There was only a scattering of mortars and no artillery. The only vehicles were two-wheeled grain carts, each drawn by two or three mules in single file.

Puller and his men counted steadily, for their mission was to estimate the strength of this army. They met a few officers who spoke English and from them gathered the mood of the troops: They were depressed but not defeated. The men felt that they had been sold out in a truce and wanted only to return north and fight the Japanese. It was a scene Puller did not forget.

His count of the Chinese, reported in Peking, was 105,000; he was pleased to see a newspaper announce a few days later that the strength was 107,000.

One of Puller's duties was locating and tracing Americans in Peking, missionaries, businessmen, tourists and retired service men. In an emergency he would gather them in the Legation compound for protection, and Marines made regular checks of the residences.

Peking's weather varied from 120 degrees in summer to 20 below zero in winter and for months ice made the Horse Marines of little use, for even when roughshod the animals could barely walk on the stone-paved streets.

The U. S. Minister in the city was Nelson T. Johnson, a veteran of thirty years in China, with an intimate knowledge of its people and customs. Johnson took a daily walk through the streets and often stopped for a conversation in Puller's office. He was full of stories of his career in China, dating to 1907, when he was an interpreter; he was the first man to make Puller aware of the growing menace of Japan and China to world peace. He also inspired Lewis to learn spoken Chinese, as he had learned native tongues in Latin America.

Puller was impressed by Johnson's diplomatic parties, where only tea and lemonade were served, to the obvious delight of Oriental guests. Johnson spoke Mandarin and many other dialects and was evidently an ideal Minister. Lewis followed his later career: "At the outbreak of war with Japan Mr. Johnson was pulled out of China and stuck down in Australia, despite his priceless knowledge of the Chinese. I never knew why. It was little wonder to me that China went Communist, the way American affairs were handled out there. From what I saw, *The Ugly American* spoke the truth. During my twenty-seven years of foreign duty I saw all too many of our diplomats whose only qualification was private wealth."

Puller was put in charge of the boxing team and drove the fighters with such vigor that there was soon a waiting list for the victorious team. Evening fight cards became a leading social event of the Peking season and drew service teams from throughout the Far East to meet the Marines. Once when Puller found that his team was out of condition a few days before a match he put all of them on a big coal pile and had them move it back and forth with shovels until they made the weight limits. They won the next match.

Another attraction of life in the city was the succession of fancy-dress balls, which drew most of the foreign colony. Once, when Puller's friend John Thomason heard that some Marine officer was going to one of these balls as Robert E. Lee, he said, "I'd sooner go as God." He expressed Puller's feeling exactly.

Thomason, who became Puller's most intimate friend in Peking, had been a platoon and company commander in the World War and was winning a name as an author and illustrator in these days. He was so senior in his rank that he often threatened to write a book titled *Fifty Years a Captain in the Marine Corps*.

Puller enjoyed Thomason and he often spent evenings listening to his talk with Jimmy Devereux and Marty Sommers, the foreign correspondent:

"John was writing for American magazines, and was always fighting a deadline. Often he would get a check for about two hundred seventy-five dollars and an order to deliver a story within six weeks. His first move was to call his Number One Boy, hand him the check and a list of whisky, and send him to the bank and the club. Mrs. Thomason would leave the apartment for a few days, and John would call up all his friends in Peking. We had some great old times, and they lasted until the checks ran out.

"All John ever did, then, about the story, was to circle a date on his calendar—and on the night or so before the deadline, when he knew he had to catch a mailboat to Frisco in order to get the story in on time, he sat down and wrote furiously and drew the pictures, too. He always made it. A great guy."

Through Thomason, Lewis made an effort to modernize the post: "John, our evacuation plans call for taking our people out on horseback. You know we couldn't do that in time. We have about thirty big trucks, and they would carry thirty or forty people each. Why do we have to keep up this nonsense?"

"Because it's always been done, I suppose. Write out a new

plan and bring it to Headquarters and I'll help you get the Colonel's approval."

Thomason telephoned soon after Lewis submitted his scheme: "My God, Puller, don't you realize that Washington will disband the Mounted Detachment when this thing reaches the Quartermasters? They'll cut it out to save money."

"Why shouldn't they?"

He never got a satisfactory answer, but was told unofficially that, in case of trouble, civilians would be evacuated by truck. "It took me just twenty-four hours to learn to play this kind of make-believe game," Puller said.

Lewis never forgot Virginia Evans and faithfully wrote her of his experiences in China and sometimes sent rather unlikely gifts. One of the better gifts was a copy of John Thomason's book on service in the Far East, *Salt Winds and Gobi Dust*, with a scribbled note on the flyleaf: "Thomason can describe the life better than I."

In one letter he wrote so emphatically that she could almost see him blurting out the words he wanted to say to her: "But dear, even if you do marry me and make me a happy man, even then, if I hear the beat of the drum, I must leave you. I want you to know that."

The chief charm of Peking for Puller was polo. He had never played before, but he threw himself into it as if he were re-enacting a Civil War cavalry charge. His early training had prepared him for the rough-and-tumble, and he became the most daring of Marine riders.

Puller was chosen No. 1 "Griffin" of the season in 1933, the best beginning player—and was thus the finest of about a dozen neophytes. His detachment team also won the Hôtel de Pékin Cup for the championship, and the next year won the Major McCallum Trophy. In two seasons of polo Lewis often played ten chukkers or more daily and finished his career there with a four-goal handicap.

Lewis had one serious accident, the most painful of his career, when a pony rolled over on him and pulled his rib cage loose from his spine down one side. Doctors were concerned, but though he remained in a cast for months, Puller was out of the hospital in a few days and back on limited duty.

In September, 1934, Puller joined the U.S.S. *Augusta*, flagship of the Asiatic fleet—but it was not his first choice. He had requested more schooling, at Quantico, or one of the Army schools. Even so, he went to sea with enthusiasm.

He came in from a cross-country ride at Peking one afternoon and was summoned to his colonel's office. He was handed a letter from Admiral F. B. Upham, asking help for the *Augusta*, whose last two Marine commanders had been dismissed as unsatisfactory.

"It would be a fine tour for you," the Colonel said. "They'll call at every port in South Asia, and if you wish you can stay aboard a couple of years longer."

"I'll take it," Puller said. But he first had to face a going-away party that caused a tumult in the Peking railway station.

After a few glasses had been raised at the Club the entire Mounted Detachment, on horseback, pushed through the doors of the station, thrusting back confused crowds of Chinese, and rode solemnly down the platform, escorting Lieutenant Puller to his car. The crowd made the horses frisky and it was only by a minor miracle that Puller was put safely aboard and sent away without accident.

He boarded the *Augusta* at Chingwangtao and passed immediately under the eye of Admiral Upham: "Lieutenant, they say you're a soldierly fellow, a fine Marine. I hope that I'll be able to say I was happy to have had you aboard, some day. I was not impressed by some of the officers who preceded you—and if you don't improve the Marine guard, you'll go fast."

When he was dismissed Lewis assembled the seventy-five men of the ship's detachment, and kept them less than two minutes. He rumbled at them: "My name's Puller. I'm glad to have been assigned to command you. We're going to work together, starting from scratch. We'll see if we all can't learn something, and do a little bit for our country. Dismissed."

The next day he took half the landing force to a rifle range in Chingwangtao and for ten days drilled them with their weapons; the other half of the detachment followed before the ship sailed. Lewis acted as small arms officer as well as Marine commander, and soon became legal aide to Captain Chester W. Nimitz, the skipper.

Their first cruise took them to Shefoo and Tsingtao and other ports for two days each, to Shanghai, then on a six-day speed run to Guam, much of it in the wake of a typhoon which felled many men with seasickness and left too few officers to stand watches. Puller was one who escaped.

Admiral Upham soon left the ship, succeeded by Admiral Orin G. Murfin. In the change-of-command ceremony, as Murfin came aboard, Upham carried his game with Puller to the final moment. The Admiral shook hands with his officers, the band played, pipes wailed as he stepped toward the gangplank, and the Marines presented arms. Puller thought he would leave without a sign of approval for the improved state of the detachment—but just as his head and shoulders were on the point of disappearing, Puller caught Upham's eye.

The Admiral returned to the quarter-deck, reached for Puller's hand and said, "Glad to have had you aboard, Puller." He vanished.

Lewis exhibited his well-trained Marines on several trips ashore, once in Japan, as an honor guard for the funeral of Admiral Togo, the Japanese hero of the battle of Tsushima during the Russo-Japanese War. The Marines were handpicked men, all six feet tall or over, and Ensign O. D. Waters, a future admiral, thought Puller's bearing so impressive that no one noticed that he was not as tall as his men, who towered over the surrounding Japanese.

Puller was aware of some American military errors aboard the *Augusta,* and he never failed to expose them in talks with his intimates: "Here we have a ten-thousand-ton heavy cruiser, with about eight hundred men aboard—just one on the Asiatic station. The British have three cruisers on duty here. You ever notice that we have thirty-seven typewriters on this ship? The British have just one machine on each of their cruisers. Why do you suppose that is? You know damned well they don't read all those reports back in Washington, when they get there. Paper work will ruin any military force—they should have learned that from Smedley Butler. They'll shed this monstrosity when war comes, though, and the fighting people take over."

The *Augusta* turned south. When she crossed the Equator, Puller suffered the horseplay of Neptunus Rex with other "polliwogs"—and his detachment whooped with laughter when he was dragged before the tribunal, charged with "unmilitary bearing" and "gross display of medals."

During a stay at Melbourne the Marines shot a match

against Australians on a rifle range ashore and as they returned to the ship, crossing a river by ferry, an automobile carrying several young women plunged into the water. The vehicle floated briefly.

Puller was standing on deck and when he saw that no one was helping dived overboard. He wrenched open a door of the car and helped out two bedraggled and hysterical women, but the car then plunged downward, bearing the woman driver. Puller dived from the surface and found the car upside down, wedged tightly in mud. He came to the surface for air and returned several times, in vain.

Puller had no idea of the identity of the rescued girls and when the father of a survivor, Sir Frederick Mann, came to the ship to express thanks and invite the Lieutenant to dinner, Puller declined. Talk of the exploit seemed to embarrass him. Ensign Waters and other officers joshed Puller when he came aboard in his dripping clothes, supposing that he had fallen off a pier in horseplay. His shipmates knew nothing of his heroism until news of it appeared in the local newspapers.

The *Augusta* visited other Australian ports, then Borneo, Java, Sumatra, Celibes and Bali. They were in Manila over Christmas, and into January, 1935, where Puller acted as legal aide to the Commander-in-Chief of the Asiatic Fleet. On this run the equatorial crossing found Lewis one of the robed judges of King Neptune's court and he enjoyed the discomfiture of Lieutenant Colonel Joe Stilwell, the Army's Vinegar Joe of future fame. Stilwell recognized Puller. The conspirators had dressed a fat fireman of some 260 pounds in a baby's pinafore. The senior judge ordered Stilwell to kiss the Royal Infant:

"Kiss the baby's belly."

Stilwell turned to Puller: "Do I have to obey that order?"

"Quick, Colonel, before they turn the baby upside-down."

Stilwell leaned to kiss the huge stomach, and two sailors thrust his head until it almost disappeared in rolls of fat.

There was gunnery at sea and overhaul at Cavite, the annual speed run for Hong Kong, then up the China Coast to Amoy and Shanghai. Puller's first year aboard was over.

The second year promised much the same schedule, but with a swing through the Dutch Islands and the Malay Peninsula, Singapore and Siam.

In January Puller's name appeared on the list of Marine

first lieutenants up for promotion to captain, and a note of congratulation came from John Thomason, now in Headquarters at Washington:

> I am very glad to see your name on the selection list and I write to offer my congratulations. All that I hear of you confirms the opinion I formed of you in Peking, and I consider you one of the few officers I know who have a genuine military aptitude.
>
> I knew a number of fine officers in the German war, men who, as platoon and company commanders, showed much promise and some talent in 1918. A good many of these same officers have shown nothing since then, and their names are not on any selection lists—that is, most of them are not. . . .
>
> Napoleon's receipt for proficiency in the military art was: to study and reflect upon, the campaigns of the great captains. He named Hannibal, Turenne, Saxe, Frederick the Great and Gustavus Adolphus and Charles XII. You can add Napoleon's name, and much is to be learned from Lee, Jackson, Forrest, Sherman and Grant in our war.
>
> Take care of yourself. The world does not promise peace, and they will need us combat officers before our time is up.

Puller smiled over the list of military reading, most of which he had been sampling since boyhood, but he pasted the letter in his copy of Thomason's *Marines and Others,* which became a gift to Virginia Evans. As he did so he thought once more of Thomason's oft-repeated threats, in Peking, to write a book about Puller and his exploits in Haiti and Nicaragua.

Lewis still made a great show of bachelorhood in these days, and he told his cronies, "The Marine Corps ought not to permit marriage. A monastic order, all the way. Married men make poor soldiers. If the Government wanted you to have a wife, they'd issue you one."

There was, all the same, a steady correspondence with the brown-eyed girl in Saluda, Virginia.

In April Lewis requested an extended tour of duty on the *Augusta* so that he could become more proficient in naval gunnery. Nimitz approved, saying, "The work of Lieutenant Puller on board this vessel has been excellent."

Yet when Puller took his examinations for Captain, the board turned him down for failure in ordnance and gunnery —four of his ten questions dealt with an obsolete antiaircraft gun. A new examination was ordered, however, and Puller passed with ease. His commission as Captain was dated from July, 1935.

In the spring of 1936 another honor came to Puller. Headquarters radioed that the Haines Bayonet Trophy, sought by every active Marine unit, had been won by the detachment of the *Augusta*.

Once more there was a call to unexpected duty. Colonel Hal Turnage, commander of the Basic School in 'Philadelphia, where all young Marine officers of the time were trained, needed the help of Lewis Puller. The Captain reported in late June.

Colonel Turnage explained his wishes simply: "Captain, we had a great class of young officers here last year, and a finer crop is coming up. They get all they need in the classroom and know military theory—but they don't get the real Marine training I like."

"You mean recruit training, sir?"

"Something like that. I'll leave it to you. You have a reputation for discipline and common sense. You do the job, and I'll back you all the way."

Lewis simply added the hard routine of boot camp to the already-full schedule of the incoming officers, and was forced to begin at 6:00 A.M. Turnage soon took note of the change that came over his school:

"When Puller got to work, we needed no bugle in the Navy Yard. He had his men out before day working them on drill and command—teaching them to shout commands in turn. It woke up everybody on the post.

"Lewis left nothing undone. We had the best classes in 1935 and 1936 that I ever knew in the Marine Corps, and Puller did a great deal for that second class."

His class of '36 was made up of ninety-four honor graduates of college ROTC units and twenty-five Annapolis Middies. Among them were nationally known football stars, including Ben Robertshaw, Navy's All-American center, and Lew Walt, a burly star of the Colorado Aggies who was destined to become a general. A little-known member of one class who would rise to fame was Gregory (Pappy) Boyington, who began here to form his opinion that Puller was "the greatest Marine of all."

Lewis began well with these young men when they saw him decorated with two combat awards on the parade ground: the Nicaraguan Presidential Medal of Merit and Cross of Valor.

They also found him refreshing as a classroom instructor. Lewis knew that students frequently slept through the dull classes. He tried new tacks, adding hair-raising stories of battle to put over his points, but he did not always succeed. One day he saw a student snoring away with his chin on his chest and, speaking in a lowered voice, walked to the rear of the culprit, yanked the chair from under him with a foot and roared as the young officer candidate scrambled to his feet: "Now, sleeping beauty! Take your somnolent duff up to your sack and sleep it off. You stay there until you can remain awake in my classes!"

It was the last of that difficulty.

Lew Walt remembered much later, after combat in two wars had made him a general: "Puller was my company commander, and to me was the epitome of what Marine Corps training should do. Not only in weapons, or classroom or field training—he gave us everything hard. At every break in the field, though he drove us until our tongues were hanging out, men still gathered around him. He told us tales about fighting in Haiti and Nicaragua, of his patrols living off the land, and fighting natives—all his experiences, not just guff. Every tale had some point.

"Being under Puller in Basic School did more for me than anything I experienced until I got to Guadalcanal. He taught us the use of terrain like a master, how to use the tiniest bit of cover to our advantage. Ground form really meant something when he explained it. He taught us to use the bayonet with all the tricks of close-in fighting. You couldn't mistake it, he knew the stuff cold."

Lewis also intensified his siege of Virginia Evans, and had persuaded her to come up for the Army-Navy game of 1936. She was much interested in a young man in Boston but agreed to the trip.

The Turnages were amused by the Captain's shy announcement: "I have a girl. Down home in Virginia, you know. She's coming up for the game. I'm sort of looking for a place where she can stay."

"Why, she'll stay with us," Mrs. Turnage said, and when Virginia Evans arrived she was installed with the commander's family. After the Navy Ball during that weekend Colonel and Mrs. Turnage concluded that the two were in love, and were not surprised by later signs that Lewis was a lost man.

He made the long trip to Saluda almost every weekend now, courting Virginia with growing confidence. The girl told her mother: "I never had a beau like him. He's always so positive about everything. He never pays the least attention to what I say. If I tell him not to come down for the weekend, there he comes, anyway. Yet, he's the most attentive thing you ever saw. He writes me every day."

In April, soon after she promised to marry him, Lewis wrote:

> I, too, miss you dreadfully, but, as you know, I can stand on my head until *The Day.* Oh! Virginia, I am so very happy and contented and we will always be ever so happy. You have made my life worth while now.
>
> Colonel Turnage showed me my fitness report today for the past six months and the report was perfect. . . . You are responsible, Darling, and from now on all my reports will be likewise. . . .
>
> The weather is quite wet here now. Rain most of yesterday and all of today. The sun is shining for me, though, and always will. . . .
>
> I would like to phone you every evening but will continue to confine myself to Sundays in order to save *our* money. . . .

On a freezing, rain-swept day just before Puller's marriage the Class of '37 had an uncomfortable experience with him on the drill field. They wore no overcoats as they marched. Teeth chattered, but the ranks moved with precision.

Lewis saw stray glances at the barracks detachment which came out for a brief drill wrapped in heavy overcoats, and then disappeared.

"Those are *barracks* Marines," he said with an edge in his voice. "You're *fighting* Marines."

They completed the full schedule for the day, chilled to the bone and soaking wet.

Before the wedding Puller had made his annual request for choice of new duty: "It has been five years since I have attended school and this request is made in order that I may improve my professional qualifications." Headquarters seemed to think more schooling for him unnecessary, for he remained a Basic School instructor three years.

Lewis and Virginia were married November 13, 1937, in

Christ Church, Middlesex County, Virginia, near the homes of their childhood. The old church stood on land donated by a seventeenth-century Puller ancestor, one Captain Bocas. Despite the cold weather Virginia had asked if the Marines who came down with him couldn't wear their summer whites to match her color scheme and he had replied patiently with a small joke: "Dear, perhaps we can persuade the Secretary of the Navy to change the regulations, or Someone Else to change the weather."

Half a dozen Marine officers took part in the ceremony and formed an arch of swords as the couple left the church.

Virginia told the groom afterward that he was a source of embarrassment to her through the entire ceremony. Before the soloist began to sing "O Perfect Love," Puller marched from the side room where he was told to remain until the Rector appeared. Spectators heard his hoarse whispered order: "Come on, Doctor!" as he prodded the minister, Rev. William D. Smith.

Virginia went down the aisle on the arm of her brother, Bill Evans, and when they came to his side, Puller said in a voice audible to the back rows, "Thanks, Bill!" There was a subdued tittering; Mr. Smith later proposed that he make this line a part of the marriage service.

When the couple walked from the church Lewis brought grins to faces of friends with his growls of affection: "You're so lovely, dear!" He did not cease despite her desperate whispers of protest.

They spent a brief honeymoon in Atlantic City and Lewis was soon back at the school. They were installed in a two-bedroom apartment overlooking the parade ground, their happiness increased by Patsy, a maid Virginia brought from home.

The newlyweds drew much attention from the student Marines. One young lieutenant never tired of braying at cocktail parties: "When I got Puller's wedding announcement I thought it must be a mistake. Hell, I thought he was hunting birds, all those trips he made down to Virginia. It beats me. I can't conceive of Lewis Puller making love to any woman on earth."

The students noted changes in Puller's nature and those who had marched in the cold rain under his relentless eye so recently now detected a softening. One of them, Lieutenant Parker Colmer, saw that they were dismissed if the days were even slightly cool or rain threatened. The officers surmised that the pretty bride peeping from the curtained windows across the parade ground had wrought a permanent change.

But Lieutenant Colmer decided not: "It must have been the first blush of wedded bliss that changed the Old Man. In later years I saw a decided return to the original Puller."

Virginia Evans managed to housebreak the field soldier, however, and the Navy Yard discovered that he was a genial, hospitable host in his apartment, where Patsy soon learned to serve small dinners with grace and skill.

Puller's social achievements were never greater than on the night the Pullers arrived at the home of the new commanding officer, Colonel Gilder Jackson, to hear the mournful plaint of Mrs. Jackson: "Here I am, with a dozen people due here any minute. I've nothing on earth for dinner except crabs, and they haven't even been cleaned—neither maid will touch them."

Puller busied himself in the kitchen and in less than half an hour the chore was done. Mrs. Jackson regarded it as sorcery. "Any kid brought up on the York River could do it with one hand," Puller said. "All you needed was a water rat."

The Pullers once went to a Navy dance in Washington, where Virginia met Lewis's old friend Chester Nimitz for the first time. He reminisced about the old days on the *Augusta* as they danced, and told her of her husband's rescue of the two women in the Australian river.

She was astonished: "I never heard a word about that! Isn't it just like him, not to mention it to me?"

"He's a fine officer and a fine man. You're a lucky girl."

"Don't I know it? But, Admiral, I've made lots of changes in Lewis since we've been married."

Nimitz smiled, but his frosty eyes did not: "Perhaps if you change him too much it won't be for the better."

She laughed: "You know that nobody on earth could change Lewis Puller as much as all that."

"I hope not. He's the kind we're going to need, one of these days."

Mrs. Puller knew that her husband was a warrior first of all; one of her gifts to him this year was *Stonewall Jackson*, by Colonel G. F. R. Henderson.

The Pullers left the pleasant life of the Philadelphia

Navy Yard in the spring of 1939, bound for the Orient. Puller had asked for duty with the 4th Regiment in Shanghai, but had been reassigned to the *Augusta* instead. The voyage out was like a second honeymoon.

Several friends were aboard their ship, including the promising Basic School graduate, Lieutenant Lew Walt, with his bride. Puller played acey-deucey with some cronies during the days, and as they reached the islands enjoyed pointing out familiar scenes from his former tours. They had a few days in Hawaii, and went to Waikiki one morning to ride surfboards with another young friend, Lieutenant Gordon Warner, a champion swimmer who had studied under Lewis at Basic School.

The two men went out to sea in a canoe, and to Virginia's astonishment Lewis rode in with Warner, balancing with skill as rollers hurled them to the shore. Lewis then returned and rode in on a surfboard alone and turned to Virginia: "Come on, you're going to try it, too. You never had so much fun."

Mrs. Puller went out with some trepidation and when the canoe halted she hung back, until Lewis snapped: "You aren't yellow, are you?" She jumped to the board just as a wave approached, and rode in, seated, with Warner standing above.

When she reached shore she laughed to Lewis: "You hound! That was the only thing you could have said that would have made me ride that thing. You're terrible—you always know what to say."

They had a lunch of hot dogs and poi on the beach, and swam and sunned in the afternoon with a party from the ship; both were badly sunburned.

Lewis rose at dawn when the ship reached Manila and climbed down the gangway among the bumboats, where he bought an armload of orchids, paying about ten cents apiece for them. When he took them to the stateroom and spread them over Virginia, she was radiant with happiness.

"You've kept your promise," she said. "Even more than three dozen orchids."

"One more promise, dear."

"What's that?"

"The beat of the drum. You remember that."

"Oh, Lewis, there's not going to be another war."

"Virginia, there will always be a war, and when it comes, I'll be there."

She found him unfailingly attentive, and on the thirteenth of every month after their marriage—their "anniversary" —he sent her a dozen red roses.

The Pullers sailed to China, and after he had settled his wife in a hotel in Tsingtao, where there were many American Navy families, Lewis boarded the *Augusta*. He found the ship little changed, beyond the addition of some new antiaircraft guns; her commander was now Captain John Magruder. Puller was aboard the flagship from July, 1939, to May, 1940, a time when she avoided Japanese-held islands in her cruising.

In May, 1940, Lewis was promoted to Major and abruptly ordered to Shanghai, and the 4th Marines. Virginia met him there—and he was none too soon, for their first child, Virginia McCandlish Puller, was born a few days later. Lewis soon had them housed in relative luxury in a three-bedroom home in Shanghai, attended by five servants.

In the city outside were distressing contrasts. Each morning about a hundred bodies were found in the streets, victims of starvation. In one quarter of the city, behind barricades, were the troops of the conquering Japanese; tension was greater here than in the days in Peking. The threat of war was in the air.

Lewis worked hard as executive officer of the 2nd Battalion of the regiment, serving on the administrative and exchange councils and audit boards in addition to training infantrymen. His superiors, who changed rapidly, gave him invariably high rating on his fitness reports: "An outstanding officer of his rank . . . exceptionally keen, interested in his profession . . . a most excellent officer in all respects. I would like to have him serve with me in any capacity at any time."

Virginia Mac was not christened until late fall, after many postponements to enable her godmother, Isabella Hart, to attend. At last Miss Hart, daughter of Admiral Thomas C. Hart, sent her gift in emergency haste: a hand-made christening robe which was delivered in the nick of time only by being sent on the flagship, *Augusta*.

Admiral Hart sent for the Major, who entered the office a bit nervously on the unusual call. Hart's seamed face wrinkled into a smile: "Puller, take this damned dress. First time I ever heard of one being delivered by an Admiral's barge."

The child was christened by the Rev. Francis Cox at St. John's University in Shanghai.

The first official sign of growing concern in Washington was a questionnaire which passed among military men in Shanghai, asking whether they wished to evacuate their families. Puller applied to send his wife and child home; they sailed on the *President Coolidge* in November, 1940.

Puller joined a Navy captain for dinner one evening, their companions two Japanese Navy officers. One of the Japanese, in his cups, soon dropped his polite, formal air and snapped at Puller's friend:

"Soon, American, we will be at war. I will meet you—you in a cruiser, me in a destroyer. We will sink you, and as I steam by, you will shout from the water, 'Help me, friend!' Then I will stop my ship and kick you down with my foot in your face and say, 'Die, you American son of a bitch!' "

The Japanese left them with the soberer officer spluttering apologies.

Puller needed no such warning. He kept a Mongol pony on the outskirts of the city in a stable, saddled and ready under the eye of a friendly Chinese hostler. In case of surrender, Puller planned to run for the stable, put on Chinese clothing and make his way through bandit country until he could join the Chinese armies.

When he entered the Noncommissioned Officers' Club one day a sergeant of the regiment hailed him: "What're you going to do if the shooting starts, Major?"

"I don't know what the Government will do, or Headquarters, either. But with no orders to the contrary, I'll take my battalion and fight my way the hell back to Frisco."

Puller did not conceal his restlessness from fellow officers: "Here I am, five months overdue in this station already, and things are going to pop just any day. When they do, we'll be caught out here where we can do nothing."

"Why don't you remind them you're overdue?"

"Hell, I can't do that. They'll think I'm yellow." This fetched gales of laughter in the Officers' Club, and was recalled a few nights later, when Puller met the Japanese Army in its first recorded clash with the Marines.

After dark a party of eighty Japanese troops violated the neutrality of the International Zone and marched through the American sector, where they rounded up two hundred Chinese, intending to take them back for trial on nameless charges.

Puller was detailed to get the Japs out of the settlement without creating an incident, if possible. He led twenty-two Marines to the compound where the Chinese were being illegally held. Lewis drew his pistol on the Japanese officer he found at the gate: "I'll give you five minutes to free those men and get your troops back across Soochow Creek where you belong."

The Japanese did not seem to understand English, but he could not mistake the meaning of Puller's tone of voice nor his expression—and over the Major's shoulder he saw Marines setting up two heavy machine guns. He barked his orders to retire, and Puller sent the Chinese back to freedom.

Puller said afterward: "I wish now I had killed him. It would have started the war, perhaps, but we'd have lost only one regiment, instead of all those men and ships at Pearl Harbor."

Lewis drove his men harder in these days, but spent some time at the clubs, and an occasional dance for members of the American colony; he was also an honorary member of a club of ex-Czarist officers. He was lonely, and his letters to Virginia did not conceal it. He wrote her of dining with some lieutenants one Saturday evening and of playing poker: "I lost eight Mex. Lucky in love, unlucky in cards. You must have been loving me a lot this evening, as I could draw absolutely nothing."

He wrote her daily, in a way that made the spirit of the city unmistakable:

 . . . The Battalion had its weekly hike this morning, almost three hours with full field equipment, and maintained a four-mile-an-hour pace. I can walk fast! Do you remember when we used to walk together and you thought I was too slow? . . .

I had a good ride this afternoon. I believe my pony could gallop from here to Burma. . . . Yesterday the exchange rate in shops was about eighteen to one. Prices are still going up, food and coal particularly. . . . Tomorrow we will have been married three years and two months and the time only seems a day, and then again it seems as if I have always had you. . . .

The situation here has eased a bit. After the war is over in Europe, I certainly hope we put the Japs back to where Perry found them. . . I do not understand why we have taken all the guff from the Japanese these past few years. England backed the Japanese up before the Russo-Japanese

War, and the British have certainly gotten what they deserved. Of the two evils, England or Germany, I prefer the former, but they have never been the first line of defense of the United States, and they never will be, even after we save them now, from the Germans. Our leaders do not know history or else are blind to it. . . .

I check the days off on a calendar. I will come to you safe and sound. Do not worry. . . . How I would love to have you and Virginia Makkee with me, but China is no place for an American woman now. Sooner or later we will be involved with the Axis powers. I thank God every day for your being safely home. . . .

In August, 1941, he was ordered back to the States, to report to Quantico; he sailed on the *President Coolidge,* and soon had a happy reunion with his wife and daughter.

Puller spent a day or two in Washington prodding friends at Corps Headquarters: "Why don't they get the regiment out of Shanghai, and the detachment out of Peking? The Japs will jump any day now. The British have moved their people—and we can ill afford to lose the few trained men we have." He got no satisfaction, and when he persisted by going to the Navy Department, got the same reply: "Mind your own business, Major. We are aware of the situation up to the last minute."

With little further delay, Lewis got what he sought for himself: He would report to the new Marine base in the North Carolina swamplands, at New River, where he would command the 1st Battalion, 7th Marines, to prepare them for war. He arrived in October.

IX

DRESS REHEARSAL

WHEN his battalion returned from the field in late afternoon Puller called a conference of his company officers:

"Gentlemen, my name's Puller. Your new commander. We have a good deal of work to do together. I'll be slow to make changes, but one of them begins tomorrow morning. At the first rest period after we leave camp, camouflage every man and piece of equipment."

"We've got no camouflage material, Major."

"We'll do it anyway. The best is in the field. Find a mudhole; smear mud on faces and hands. Twigs on helmets, in blouses, anywhere you can stick 'em. Pine foliage is good. You'll learn."

That night when he conferred with his new regimental commander, Puller did so with a cool reserve—his colonel was the same officer who had consistently bungled the affairs of Company M in Nicaragua with his ignorance of field conditions. There was no need for Lewis to mention the ineptness of this officer, for one of the young men of the battalion wrote in his diary: "The Colonel gave all officers a talk today. Meant to be a pep talk, but was flat. He read some of it. Encouraged us to appear 'bright-eyed and bushy-tailed.' He waddles like a duck."

The battalion was camouflaged to Puller's satisfaction within an hour on the day of their first hike together. Passing troops sniggered, and Lieutenant Zach Cox of A Company heard derisive yells: "Heigho! The Walking Forest!" The self-conscious men soon grew accustomed to the attire and they had little time for reflection. The unit marched all day through forest, swamp and streams, so that company and platoon officers could learn to keep the men properly aligned. After five exhausting hours they turned about and marched to the starting point, still in skirmish line. Some units strayed and Puller solved the problem simply during a halt: "All men who were raised in the country, step out!" He sprinkled several dozen farm boys among the platoons to act as guides in the rough terrain. There was no more straying.

The regimental commander came out in a staff car while the men were at work, and stared at the pine-tufted helmet the Major wore: "Who do you think you are, Puller, Daniel Boone? Looks like a damned Halloween party. Get these men cleaned up and looking like Marines, or I'll relieve you."

"Yes, sir," Puller said. The commander bounced away in the staff car, and the battalion completed the drill.

In the evening the division commander, General Philip Torrey, called Puller into his office: "Major, I saw that camouflage work out there today. Good. Where'd you pick it up?"

"In China. The Japs and Chinese use it to perfection. If you fight in their country, you can't beat it."

Torrey questioned Puller, then issued an order for the First Division to use camouflage in the field.

The battalion began with marches of twelve miles daily, was pushed to fifteen and then twenty miles. Puller punctuated drills with fight talks to the men. They were very young, many of them beardless boys under sixteen, who must have lied about their ages. They were the most obscenely profane men Puller had encountered. Edward L. Smith, Jr., a young battalion doctor educated at Yale and Harvard, confessed that the constant flow of filthy language actually sickened him. Puller told his officers that the problem was to toughen these swaggering young men, teach them battle skills—and convince them that they were by no means bullet-proof. He also gave them pride in their outfit. In one talk after a hot, dusty march on which some had fallen from heat prostration, the Major roared at them, "When you were marching this morning, I heard a Marine on the roadside say, 'There goes the goddam Seventh Regiment.' I was amazed that one of you didn't step out of ranks and knock him cold." Dr. Smith wrote in his diary that night: "I think we are going places now."

A few days later Puller called together all officers, platoon and first sergeants for a more fiery talk: "Gentlemen, this is not only going to be the first battalion of the Seventh Marines. It's going to be the first battalion of the whole

Marine Corps from now on. . . . Now, if you want to get the most out of your men, give 'em a break! Make 'em work, but not completely in the dark. If you do, they won't do a bit more than they absolutely have to do. Get 'em on our side."

As an afterthought he growled: "And for Christ's sake, don't swear at your men!"

Puller drove the men until they were near exhaustion, and on one day when it rained, had them sleep in the downpour, then roused them for a meal at 1:00 A.M. and marched until three o'clock the next afternoon. "For reward," Dr. Smith noted, "we got two sandwiches and an apple each."

Smith took note of Puller's firm, aloof discipline, and also of his scrupulously fair treatment of men. Once when a four-time offender was brought to him, scheduled for court-martial, Puller spent an hour or more in his tent talking with the young Marine, trying to find the reason for his troubles; then he called Dr. Smith, explained that the boy might not be entirely responsible for his behavior and asked his advice on releasing him from the brig for psychiatric study. Smith gave quick agreement to the scheme.

One of his privates, Gerald White, a Yale man from Eastport, Maine, also a diarist, began to take note of Puller: "He is never obscene, remarkably, for the vigor with which he handles us. He is tough and demands the utmost, but there is always a kindly approach even when he is chewing you out that displays a touching sympathy with the miscreant."

There was an increasing firmness in the Major. At the end of one talk, Puller said: "One more thing. Wherever we are at chow time, the privates will be fed first. Then the noncoms, and the officers last of all."

To those who grumbled afterward an old gunnery sergeant said: "You're lucky. When I was with the Old Man down in Nicaragua, the order was mules even before privates, and brother, them mules could eat! You'll find out there's method in the Old Man's madness."

The battalion was soon isolated from others. Puller snatched them from the comforts of tent camp, and for most of the training time left to them they spent their weeks, from Monday morning until Friday afternoon, in the wilds. They slept in pup tents, or in the open, in the winter's bitter weather.

The men felled trees, built rifle ranges and cleared firing

lanes. All hands were at work, including medical corpsmen, who also wore heavy battle gear and walked on every hike. They were up with the others before dawn, went through calisthenics dancing with cold and often marched twenty miles through the woodlands to spend the night in snow banks. When they were toughened to that, Puller put them through a series of night marches, beginning after midnight. The doctors, like others, learned to read maps and compasses and to handle weapons, including mortars. The practice of identifying ships and planes, a joke in most units, became a serious business in 1/7. Some medics learned Morse code, and Manila John Basilone, an Army-trained veteran machine gunner, traded semaphore lessons for instruction in first aid.

The cooks were dragged from comfortable mess hall kitchens into the woods, where they were sent to companies, platoons, and even squads, to learn field cooking. Puller clung to the notion even at the end of his career: "What will we do for good cooking in the field in the next war? We have no cooks for units smaller than battalions, and they are used to electric stoves and dishwashers and every kind of gadget. How the devil can such men switch to field cooking? The troops will starve."

Few details escaped Puller's eye. One day he watched a platoon under Lieutenant Willie Dumas practice an assault on a hilltop position and became impatient with an elaborate flanking maneuver which wasted time.

"Old man, there's mighty little room for fancy tactics below division level. The enemy are on the hill. You go get 'em. In the end you'll save men. There are times when you'll have to flank, but don't forget that the shortest distance between two points is a straight line."

Lieutenant David Condon, who heard the tale as it spread among junior officers that night, summed it up: "Well, we know now. He's going to be hey, diddle diddle, right down the middle. Somebody's going to get hurt—but when the real stuff starts, I want to be with the Old Man, myself."

Puller gave a practical lesson in field communications to his runners that they never forgot. He lined up a couple of dozen message-bearers in two groups, about a hundred yards apart, and had them count off. He whispered a message into the ear of the first runner: "Find Captain Jones of C Company. Tell him to pull out and come in on the right flank and hook on at a 45-degree angle. Have him move at 1100."

He slapped the runner on the rump and yelled: "Hustle! Take it to Number 2! All of you make top speed!"

The young men sprinted over the open in sequence, passing the message down the line, until it had passed to the last man. "Let me hear what you got, old man," Puller said.

"B Company comes in off the right flank at 1145. Order from Captain Jones."

Puller shouted the original message to them, and put them to the exercise again: "Open your ears. You'll have to do this until you learn. When you carry a message in combat, the life of every man in the outfit may ride with you."

Training came to a climax with Puller's battle against the battalion of Lieutenant Colonel Herman H. Hanneken, who was also a hero of the Haitian campaigns. Puller entered the exercise as if it were war to the death. He led his men to the tip of a peninsula overgrown with brush. They were assumed to have landed by boats on this point and were to drive inland against Hanneken's line and attempt to capture the small town of Verona, North Carolina, in the enemy's rear.

The distinguishing marks between the warring battalions were arm bands, white for Puller, red for Hanneken. Lewis opened his assault by tying red bands on half a dozen of his men and sending them through enemy lines to the rear—where they cut the communications wire.

Puller sent a handful of men forward to distract the attention of Hanneken's main line by firing rapidly, then led his force through the flanking swamp, overcoming briars, vines and cypress stumps until the column was in rear of Hanneken's lone tank. The vanguard approached so swiftly that the tank commander was pulled through his hatch, a captive. The leaders dashed toward the enemy command post.

Hanneken escaped by fleetness of foot but confusion was so great that two colonels, who were on hand merely as observers, broke into a run themselves at sight of the oncoming troops and were "captured."

Puller's young men pounded into the road in rear, toward their village objective, as Puller bellowed from the roadside: "On to Verona!" First Battalion, Seventh Marines, returned to camp in triumph.

Not all the lessons were in combat techniques. Lewis came upon a strange sight in a company street one day: A private at rigid attention saluted over and over, like a robot, a beardless second lieutenant who stood before him, hands on hips.

"What's going on, old man?" Puller asked.

"This Marine, sir. He neglected to salute me as we passed, and I've ordered him to salute one hundred times."

"You're right, Lieutenant. So right. But you know that an officer must return every salute he receives—now let me see you get to it, and do your share."

He stood nearby until he had seen justice done, and thereby won the heart of every enlisted man in the unit and put junior officers on their guard. Dr. Smith made note of the Major's control: "Puller becomes so angry sometimes that words seem to stick in his throat, and he has to cool off— but he is very fair, and every man knows it."

Sunday, December 7, 1941, found Puller on leave in Saluda, in the home of Mrs. Puller's mother. When breathless announcers interrupted radio programs to shout news of the attack on Pearl Harbor, the women noted that the Major behaved as if he had heard the news long before, and this was only confirmation. He hung about the radio with his family for an hour or more, until it became clear that they would learn few more details of the disastrous strike, and then became impatient to return to his troops.

"Why don't they say something about the Marines in China?" he growled. "I know they got the Fourth out in time—they're down in the Philippines. But you know they've nabbed everybody left in Peking! How can people be so blind?"

He drove back to New River during the night, leaving the instant his wife returned from an early evening meeting at church. He had no radio in the car, and learned little more news from the Pacific until he was back in camp. Men of his battalion thought that he was the only officer at New River who had always been certain that war with Japan had been coming; training methods in the First Battalion, Seventh Marines, remained unchanged except for their tempo. There was a kind of inner calm in Puller's ranks, despite the national frenzy of preparation for war in these days.

After Pearl Harbor, Lewis drove the men as if his battalion were destined to halt the onward march of the Japanese alone. The only warm place in the camp after dark was the shower buildings, and Puller's officers congregated there often, to hear their commander's tales of combat in the tropics and stories of the Russian Revolution gleaned from Czarist officers in China. He never failed to speak of the disquieting news from the Pacific and gave them a candid view of the growing list of American defeats.

As the tragic drama of the Philippines unfolded he explained the situation to the new officers:

"Our plans were based on the existence of the Pacific fleet. Since it is no more and there's no sea power to help General MacArthur, he will develop a plan as he goes."

But as weeks passed and Japanese victories continued unbroken, Puller expressed his amazement: "MacArthur is following the old plan to the letter. He's not adapting to the situation at all. He has enough troops to fight, but we're headed for a terrible licking."

Bad news only increased the tempo of Puller's training. He cornered Colonel Pedro Del Valle, the great gunner who commanded the 11th Marines: "Colonel, you'll be starting artillery training next week. I want you to let me know when you'll fire. I want to get my troops under it as often as I can."

Del Valle understood Puller's need for actual battle conditions, but warned: "There may be accidents."

"We can chance those. What I won't chance is taking a bunch of green kids to war before they know the sound of big guns. I know shells aren't the same, going out and coming in—but this will help."

"You're the only one who's asked me. They're all yours."

Every day afterward, when the men of 1/7 were in the field and the 11th Marines were firing, shells streamed overhead, until the *whoosh* of flying metal became as familiar as rifle fire. There were many bursts nearby but no accidents. Puller's was the only battalion with such training.

Lieutenant Cox, now the executive of A Company, was impressed by Puller's thoroughness: "Major Puller never stood aside and said, 'Carry on, Sergeant,' and most other officers did. He was in there with us, pack and all. He could walk down the best of us, even the kids. Other commanders rode cars in the woods, but not Puller."

The Seventh Marines, including Puller's battalion, were combined with a battalion of the 11th Marine Artillery into a new unit—the Third Marine Brigade. It was the first expeditionary force to leave the United States during the war; its men began boarding ships in Norfolk, Virginia, on Easter Sunday, April 5, 1942. The rest of the First Marine Division was soon to follow.

In their last meeting Puller tried to reassure Virginia that all would be well and told her that his battalion was the best in existence. He could truthfully report morale at a peak, for when word of the embarkation leaked out two deserters returned and there were miraculous overnight cures in the base hospital. Mrs. Puller gave him a last-minute gift, a bathrobe. He thanked her tenderly, but growled to his staff: "I've got the world's greatest wife, but my God, what do you do when she sends you off to war with a new red flannel bathrobe?" He had it secretly stowed away before boarding his transport, the U.S.S. *Fuller.*

His final act ashore was to turn over a sizable bank account to his young brother-in-law, Bill Evans, with simple instructions: "Please see that Virginia gets a dozen red roses on the thirteenth of every month. If you have to leave, make sure some florist keeps it up until I get back home."

The troops lay just off Norfolk for several days as their convoy gathered, including the battleship *Texas,* the cruiser *Brooklyn,* half a dozen destroyers, four troopships and a number of supply vessels. They left Hampton Roads early on April 10, in heavy seas which made half the men ill.

On the first day they passed a foundered freighter with only her superstructure visible, the victim of a submarine just off the Virginia coast. There were blackouts at night and abandon ship drills by day. Rumors of submarine sightings were frequent as they sailed southward; planes were catapulted aloft to search nearby waters. Dr. Smith coped with cases of German measles, scarlet fever, mumps, colds, gonorrhea; on one day, medics on the *Fuller* gave 1300 cholera shots. They passed through the Panama Canal under a covey of barrage balloons, and were far into the Pacific before accurate word of their destination reached the lower echelons: Samoa.

There were weapons drills, especially on machine guns, and endless inspections. Fresh water was rationed. A ship broke down, and the convoy slowed to a crawl. An albatross hung over the *Fuller* for the last few days and nights. On the evening of May 7, when the ships lay within sight of their Samoan island, Puller wrote Virginia:

One month ago today I left you and you have not been out of my thoughts for a moment during those days. . . . Heretofore I have always been eager to go on an expedition. But that was before we were married. The only thing I want now is happiness with you. . . . Please do not worry. I am coming back, and then we will have the home with two chimneys. . . .

Germany and Japan must be stopped, and then perhaps I can retire. . . . I am well but I do miss you dreadfully. I have a fair sunburn, but there has not been much room for exercise. Last night the stars seemed very near.

I have re-read "Jackson"; remember when you bought a new copy for me in 1937? Thirty-seven was a great year for me. I know how hard it is to tell Virginia Mac of me, but do not let her forget me. I love you, Virginia, and I always will.

The Major drove them so relentlessly on Samoa that the men forgot the hardships of New River. For two days after docking at Apia the men acted as stevedores, working in relays with only three hours' sleep each night. When they were off that duty, they carried heavy machine guns in advanced gun drill. Only the most observant, like Dr. Smith, noted the beauties of the place: "Mountains come gently down to meet the sea. In Apia, low houses with red or green roofs. Few stores. No hurry. Flowers and trees blooming, few autos with right hand drive, horses ridden bareback. We march down quiet streets, carrying packs and rolls, natives laughing and giggling. We stare at bare feet, handsome draped bodies, graceful carriage. Camped under banyan tree on the shore. . . . In the moonlight could hear guitars in huts where Marines had gathered with natives to sing and dance."

Training was uninterrupted. Their first march was ordered by a directive which said that Puller's old nemesis, the regimental commander, would march at the head of the column. Junior officers were so amused by this unlikely announcement that they made a pool, guessing when the commander would drop out. The man who held First Mile won, for the colonel rode in a station wagon all the way. In the camp men were soon singing an irreverent ditty: "Roll Out the Wagon, We're Off to War Again."

Puller led many marches, but on one broiling day he pushed them near the limit: "I want nobody to fall out today unless he falls on his face, unconscious. You're going to need every ounce of endurance you can build up, when you get into combat. Anyone who staggers to the roadside, and then sits down, will be court-martialed or surveyed out as medically unfit."

The march was twenty-two miles under a searing sun, over an asphalt highway. Many strong youngsters were felled, including Captain Regan Fuller, who was only two weeks out of bed from a shipboard appendectomy; Puller stopped by to congratulate him on his courage in keeping up for so long, for there were then only two miles to go. Captain Jack Stafford lost consciousness, and was carried in.

Private Gerald White wrote for his diary: "Puller must have marched twice the distance we did, for all day long he kept marching up and down the column, jaunty as a bantam rooster, pipe clenched in his teeth, ever alert to see that men who were succumbing to the heat, exhaustion or blisters were taken care of by corpsmen. Many times today I saw him take a BAR, machine gun or mortar off the shoulder of some Marine whose fanny was dragging and carry it to give the poor guy some respite."

Dr. Smith looked at the Major expectantly at the end of the march, but got a surprise: "Puller never even batted an eye over the march. He came steaming into camp as fresh as when he started."

Lieutenant James Hayes, the battalion judge advocate, never forgot the day:

"When we got to Apia my feet were so blistered that I could hear them squooshing. Almost all the men fell in their tracks when we were dismissed, and fell asleep without chow. Some of the younger officers were critical of Puller the next day. They thought he was too tough."

Puller explained once more to his company officers, when he had seen the worn men: "Gentlemen, remember to have every man carry a one-inch square of beef suet in his pack. If they'll grease their feet daily, and avoid so much washing, they'll have no blisters. An old trick from the Haitian soldiers, and it never fails. You can't march men without feet, gentlemen."

There were other hard marches and the battalion became tougher as the weeks passed. Private White, who went AWOL briefly one day to climb a mountain and find the overgrown grave of Robert Louis Stevenson, wrote of Puller's unexpected kindness to a boy he caught asleep on guard duty at an ammunition dump. Puller shook the boy awake: "Old man, it's dangerous to pull a trick like this. Suppose Captain Rogers had caught you. He'd have made a big fuss, and then I'd have to court-martial you and slap you in the brig. Maybe that's what I should do—but I'll give you another chance. Pretty soon, now, we'll be fighting for keeps, and you'll stay awake, or risk the lives of every one of us. You understand me?"

"Yes, sir, Major."

Puller began to mourn his fate to staff officers: "Here I am, stuck out here to rot on this damned island while other people fight the war. They've marooned us. Did you know the Division landed on Guadalcanal yesterday?"

It was true. The first offensive blow of the war against the victorious Japanese had been taken by the landing of Marines under General A. A. Vandegrift, Puller's old chief in Haiti. There was no opposition to these August landings, but the Division was soon fighting desperately to hang on to an air strip, Henderson Field. The enemy still controlled the sea, and to a large extent the air. From Samoa the news had a strange, unreal sound, and every day made Puller more impatient to join the action.

Morale on Samoa was high. There was a beer ration, two cans a day and more from the underground; there was a well-stocked ice house and plenty of hot food from the galleys. But the favorite pastime of the Seventh Regiment, or at least of its First Battalion, was keeping watch on Major Puller.

Private Bob Cornely, a twenty-year-old machine gunner from Philadelphia in Dog Company, was impressed by Puller on the softball field: "He got in there and played like a kid himself. He was catcher on a team one day, and when he came to the plate the pitchers hesitated to knock him down like they did the other guys, and that made the Old Man sore. He yelled at 'em: 'I'm as tough as the next one, old man. Go ahead and dust me off if you can.' They did, and he took it okay. He wasn't such a bad hitter, either."

Lieutenant Hayes took careful notice: "Puller was more peremptory with his officers, and expected more of them than of enlisted men. He always saw to it that the men were fed first, and many a time I saw him hang around a chow line, watching to see that the men got what they needed. He never took a bite until all had been fed."

Puller was promoted to Lieutenant Colonel on Samoa, and his first move was to increase the allotment sent monthly to his wife—from $250 to $300.

He wrote her:

> . . . I am just living for our life together when this war is won and I will return to you and Virginia Mac. . . . Please do not worry, even a little bit, sweet. . . . I would give anything that I may ever have, except your happiness, to see you smile at me again.
>
> Life is so short. And when I was a child, I thought it would last forever and ever. My love for you will, Virginia, even into the next life, and then on. The hardest thing that I have ever done was to tell you goodbye. That was a black Tuesday and I pray there will never be another separation. . . .

One evening in early September when Puller was playing bridge in his hut with his executive officer, Captain Otho Rogers, and the doctors, Smith and Schuster, he was unusually inattentive to the cards. He had heard by radio in the afternoon of a battle on Guadalcanal, in which one unit had counted 670 dead Japanese before its position: "Think of that," Puller said over and over. "Six hundred and seventy! They mowed 'em down. One of these days we'll be giving 'em hell like that, too. *Better* than that."

In the second week of September, at last, they sailed for Guadalcanal.

X

A WAR WITHIN A WAR

SEPTEMBER 18 dawned on the convoy as it ran the narrow waters of Sealark Channel and the ships began to lose way. The holds were like ovens and those who could crowd on deck took the cool morning breeze as they looked toward the island which humped against the sky in a curious pie-bald pattern, jungle masses crowned by pale grassy hills. Two planes circled over the landing beaches, and as the sun rose, men swarmed down the nets and boats bobbed away for the shore.

Lewis Puller was just over forty-four years old, with more than half his life spent in the Marine Corps. The other battalion commanders of the Seventh who landed with him, Herman Hanneken and E. J. Farrell, were also hardened by service of more than twenty years. Veteran officers who watched from the shore realized that "the first team" was in, and that with the Division complete, there would be more than perimeter defense. One of those who saw Puller land, at about 6:00 A.M., was Red Mike Edson, the Nicaraguan veteran whose Raiders had saved the Division in a bloody battle four days earlier. Edson turned to his executive, Hank Adams: "There comes the greatest fighting man in the Marine Corps. We'll have some competition now."

There was a noisy reunion between Edson and Puller and the next moments became part of Marine legend. "Now show me where they are," Puller said. Someone handed him a map, which he took absently, holding it upside-down, looking to the jumbled terrain beyond the beach: "Hell, I can't make head nor tail of this—why don't we have something better

108

than a National Geographic map anyway? Just show me where they are!"

Hands waved toward hills which rose behind the jungle. "All right," Puller said. "Let's go get 'em."

Guadalcanal was a jumbled land mass almost ninety miles long, a little-known British copra station which was now the nearest Japanese outpost to Australia and a threat to American supply lines in the South Pacific. There were no accurate maps. On the north coast, a country of plains, slow jungle rivers and rain forest, the Japanese had begun an airfield, now being completed by the First Marine Division. To the south lay a backbone of mountains, the tallest peak 7500 feet high. The average temperature was 80 degrees; the small black natives were afflicted with malaria, dengue fever and fungus infections.

General Vandegrift had landed with the First Division, less the Seventh Regiment, on August 7, and quickly threw up a defensive line around the airstrip now known as Henderson Field. The perimeter was about six miles long and three miles deep, and lay along the northern beaches around the Lunga River. Deep jungle alternated with grassy plains within this area.

Unknown numbers of Japanese patrolled the jungles beyond, and were concentrated westward near the coast, at the Matanikau River. Vandegrift at first attempted nothing more than the defense of his post; his strength did not permit him to probe outside his lines. With the coming of the Seventh Marines, he could open a new phase. The first Allied counteroffensive of the war might now become truly offensive.

There were 4262 Marines of the Seventh, a welcome reinforcement in a cause not yet won, and with them the first supply of aviation gasoline and ammunition for the hardpressed men of General Vandegrift. The newcomers worked until late afternoon, unloading landing craft. Stacks of cases grew on the sands and captured Japanese trucks bore loads into the grove beyond. Puller urged his men to get every possible case clear of the beach.

General Vandegrift and his staff came to see the landing and the commander's face grew grim when he saw the commander of the Seventh Regiment step ashore—the colonel wore a natty uniform, complete with low-quarter shoes and

GUADALCANAL ISLAND

0   5   10   15   20
MILES

N

FLORIDA I.

SAVO I.

Cape Esperance

VANDEGRIFT
7 AUG. 1942

XX
1 MARINES

Lunga Point

Point Cruz

Koli Point

Kukum

Mt. Austen

Lunga

Tenaru R.

GUADALCANAL

S BRYANT

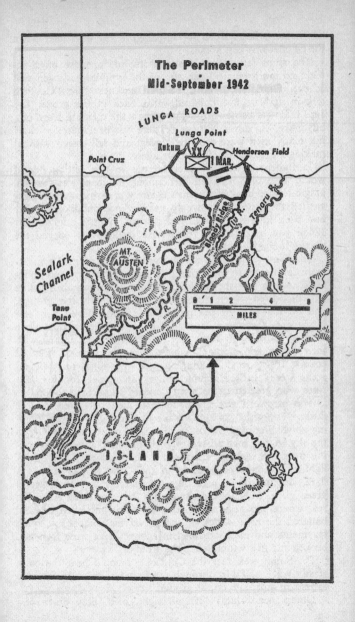

The Perimeter
Mid-September 1942

LUNGA ROADS

Lunga Point

Kukum

1 MAR.

Henderson Field

Point Cruz

Bloody Ridge

Tenaru

Sealark Channel

MT. AUSTEN

Lunga

0 1 2 4 8
MILES

Tanu Point

I S L A N D

silk hose. Officers were not surprised a few days later when the colonel was sent home.

The ships left before dusk, fearful of Japanese naval attack; no more than 60 per cent of the supplies had been sent ashore. Puller drove his men until darkness fell: "Get 'em dug in at least five hundred yards back in the grove. The Japs may wet us down tonight. I know the men are worn out, but make 'em dig if you can." There was beef stew for chow but many men were too tired to eat and fell asleep without making a pretense of digging foxholes.

In Puller's pocket, so preposterous in this setting that it would have provoked laughter among his men, was the old, jungle-stained copy of Caesar's *Gallic Wars* which he had now carried for more than twenty years. Since childhood Puller had been impressed by Caesar's common-sense admonition: When you make camp, fortify. He instinctively obeyed the maxim tonight.

The First settled in a coconut grove which seemed a nightmare landscape to Dr. Smith: "Between the torn and splintered stumps flew shrieking and wildly screaming birds, white and blood-red. Deep zigzagging trenches split the ground, and on the edge of the jungle were camouflaged gun emplacements. Scattered through the pockmarked groves were charred remains of Zeros that had crashed and burned with their pilots; and along the shore were the ruins of wrecked enemy trucks and landing barges. Peopling this violent scene were bearded, gaunt, hungry and lonely-looking Marines who greeted us with no outward show of emotion."

The password was given out and men fell asleep in the dusk. Dr. Smith was kept awake by grotesque shapes looming about him, and the unfamiliar Southern Cross glowing in the sky. A few men stirred after midnight. Planes were droning over the sea, but the motors were suddenly cut off. A light explosion brought men to their feet in the grove. A flare, drifting on a parachute, lit the camp with a weird green glow. Men looked for planes, but fire came from the sea, where Japanese ships stood close in, unchallenged, and battered the area. Much of the grove was combed by flying fragments and men screamed in agony. Trees were torn and broken and many tumbled to the ground.

Dr. Smith was near the Colonel: "I could hear the calm steady voice of Puller through the thunder, ordering the men to remain quiet and on the ground."

Others heard him: "It's all right, men. Stay down and

they can't hurt you. This won't last forever. Tomorrow it'll be our turn."

Men who had not dug holes now attacked the earth with helmets and bayonets. Three were killed, two of them near Puller, and Dr. Smith and Dr. Lawrence Schuster treated twelve wounded.

An old truck removed the bodies for burial after dawn, and Dr. Smith thought the faces of men in the grove were already much older.

Puller went to Division headquarters, where he spoke with General Vandegrift. The command post was in a ravine shielded from fire by land, sea and air, a chain of dugouts and caves piled high with sandbags. Puller saw two other old friends there: Lieutenant Colonel Merrill Twining and Major Edward Snedeker. He left with orders to take his men on their first patrol, a probe of the jungle in the Lunga River area. Puller prepared to leave immediately.

The battalion left the perimeter that afternoon, a file of more than eight hundred men, winding along a trail. Puller had a few last words for the men: "Keep those canteens out of your mouths. If you don't save water, you'll regret it. That drink will mean more to you in this place than you ever dreamed it could."

The lead squad went through the tunnel of the trail; tree-tops laced together a hundred feet overhead, shutting out the sun. There were strange bird calls like human cries—one sounded like someone being strangled, shouting, "I'm all right!" One squawk was like the sound of boards being clapped together. The steamy heat increased with each step.

Puller was near the front of the column; behind him, heed-less of his warning, men began to drink water. The tail of the battalion had hardly cleared the perimeter when there was firing ahead. Captain Hayes was near the Colonel at the moment:

"Every man hit the deck, except Puller. We dived for the growth beside the trail but he walked up and down the line talking as if he were on parade. He told us it was all right and that this was nothing to worry about, just small stuff. We began to get up again. Then and there he commanded that battalion as it never imagined it could be commanded. The men saw what kind of a man they had and the word went down the column as fast as light. We lost our fear— or some of it."

Puller found that three Japanese had been killed at a bridge of the Lunga River and a sniper had fired from the far side of the river. He went ahead, beyond even A Company, which had deployed and lost contact with the column. Captain Bob Haggerty ordered Corporal Frank Cameron, a squad leader, to take his scouts across. Cameron gulped and looked uneasily across the river; his men tiptoed over the bridge, ready to dive into the water at the first sound. There was a stir in the growth ahead of them as they neared the bank—and the scouts were stunned to see Colonel Puller emerge. Haggerty, who was watching from cover, groaned with relief: "For a week those scouts walked around like men who should have been dead."

There were no Marine casualties here and the column pushed on. The battalion suffered from thirst late in the day; tongues were swollen, dry and scratchy, and some men became dizzy. The jungle changed; they climbed hills so steep that they pulled themselves up the trail by the undergrowth. On a grassy knoll above the tangle, where the night's bivouac was planned, the column met an ambush. Two of Bob Haggerty's platoon were killed and the unit broke into tiny groups, leaving Haggerty without a command. He lay in cover and watched Puller: "It was the greatest exhibition of utter disregard for personal safety I ever saw."

Puller exposed himself to cross fire from concealed enemy machine guns, organizing resistance. He bellowed: "A Company, machine gun squad!" Gerald White, Hurley Edwards and Roland Robey ran up as fast as they could, and Puller placed them in the clearing to cover the advance of the infantry, where enemy weapons showered them. Men were hit near them but until White's skull was creased by a bullet which tore a hole in his helmet the gunners were untouched. Private Willie Rowe, a rifleman who was wounded near them, called in the dark when fire had ceased: "Leave me alone. I'm going to die where I am."

Puller would not permit it. Squads crawled over the area until all men were accounted for and the wounded were brought into the lines. Gerald White's throbbing head prevented his sleeping and he often saw Colonel Puller: "He paced up and down that weary, dejected band all night, reassuring the wounded that they would get good care the next day. He told us we were in no danger of a night attack—but I didn't think he *knew*. He must have been twice as dogtired as we were."

Another Puller story spread through the camp before men fell asleep: In the dusk, the Colonel had deliberately lighted his pipe in the open, then quickly fallen and rolled over in the dirt, to draw machine gun fire and spot the location of an enemy nest. His own gunners then cleaned it out by firing at the muzzle flashes.

Quiet fell late that night, after Puller had halted a bit of nervous firing by some of the men: "I don't want another man to fire a round, unless he can point out the target to me."

In the morning they tackled the cruel ridges and ravines once more and the vanguard met still another ambush—this one lightly manned and quickly brushed aside. There were two casualties, one of them serious. Captain Jack Stafford, who had mishandled a rifle grenade, or used a faulty one, was torn by an explosion; blood gushed from his face and throat. Puller reached his side as a corpsman gave the officer morphine.

A red tide oozed over Stafford's chest, and the Colonel saw that he was on the point of strangling in the gore. Puller snapped a large safety pin from a bandoleer, reached into Stafford's mouth and deftly pinned the tongue to the up-turned collar of his uniform. He sent the stretcher off with five four-man teams to act in relays, and even so it was a punishing burden on the rugged terrain back to the perimeter. Puller had saved Stafford's life.

The column at last reached another river, and here most of the men, half-maddened by thirst, lost all discipline for a time. Those near Captain Hayes "acted like dogs, lying and lapping the water." Hayes, like several other officers, used canteen cups and laced the water with iodine. Many men plunged into the muddy stream.

Near this point Puller met Company A of Edson's Raiders, led by a familiar figure. The new commander was Captain Lew Walt, his old Basic School student. Walt's strong round face beamed as they shook hands and he said earnestly: "I'm sure honored to be in a fight with you, Colonel."

The crew carrying Stafford rearward had an adventure at about the same moment: When two snipers opened on the stretcher party Stafford hopped from the litter into a nearby hole despite his severe wound and directed fire against the enemy by his gestures. Bob Haggerty thought: "We'd have been firing in the trees all day if he hadn't taken charge."

With the main column, Walt's men found a wounded Jap who had a mangled leg but seemed likely to survive. Walt picked six men and put a sergeant over them with precise orders: "Get him back to the perimeter alive. I don't want to hear of his death by accidental discharge. Get him back for questioning. Alive."

When the patrol returned to camp Walt heard the story of this wounded Jap's end: The stretcher party had faithfully carried him back, guarding his life from passersby who were suspicious of oft-repeated Jap treachery. The prisoner had gone to a hospital tent and onto an operating table, and while doctors worked over him had snatched a scalpel and buried it in the back of the nearest man. The doctor was expected to recover. The Jap did not survive for questioning.

The battalion came back into the lines before dark and took a defensive position for the first time. The men crawled into foxholes and peered out across fifty-yard fire lanes cut into the thick growth.

A fury of fire broke out in the adjoining Third Battalion sector about midnight. Puller called assurances to his waking men: "No Japs. If they were firing, there would be stuff coming over. Stand up and you'll see. This is what I told you about in training. Never duck until you hear a shell coming —and then it'll be too late."

Hank Adams of the Raiders stopped by Puller's command post and found the Colonel lying on his blankets as if listening to rifles on a firing range: "Listen to those poor green devils banging up the ammo, Hank. It'll be a wonder if somebody doesn't get hurt." When this firing continued Puller was ordered to the troubled area with his troops. He found the battalion command post in disorder; a staff officer had shot a canteen from a friend's hip with his pistol, and tracers now flew in every direction. Puller halted one addled marksman, a veteran warrant officer who was firing furiously up into a tree: "Stop it! Nothing up there. If you fire again, I'll bust you."

Daylight revealed only empty cartridges on the ground —all Marine.

The next day, September 23, the First Battalion moved on its first major action, a patrol across the slopes of Mount Austen, a dominating hill near the headwaters of the Matanikau River. Puller was to lead one arm of a pincers movement against enemy forces concentrating in that region: The First Raider Battalion would march up the Matanikau from the sea,

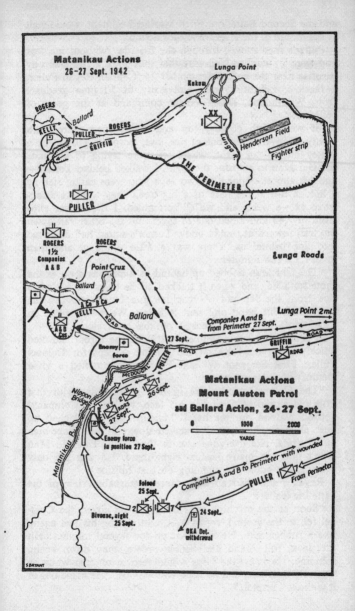

Matanikau Actions
26-27 Sept. 1942

Lunga Point

Kukum

ROGERS
Ballard
KELLY
ROGERS
PULLER
GRIFFIN

1 XX 7

Lunga R.

Henderson Field
Fighter strip

THE PERIMETER

1 II 7
PULLER

---

1 XX 7
ROGERS
1½ Companies A and B

ROGERS

Lunga Roads

Point Cruz

Ballard

A Co B Co

KELLY

A & B Cos.

Ballard

ROAD

Enemy force

McDOUGAL

PULLER

2 II 5
26 Sept.

Nippon Bridge

2 II 5
RDRS
27 Sept.

Enemy force
in position 27 Sept.

Matanikau R.

Companies A and B
from Perimeter 27 Sept.

Lunga Point 2 mi.

27 Sept.

ROAD

GRIFFIN

1 II RDRS

Matanikau Actions
Mount Austen Patrol
and Ballard Action, 24-27 Sept.

0   1000   2000
YARDS

Companies A and B to Perimeter with wounded

PULLER 1 XX 7
From Perimeter

Joined
25 Sept.

2 II 5 1 II 7

24 Sept.

OKA Det.
withdrawal

Bivouac, night
25 Sept.

S BRYANT

and the Second Battalion, Fifth Marine Regiment, would wait at the mouth of the river, ready for action.

Puller's men moved through the first day without incident and were by now so trail-wise that they took a Jap camp by surprise near the end of September 24. Captain Regan Fuller, a fearless, rail-thin young University of Virginia graduate from Washington, D.C., was in command at the point of collision:

"It was rough country, up and down everywhere, with plenty of cover. I sent one of my boys, Corporal Turner, up a grassy hill to our right, where we were trying to persuade the Old Man to stop for the night. I walked behind Turner—and we almost stepped on two Japs who were eating rice by a hidden fire at the base of a big tree. They were as astonished as we were, and we all scrambled. I fired three clips from my .45 and killed one of them, but the other ran down the trail toward our main body. Turner's squad had deployed into line behind us. There was a little shooting, and then quiet for a few minutes.

"The Old Man bobbed up behind us almost as soon as the shots sounded, and when it slacked off he began to eat some rice from the Jap pot. A machine gun bullet knocked the bowl from his hand and sent it flying. We were caught in some cross fire, pretty wicked on the open slopes."

A runner just behind Puller was hit in the throat and died quickly. Everyone else hit the ground, except for Colonel Puller. First Sergeant William Pennington retained a vivid memory of the moment:

"The Colonel stood there in that grazing fire with that little old stump of a pipe in his face, yelling, 'B Company! Second platoon, in line here!' Machine gun fire kicked up dust all around me, and I stayed down in that knee-high kunai grass, like everyone else in the ranks. The Old Man didn't find too many leaders right there. He was the only Marine you could see standing on that hillside."

Regan Fuller had an even more remarkable view of the battalion leader:

"Soon as the machine guns opened from cover, the Colonel fell to the ground, rolled over, and was on his feet again, like a rubber man. He kept that up for several minutes: Hit the deck, roll. Stand and bellow orders, then down again, spinning. He knew the Nips would zero in on him while he was yelling orders, and he kept 'em buffaloed. He came out of it without a scratch."

Puller continued to shout orders until he got Captain Chester Cockrell's B Company into line as a screen against the concealed Jap force:

"Cockrell! Get 'em up!" And for a moment the outrageously loud curses of the Colonel echoed in the jungle through the fire fight. He soon had a skirmish line moving forward and the enemy was pushed beyond a ridge.

A grenade fell near the Old Man—no more than eight yards away, Captain Zach Cox estimated, but Puller turned when he saw A Company scatter and yelled: "Oh, that damned thing ain't going off." It helped to steady the men. The grenade was a dud.

Cockrell's B Company was being cut up in the woods by snipers in trees with light machine guns, and fire from Puller's front became spotty. The fight was now at close quarters; the Colonel had killed three men with his .45—one of them a Japanese major.

Fire near the rear of the position was so heavy that Dr. Schuster was forced to snake on his stomach to reach the wounded. It was now almost dark and the doctor shielded himself as best he could, using a flashlight in brief intervals to pack bleeding chests, tie off torn arteries, and administer plasma.

A runner brought word that Cockrell had been killed; Puller called for Zach Cox: "Take over B down there and pull 'em together. They're scattered over hell's half acre."

When Cox found a sergeant and half a dozen men of the front company and asked where the men of B were, he got the reply: "This is it, Captain. These are all we've got." A search turned up most of the other men; the wounded began to move rearward.

The skirmish closed when Cox led a charge which drove the enemy and exposed a Jap camp. Puller estimated that five hundred men had bivouacked there. Looters brought him canned crab and tangerines which he tried at once and found delicious. He took a beautiful dress sword from the body of the major he had shot, as well as a map case and a war diary. He gave these to Pennington: "When you get back to camp, have an interpreter go over the papers. I want a copy of the translation."

Puller then fell back to a ridge in the rear and had the men dig in for the night. Thirty or more Japanese bodies lay within their new lines. Radiomen called the perimeter with Puller's report on Marine casualties: seven dead, twenty-five wounded, eighteen of them stretcher cases. The Colonel also asked for an air drop of stretchers and said that he would pursue the enemy. A reply crackled from headquarters: A battalion of the Fifth Marines would reinforce him, the wounded would be sent back, and the probe would continue to the Matanikau, if Puller thought it advisable.

The night passed in quiet, with a light rain. A sleepless officer discovered the depths of Puller's concern for the dead and wounded in one of the Colonel's rare intimacies: "God, I hated that I had to curse at Cockrell out there tonight. He was a good, brave Marine—the fighting kind. It was something that had to be done."

The reinforcements from the Fifth Marines were up at 8:45 A.M. and Puller sent Major Otho Rogers back with the wounded, with A and B Companies as bearers and guards, then led his combined force westward. The trail toward the river was narrow and overgrown and progress was slow. A lone Jap was sighted during the morning. Puller walked into an open field for a look around; an enemy private leapt from cover and raced toward the jungle. The Colonel helped half a dozen men run him down but the small, frightened man told them nothing. He seemed to speak no English and was unarmed. In his hiding place they found a radio. "They're smarter than we are," Puller told his officers. "They had him lying there to report our patrols. I expect they know every move we make."

They carried the prisoner and his radio toward the Matanikau.

The force reached the swift brown stream on September 26 and since his original orders directed Puller to return to the perimeter on that day, he did not cross the river but turned northward toward the sea. At about 2:00 P.M. there was mortar and machine gun fire from across the river and a bitter fight ensued at the mouth of the stream; Puller waded almost across the river under fire which caused twenty-five casualties—most of them in G Company, Fifth Marines. Once more, he escaped unscathed.

During this night headquarters radioed a new plan: Puller, with the single company of his battalion, plus the Second Battalion of the Fifth, would hold their position. The Raiders would march upstream, cross, and come into the Japanese rear. Colonel Mike Edson was sent out to take charge: Puller would act as his executive officer for the operation, but this chain of command was not made clear, at least to junior officers, and added to the ensuing confusion.

Sunday, September 27, was a day of tragic blunders. Puller remained with Edson at the river's mouth, where a white sandspit thrust through the shallows toward the enemy. To their right was the sea and to their left the tangled growth through which Lieutenant Colonel Sam Griffith now led the Raiders upstream. Planes bombed the enemy on the far shore but planned artillery barrages did not come. There was a long delay. The coastal force did not attack.

Radio messages from the Raiders passed through Puller's communications men late in the morning. The first was garbled and led Edson to believe the Raiders had crossed the river. The commander called on headquarters to send reinforcements—and was promised the men Puller had sent back to camp. They would come down the coast in Higgins boats, land on the far side of the Matanikau, and aid in surrounding the enemy. Puller did not learn of this move until he saw the boats themselves, driving past him just outside the surf; he tried in vain to hail them.

A few minutes later there was another radio call from upstream: The Raiders had been stopped. Griffith was wounded and Major Kenneth Bailey, his Medal of Honor exec, was killed. The radioman, assuming Puller to be in command, handed him the message, which he read and passed on to Edson.

Edson studied the message with care. "All right," he said. "I guess we'd better call them off. They can't seem to cross the river."

"Christ!" Puller said. "You're not going to stop 'em when they've had only two casualties? Most of my battalion will be out there alone, cut off without support. You're not going to throw these men away."

The officers could not agree on the next move. Puller never forgot the long afternoon: "I walked away from Edson and his officers, with a signalman. I just went down to the sea and hailed a boat from the old destroyer that was out there, heading for Point Cruz, where my men were. I got aboard the ship, the *Ballard*, she was. Her skipper took her right in close, and when we spotted my men on a hilltop, a few hundred yards inland, I began sending blinker and semaphore messages. It was only a minute or two before I could spot, in my field glasses, a Marine with semaphore flags, answering us from the hill. It went about like this:

" 'Return to beach immediately.'

" 'Engaged. Cannot return.'

" 'Fight your way. Only hope.'

"There was no reply, and so I had one more signal sent:

" 'Give me your boundaries right and left. Will use ship's fire.'

"I got no answer. The ship turned its guns on the jungle, and blasted hell out of it, from the sea up the hillside. We could see just about where the battalion lines were, and those gunners laid it on, right up to the limit."

From the hilltop, the furiously firing *Ballard* was welcomed as an avenging angel. The survivors had almost given up hope.

Major Otho Rogers was a small, quiet, inoffensive reservist, a Washington, D. C., Post Office employee who had never seen combat. Puller had grown fond of him in their months together but realized that his executive officer-was beyond his depth in jungle warfare.

Yet on this Sunday morning, ordered to lead a relief force beyond the Matanikau, Rogers had briskly rounded up the company and a half of 1/7 which had brought in the wounded from Mount Austen, and scraped together every cook, baker and headquarters man in sight. Rogers wore fresh clothing which would make him a conspicuous target: starched breeches and a clean shirt, both faded almost white from washing. Bob Haggerty thought his little speech pathetic, as the three hundred gathered on the beach to board the boats: "Men, you belong to the world's finest body of fighting men, the U. S. Marine Corps—and you're with the best officers and noncoms in the Corps. There's only two or three hundred Japs where we're going now. Let's wipe 'em out. I hope every man gets the Navy Cross."

They landed in two waves, and at 1:10 P.M. were ashore without incident, just west of Point Cruz, a wooded peninsula west of the mouth of the Matanikau.

There was no opposition; the men went through an old coconut grove to the grassy heights above. Private McGuire, of Haggerty's platoon, killed two fleeing Japs—and in the rear there was a burst of machine gun fire. The landing boats had now pulled out of sight and the unit was alone. A column of Japanese appeared on an old coastal road, coming from the river. Captain Zach Cox ordered the 81 millimeter mortars to fire on them. Rogers looked at the big force with concern: "They told me the Jap strength in here was no more than two or three hundred." The column below, which scattered briefly under mortar fire, began working its way up the hill. The Marine force was surrounded.

Captain Cox retained a memory of a moment of relative calm: "There was an air raid on Henderson Field and our fighters went up after the Japs. I saw an enemy bomber fall apart, high up, and it seemed to take forever for the wing to fall into the sea."

This raid knocked out communications at division headquarters and thereafter the isolated men were on their own. Artillery fire burst upon them; it was American artillery, firing from far down the coast, trying to aid the attack which had disintegrated. The Japanese now closed in.

A mortar shell exploded almost between the feet of Major Rogers and the commander was killed. "There was so little of him left we rolled the remains in a blanket," Sergeant Pennington said. The same blast tore the arms and legs of Zach Cox and he was out of action. Dr. Schuster attempted to give him drugs and bind the arm with splints, but Cox refused until he was told it was the only way he might live. Schuster tended him and crawled to other wounded. Captain Charles W. Kelly, Jr., took over Rogers's command.

The perimeter, narrow and winding, snaked around the crests of irregular hills and men could see few of their companions in the attack which followed; machine gun and mortar fire literally sprayed them. Losses mounted.

Marine mortars, firing at an almost impossibly close range, were held in place by men who lay on their backs to support the tubes with their feet. Captain Kelly tried to gain contact with the units beyond the river, but got a grim report from the communications man, Sergeant Robert Raysbrook —the radio had been forgotten, left at the base in the perimeter.

Help now appeared in the sky, a scout dive bomber which was prowling the coast for targets. Kelly's men laid out white undershirts to signal: H E L P. The plane circled and its pilot, Second Lieutenant Dale M. Leslie, dipped his wings in acknowledgment. He sent word of the unit's plight by radio and circled overhead, waiting for a chance to help.

Bob Haggerty was hit, and as Dr. Schuster worked over him, the wounded Captain saw enemy coming up the hillside, under the trees: "The little bastards, dressed in green from head to foot, were sneaking through the bushes toward us. I told the machine gunners and mortarmen to stand by." The firing order never came, for the *Ballard* hove into sight.

From his promontory on front of the hill, Captain Regan Fuller saw her with disbelief: "An old time four-stacker, and she was boiling, with black smoke trailing out behind her. Almost as soon as I caught sight of her the guns began to swing upward, hoisting into position. It was a lovely sight." Fuller's men had sustained only one casualty to this point—but in Haggerty's sector, where artillery shells still fell, many men were lost. Some of Haggerty's men were demoralized by the time the *Ballard* appeared.

Sergeant Raysbrook now redeemed himself for failure to bring the radio and under fire from snipers and machine guns semaphored the destroyer and called Puller's messages to Captain Kelly. The survivors made ready to abandon the hill.

As they watched, shells from the *Ballard*'s five-inch guns tore the jungle growth, blasting a path to the beach. Captain Cox peered down beneath the foliage, where in the dim green thickets he could see groups of the enemy blown apart. The noise and smoke grew and within a few minutes the descent began.

Regan Fuller's men gave a Rebel Yell and plunged down the slopes, taking Dr. Schuster with them. They reached an open space near the beach before meeting opposition from Japanese, still half-seen, who were no more than twenty feet away. Schuster was hit in the elbow and attempted to bandage himself. Fuller helped him and sent him forward with other wounded.

Platoon Sergeant Andy Malanowski of Baltimore was nearby with a BAR taken from a casualty. "Captain, you take Doc Schuster and the other wounded on down, and I'll handle the rear. I'll be with you in a few minutes." Malanowski set up his gun on a log across the trail.

Fuller had to clear a path once more, and with a grenade tossed a few yards away brought a Japanese toppling from the thickets. A Japanese officer darted from cover, holding a sword in two hands, and beheaded a private marching near Fuller.

The other units trickled down the hill but, except for Fuller's men, met no organized Jap parties. Survivors gathered on the beach, where a small perimeter of defense was set up. Fuller waited for Malanowski but he did not come. There was one rapid burst of fire from the undergrowth where the sergeant had waited, then silence. Malanowski was later awarded the Congressional Medal of Honor posthumously for his brave rearguard stand.

There were conflicting memories among survivors as to what happened on the beach. B Company arrived first and was first to get in boats sent out from the *Ballard*—the small craft commanded by Coast Guard coxswains. They were held up for a time by Jap fire from Point Cruz but at last got in, when a boat's gun knocked out an enemy machine gun. Sergeant Pennington remembered a big coxswain swearing at the Japs, holding a tiller in one hand, and firing with the other. One coxswain, Douglas Munro, was killed, and won the Medal of Honor; two others, wounded, won Navy Crosses.

Captain Kelly had his men bearing wounded to the boats, which had grounded some thirty yards from shore; he watched proudly as the stretcher bearers returned to the beach to await other boats rather than climb in with the wounded. More boats hovered far out, despite efforts of Lieutenant Leslie, still overhead in his plane, to herd them to shore.

Dr. Schuster got into a boat which stuck on a coral reef and was almost sunk by Jap machine guns before Marines from the beach gave covering fire.

A few minutes later, near 5:00 P.M., Regan Fuller experienced trouble with the coxswains. With only a few of his wounded aboard, Fuller was forced to hold a pistol on one coxswain to force him to wait for other men. The last of them got away under fire, with Japs pushing to the very edge of the undergrowth at the beach.

Puller could see little of the action from the *Ballard*, but when he caught sight of his men on the beach he quickly went overboard and into one of the small boats. Puller's boat neared others which were circling far from shore, hesitant to go in; he bellowed orders and led them to the beach. The coxswains moved. The Colonel went in with them, and was at the water's edge for ten or fifteen minutes, under sporadic fire, as the evacuation came to an end.

Puller's battalion had twenty-four dead and twenty-three

wounded in the fiasco—and the Raiders and the Second Battalion of the Fifth Marines, who withdrew at about the same time, had another one hundred and seventeen casualties. The only benefit of the operation was the ominous intelligence that a bigger Japanese buildup was under way.

Colonel Puller saw some of his officers and men in the evening, but had little to say. The next day, back in the main defense line of the perimeter, he called together the battalion officers. His voice was hard and his face unsmiling:

"Gentlemen, at least we've all been blooded now. I don't want you to be mooning over our losses and feeling sorry for yourselves or taking all the blame on your shoulders. We've all got to leave this world some day; we're all in the same pickle. And there are worse things than dying for your country. Some things about our action in the last four days I want you to remember forever. There are some we'd all like to forget—but they'll be in your mind's eye as long as you live. I hope we've all learned something. Now take care of your men, and make yourselves ready. We haven't seen anything yet.

"One other thing. Back there on the hillside at Mount Austen, I had trouble getting company officers up. I hope you saw what that cost us in casualties. Never do I want to see that again in my command. I want to see my officers leading. I want you to know that you're leaders, and not simply commanders. You cannot operate a military force in the field under these conditions with commanders alone. Civilians wouldn't know what I was talking about, but you've found out now that it's true: There are many qualities in a man, but one that is absolutely necessary in an infantry leader is stark courage. Give that idea to your men in your own way.

"Don't worry over things that are done, that we can no longer help. Concentrate on building a better combat unit, because that's the best hope of all of us surviving. None of us could help the fact that I was the only combat-trained man in our outfit when we began. I was lucky enough to get the jolt when I was young. You'll come along fast, and there'll be work for us. Let's be ready when our time comes."

Regan Fuller noticed that a thinly disguised scorn came into the Colonel's voice as he spoke of details of the bungled operation, especially in the phrase, "the much-vaunted Raiders." Fuller was so impressed by the Old Man's manner, and his words, that he took the same theme to his company, and talked with them long and earnestly. They seemed to buck up.

One night soon after, an interpreter brought Puller a translation of the diary taken from the Japanese major he had shot on Mount Austen. The Colonel read it with interest. The officer, who had fought for ten years in Manchukuo, had studied the great military leaders of the world—half of them Asiatics whose names meant nothing to Puller. But there was Genghis Khan, and among Americans were Lee, Jackson and Grant. Puller read a few lines aloud to officers who were visiting his command post—Mike Edson, Hank Adams, and an old World War I flier of the House of Rothschild, now the battalion paymaster, Major Henry Heming:

> The Americans amaze me. I never violate the principles of warfare, and they never obey them. We never move without an advance guard, but when we attack Americans, it is always the main body we meet. We Japanese take advantage of the country; the Americans use great machines to clear the jungle.

Puller laughed: "Right now I'm mystified by some of the tactics we use, myself."

A day or so later the beautiful sword of the Jap major was stolen from the command post. One of Puller's aides was indignant. "We'll have a shakedown. We'll turn it up in one of the bedrolls, Colonel."

"Hell, no!" Puller said. "I don't know who got it, but any one of those boys rated it more than I did. They carried the big load. Let him keep it."

A week later Puller heard that one of his Marines had sold the sword to a souvenir-hungry sailor for $1000. He laughed: "Those idiots will buy anything."

He was writing his wife daily, and on October 4, just a week after the return from Mount Austen and Point Cruz, wrote her:

> Merry Christmas (make it a merry one for our precious daughter's sake). I will be merry because you two are safe and well. I love you with all my being.

He enclosed a $500 Government check, as first payment

for a diamond pin for Mrs. Puller, and promised another later. He ended the letter:

> I will return to you safe and well; never doubt it, not even for a moment. . . . Lewis.
> My command is one to be proud of. It has proved itself to be such.

The keeping of records was now primitive and rather casual, for there was seldom a day without enemy contact, bombing or naval shelling. Puller wrote his reports in longhand and had Sergeant Pennington type them on the antique typewriter owned by the battalion. He soon had statements from the survivors of the stand at Point Cruz and recommended several men for medals—including Andy Malanowski, the Medal of Honor; and Robert Raysbrook, the Navy Cross.

He still missed nothing involving the morale of his men. Regan Fuller, who began to feel the stark drama of the situation after the first severe fight, grew a beard and swaggered around the perimeter like a desperado.

Puller took him aside: "Old man, you're carried away with this war business. You're feeling too self-important about it. That's dangerous. This is just a matter of kill or be killed, and we've got to stay on our toes to have a chance. Clean yourself up. Here's some shaving gear. And when you're through, you can take a drink from that bottle, if you like."

General Vandegrift had been promised reinforcements. Army troops were on the way and there would be a naval buildup, too, in an effort to halt Japanese attacks from the enemy base at Rabaul. Vandegrift determined to repeat the stab across the Matanikau, this time in greater force, for his aerial photographs showed him Jap concentrations there, a threat to the whole perimeter and to Henderson Field. If the Japanese could cross the Matanikau, they could place artillery within 5000 yards of the airstrip.

Even as he made the decision to attack once more, the enemy was gathering to spring. The fresh 4th Regiment of the Sendai Division, conquerors of Java, had just been put ashore. The enemy was in place to storm the Matanikau on the night of October 6.

The Marines launched their move on October 7. Mike Edson's Fifth Marines marched along the coastal road to hold the mouth of the river. Lieutenant Colonel Bill Whaling, a skilled woodsman without a command, was given a small force of picked men, including snipers and scouts. He would follow Edson, then turn upstream, cross at Nippon Bridge, and drive down the opposite side of the stream to the sea. Behind Whaling was the Seventh Regiment, now under a new colonel. Its assignment was to follow Whaling and cover the left flank of the operation, then to attack and drive for the sea if possible.

Edson soon met the enemy and in a fierce fight pushed them into a pocket on the east bank of the river. In the night, reinforced by the Raiders, Edson fought hand-to-hand to hold his position under fresh attacks. The men of Whaling and the Seventh Regiment, meanwhile, pushed toward their objective upstream.

On this march, for the first time, Puller used native bearers and guides in his column, stocky, muscular black men with six-inch shocks of dirty red hair, a coiffure achieved by rubbing raw lime into the hair. Puller had bargained for these men with Captain Martin Clemens, the British labor boss of the island; the price was one twist of chewing tobacco daily for each man.

Late in the morning the head of the battalion came upon a slightly wounded Japanese soldier after a sniper hunt. Puller looked at him from a distance of several yards.

"Don't take chances with him," he said. "He may have a grenade ready to go off. We can't slow down to carry him anyway. Kill him."

The Colonel led the file ahead. Marines in the rear prodded the prisoner to his feet and after a gingerly inspection loaded him with packs, two or three at a time. They drove him all day, lightening their own loads, but near the end of the march passed Puller, seated on his helmet at the trailside.

"Say, old man, why didn't you kill that bird? Didn't you hear my order?"

"Sir, we thought he could carry today and we could kill him tonight."

"No you won't," Puller said. "He did your work all day, and you'll sit up and guard him all night."

The discomfited Marines kept watch over the prisoner, vainly tossing bayonets within his reach, hoping to tempt

him to make a dash for freedom. In the morning the survivor went rearward with a party carrying wounded.

On this day, October 7, the *Life* magazine reporter John
Hersey marched with the interior column. On the trail Colonel Julian Frisbie, the executive to Colonel A. L. Sims, gave
the plan of operations to Hersey in simple terms. He ended:
"This is very much like a plan Lee used at the Chickaho-
miny . . . with Jackson closing the trap at the rear. . . . The
units will not be sent out in quite the same pattern, but the
same general idea. Our advantage is, if Whaling finds the
going impossible, we haven't committed Hanneken and
Puller. I think it'll work."

Hersey heard his first sounds of war on the march. Rifle
fire, he wrote, was constant, falling on the ear "like the sound
of a knife tearing fabric." He was impressed by the shouts
of the mortarmen at work, and most of all by the weird
sounds shells made overhead, "like a man blowing through
a keyhole."

Late in the afternoon Hersey saw Puller's meeting with
the commander, Colonel Sims. Hersey's account of the moment as Sims ordered a push forward:

"Puller blew out his cheeks, thrust out his chest: 'That's
fine. Couldn't be better. My men are prepared to spend the
night on the trail. Best place to be if you want to go anywhere.' "

Puller and Frisbie yelled some jokes back and forth, and
Puller moved on.

Hersey joined Whaling's force the next day and from his
experiences wrote the book, *Into The Valley*—but it was
Puller who fought the spectacular engagement of the operation, one of the most bloody of the island campaign.

There was a quiet night by the river, but at 5:30 A.M. on
October 8 a severe rainstorm broke, ending visibility and
turning the trails into streams. Whaling and the Seventh
Regiment managed to cross Nippon Bridge, a small affair
of coconut logs, but made slow progress through the hilly
jungle. The attack was postponed a day and at headquarters
Vandegrift got disquieting news of an even larger Japanese
buildup west of the Mantanikau.

The morning of October 9 dawned clear and refreshingly
cool. The force from the interior moved down the west side
of the Matanikau toward the sea. Edson still held the river's

mouth, on the east bank, and the little offensive thus bore the shape of a crude horseshoe.

Puller noticed that his regimental commander did not accompany the attack, but remained on the east side of the river at Nippon Bridge. The movement developed with Whaling nearest the river, then Hanneken with the Second Battalion of the Seventh, then Puller with the First Battalion. Japs were out in full force and there was constant action against snipers and small parties; this did not impede progress and the front soon neared the sea in the area of Point Cruz.

Hanneken fell into a brisk battle in the broken country and while he was organizing his defense was called from Nippon Bridge: A change of plan by headquarters had called them back to the perimeter. He was to break off and return by the beach road.

Hanneken obeyed orders and in the move left Puller's Company C, commanded by Captain Marshall Moore, to hold the front alone. Puller hurriedly threw A Company onto the ridge to help, but there was little room for maneuver. Bob Haggerty placed his B Company on an adjoining hill and opened furiously with mortar fire, and though he could not see its results, was told by men from C that the enemy was being cut to pieces by the shells.

At the peak of this Puller had a telephone call from the regimental commander, in the rear: "Puller, we've got a change in orders. Execute a reconnaissance in force with your battalion along the coast road toward Kokumbona. Do not become involved in a large action. Be prepared to withdraw, to maintain communications."

Regan Fuller was within earshot as Puller shouted, in a rage: "How the hell can I make a reconnaissance when we're engaged, down to the last man? We're fighting tooth and nail, man. If you'd get off your duff and come up here where the fighting is, you could see the situation." He slammed down the field phone.

Puller called a brief conference; Regan Fuller noticed that he held an aerial photo upside-down, obviously using it as no more than a prop. "All right, gentlemen," the Colonel said. "There are the enemy over there in those ravines. And here we are. Now go get 'em. Drive 'em into the sea."

At 1:00 P.M. the battalion's fight reached its climax and within an hour it was over: Puller saw Japanese swarming

from a circular ravine in the midst of the jungle growth—
an old crater, he assumed. Puller called for an artillery concentration. The big shells came into and around the crater
in devastating fashion, but even more deadly were the mortars of 1/7.

Puller had at last caught the enemy in an ideal situation
and pressed his advantage. When mortar fire drove the Japanese up the slopes of their crater, they emerged into the
fields of fire from his machine guns, which cut down scores
of the small figures. When the tide flowed back into the
crater the mortars opened once more. Within a few minutes the slaughter was complete and the enemy unit had
ceased to exist as an effective force.

When it was over, regimental headquarters called back,
relieving Puller of the necessity of a reconnaissance patrol
and permitting him to return to the perimeter. There was
also a call from Hanneken, a request to bring back his
wounded. Puller's men carried in all casualties from the two
battalions. Puller's battalion had five dead and twenty-one
wounded; total losses were sixty-five dead and one hundred
and twenty-five wounded for the operation. Puller estimated the enemy losses to be at least five times as great—
but it was later revealed that the Japanese Fourth Infantry
had lost almost an entire battalion, with six hundred and
ninety dead, the result of Puller's strike in the crater.

Enemy documents found in the crater told headquarters
how fortunately timed the attack had been and how telling
Puller's blows. One order to the enemy troops had read:

"From now on, the occupying of Guadalcanal Island is
under the observation of the whole world. Do not expect to
return, not even one man, if the occupation is not successful.
Everyone must remember the honor of the Emperor, fear
no enemy, yield to no material matters, show the strong
points of steel or of rocks, and advance valiantly and fe-
rociously. Hit the enemy opponents so hard they will not
be able to get up again."

Also found were atrocity tales sent back to Japan by these
troops:

"The Americans on this island are not ordinary troops,
but Marines, a special force recruited from jails and insane
asylums for blood lust. There is no honorable death to prisoners, their arms are cut off, they are staked on the airfield,
and run over by steam rollers."

General Vandegrift, then unaware of the damage inflicted, was not content with the operation. Puller was also displeased, but for very different reasons:

"The whole process was asinine. They mixed up the outfits as badly as they possibly could. There was no overall commander. Division gave orders to Hanneken, Whaling and me. Whaling was senior, but orders did not come through him. My regimental commander was behind the river, and not on the scene. Thus, when they found two battalions stopped cold in the fight, communications were so bad that they pulled these two outfits, and left me to face all the enemy. We were blindly lucky to come out as we did. Imagine them ordering me to go on some damned reconnaissance, when I was fighting with every man I had! Proper designation of authority would have made everything clear."

Despite difficulties, the enemy had been seriously checked. On October 11, as the land action subsided, the Navy, with a little fleet under Admiral Norman Scott, caught the Japanese Cruiser Division Six off Cape Esperance, "crossed the T" on the enemy, and virtually blew the division out of the war. The American ships were part of the shield for the Army's Americal Division, now on its way to Guadalcanal.

Puller's battalion now took its place in the perimeter which defended Henderson Field, the main line of resistance in the American position. Puller temporarily took a line of holes and gun positions on ridges behind barbed wire. The Colonel set to work on improving battalion morale. Dr. Smith noted in his diary that Puller seemed more concerned over losses:

"He has become almost fanatical in his desire to see that the men are properly cared for. If a man's body is lost he is greatly disturbed, and frets about the time lost before he can recover the body and give it a decent burial. Not an outwardly religious man himself, he encourages divine services to be held frequently on the front lines for the men who want them. He would much sooner give services himself than not to have any."

Puller was often dissatisfied with a chaplain's talk to the men and would grumble: "Maybe it's time I tried my hand. I think I could do better." Dr. Smith thought he would have been the island's best chaplain, and wrote in open admiration: "Whatever he says is sincere. I have never seen an officer with so little bluff."

Puller recommended other men for medals from the operation at the crater, among them Lieutenant George Plantier, who, though badly wounded, refused to be treated until he had seen all his mortar shells fired. Despite maximum range over difficult terrain his first round had been on target.

Supplies were still short, but though all outfits were limited to two meals daily Puller fed his battalion three without violating orders. He spotted stacks of Japanese rice in boxes along the shore, a neglected treasure. Some was wormy and spoiled; his men culled it, and he sent the rest to his cooks. This was a godsend during October. For three weeks there had been no coffee or sugar, and rice was so inevitable at meals that cooks colored it with food dye in an effort to divert the attention of the jaded men.

The troops were filthy; their socks were gone and their underclothing was rotting away. At the worst of this time the Army hit the beach, the vanguard of the American Division. The Colonel learned of it when he saw half a dozen of his men spruced up in Army utilities.

"Where the devil did you get 'em?"

"Colonel, the beach is loaded. Anything you want."

Puller summoned Pennington and they went to the beach in a jeep. There were vast piles of stores: boxes of socks, bacon, underwear, everything the Marines could desire. The soldiers had taken cover from Pistol Pete, a long Jap howitzer far down in the jungle which dropped a shell in the sand every few minutes. Puller and Pennington threw cases on the jeep until the sergeant feared that they would never move it.

A crouching Army MP shouted from a foxhole: "Leave that stuff alone, damn you! That's Army gear."

Puller gave him a farewell: "If you're guarding this stuff, get the hell out here and guard it."

Pennington returned for two more jeep loads and the glad news went out to the companies over the phones; every unit got fresh socks and plenty of sugar that night. Puller went back to the beach for more weapons and lugged in dozens of machine guns. There was an enticing treasure, an iron-bound battalion arms chest with a lock so sturdy that it had to be burned off with a torch. Puller had visions of hundreds of spare weapons parts he would soon dole out—but when the box was opened he saw that some soldier had replaced the contents with hundreds of cans of sardines. The cans were distributed down the battalion line, but Puller mourned the loss of the parts.

Puller's communications men had taken a radio from a wrecked plane at the edge of Henderson Field and hooked it up with five or six headsets, so that the command post now often listened to news from back home. One night Puller and his officers heard Secretary of the Navy Frank Knox say dolefully that Guadalcanal seemed hopeless, and threatened to become another Bataan.

Puller shook his head, and a young officer shouted: "How about that old bastard? Don't he know we got real Marines on this island?"

Division headquarters scolded Puller when it discovered the radio, and was still annoyed even when he explained that it had been salvaged from a ruined plane.

Malaria began to cripple the Division, with more than 700 cases in the first half of October and 655 new cases in the next week. Puller advised headquarters to try the old Haitian remedy of injecting the troops with quinine, but after a conference with medical officers, General Vandegrift declined: "They say that foreign doctors use the method, but that it's too dangerous. About one to two per cent casualties could be expected. We can't risk it."

Puller protested: "It's better to take that risk than to keep on as we are, and know we'll lose hundreds, even thousands. Sooner or later, you'll have the Division put out of action with malaria."

This was in vain; treatment of malaria was continued with atabrine.

During mid-October Japan made her supreme effort to conquer Guadalcanal and reach for Australia. On October 9, while Puller was pounding his adversaries in the crater, General Harusoyhi Hyakutake of the Seventeenth Army landed to take charge. About 900 Japanese troops were being landed each night, and on October 12, a night when the American position was hammered by Japanese battleships and planes, 4000 more enemy soldiers landed at Tassafaronga. By now more than 20,000 Japanese troops were ashore, facing an almost equal number of Americans, the latter hemmed into their perimeter against the sea, so that the Japanese retained

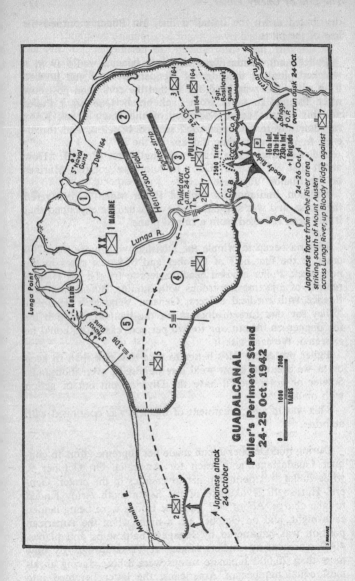

GUADALCANAL
Puller's Perimeter Stand
24-25 Oct. 1942

Lunga Point

Kukum

Lunga R.

Henderson Field

Fighter strip

Bloody Ridge

5" Naval Guns

5" Naval Guns

5 3DB Guns

Matanika R.

A Japanese attack 24 October

Japanese force from Pohe River area
striking south of Mount Austen
across Lunga River, up Bloody Ridge against 1

16th Inf.
29th Inf.
230th Inf.
+ 1 Brigade

24-26 Oct.

O.P.
Briggs
overrun dusk 24 Oct.

2500 Yards

Sgt. Basilone's
guns

Pulled out
a.m. 24 Oct.

PULLER

YARDS
1000   2000

S. BRYANT

the initiative. In "The Slot," or Sealark Channel, the American Navy still ruled by day, and the Japanese by night.

Vandegrift now reorganized the perimeter. On his left, facing inland, Sector One, along the beach, was held by a defense battalion and special troops; Sector Two, moving into the jungle, was held by the 164th Army Infantry Regiment; Sector Three, 2500 yards long, belonged to Colonel Sims's Seventh Marines—but only Puller's and Hanneken's battalions were used in the lines; Sector Four, with the First Marines; and Sector Five, with the Fifth Marines, completed the curve back to the sea at the mouth of the Matanikau.

The major Japanese attack was expected along the Matanikau, and most of the Division's strength was placed there.

The Japanese moved to attack these positions on October 15, with Lieutenant General Masao Maruyama's Second Division assigned to swing far inland and hit the Marines from the south—in the area where Puller's men awaited. Nine infantry battalions set out on this march, a total of 5600 men, excluding artillery and other support troops. The soldiers carried or dragged everything, even guns, over the rough trails. They were late in making their attack and abandoned many guns on the trail.

Heavy rains swept the island almost daily and Japanese progress was slow until, on October 22, a tank and infantry attack on the beach struck the Marines and was bloodily repulsed. This had an effect, however, for to meet the threat, Hanneken's battalion was pulled from its place beside Puller on October 24, and sent to a riverside position. Puller's men spent the day in furious activity.

Puller now had to cover the whole sector of 2500 yards with his understrength battalion, and he filled the hole left by Hanneken by spreading his men and putting all except the mortars in line. He had sent officers and noncoms among Hanneken's men before the departure, and in an hour they learned more about the lay of the land and the firing lanes than they could have learned in a day by inspection. Holes were deepened and more machine guns were put into position.

Puller had seen a couple of strands of barbed wire along a jeep road in his rear and had that taken down for the front line; there were no staples, and Marines wrapped the wire around trees. The wire was hung with tin cans filled with stones and grenades with their pins half-pulled. There were no trip-flares to warn of enemy approach and light the area.

Puller walked the line most of the day, at each gun position asking the man in charge to show him the field of fire; the Colonel checked to see that the fire zones interlocked, and ordered improvements at almost every point.

From left to right, the companies were: A, C and B. On the far left, where Regan Fuller commanded, was the only spot of open land, where A Company joined the 164th Army Infantry. During the day the field in front of the Army position was plowed, to slow attackers. At the edge of the field Regan Fuller placed a 37 millimeter gun and two 50-caliber machine guns. Otherwise, A Company had the worst of the battalion position, for their ground was low and the hill in their front was heavily wooded.

Men worked so hard in the day, carrying arms and ammunition, digging, filling sandbags and hanging wire, that many were asleep by late afternoon.

A Company was weaker by one platoon than the other companies, for despite the protests of Colonel Puller, there was an outpost of forty-six of its men some 3000 yards to their front, commanded by Sergeant Ralph Briggs, Jr., of Port Edwards, Wisconsin. These men had been out for several days, to warn of an enemy approach.

Colonel Puller was on the field phone often during the day of digging-in, trying to persuade his regimental commander to have headquarters withdraw Briggs and his patrol: "They're going to sacrifice those men—that's all. We don't need any bait on the hook, as you say. If they're coming, they're coming. It's foolishness to throw away that platoon."

Once, when it appeared that the commander had expressed agreement, officers in the CP heard Puller roar: "All right, then, if you think so, why don't you waltz your duff down to Division and get 'em back in here?"

The outpost remained in the hills to the south, out of sight, but connected with the main line by telephone.

Puller also called Pedro Del Valle, of the 11th Artillery, several miles down the coast, and asked him to be ready to fire support during the night. Del Valle was reassuring: "I'll give you what you want. I know you won't be unreasonable. Just call for all you need."

At dusk, as usual, the artillerymen registered their guns, and shells exploded in the thick growth a few yards beyond Puller's lines.

In the afternoon there was a report of smoke in the hills beyond the outpost and a rumor spread that a Jap officer had been seen studying the position through field glasses. None of this intelligence came to Puller, but as night drew on, men in the CP with him saw that he expected trouble. Sergeant Major Frank Sheppard was beside him as daylight faded:

"Shep, we'll probably get mixed up in a scrap tonight. The weather is right, and the moon won't be much. It'll rain like hell—and Nips are out there."

The Colonel had the field phones opened down the line so that all companies and platoons could hear every message. He made a final check after dark, squatting in the dugout of his CP; there was no light in the place except for a flashlight occasionally used by the radioman.

First Battalion, Seventh Marines, was ready for its night of trial. Rain began to fall.

At 9:30 the phone rang in the battalion CP. Puller answered. It was Sergeant Briggs, whispering. The company communications men listened to the conversation:

"Colonel, there's about three thousand Japs between you and me."

"Are you sure?"

"Positive. They've been all around us, singing and smoking cigarettes, heading your way."

"All right, Briggs, but make damned sure. Take your men to your left—understand me? Go down and pass through the lines near the sea. I'll call 'em to let you in. Don't fail, and don't go in any other direction. I'll hold my fire as long as I can."

"Yes, sir."

Puller had hardly put down the telephone when the bell rang once more. A company in the line reported Japs were cutting the barbed wire in its front. Puller spoke to the circuit down the battalion line.

"All right," he said. "Let's get this straight. Hold fire until you get an order from me. The outpost must get clear before we open up. If the bastards break through, use the bayonet. And keep someone at every phone. Wait."

Puller looked at his watch. It was ten o'clock. Yells rolled from the right: Japanese voices shouting in English, "Blood for the Emperor! Marine, you die!"

A Marine bellowed back: "To hell with your God-damned

Emperor! Blood for Franklin and Eleanor!" Obscene shouts followed.

Puller got on the telephone and called loudly: "Commence firing."

The front erupted with blazing weapons, and over their heads the artillery shells soughed through the rainstorm. Explosions farther back in the jungle halted Japanese columns before they could move but the vanguard pressed against the wire along a narrrow front. Grenades blew holes in the fencing and enemy troops ran into the fire of the massed machine guns. Puller had almost doubled the normal strength of machine gun companies, picking up the weapons at every opportunity. Their weight was felt now.

Sergeant Manila John Basilone's nest of guns was about the center of C Company, in the middle of the line, with a slight decline in his front; the enemy drove toward him so persistently that he covered the hill with their bodies and when the first fury of attack faded he sent men to push down the wall of enemy bodies, to clear the fire lane.

Calls for help came from several outposts and Puller sent men from headquarters; often he left the CP himself, prowling among the companies. The attacks now came in waves, each high tide lasting for about fifteen minutes, with increasing fury each time. There was at least one attack every hour. Weapons began to give out.

Regan Fuller, on the low ground at the left, saw an enemy mass in the edge of the field, crowding against the jungle for cover. His 37 anti-tank gun fired three rounds of canister and the column disappeared. Elsewhere in his front Fuller had every weapon blazing—he had a rifle platoon, a heavy machine gun section with four 50-caliber and six 30-caliber machine guns, two anti-tank guns, and a number of extra pieces, including half a dozen old Lewis machine guns, most of which jammed. There were eighteen BAR's and a 60 millimeter mortar. The mortar fired 600 rounds during the night, until it was red hot; at dawn the tube barely projected from the mud. The wire before A Company was not broken and not a man was lost during the hours of darkness. In the first light, Regan Fuller saw enemy bodies stacked "like cordwood" in the edge of the jungle, and in the field where his anti-tank guns had fired was a column of Japanese dead, each rank lying half atop the one in its front in perfect formation—a weapons company with machine guns, rifles, mines and dynamite still held by its troops.

Puller called Del Valle again: "Give us all you've got. We're holding on by our toenails."

"I'll give you all you call for, Puller, but God knows what'll happen when the ammo we have is gone."

"If we don't need it now, we'll never need it. If they get through here tonight there won't be a tomorrow."

"She's yours as long as she lasts."

John Basilone came scurrying to the CP several times during the night, at lulls in the fighting. He reported some guns in trouble and vanished, bearing heavy parts or ammunition on his back. He was barefooted. Regan Fuller saw him once on the A Company front. Basilone reported his guns burning out, and such a serious lack of water that men were urinating in the gun jackets to keep them firing.

From the rear, after a couple of hours, artillerymen reported the barrels of their 105's were white-hot at the muzzles. No one knew how long the big weapons could maintain their fire.

Regan Fuller called the CP from the flank:

"Colonel, I'm just about running out of ammo. I've used almost three and a half units of fire."

"You got bayonets, haven't you, Fuller?"

"Sure. Yes, sir."

"All right, then. Hang on."

In the heaviest of the firing, when Puller had left the CP, regimental headquarters called for him.

"Not here, sir," the wireman said. "Colonel Puller's up front."

"Find him. Get him on the phone."

After the crew had made several calls to the line position, Puller returned and talked with the regimental commander. The few remaining in the pit heard Puller's explosive reply:

"What d'ya mean, 'What's going on?' We're neck deep in a fire fight, and I've no time to stand here bullflinging. If you want to find out what's going on, come up and see." He growled angrily to Pennington and Sheppard: "Regiment is not convinced we are facing a major attack!"

Near 3:00 A.M., when six or eight separate attacks had built up and waned on his front, under almost constant fire, Puller again talked with regimental headquarters—this time with the exec, Colonel Julian Frisbie:

"Yeah, it looks pretty bad. . . . Sure, we could use help.

But if it's coming, for God's sake don't hold it back—send it on in."

The battalion was now down to about 500 men, Puller estimated. He had no way to guess the strength of the enemy waves. Japanese had infiltrated the lines by this hour, and men who could be spared were hunting them in the blackness. Frank Sheppard organized a small security party for the CP in an effort to protect Puller and his diminished staff; there were now two men left with the Colonel.

There were more talks with the regimental CP before reinforcements arrived, and some delay ensued when the fresh troops, the Third Battalion of the Army's 164th, were led to regimental headquarters, instead of coming directly to the front.

"Who's guiding them in?" Puller asked.

"A Navy chaplain here, Father Keough."

"Put him on."

Puller was soon satisfied that the priest, who had often visited the front positions, could lead the battalion through the rain-swept jungles the mile or more to his position. He hung up the telephone and went into the downpour, accompanied only by a runner.

The jeep road was lower than the battalion line and perhaps a quarter of a mile to the rear. When Puller reached the road and stood in the rain, waiting, there was an occasional tracer over his head. Within a few minutes the head of the relief column appeared. Puller shook hands with Father Keough.

"Here they are, Colonel."

"Father, we can use 'em."

Puller greeted the Army commander, Lieutenant Colonel Robert K. Hall: "Colonel, I'm glad to see you. I don't know who's senior to who right now, and I don't give a damn. I'll be in command until daylight, at least, because I know what's going on here, and you don't."

"That's fine with me," Hall said. "You lead on."

"I'm going to drop 'em off along this road," Puller said, "and send in a few to each platoon position. I want you to make it clear to your people that my men, even if they're only sergeants, will command in those holes when your officers and men arrive."

"I understand you. Let's go."

Puller, Keough and Hall led the file along the dark road

in the rain with the thunder of fire growing to their left. Every hundred yards or so they met a runner who had come back through the undergrowth to lead in reinforcements. Puller halted at each runner and gave him a squad or more of men. When they came to the end of the line all the troops had been fed in, with guides to their positions, and were ready to help stand off the enemy.

In some of the holes Marines took the fresh guns and ammunition of the Army troops and did much of the firing themselves—but other beleaguered veterans found the newcomers superb fighting material, though they did not know the ground. The Army men had the new M-1 rifles, the first the Marines had seen. The mixed men fought well together, and as dawn approached beat off two or three more Japanese attacks.

Puller went to the CP with Keough and Hall when the men of 3/164 had been distributed. It was after 4:00 A.M. An hour later the enemy drove a wedge into the line, some seventy-five yards deep and perhaps fifty yards wide. As the first light of day came Puller sent mortarmen on either side of this break and with a flurry of fire cleaned up the salient. Marines counted thirty-seven Jap bodies in the small triangle when the line had been straightened.

Puller gave the Army colonel and the priest blankets and a meal of C-rations, then left them to inspect his line. He later recommended Keough for the Silver Star for his work of the night; it was not awarded.

Reports of trouble still came from the line. Sergeant Robert Cornely had lost several guns in his position, one because a steam condenser had exploded, and his men competed with others for spare gun barrels in the morning. Dozens of automatic weapons had been fired for so long that the rifling was worn smooth. Two of the three men shot during the night in Cornely's position were killed by Marines in the confusion caused by Jap infiltrators in the rear.

Soon after dawn Puller was told that men had found a party of about forty of the enemy, lying asleep near the 80 millimeter mortar position commanded by the great gunnery sergeant, Roy Fowle. The sleeping Japs bore land mines and dynamite, evidently for an attack on the mortarmen, whose fire had wrought such havoc on the Jap columns. The sleeping invaders were soon wiped out.

There was one enemy prisoner, a sullen little warrant

officer who refused to talk when he was brought to Puller. The Colonel was so stung by the insolence of the prisoner that he slapped him with the flat of an entrenching tool; teeth spilled from the Jap's mouth, but they were false teeth. He gave no information, even then.

A later prisoner talked freely with Puller:

"Why didn't you change your tactics when you saw you weren't breaking our line? Why didn't you shift to a weaker spot?"

"That is not the Japanese way. The plan had been made. No one would have dared to change it. It must go as it is written."

The commander of the Army's 164th Regiment, Colonel Bryant E. Moore, sought Puller during the morning. "Colonel Puller, I want you to know how happy I am to have had my men blooded under you. No man in our outfit, including me, had ever seen action, and I know our boys couldn't have had a better instructor. I wish you'd break in my other battalions." Puller praised the men of the battalion in return: "They're almost as good as Marines, Colonel."

His old friend, General R. S. Geiger, the aviation chief, also visited the front and walked over the torn terrain. He was astonished by the windrows of Japanese bodies. Overhead, his planes were strafing and bombing the retreat of the enemy through the interior.

Sergeant Briggs and his men of the outpost had a hair-raising return to the lines. When the battle broke out Briggs led the way to the area before the Army regiment, where most of them hid overnight. There was a close call on the way. As Briggs told the story:

"We gained cover in the woods where it was cold as hell, and the Japs seemed to be all around us. We could hear them jabbering and walking so close that one Jap stepped on a Marine's bayonet and another stepped on the helmet of a man hit by rifle fire.

"They filed by in squads, the most unreal sensation I ever had, but they didn't want to tangle with us for fear of betraying their position to the guns."

At daylight Briggs and the party crawled into the grass. Japs turned mortar and machine gun fire on them. Private Gerald White and another man made an heroic trek from this spot. When he remembered the machine gun he had left behind in the outpost, White crawled back some 600 yards to the spot, accompanied by his friend, and removed a bolt, making the gun unserviceable. In his absence Private Robert Potter gave his life to save his companions. When Jap fire became heavy in the field Potter leapt to his feet and dashed back and forth, drawing fire, shouting to his friends to run for American lines. Most of them escaped in that way, Potter was killed. Several remaining men of the party got back into the lines aboard a Bren gun carrier sent out by Regan Fuller. Only four of the outpost failed to return.

Puller's men found two hundred and fifty Japanese dead inside their lines during the day, about twenty-five of them officers—one a major who had committed suicide, leaving a final entry in his diary on the loss of his colors and troops: "I do not know what excuse to give. I apologize for what I have done. . . . I am going to return my borrowed life today with short interest."

Puller's casualties for the battle were nineteen dead, thirty wounded and twelve missing. In his first report, the Colonel estimated that he had been attacked by a Japanese regiment with a strength of 2000 men. Captured documents revealed that his half-battalion had beaten off the suicidal attacks of three enemy regiments (the 16th, 29th and 230th), plus the remnant of a brigade—or the equivalent of a Japanese division. Two of the regiments admitted to carrying off 500 stretcher cases between them.

Two or three days later when the stench of bloated bodies in his front made his men retch, Puller persuaded Division to make a count of enemy casualties and bury the corpses. This burial detail counted 1462 bodies and spent two days at the grisly work. Bulldozers gouged holes and covered the enemy dead in great pits.

There was an attack on the night of October 26 following Puller's big fight, but it was light by comparison and the enemy did not press home. It was clear that, for the time being, 1/7, with the aid of Del Valle's artillery and the final support of the Army battalion, had saved the perimeter against almost staggering odds. It had cost the Japanese dearly to leave their artillery on the rugged trails and to confine their attacks to a narrow front. Guadalcanal saw no fighting more furious, by land, sea or air.

Puller added somber figures to his report: In the campaign thus far his battalion had lost twenty-four per cent of its men and thirty-seven per cent of its officers.

General Vandegrift sent the battalion a commendation for its "determined and vigorous defense against . . . numerically superior enemy forces. . . . The high combat effectiveness demonstrated is a tribute to the courage, devotion to duty and high professional attainment of its commanding officer, Lieutenant Colonel Lewis B. Puller, and to the company commanders, Captains Charles W. Kelly, Jr., Regan Fuller, Robert H. Haggerty, Marshall W. Moore, and Robert J. Rodgers."

The company commanders won Silver Stars for the night's fighting, but Regan Fuller, for one, thought that Sergeant Briggs, Gerald White and Robert Potter should have been honored instead. Sergeant John Basilone won the Medal of Honor, the first Marine enlisted man to win the award in World War II.

Puller won a second gold star for his Navy Cross.

The Colonel spent the next days trying to care for the men, for he had little hope of replacements. Dr. Edward Smith saw Puller almost as soon as the guns stopped firing on the morning of October 25, when the Colonel appeared at the aid station, now a makeshift hospital.

Smith and an assistant were operating on a crude table beneath a tarpaulin stretched over a gully. The doctor had on one shoe and stood in six or eight inches of mud, the last hope of sanitation gone as he worked over the battered chest of a young Marine. Blood colored the muck beneath the doctor's feet. Smith had been operating all night.

Puller had little to say: "Well, Doc, I guess when they trained you, up there at Harvard Medical School, you never thought you'd come to this?"

"We must have help, Colonel. Get us more doctors. Men will be dying."

Puller made an effort, but it was six hours or more before other doctors were sent by headquarters and all the injured began to get attention.

Smith continued to operate; there was now an added reminder of battle and a promise of more to come. A Marine set up a grinding wheel beside the doctor's shelter and at odd hours, day and night, men came to sharpen their bayonets.

Regan Fuller kept an increasingly close watch on the Colonel: "He became more concerned for the men being killed and wounded as it grew worse. I saw his eyes puddle up many a time, but he would have died rather than have any of us think that he could weep for his men, or anything else. He never lost control."

Puller frequently sent the men to the nearby river to bathe, with riflemen on constant guard. The jungle itch had become serious and was weaving red welts over the bodies of men; they were ordered to wash as often as possible.

The Colonel washed in the river with the troops, too, and Regan Fuller noticed that even when he washed his uniforms he stripped with the enlisted men in the river. "A common touch the men liked," Fuller said. "Though a few of the Clausewitz-type officers in the rear ranks snickered behind his back, the men knew he was real, that he never put on an act, and they loved him."

Puller's ill-concealed tenderness was evident to his men when he talked with one of his old gunnery sergeants, Roy Fowle, who had cancer, knew that he was doomed, and could eat only canned milk—every can of which was saved for him by the troops. Fowle was a little bear of a man, far from handsome, with a quiet manner which concealed his warlike spirit and his skill as a mortarman. "He could teach Lou Diamond tricks," Puller often told his men. The men often discussed the proposition: Who is the world's greatest gunnery sergeant—Roy Fowle, Joe Buckley, or Red O'Neill? All were veterans in the ranks of 1/7 who played leading roles in the perimeter defense.

There was little enough gaiety, for more men had malaria each day and hundreds, like Puller, suffered from it in the afternoons, when they were so weary that they could not move their aching joints. When action came they returned to duty as if they were normal.

Puller shielded the men from unnecessary work. A young officer who insisted that they police up the battalion area, removing Jap beer cans and the debris of battle, was stopped by the Colonel: "Forget it, old man. Let the boys get in their sacks and leave them the hell alone. They're half dead from fever and fighting, and they'll have to hop to it again any day now."

The first bags of mail for the battalion arrived from the States in early November, creating great excitement. Puller had Sergeant Pennington open the sacks, and there was consternation when he dumped out packages of training manuals from headquarters, material they should have had weeks ago, on Samoa. Puller gave them a long, bitter look.

"Take the damned things down the hill and burn 'em," he said. "Sort out what real mail there is. Can you think of anybody who needs training manuals less than our gang?"

There was a squabble between A Company and some of the 164th Army men, for Regan Fuller's men had bartered for, or stolen, some new M-1 rifles during the big night's fighting, and Army officers wanted them returned. The Colonel was amused by the affair. For himself, he favored the old rifle they brought to Guadalcanal: "For sheer accuracy, if you want to kill men in battle, there has never been a rifle to equal the Springfield 1903. Others may give us more firepower, but in ability to hit a target, nothing touches the old '03. In my opinion, nothing ever will. A perfect weapon, if ever there was one."

Puller's command post telephone rang at 3.00 A.M. one morning and someone shook the Colonel awake. Colonel Thomas at Division was calling.

"Puller, there's a man here who wants to see you. Come on down."

"Who the hell is it?" It was a ten-mile jeep ride to Division, and there was a downpour of rain.

"I can't tell you on the phone. Come on. Be here by daylight."

When Puller clumped into the Division dugouts, streaming water, he saw the smiling face of Chester Nimitz, who had come down from Pearl Harbor.

"Admiral Nimitz," Thomas said, "I want you to meet Colonel Puller."

"You're ten years too late," Nimitz said. "Puller and I were shipmates, away back there in China station days."

There was a warm, brief reunion between the old *Augusta* hands.

"I was delighted to see your name come through in dispatches at my headquarters," Nimitz said. "I assure you they went through my office, on into Washington. You're doing a great job, just the kind I knew you'd do."

The Admiral was soon busy pinning medals on officers and men who had gathered for the ceremony, and when it was over, Puller said goodbye and bumped down the road to his battalion.

The first week in November settled the fate of Guadalcanal and the Solomons. An even dozen big Japanese transports lay within striking distance, loaded with troops, and task forces gathered to escort them in. In the American perimeter, most of the American Division had arrived, as well as two regiments of big guns, 105's and 155's. The Eighth Marines were on the point of landing and the air force was growing—there were now five squadrons based at Henderson Field.

On November 3 Colonel Hanneken led his men across the Metapona River. He observed enemy ships landing troops and was almost cut off by a strong attack which forced him to retreat over the river to Koli Point. After hours of trying to reach headquarters with a faulty radio Hanneken got through a call for help. The force sent to extricate him was led by General W. H. Rupertus, the officer who had persuaded Puller to go to Haiti so many years before. Rupertus took three battalions of infantry, some artillery and tanks. One of the infantry outfits was Puller's 1/7.

The battalion joined Hanneken at the mouth of the Malimbiu River, crossed in landing craft, and with the aid of an Army battalion upstream Hanneken and Puller tried to surround the enemy. Puller pushed from the west against the enemy, Hanneken from the east, and the Army's 2/164 from the south.

The country, as usual, was rugged and well screened and Japs were everywhere. At 6:00 A.M. on November 8 Puller's men left the beach at the mouth of the Metapona River and on a front of about 600 yards moved toward an unnamed stream about 1500 yards away. They skirmished through the morning and at 2:00 P.M., without warning, enemy artillery and machine guns opened on the column from across the nameless river.

Puller was 300 to 400 yards behind the point of his column. The first salvo of Japanese fire burst just in front of him. For the first time in a combat career spanning twenty-three years, his luck ran out under enemy fire. He was blown from his feet by a spray of flying metal; shell fragments had torn his legs and lower body and he was bleeding freely.

The field telephone was carried by a Marine just in his rear.

"Call headquarters, old man," Puller said.

"I can't, sir. The wire's been cut."

The Colonel struggled unsteadily to his feet and tried to help the communications man repair the wire. As he stood an enemy sniper shot him twice through the flesh of his arm with small caliber bullets. He sank back to the ground.

Frank Sheppard was leading the column with a party of cooks who carried ammunition. The point halted when enemy fire came in and Sheppard instructed the cooks in operating the light machine guns, which he set up for them. A runner brought him word which he could not at first believe:

"The Old Man's been hit. Bad."

Sheppard soon reached the spot, which was still under fire. Bunky Davis, a brave corpsman, was darting about the clearing, hanging plasma bottles over the wounded and treating all he could find. None of the doctors had come up from the rear.

Puller nodded toward Davis: "I want that man recommended for a Silver Star."

Sergeant Pennington had come up by now, and he helped Sheppard lift Puller into a poncho to get him off the ground and avoid tetanus infection.

Sheppard bent over Puller: "Are you able to stay here in command, sir?"

"Yes. Of course I am. I'll be okay. I can't leave these men."

"May I call for artillery fire, if I can get the radio or phone working?"

"Yes, if you know how."

Men shoveled out a foxhole for Puller and lowered him in the poncho. The telephone was placed in the hole with him and when the line was repaired he cradled the phone in one arm and talked with headquarters. Pennington listened as he discussed a mortar barrage across the river the next morning and the launching of a dawn attack.

Sheppard called in the artillery fire; shells soon burst in the thickets across the stream and the enemy was quiet for the rest of the evening.

Late in the night Puller realized that he could no longer walk and called Division headquarters.

"I find myself unable to proceed by leading my troops," he said.

After a delay word came back: "Major John C. Weber will assume command of your battalion within a few hours. He is leaving the perimeter immediately."

Weber arrived about 3:00 A.M.

Amphibious craft came into the river after daylight to pick up the battalion's dead and wounded, but not until all others had been gathered would Puller consent to move.

A corpsman leaned over him with an evacuation tag,

preparing to tie it to Puller's uniform. The Colonel snarled: "Take that and tag a bottle with it. I can go under my own power. Go and help the men who need it."

Pennington said, "Colonel, the boats are here, and are all loaded. They're ready for you now."

Puller got slowly to his feet. A doctor reached for his arm, but the Colonel wrenched away. "No, dammitall. Let me be. I can go." He limped down the trail. He made it to the beach on foot, a distance of about a thousand yards, then crawled onto a landing craft and was taken down the shore to Kukum, in the perimeter. There was a long, painful jeep ride to the field hospital, which was no more than a canvas stretched overhead against the weather.

Mike Edson and Hank Adams saw him on the way back and stopped to ask if he needed help.

"Nothing to it," Puller said. "Hell, these are just Band-Aid wounds."

When the doctors examined him in the crude shelter they gave him drugs, and went to work. They dug out six of the smaller fragments of shell without using an anesthetic. It was a burst from a 77 millimeter which had felled him. When they reached a bigger wound in his thigh the medics halted.

"If this is coming out, Colonel, you'll have to fly south tonight. Nothing this side of Australia can do the job. It's for a real hospital."

"How long would I be laid up?"

"Maybe a month, maybe only three weeks."

"Wouldn't it take care of itself—won't tissue cover that chunk without having to operate?"

"Nobody knows. You can't keep going forever with it embedded there."

"Hell, when I was a boy in Virginia half the old men in the country carried around enough Yankee iron in their bodies to open junkyards. I can't go to Australia while my men are fighting."

The doctors shook their heads but did not insist. The Colonel went to bed for recuperation.

Frank Sheppard visited him when the battalion had come back from its latest adventure and together they composed Puller's report on the action, a detailed account which ended: "Casualties inflicted on the enemy during this period are known to be more than twice our own. Our losses were twelve killed and twenty-seven wounded. Our total casualties to date are officers, fifty per cent, and enlisted men, twenty-three per cent; combined, twenty-five per cent."

Dr. Smith passed one day and Puller yelled: "Hey, Smitty, let's get together for a bridge game," but both knew the old foursome was no more. Puller proudly showed the doctor a snapshot of his daughter which had recently arrived by mail. He seemed optimistic about the war, too. On the day after he was wounded there was news that the German Rommel, the Desert Fox, was in retreat after so many victorious months in the North African deserts.

Nearby, the tide also turned. Off Savo Island an inferior task force under Rear Admiral Daniel J. Callaghan and Norman Scott gallantly assailed a big Japanese fleet, and though both were killed and six ships lost, the enemy was shot to pieces. The Jap losses were two cruisers and a destroyer sunk, five others burning and presumed sunk, and a crippled battleship which was finished by American torpedo planes the next day. Guadalcanal appeared to be safe, but Puller could see even from his confinement in the canvas shack that the First Marine Division was near the end of its usefulness.

By the time Puller was wounded the few surviving original officers were unsteady on their feet, ill with malaria, dengue fever or skin diseases. Regan Fuller had left at last, for after the fight at Koli Point he had weighed only one hundred and seven pounds; his evacuation tag read: Malaria and semi-starvation. He left the island ruefully, realizing that he was afraid to face Puller, because he had been evacuated. The feeling endured for years.

One day a new patient was placed in the cot next to Puller, just a foot away. The boy had come from the Fifth Marines, a shell shock case; he trembled and whimpered constantly, and babbled in the night. The Colonel made efforts to help him, but the boy was hostile. After the first few days Puller noticed that the young man no longer had tremors except when he knew he was being watched.

"There's no such thing as shell shock or battle fatigue," Puller said. "All in the mind. Until I got in this war, I never saw a bit of it. We fought all up and down Haiti and Nicaragua without it. You'll be okay."

After an air alert one day, when the boy had crouched in an underground shelter for a long time after the all clear sounded he returned to his cot, took from his billfold the photograph of a pretty girl and began to cry. Puller looked over his shoulder.

"Too bad you'll never see her again," he said.

"What do you mean?"

"Why, she'll never look at you again after this. She wouldn't spit on you."

"She'll never know. How could she hear?"

"Oh, she'll find out. You ever see those big Wanted posters in the Post Offices? That's what the Marine Corps does with its goof-offs. Your picture will go right up there. She'll find out, all right."

The boy reached under his cot and Puller tensed, thinking that he was after his pistol. The sobbing boy dragged out his pack and hurried from the tent. A medical corpsman soon entered.

"Colonel, you shouldn't talk to a man like that. You brutalized him."

"It's just what he needed. You mind your business, old man."

The doctor appeared the next morning at Puller's cot, grinning. "Colonel, I told you that I'd send you back to your battalion within a week, but I'm going to recommend that you stay right here, instead. You could do more for the war effort. Did you know that corpsman of mine put you on report this morning?"

"No, and I don't give a damn."

"He reported you for roughing up that kid you sent out of here—but do you know what? I called the Fifth Marines, and damned if he isn't back on duty, chin up and ready to go. Whatever you did was just the medicine for him."

Puller later heard that the boy was decorated for bravery on the island.

On the last day of his eight-day stay in the field hospital Puller had a visitor from Washington, Lieutenant Colonel Russell P. Reeder, Jr., of the War Department's General Staff, who had been sent out by General George C. Marshall to evaluate the fighting against Japan.

Reeder questioned Puller closely for an hour or more and took notes. These observations were later published in a classified booklet used as a guide in Pacific operations. Puller offered his criticisms with complete candor: "The staffs are twice as large as they should be. The regimental staff is too large. I have five staff officers in the battalion and I could get along with less."

He also blasted some of his superiors: "Calling commanding officers from the front lines back to battalion and regimental command posts to ask, 'How are things going?' is *awful*."

The booklet introduced Puller with a note: "Lieutenant Colonel Puller is being recommended by General Vandegrift for the Medal of Honor for leading his battalion, with seven holes in him, continually for twenty-four hours." This did not develop, but the division commander, in addition to commending Puller's battalion for its perimeter defense and putting in for a third Navy Cross for its commander, also wrote:

"I have known Lewis Puller since 1919. He was one of the best combat patrol officers I knew—just as he is an outstanding officer today. He did a wonderful job with his battalion on Guadalcanal, in every phase of the operation. I am as proud to have him as a friend as I was glad to have him as a Marine."

Puller did not forget his men. Of the commanders on Guadalcanal he alone wrote letters to all wounded men from his outfit who had been evacuated to hospitals or home. Captain Zach Cox got one of these letters:

> The officers and men of the First Battalion, Seventh Marines, recall with pride the part that you played in our successes against the enemy until you received your injury in action.
>
> They employ this medium to express their appreciation for the part you played while you were here, wish you a speedy recovery and hope that when you return to further action, it will be in the same outfit.
>
> They further assure you that until you return and thereafter until the enemy is destroyed, they will continue the fight with ever-increasing vigor and determination.

January 1, 1943, was warm and sunny and the loading went smoothly. The gear was all stowed and the last of the First Marine Division troops were going aboard. It was only then that their condition became apparent. Men who had fought for four months in the foulest climate in the Pacific and had been shelled, bombed, or shot at by snipers almost constantly between battles, seemed to collapse at the same moment. Scores were unable to climb the nets into the ships and had to be carried aboard. They had shocked expressions, with glazed, sunken eyes. For weeks most of them would be patients with malaria, dysentery, assorted fevers and fungus infections. Virtually every man in the Division had malaria by now.

Puller said: "It isn't so much that they're sick, or even worn out. It's the reaction, from the discovery that they're finally leaving this damned place, and yet, a lot of them grew into men here."

The Division's dead were 1242, and 2655 had been wounded; sickness was nearly total. No one could yet grasp the importance of the island fighting on the day of loading out: The longest of the Pacific island campaigns had been fought and the pattern of future victories had been set. The Japanese had paid a higher price here than they would pay again and had thrown in all at their disposal, ships, planes, men and machines. More than 50,000 men had been lost on the island or on ships trying to reach it. In Japan it was already known as the Island of Death. For more than a year Radio Tokyo was to call the First Marine Division the Guadalcanal Butchers.

Though the Division had covered itself with glory, it was the First Battalion, Seventh Marines, which led all the rest. Other outfits had been more highly publicized, but the Seventh Regiment had won thirty-seven medals and nineteen commendations, fifty-six in all. Of these, the First Battalion had forty-three—twenty-eight of the medals and all but four of the commendations. And 1/7 had 264 casualties of its own, 93 of them dead.

Puller spent the last day idly. After a swim that lasted most of the morning he saw a half-naked Marine barber cutting hair and had his skull shaved. After lunch he lay in the sun for an hour and fell asleep. Frank Sheppard shook him awake.

"Colonel, they want you to go to Henderson Field and see General Geiger. You've got orders to go to the States by the first transportation."

"What's it all about?"

"I don't know, Colonel. The Division adjutant called, and he made sounds like he was in a hurry."

Division headquarters knew nothing of the mysterious change in orders, but it was clear that he would not now join the Division in Australia while it refitted. He went in a jeep to the airfield, where General Geiger told him that he could take off for Noumea the next morning.

He left in the first light of January 2, with a long backward look at the dappled island where he had fought for so long, and then there was only the sea. He transferred to a commercial plane at Noumea and almost as soon as it was airborne he fell asleep. He was on his way home.

XI

WINNING THE WAR AT HOME

VIRGINIA met him at the Washington airport on January 9, 1943, almost speechless with happiness and relief. She saw that he was thin and drawn, his skin yellowed from malaria or atabrine, but there was not an outward sign of his wounds. His walk was brisk.

An aide in the office of the Commandant, General Thomas Holcomb, jolted him with the news: "The General has given you to the Army, Puller—I mean on loan, for three or four months. General Marshall wants you to explain the Guadalcanal fighting to his troops all over the country.

"You needn't fret about leaving your men. The Division will be in Australia for six months before it can get back into action. I expect you'll rejoin it in time for another big show."

The Pullers drove home to Saluda that evening, and though it was late when they arrived, he went upstairs to see the baby. Virginia Mac was not quite three years old and it was nearly a year since she had seen him, but she stirred and climbed to her feet, holding out her arms. "Father!" she said.

He was in the village for two or three days and the highlight of his visit, to the neighbors, was the sight of the hero of Guadalcanal skipping down the walks under the huge elms, holding hands with Virginia Mac, who issued imperious commands as if he had been sent home for her entertainment.

The Colonel soon returned to Washington and reported to the Pentagon, to the office of General George C. Marshall, the Chief of Staff. An aide talked with him:

"General Marshall has asked you to come home to help improve the morale of our people. They have the idea that the Japanese are invincible. The General has known you for many years and he believes that no one can do the job better than you. I can't tell you how important this assignment is —it's a lot more than a road show, or a Chautauqua. We could easily lose the war, or prolong it for years, if our people lose heart. You've no idea how jittery some of our civilian population has become, and the outlook of the troops is sometimes none too good.

"The General has asked several other officers to come from all over the world, and not only Americans. They will work with you in trying to destroy the myth of the invincibility of our enemies. We want you to tour the Army's camps where divisions are in training. Marshall would like you to visit every one of them, and had asked for you for six months, but the Corps will let you go for no more than three months. It isn't strange, from what we hear of your work on Guadalcanal."

"I never made a speech in my life. What do you want me to tell them?"

"The General wants the truth, Puller. There will be no wraps on you. Say what you like about command, men, performance or anything that you think will be helpful. But the one idea he wants you to get across is that we will whip the Japanese in the end."

"I'm no speaker, but I'll try."

"We're not worried about what you'll say. It may be rough on you, hopping around the country. We know you're impatient to get back into action, but try to remember that if we don't do this job, it's going to be so much the harder out there in the Pacific. Good luck."

There was a press conference at the Navy Department, where half a dozen reporters quizzed him, and since he was the first front-line officer fresh from the fighting on the island, the interview furnished headlines. He told them that there were only 4000 Japanese left on the island, and that they could be mopped up in ten days if the commander launched a full-scale offensive. He estimated that 15,000 Japanese had been in the fighting, and that 8000 had been killed in battle, with another 3000 dead of wounds or starvation.

Charles Hurd of the New York *Times* sensed the value of Puller's candid message:

Puller's description of operations on that hard-fought island gave a far more confident picture than any official information heretofore released. . . . gave the impression of a securely held American base, complete with landing fields and ship anchorages, available at any time for the start of any action northward.

As to the enemy who remained on Guadalcanal: "There should be no trouble in cleaning out the rest. The Japanese on that island have had enough of it."

Reporters noted that he said nothing about his wounds and little of the action in which his battalion had saved Henderson Field.

The following day, Puller saw General Marshall and General Holcomb, and was off on his tour. There was a preliminary stop at Aberdeen Proving Ground, where he was shown several new weapons, among them the carbine soon to be issued to troops. Puller fired it on the range. "It's no good," he said. "Lots of fire, but neither heavy enough nor accurate enough. Give us the Springfield." Watching officers were crestfallen.

His orders listed stops at Fort Benning; the Army Amphibious Training Center at Carabello, Florida; Fort Sill; Fort Riley; Fort Leavenworth; and Fort Ord—but there were many additions, and he seemed to make almost every post where troop concentrations were in training; he often spoke three times daily, and was on and off planes until he all but lost track of his route. He told the story of his fight for the perimeter, of Basilone pushing the wall of enemy bodies down the hill, of the burials by bulldozer, and of the weapons they used. He told of patrols in the thick growth, but never of his wounds.

"I can't tell you the Japs are no damned good," he said, "because they are good. But we're better. One American, properly trained, can handle two of the yellow bastards. They have discipline, and they use the jungle cover better than we do, but they can't think on their own. They never change battle plans once they're made, regardless of cost. They think they'd lose face.

"They have no artillery to compare with ours, and our guns chew them to pieces. They get the jungle rot just as much as we do.

"They're not supermen, and we can whip hell out of 'em,

and you'll be helping to do it soon, I suppose. If you take
your training seriously there's nothing to worry about. But
you'll have to be hard—and you can be hard when you
write to your families, too. Try to convince 'em we're in a
war to the finish, and that all these strikes and softness
and confusion will have to go. I can tell you one more
thing: There are worse things than dying for your country."

His audiences invariably cheered him to the echo, even
when he spoke to War Production Board officials in Washington:

"I want to ask you why American troops shouldn't have
the world's best fighting equipment. On Guadalcanal we saw
our trenching shovels break at the first use. All of our men
now have Jap shovels, because they're better and more de-
pendable.

"Jap field glasses are better, too. I have good ones myself, German glasses that I've carried for twenty years. Why
should American glasses be so poor? Not worth a damn in
the tropics. They fog up because they are improperly sealed,
and once they get damp, they're done for. I've seen hundreds
of pairs tossed away in the jungle or the sea, because men
know they can see as well with the naked eye. What kind
of American ingenuity—or patriotism—produced those?"

He told them stories of Sergeant Raysbrook and Basilone,
and of Tex Conoley and Mitchell Paige, the heroes of the
Fifth Marines. He described the rescue of his men with the
aid of the destroyer *Ballard*.

Some men pressed him during the question period: "You
don't really mean American equipment is inferior on the
whole?"

"Not all of it, of course—but it makes no sense to me
that any of the enemy stuff should be better. It may sound
simple and harmless to you here in this room, but there's
the matter of the canteen. They gave us plastic ones, and
we found out in a few days in the field that they weren't
worth carrying. They crack and leak under hard use. So
we went back to aluminum.

"Now, our ordnance people spent billions, and we went
to war with nothing better than the little 37 millimeter as
an anti-tank gun. They can outgun us, as little as they know
about artillery.

"If you don't believe me, you can ask the Navy. I understand our first reliable torpedo is being developed only after
we captured one from the Japanese.

"I could keep you here longer than you'd like, telling you about how we've fallen down on the job. The truth is that war caught us unprepared, as usual. We were supposed to have fine smokeless powder, but on Guadalcanal our guns smoked so badly that they gave away our positions.

"The Japs outthink us in other ways. They developed infiltration tactics that were hard to combat. They'd slip in from several directions, and to avoid casualties to their own men, fired wooden bullets, so that they would burn up after a hundred yards or so—but at short range, they'll kill you dead as the finest American lead.

"We'll have to get over the idea that we're the greatest people on earth in every respect, that we're infallible and that no one else has ideas worth considering. One of the reasons we had to fight against odds on Guadalcanal was this insufferable American notion of superiority, and our carelessness in face of danger. It goes back to Pearl Harbor and far beyond."

He got a standing ovation, and a few days later a letter from Frank A. Patterson of the Training Section, Personnel Branch of the War Production Board:

> I have never seen such a stirring demonstration as the one the members of the Board's Operations Training Course recently tendered you.
> It was grand of you to appear for us and tell us your story and we like you for it. If I were asked to tell which event of the week was the outstanding one, I would say Colonel Puller's talk about Guadalcanal. It is too bad that more people could not have heard it.
> Colonel Puller, we are proud of you!

He was summoned before the high command of the Marine Corps and gave the same forthright picture of fighting he had seen. He handled ticklish questions without flinching:

"Gentlemen, we have some of the same old troubles: Staff officers, who have never seen a combat, issue unrealistic orders that cost lives, time and money, and ruin morale. For example, we were out there on that island trying to defend a perimeter. When they wanted to send a patrol outside, the command never used a single regiment—but sent out three mixed battalions.

"The logical thing would have been a regular regiment, with one battalion leading and the other two covering. Officers and men would be familiar with each other, and there would never be questions about just who was in command. But when we did go out, it was almost always with mixed battalions. It may look good in a staff officer's chart here at headquarters, but it didn't work, brought us only stumbling and confusion and casualties. More than once, when we were out in the jungle, nobody really knew who was in command. I could cite you the names of many a man I lost because of that. It was inexcusable."

He told them that malaria had been badly handled, and of his futile proposal for the quinine injections: "If I'd been commanding, I'd have accepted the lesser casualties on behalf of those boys and the American people. The death rate from malaria was perhaps ten times greater than it should have been, the way we handled it. I take atabrine myself, every day, and I know that when I stop it, I'll go down with malaria again."

General Holcomb asked: "Puller, what do you think of the Raiders?"

"Nothing special about them, sir. They're just ordinary Marines, when they're good. No better than our good men in the ranks. There's too much guff about them, I mean too much Hollywood stuff. It isn't good for the Raiders, and it's mighty bad for the regular Marines. The First Raider Battalion is just a battalion of the Fifth Marines. The Raider idea should be abandoned."

A few minutes later, as Holcomb went down the hall, an officer overheard him rumble to a friend: "I must be getting old. I ought to know better than ask Puller a question like that."

Soon afterward Puller faced a board which was planning changes in Marine Corps organization. On this day it was dealing with the problem of handling machine guns. The senior officer explained:

"We've decided to do away with machine gun companies, and have machine gun platoons instead, as an integral part of each rifle company. That order is already out. What do you think?"

"It doesn't matter what I think, if the order is out. I'd like to have been asked about it before the decision was made, because it shows an utter lack of knowledge of the art of machine gunnery.

"These guns are the most important fire power to infantry, and after World War I, when they were in battalions, and their commander was a senior lieutenant colonel or major, the system was ideal. The officer had rank enough to demand sufficient time to train his gunners. You need time for this, as much as for artillery, and you need officers with seniority in order to get it.

"These platoons of yours will be commanded by lieutenants who can't demand anything, and the guns will be treated more or less as toys."

"Puller, isn't it a fact that on Guadalcanal the First Division habitually had machine gun platoons attached to each rifle company?"

"Yes, but you don't realize the reason. The terrain and close jungle growth dictated it. Overhead machine gun fire is feasible in open country, but not in the jungle, so the guns were not massed on Guadalcanal.

"I understand there is a plan to land in China before we land in Japan. If so, we'll operate on a great open land mass and machine gunnery will come back into its own.

"Our staff officers have never served on Guadalcanal, or plains like those of China. I can tell you one thing, you're one hundred per cent wrong. When this order goes into effect the Marine Corps will never afterward have properly trained machine gunners, and the art will disappear from this country—and don't think for a moment that it isn't an art."

Among other command groups, Puller sat with that of General Walter Krueger, the Sixth Army chief, who was planning for Pacific operations with his staff. Puller advised them on problems in the area, and was impressed by Krueger's direct and common-sense approach to his assignment.

Mrs. Puller was with him in Washington for two weeks but saw little of him, for he was seldom home before 11:00 P.M. One evening they called on the widow of Major Otho Rogers. Puller spoke gently to her of the service of her husband and his death at Point Cruz. Mrs. Rogers handed him a package.

"They're yours," she said. "Otho asked me to send them to you for Christmas, not long before he was killed. Your favorite cigars. Please take them."

Mrs. Puller barely escaped the door before she burst into sobs.

Puller went back on the road, covering Army posts in the Midwest and Far West. As usual, he did not shun sacred military precincts, and he expanded on previous talks:

"We just don't know all we ought to know about warfare, on land or sea. Just off Guadalcanal, not long ago, we lost three cruisers, blasted down by Jap guns as they sat there—sitting ducks, that's all. I'll tell you exactly why we lost 'em. The admiral in charge got a plane report that a Jap force was approaching at fourteen knots, by daylight. So he figured that, at this speed, the enemy couldn't arrive in his waters before the next dawn. After dark, of course, the Japs stepped up their speed to twenty-eight knots, and got to the scene at 3:00 A.M., when our men were not even at battle stations.

"It happened like that, I'm positive. And instead of keeping such things secret, we ought to have 'em emblazoned on the gate at every naval station. We must not be too proud or too stupid to profit by our mistakes—and God knows we make 'em."

He also dared to speak in a rather critical vein of American prisoners of war, but the force of his logic won his audiences:

"Japanese soldiers aren't allowed to return home if they are taken prisoner. They have made captivity the ultimate disgrace for a soldier. It would be a good thing if we thought about our own policy—which is just the opposite. We double the pay of men who are taken prisoner, and we're the only nation doing that. Not even the British go that far—in fact, they stop the pay of captured men. In a way, Americans make it profitable to be captured, and remove the onus from it.

"I know you soldiers can see the effect of this on morale, when you're in a hard fight. There is less pressure to resist. Lots of our boys who were captured on Bataan were lieutenants. Under our policy, they will become lieutenant colonels or even colonels when they are released at the end of the war—with their only qualifying experience that of living in a prison compound. Does that make sense to you?

"God knows I have sympathy for a prisoner of war, and I know all of you have, but we're not following an intelligent line on this. It sounds like a policy dreamed up by inexperienced staff officers to me. From the field commander's point of view, it is ruinous."

He then attacked an even more sacrosanct topic—the problem of the thousands of American troops suffering from shell shock:

"I know something about the strain of combat. For five years, in Nicaragua, I marched at least twenty days a month, under the constant threat of ambush. But I never saw in those Indian troops any sign of battle fatigue, or anything resembling it. In the Pacific, I saw a lot of our people break down.

"My reaction is this: What does it matter how you're killed, if you're killed in battle? Why does the louder noise of a fight with heavy artillery and bombs make such a difference? I think the difference is entirely in the mind, in the preparation of men for combat. In the constabulary actions I fought, the men were all picked volunteers, professionals, who were paid to fight and realized that they might have to die in the trade.

"I'm sure from my own experience that it's the mental attitude. I went through the worst days they had on Guadalcanal, and I didn't suffer a bit. I lost some weight, but that was because we didn't get the proper food. If we make our men tough in mind, before they go to war, and give them an honest idea of what war is like, we won't have so much of this trouble. Why do we have to baby them with all this crap about careers and opportunity and foreign travel?"

At Fort Leavenworth, the Army staff college, Puller opened his talk cautiously: "Anything I say in criticism is meant only for the Marine Corps, and in Marine Corps terms, since I know nothing at all about the Army, and I don't want to insult anybody."

The atmosphere became heated in a questioning period when an officer asked: "What's the most serious military problem we face?"

"The practice of having command post exercises," Puller said—though he realized that he was treading on prominent toes in his audience. "We take skeleton forces of headquarters troops and the like, just a handful, and go through exercises so often that we forget we aren't simulating actual warfare. It has become so bad that even platoons are carrying out command post exercises. In battle, of course, once you set up a CP, you stop all forward motion, because the commanders sit on their duffs in its relative security. And when you halt forward motion you get into trouble, immediately. I admit we have to learn to handle commands, but we've carried it to a ridiculous extreme."

Later, when the commanding general took Puller home to dinner, he said to the Marine: "Today you cut the ground clean out from under us at Leavenworth. Everything we've been teaching is swept away if you're right."

Puller protested his innocence of purpose, but the general brushed him aside: "No. You're right. That's the hell of it, how right you are—and yet we won't stop it. We'll keep on, building right on top of our mistakes."

One of Puller's companions at Leavenworth was a British brigadier who had been imported from Africa by Marshall to speak on desert warfare. He was not a glib speaker, but Puller was fascinated, and heard him lecture three times. One thing stuck in his memory:

"When I left North Africa," the Briton said, "half the equipment the Germans had—tanks, guns and vehicles, too —was British-made. They snagged everything they could capture from us, and made good use of it. On the other hand, we never captured anything from them intact. The Germans had destructive charges built in or attached as part of the equipment, so that before its capture it was blown to bits. Sensible warfare, that."

When it was all over and Puller was ready to fly back to the Pacific, he had had more than enough of this duty, but he was touched by the letter he got from General Marshall, who was not given to flattery:

> I want you to know of our appreciation for your splendid services.
> You were given a very heavy and tiring schedule but reports from every organization you visited indicate that your inspirational talks and first-hand information which you brought from actual combat with the Japanese have been of tremendous value in preparing our soldiers for the type of enemy they will soon face.
> Undoubtedly you have saved the lives of a good many soldiers and have given the veteran's touch to some of our training. I am sure every soldier is grateful.

On March 23 Puller flew westward from San Francisco,

bound for the First Division in Australia. He had grown tired of taking his daily dosage of atabrine before leaving the States, and when he reached the Division at Mount Martha, Victoria, he went down with malaria. He spent two weeks in bed.

XII

CAPE GLOUCESTER

PULLER emerged from the hospital to find that he had lost his troops—through his promotion—but though he was now executive officer of the Seventh Marines, he worked as hard as ever at the training of troops.

When the regiment visited a rifle range at nearby Williamsburg, adjoining an abandoned race track, an Australian major offered the grandstand as shelter. Puller declined: "Thanks, Major, but we'll bunk in the field. We would like some of your tent floors, but we won't get under cover. We've just taken the boys out of the boondocks. They've got more jungle work coming up and it might give 'em pneumonia to sleep in out of the weather."

Puller's personality was still a leading asset of the regiment and the troops found him constant, with none of the pomposity so common in officers.

One morning as he approached a company of his men lounging among their tents a newly arrived lieutenant barked an order and the Marines scrambled to their feet, standing at attention.

"What the hell's wrong with you?" Puller roared. "Don't you think I've got more sense than to demand that you put on a show every time I come within pistol range? Get back down on your duffs. You ought to know me well enough to realize that I'm no damned bandbox soldier. Take it easy—there's enough for you to do when we get our next assignment."

The red-faced lieutenant looked on miserably.

A brand-new chaplain from the States glimpsed Puller in the sergeant major's office one day, a dazzling sight in his greens, with a great patch of ribbons on his chest. Puller was on his way to a review. The chaplain spluttered praises on the display of decorations. The Colonel dismissed him quietly: "Just the rewards of a misspent youth, Padre. Nothing to it."

The replacements who had joined the regiment felt Puller's appeal as much as the veterans and were awed by tales of his career. Junior officers noted hero-worship in the faces of men, especially on parade or inspection. When other officers passed among them the troops were impassive, eyes straight ahead, as if unaware they were being inspected.

Lieutenant David Condon saw what happened when Puller walked the ranks:

"His inspection was always different from that of anyone else. He stopped one morning going down the line and looked at a young BAR man. 'How well you shoot that thing, old man?' he asked. The kid said, 'Expert, sir.' And Puller growled, 'That's the way,' and walked down the line.

"Then you could see on the faces of the troops what he meant to them. Every eye rolled after him as he walked on and their expressions said better than billboards that he was their kind of an officer. They would have followed him anywhere."

As the time for a new campaign drew near, Puller drove his staff to complete the last detail in preparation. He warned the regimental supply officer that an Army Quartermaster general was to check their requisitions.

"Notify me at once when he arrives," Puller said. "I want to explain things in person."

The Army general arrived when Puller was out, and the lieutenant took the inspector to the supply dump. Puller found them there and overheard their conversation:

"Lieutenant, your requisitions are excessive."

"I'm sure Colonel Puller would never have signed for more than we need, sir."

"But he's asked for ten thousand brass buckshot shells. What the devil does he want with those?"

"To kill Japs with, sir."

"Doesn't Colonel Puller know that buckshot is prohibited by the Geneva Convention?"

"Sir, Colonel Puller doesn't give a damn about the Geneva Convention—any more than the Japs did at Pearl Harbor."

Awards for heroism during the Guadalcanal campaign

finally caught up with the Division in July and Puller led
a line of the noncoms on the parade ground before the
massed Division. The Congressional Medal of Honor winners, Mitchell Paige and John Basilone, flanked by a row
of Navy Cross and Silver Star winners, marched down the
field in imitation of the soldierly pace of Lieutenant Colonel
Puller. General Vandegrift pinned on the medals, and
memories flooded the ranks of veterans as an officer bellowed the citation for Puller's second star for his Navy Cross.

When it was over Puller complained to his officers that
the business of medals was being overdone by American
forces: "Take a look at the Australian veterans. Lots of
them have fought all the way through this war, including
the African campaign, yet most of them rate only one medal.
Lots of old-timers have only the Victory Medal of World
War I. Yet the merest seventeen-year-old kid from the First
Marine Division with not more than a year of service is
wearing three medals, and if he's been decorated for bravery,
he'll wear up to half a dozen. They're making 'em too cheap."

Puller embarked with the Division in a convoy for New
Guinea on September 23. They landed on October 9, and
scattered to staging areas for the forthcoming operation.
Japanese planes from Rabaul bombed the camps every night
or two, but the nuisance raids hardly interrupted final training.

Puller was made a full Colonel in November, the rank
to date from October, 1942, the month of the perimeter
stand on Guadalcanal. He attended most staff conferences
on New Guinea, one of which confirmed his earlier impression of the Sixth Army commander, General Walter Krueger,
whom he had seen in Washington.

Krueger consulted with Marine officers on projected invasion of nearby New Britain:

"What is your plan, gentlemen?"

General Rupertus, who was now the Division commander,
explained in general terms; it was clear to Puller that there
was no real plan.

"Exactly what is the sequence of your moves?" Krueger
asked.

"Well, we will land here on the cape, establish a beachhead and carry on from there. Just as we did at Guadalcanal."

"Ah, yes. You will land, but no beachhead. You will form

your division in column and drive for the Japs where you find them, and then destroy them. Plan no beachhead at all. We will not stagnate on New Britain as you did on Guadalcanal."

Puller's admiration for Krueger grew, and he said to an intimate: "Wouldn't you think that Washington would have put him in command in Europe? He's so obviously the finest soldier we've got who's qualified for the job. But, no, because he was German-born, they wouldn't trust him to fight his old countrymen, though he's been an American citizen for about fifty years and most of that in the American Army. Does that make sense to you?"

The Army-Marine controversy over the plan had dragged on for months, and it was not until General Douglas Mac-Arthur, the old "enemy" of the Corps, came to New Guinea in late November that the Krueger plan of landing one Marine regiment and a regiment of Army paratroopers was overruled. In the end, Marine officers had their way: Two regiments of the Division would land together, with the third standing by—but there was no Guadalcanal style beachhead involved.

A regimental chaplain came to Puller's tent one night in December.

"Colonel, I want you to get out an order for me."

"I can't get you an order. See Colonel Frisbie, he's your man."

"I'm afraid of him."

"His bark's worse than his bite. If you have a reasonable request, he'll help you. What's on your mind? Maybe I can give a hand."

"Well, I want you to prohibit all these good Protestant boys from joining the Catholic Church."

"Holy smoke, man, we can't do that! If they're deserting you, there must be a reason. If you fellows would get down to work like the Catholic chaplains, you'd have no trouble."

The disgruntled minister went away.

The enemy also had word of the coming assault upon Cape Gloucester. Radio Tokyo blared one afternoon in late December: "The First American Marine Division, assorted cutthroats, degenerates and jailbirds, has been chased out of Melbourne, is now in camp in New Guinea, and will try to invade Cape Gloucester. I am pleased to add that our soldiers are fully prepared to repulse this insolent attempt. The jungles will run red with the blood of the Guadalcanal butchers."

New Guinea lay just 63 miles across a strait from New Britain, a large, mountainous, overgrown and undeveloped island some 330 miles long and 50 miles wide. An estimated 70,000 Japanese defended it, most of them in the northern area, near Rabaul. At Cape Gloucester on the northwest tip there was a good air base and scouting parties had found it lightly held. That was the target.

Transports gathered in Buna Harbor on Christmas Eve, 1943, and left with an escort of destroyers and cruisers; ahead of them, Marine and Air Force planes from many fields pounded at Rabaul and opened the attack on Cape Gloucester itself. Marines tried singing Christmas songs as the craft pulled out of the harbor but few joined in until one outfit tuned up on "Pistol Packing Mama." The holds were so hot that the troops spent most of the run on the decks until, on the early morning of December 26, they stood off Cape Gloucester.

Big guns of the fleet rolled for an hour and a half, beginning before dawn, and Marines ate their traditional D-day breakfast of steak and eggs while the salvos shook the hulls beneath them. As the light grew the troops had a look at the tangled green landscape: The two landing beaches, which were split by about 100 yards of jungle growth at the water's edge, were so narrow as to be almost invisible to the naked eye. To the right, westward, ridges rose to a 6500-foot peak and just beyond, an active volcano trailed a plume of smoke. On the left an imposing hill, some 450 feet high, bulked near the water. This hill was found to be covered with enemy troops, and planes began blasting it. Soon there was a brown smear amid the foliage where bombs had caused a landslide.

The first bombers were in about 7:00 A.M., flying almost out of sight; their bombs walked in gray puffs from the beaches up the hills. A fuel dump exploded near the airfield. Bombers then came in lower—B-25's followed by A-20's, which worked very low, strafing. About 7:30 a smoke screen was laid along the beaches and landing craft went in.

Puller had insisted that the assault on the largest visible hill be made at a dead run: "You've got to shove 'em in there right under the shells. As soon as the bombardment lifts, make 'em scramble. They'll get there before the Japs get back into position—because those devils will leave while the big stuff is flying, and count on getting back before we can move."

The attack went on that schedule. The Third Battalion, Seventh Marines, landed first, followed quickly by Puller's old battalion, which floundered through a morass behind the beach and pushed up the tall knoll, already known to aviators and ships' gunners as Target Hill. The slopes were blackened from fire and shrouded with fumes of bombs—and clear of the enemy. Marines occupied the ridge in strength and settled down around the unmanned Jap guns. They beat back a Jap counterattack on the position with ease soon after.

The reserve battalion of the Seventh, the Second, met opposition 1500 yards inland and was pinned into line, settling to fight it out.

An hour after the Seventh was ashore the First Marines came, turned toward the airfield and walked into a well-laid Jap ambush. Tanks came in to clear the enemy from their hidden bunkers and by nightfall the First was well on its way to the airfield.

A falling tree in the soggy forest injured one Marine, and otherwise there were only twenty killed and twenty-two wounded on D-day; enemy casualties were estimated at fifty. The Division was on the way to what one historian called the "most nearly perfect amphibious assault of World War II," but there was trouble to come. The Division staff was puzzled for the next two days by the absence of the enemy as the troops pushed forward through the rough terrain. On the fourth day the Second Battalion of the Seventh stumbled into Japs in bunkers in company strength, and killed almost four hundred of them, against Marine losses of twenty-five dead and seventy-five wounded. After dark that night the Fifth Marines, who had now been brought up from New Guinea, gained the airfield.

On December 30, the First and Fifth secured the field, after hand-to-hand fighting in which they had to call on tanks for help. Rupertus sent a triumphant message to Krueger, offering the field as a New Year's gift.

Puller was still much in demand. On the fourth day of the assault he was called from his post as exec of the Seventh to repair the ruptured front of the regiment. The First and Second Battalions, under Majors Jack Weber and Tex Conoley were split by a gap of about 1000 yards; casualties were mounting as the stalled units fought blindly in the overgrown terrain. Marines in many foxholes sat with water up to their necks, for the rain still poured in torrents; more trees crashed in the jungle, and about twenty men were killed as artillery fire felled the rotten giants.

Colonel Julian Frisbie sent Puller forward: "Pull the line together so we can hold. They'll be sending an attack through the gap on us soon."

Puller hurried off with a runner—and ideas of his own. From the top of Target Hill he saw the problem: "Both battalions were lightly engaged. I could see firing and by using my glasses, though Conoley's position was mostly in jungle, I could pick out a few of his men from time to time. I got Frisbie on the field phone and told him I was going to Conoley's position. I hung up before he could stop me, and went across.

"I got over the gap—at least 1000 yards—without running into Japanese. I ordered both Weber and Conoley to extend their lines until the battalions were joined. They soon had them linked up."

Nothing else was quite so easy as seizure of the airfield. The force now turned to secure its hold on the island by driving into the jumbled, ravine-cut country around Borgen Bay. The toll mounted rapidly.

Brigadier General Lemuel C. Shepherd, Jr., the assistant division commander, directed the assault in semi-independent command of the scattered division. He ordered an unusual scheme of attack, with an unbroken line hinging on the beachhead, swinging to attack southeastward on a front of about 1000 yards. Headquarters seemed unaware of the difficulties of terrain for this drive; trouble developed quickly. A five-man scouting party sent out on December 30 was ambushed and four of its men stabbed or clubbed to death. Three days later the push opened, with the three battalions of the Seventh and the Third Battalion, Fifth Marines, in line.

The skirmishers were stalled at a swift jungle stream, soon known as Suicide Creek, from whose banks automatic weapons fire decimated the first platoons to cross. For all of January 2, two battalions fought their way back and forth across the stream, to be driven off and return. Some men crossed the creek four times. One sergeant remembered a moment from a mortar attack by the enemy: "A kid sitting there in his foxhole. He didn't have any head. He just had a neck with dogtags on it." A gray-faced youngster nearby was muttering as he fired his rifle: "It don't do any good. I got three of 'em, but it don't do any good."

Japanese snipers had infiltrated the line, and killed Marines at short range; and one unit which tried to wade the stream was broken, its survivors driven to hide in the weeds at the edge. From mid-stream a boy who failed to make it hung over a log, his body riddled by a score of bullets. For half an hour or more he called to his mates before he died: "Here I am. Here I am."

The attack had stalled; the line now became U-shaped, with a pocket of the enemy holding back the center. General Rupertus, from Division, relieved the commander of the Third Battalion, Seventh Marines, and sent Puller into action once more, with orders to reorganize and drive forward the unit. Puller retained a memory of the next twenty-four hours:

"Rupertus didn't ask my advice about relieving that commander—but he did ask me if another senior officer should be relieved. I told him no. The trouble was the same old thing—staff officers don't know the meaning of terrain, and how it can slow down troops and cost lives.

"I went up to the front about two in the afternoon. I called the company commanders in and told them as briefly as I could what I had in mind:

" 'I've been sent to take over. Your commander has been relieved. I don't intend to be relieved, you can bet on that. We're going to attack here in the morning!'

"There were protests that the Jap bunkers could not be seen, and that they were cutting up our line. I told 'em I had the medicine for that. I ordered up some of Joe Buckley's half-tracks, because I knew their guns could deal with the bunkers. The resistance was fairly light—but the staff orders were so foolish that we were just making sitting targets of our people. Buckley did a great job there, as he always did.

"They had orders in these battalions to guide both right and left—an order that can't be followed well even on parade ground. Any beginner knows that you can guide left, or you can guide right or even center, but you can't follow two leaders on either side at the same time. The line will buckle and cause gaps. We were frustrating the troops with delays to re-form the line.

"I just said, 'Now, we'll go forward and forget all about this guiding business. Just forget there's anybody on the flanks. We have enough power here to drive, and we're going to drive. Blow your way through, and think of nothing else.' "

The half-tracks, a bulldozer and tanks were up by dawn, and at 8 o'clock the push began. A bulldozer driver was shot in the mouth as he began work at Suicide Creek, but under sniper fire other volunteers manned the machine until the banks had been cut for the entry of half-tracks and tanks. Puller mounted the vehicle himself several times. The big guns soon located and destroyed Jap bunkers, built of logs just above the surface of the ground, and the way was opened. The vanguard drove several thousand yards before the end of the day. Once more Puller's leadership had been crucial.

After the infantry had crossed the creek, hanging about the tanks and other vehicles, the whole force moved. With the line straightened, a Jap pocket was wiped out and Marines were ready for the next objective, known to the Japanese as Aogiri Ridge. Heavy fighting raged on the thickly covered slopes and there was danger of another stalemate. Puller took over another battalion on January 8—Third Battalion, Fifth Marines—when its commander, Lieutenant Colonel David McDougal and his successor, Major Joseph Skoczylas, were both wounded. Puller held the scattered troops together for the day until the new exec of the Fifth Regiment, Lew Walt, came up to take over.

Young Walt, now a lieutenant colonel, won further praise from Puller in the next day's assault as he led his men up a fire-swept hill—dislocating a shoulder as he helped haul a 37 millimeter cannon to the top by hand. By his courageous exposure Walt inspired the troops in the Puller tradition and at nightfall, when opposing lines were only ten yards apart, the injured Walt prepared his men to meet an attack. He held fire until the Japs had charged uphill with shrill shouts. All Marine weapons, including the 37, fired at the final moment, and at dawn, after five assaults had exhausted Walt's ammunition, he counted more than two hundred Japanese dead in his front.

General Shepherd renamed the hill that morning: Walt's Ridge.

With the fall of the next ridge, Hill 660, Cape Gloucester was made safe. Puller inserted himself into the final fighting though he had no battalion to command.

Before the guns stopped, a staff officer from Division was spreading a new version of Puller's magic formula for handling men in battle:

"I went up there in the heaviest of the action, when fire was flying all around us. Puller walked around the *outside* of the wire at Hill 660, and he stopped at every dugout to talk to some kid. He'd say, 'How's things going, old man?' just as if he'd come from next door to borrow a cup of sugar.

"Those kids thought it was the greatest thing that ever happened. You'd think he had been handling out thousand-dollar bills down the line, and that there was some place here to spend 'em."

Puller had found one demoralized boy sitting stonily in his hole, looking out with the telltale "thousand-yard stare." He muttered over and over: "Colonel we got to get the hell out of here."

"That's no way to talk, old man."

Puller led the boy a few paces to the rear and sat with him for ten minutes or so: "Look, old man, I wanta go home, too. I'm not getting any younger. Hell, I'm forty-five years old, you know that? I got a family at home. I know this dump is no good, but neither of us is going home until we lick these bastards. We've got to help make our folks safe back home. I'll try to get you some hot chow up here, old man."

The boy went back to his hole with a brighter look in his eye.

Private Dick Rowland, who became Puller's jeep driver on the island, had a similar dose of Puller's morale-building. The seventeen-year-old Californian, a recent high school football star, was talking with his sergeant major one day when Puller walked past: "That old man can walk you into the ground any time," the sergeant said.

"Nobody forty-five years old can keep up with me," Rowland said, but he learned. He later recalled: "In the next two years I found that he could outwalk me and most others. I chased him all over New Guinea and twenty-eight days on the long patrol on Cape Gloucester, and him with all that shrapnel still in his leg!"

Rowland applied for the job of the driver. "You don't have to take it," Puller said. "Eight others before you have been killed or wounded. I get around a little bit."

When Rowland persisted, Puller called a war correspondent, posed for a home-town newspaper picture with the private and asked the reporter to be sure the photograph was sent to California.

Rowland cherished memories of Puller for almost twenty years: "He was a very real and good man, and made quite an impression on me at that age. He was offered dates with nurses and Red Cross women and invited to parties when we were back from the front, but he would never go. He kept a picture of his wife in a little case and looked at it often. He had the respect of every man who got to know him."

Rowland's first outing with Puller was a revelation. They walked out in front of the skirmish lines at Cape Gloucester: "A Jap machine gun let go toward us. I hit the deck and looked up to see him looking down at me. He told me never to do that again. He said I could scare half the men on the line, and they were spooky enough without me helping. To this day I can take a loud noise without flinching.

"He could not stand it when Colonel Frisbie would make him stay in the command post, and every chance he had, off we would go, checking the line companies."

Puller had been puzzled over the number of men with chest and head wounds, as his casualties mounted during the drive against the enemy. Japanese marksmen were not reputed to be expert, yet they had run up a serious total. As captured enemy rifles came in he found the answer.

"No wonder we're getting hit," he told his officers. "Look at these rifles. One in three has a telescopic sight, and a damned good one—one devil of a lot better than ours. We're lucky if we get one to a squad, and they've got all they want."

He also found that the enemy scopes were more durable and could be used for weeks without correction, whereas American models were so delicate that they must be zeroed in afresh each day to maintain accuracy.

Lewis wrote to Virginia on January 16, saying that conditions were "very good and steadily improving," though he had been too busy recently to write. He added:

> There is no reason for you to worry, so please do not! In my own mind I have done my duty and I have personally been thanked by Rupt. for my efforts. The men and junior officers have been splendid. . . .
> I regret to say that your Christmas picture has been completely ruined and Virginia Mac's almost, from continual

wetting; I had them on my person and the rainfall has been heavy. . . .

The Almighty has been good to us and I am indeed thankful.

When the fighting was over at Borgen Bay, Puller tried to boost morale with an order for an immediate movie and band concert, and bulldozers hacked away at a ravine near the command post under Hill 660. One night later Bandmaster Leon Brusiloff led the musicians who had so lately fought as the Headquarters Defense Force. They played the *Grand Canyon Suite* and Dvořák's symphony *From the New World*. Major Henry Heming, the paymaster, saw that though most of the 4000 men were not familiar with the music, hundreds of them wept openly.

Puller stopped by Heming's tent one night in a rare mood, and talked for hours.

"I'll tell you, Major. There are three words that I never want used in my presence again—Kike, Wop and Harp."

"Why do you say that?"

"Well, the first three good sergeants I lost on Guadalcanal were a Jew, an Italian and an Irishman, and it helped me to realize the secret of our strength—it takes all kinds, and we've got 'em."

He also made an unusual confession: "The only thing we regulars are good for is to keep the guns clean for you reserves, and to lead you in battle. When war comes, there will never be enough professionals to do the job."

With the clearing of the Cape, General Rupertus planned a patrol far across the island to the village of Gilnit on the southern coast, near the Itni River. The route lay through territory perhaps untrod by white men and required a commander wise in the ways of jungle and Japanese. Rupertus chose Puller and sent him off late in January. The Colonel left the Cape with two enlisted men in a jeep, empowered to pick up all the the men needed. He swept them up by squads, platoons and even companies. In two days he gathered 1300 men.

One of the hundreds he abducted was Corporal W. B. Winterberg, an eighteen-year-old from Ludlow, Kentucky, who belonged to the headquarters company of the First Battalion, Seventh Marines. He was sitting in his company area when the Colonel's jeep halted.

"What're you doing, boy?"

"Resting."

"Fall in. Come with me."

Winterberg found himself in a rear file of the patrol as it moved off toward the interior. None of the strangers near him could explain where they were going, or why, or when they would return to their outfits.

An hour or so after the start Winterberg was astonished to see the Colonel approaching on foot: "He was running, and I don't mean walking, and he'd come back all down that column, at least a mile and a half, to see if I was still at the rear. Imagine an old bird like that. He ran back to the front, too. We all thought he was a wonderful son of a bitch."

Farther along the trail Puller spied an overweight officer with an artillery battery: "Hey, old man, where you going?"

"I'm hunting my C.O. I'm in Parish's company."

"Where is it?"

"I don't know, sir, but I'm going back."

"No, you're not, Fat. You've just joined the Puller patrol."

The young man was so downcast that Puller made an effort at conciliation: "Fat, it'll do you good to get away from that jeep. I'm looking out for your own good."

After a two-day march into the interior it became clear that Puller could not feed all these men; headquarters had been unable to keep its promise to stock him with eight days' rations at the start. The Colonel ordered supplies brought in behind him by jeep, but some staff officer improved on the suggestion and sent out a heavily loaded ten-ton truck, instead. It bogged in the mire and a bulldozer sent to its rescue also stuck fast.

Puller called for air drops of food but the planes, B-17's, flew so high that they spewed K-ration cases all over and through the jungle and when they came near the patrol, struck some men. Puller radioed headquarters and asked for Marine Cubs instead, and the small planes fluttered over the jungle party, each dropping three cases of rations per flight —on target.

The first satisfying food came when Major John Mather, an Australian Blackbirder, came through the jungle from Sag Sag at the head of a long column of blacks, and shared his fresh rations.

On its fifth day the patrol reached a deep stream where engineers built a stout, crude bridge, much like those Puller had used in Nicaragua and Haiti, and like those described by

Caesar—tripods of poles thrust into the river, lashed together with vines, with logs across them to bear the traffic. The bridge would pass his two jeeps, but the trail beyond was so poor that Puller sent them back. He also cut the force to 389 men.

He reached the village of Agulupella on January 30, where he picked a staff. When he was choosing his intelligence officer, his exec pointed out a major sent up for the purpose by headquarters. Puller scoffed loudly, "Hell, that man hasn't even got on a weapon. Find me another one."

From this point he sent forward a small patrol under a brave captain, George Hunt, a newspaperman in civilian life. Hunt was ordered to the banks of the Itni River to scout the neighborhood for Japs and told to return in the evening. The night passed and Hunt did not reappear. Puller took the trail himself and within a few hours found members of the party: "Where's Captain Hunt?"

"He crossed the river, sir."

"Your orders were to stay on this side. What did he say?"

"He said he was going to get the Medal of Honor or go to China, sir."

Several officers corroborated the story and Puller sent runners to find Hunt, and tell him that he was under arrest. The aggressive captain had taken off the entire vanguard of the column and in violation of orders, Puller concluded, had deliberately disregarded instructions. When Hunt returned it was at the tail of his column, the men under command of a lieutenant. Captain Hunt remained under arrest only until the return to Cape Gloucester, for Puller recognized his value and preferred no charges against him.

As the column pushed on toward Gilnit, Major Mather assured Puller that the country was free of the enemy, and that he need have no fear.

"How do you know?"

"My native boys. They've volunteered to cross the river, and if there was one Jap there, I know damned well they'd never stir."

Mather took advantage of one pause at a stream to persuade Puller to remove his battle-soiled khakis so that the natives could wash them. Mather marveled at the trousers: "They literally stood up like boards with dried sweat and must have been awfully uncomfortable. It took quite a lot of argument to get them off him; he was determined not to get caught in ambush."

Puller finally removed the trousers and donned a towel offered by Mather. Two natives washed and dried his clothing.

The patrol left Agulupella on February 6 for the hike to Gilnit; it was only twenty miles by air, but seemed hundreds on the rough trail. Puller kept the pace fast and the men were constantly wet from rain or sweat. The few Japanese they found were diseased and crippled wretches by the trailside and were bayoneted by Marines, furnishing a grim line for Puller's later report on the action: "The pig-sticking was fine."

They reached Gilnit on February 11 and there was not a sign of the enemy—nor of an Army patrol they were to meet there. Puller sent a party to inspect a hill across the Itni known as Attulu and found it unoccupied. He had a puzzling message from the Army patrol: *Held up before Attulu Hill.* Puller sent another patrol to the hill, found no trace of the Japs, and left in disgust. He left one platoon to remain for twenty-four hours, with the message that he had returned to the Cape.

When he saw that danger was past, Puller slowed the pace and during halts used his Nicaraguan experience to find food. He had men toss grenades into streams and remove hundreds of dead and stunned fish. Within minutes natives had fish broiling on twig racks over fires; the upper racks were covered by heavy green leaves, reflecting heat and hastening the cooking.

Puller thought he had never eaten better food. "It's a damned wonder," he said, "that someone at home doesn't think up something as sensible as this kind of cooking rig and put it on the market."

Puller had liberated and returned to their villages 1700 natives, after proving that the area was free of Japanese. His report stressed some lessons of the patrols: The newer 610 radio should be used for air-ground communication, since interference by active volcanoes interrupted less powerful radios. Inland patrols needed hob-nailed shoes, and jungle medical kits. The skirmishes of the companies of Captains George Hunt and Nikolai Stevenson showed the need for 60 millimeter mortars on patrol, in addition to BAR's and light machine guns. He warned that the building of a motor road from Cape Gloucester to Gilnit would be a major undertaking.

Puller judged that the enemy was suffering, since their

equipment was inferior to that used on Guadalcanal; Japanese troops now used linoleum as a substitute for leather.

There was a final Puller admonition: "Both officers and men must be taught the absolute necessity of silence on patrol in order to surprise the enemy and not be surprised. There is no excuse for either officers or men speaking above a whisper unless engaged with the enemy."

The patrol rode the last few miles into the camp at Cape Gloucester. As Puller jumped from a truck he was confronted by an outstretched hand—it was his acquaintance, the Protestant chaplain who had complained of Catholic inroads on New Guinea. Puller was in no mood to befriend him.

"Where've you been all this time?"

"Why, I've been here doing my best to help out."

"You weren't up where the fighting was. I think I'll prefer charges against you for being absent from your regiment."

"Colonel, I was with the medical battalion, aiding the wounded. We worked around the clock."

"They've got a chaplain of their own. Your place was with the fighting men—your own battalion. You remember our little talk about Protestant boys joining the Catholics? Well, conduct like yours is one reason for it. They see those priests doing their duty and see you evading it. I can't work up much sympathy for you."

Puller told his officers: "In all our fighting I've known only a few Protestant chaplains worth their rations." Years afterward, when he was home from the wars, Puller bearded his Episcopal bishop in Virginia: "I can't understand why our Church sends such poorly prepared men as chaplains when fighting breaks out—they look to me like men who can't get churches, for the most part. The Catholics pick the very best, young, virile, active and patriotic. The troops look up to them."

The Bishop replied that the work of the Church must go on at home in wartime. Puller retorted indignantly: "How can they do that work better than with the troops who are fighting to keep the country safe? What difference does it really make, so far as the survival of America goes, about the people who stay at home, and shirk their duty?"

An exception to this charge against Episcopal chaplains, Puller always added, was Rev. Robert Olton, of All Saints Church in Richmond, a brave man in the war zones, and an exemplary Christian.

In February, 1944, Puller had a physical examination in the camp at Cape Gloucester and aside from a notation of a recent attack of malaria was found in perfect condition. On the same day, upon hearing a rumor that one-third of the veterans of Guadalcanal were to be rotated back to the States, Puller wrote General Holcomb, the Commandant, in terms which would have been appreciated by a Caesar or a Napoleon:

> It is respectfully requested that my present assignment to a combat unit be extended until the downfall of the Japanese Empire.

He enclosed a copy of his physical examination report; General Rupertus scrawled his approval on the document.

In April, when the Division was nearing the end of its stay on New Britain, another decoration came through for Puller—a gold star in lieu of his fourth Navy Cross.

The Division moved back to a rest camp on Pavuvu in the Russell Islands in April, to prepare for still another invasion. The new island was a hellhole in the first weeks. Tents were pitched in bogs and the bottomless roads had to be filled by Marines in coolie brigades who hauled coral in buckets.

Hank Adams stalked into General Oliver Smith's tent at headquarters and shouted: "Great God! Who picked this dump? More like a hog lot than a rest camp."

Puller indicated half a dozen officers. One of them grinned: "It didn't look quite like this from the air. We thought it was a paradise."

The Division recouped and drew replacements here; the first of the new weapons began to appear in quantities. The Springfields had almost disappeared now, to Puller's sorrow. He was interested in the first of a new-style flamethrower when an officer brought one by. The youngster proudly explained the work of the deadly torch and looked to Puller for approval.

"Where's the bayonet fit on?" Puller asked.

Puller's men rigged for him the only shower in their section of the island, a crude arrangement fed by a barrel mounted over a canvas shed. Men climbed the hill to wash up after hours of working in the black muck, and because of the long uphill carry limited themselves to a bucket or two of water. Puller kept a close watch on the shower. One afternoon as he played cribbage with Henry Heming a freshly arrived lieutenant swaggered up the hill with a towel and stiffly starched khakis over his arm. The boy officer kept the shower running far beyond the limit; when he reappeared Puller beckoned:

"Lieutenant, you enjoyed your shower?"

"Yes, sir, Colonel. Great!"

"That's grand. Lieutenant, how do you suppose that water gets up there into that barrel?"

"I never thought of that, sir."

"This is your chance, Lieutenant. Every drop of water passes up this hill on the backs of enlisted men. Now you grab those two cans over there and see what you can do about it, Lieutenant."

"Yes, sir."

"And don't let me see you stop for one minute until that barrel is full."

Puller and Heming played cribbage far into the night, but the paymaster's mind was not on the game: "That poor, silly kid labored up and down that hill all night, so far as I know. He was still going when we gave up on cribbage."

Puller's men had a hard routine of setting-up exercises; Henry Heming thought the Colonel worked at them harder than anyone else. But when Puller once caught the overweight banker in the rows of puffing men he shouted: "Cut it out, Heming! Get back to your tent and don't let me catch you here again. Can't afford to lose the paymaster, above all others."

The veteran sergeant, Red O'Neill, remembered for years Puller's early-morning instruction when he halted an exercise period: "Now, when this regiment goes into action, there will be platoon leaders in front of the platoons. And company commanders in front of the companies. The battalion commanders will be in front of the battalion—and your regimental commander will be in front of all." It was not idle talk.

Puller had only lately got the promotion he wanted most —as a commander of troops. He was given a regiment, the First Marines; he began training them with characteristic thoroughness.

Oliver Smith, the assistant division commander, who came to observe Puller's work, arrived when Lewis was off on a command post exercise, simulating an assault landing. Puller, taking only his staff and communications troops of the regiment, had crossed a bay near their camp to land on the far shore. Smith followed in search of Puller; he went in from the beach on foot and soon found the command post of the two assault battalions, where their officers awaited developments. Puller was not to be seen. "He's up ahead," an officer said. Smith trudged inland. When he overtook Chesty, Smith laughed: "Lewis, don't you know that by the book you've got to have the regimental CP *behind* the battalion posts?"

"That's not the way I operate," Puller said. "If I'm not up here, my people will say, 'Where the hell's Puller?' "

When Smith had gone, Puller spoke to his staff: "I know you'll hear 'em say I'm a damned fool for exposing myself, and running along the front lines, and that I'm just a platoon leader at heart. I go up there because that's the only way a field commander can handle a force in combat. It was the reason Lee and Jackson exposed themselves so often in the War Between the States. I recommend it to you. It has nothing to do with bravery. I can feel fear as much as the next man. I just try to keep my mind on doing my duty."

A young officer spoke up: "But Colonel, you expose yourself like a private, and you're the most valuable man in the outfit."

"No officer's life is worth more than that of any man in his ranks," Puller said. "He may have more effect on the fighting, but if he does his duty, so far as I can see, he must be up front to see what is actually going on with his troops. They'd find a replacement for me soon enough if I got hit. I've never yet seen a Marine outfit fall apart for lack of any one man.

"I don't want you to go up under the guns just for show. It's only the idiots and the green kids who think they're bullet-proof. But if you don't show some courage, your officers won't show it either, and the kids will hang back. It's that kind of an outfit that always has trouble."

There were several award ceremonies on Pavuvu and Puller, decorating some of his men for valor on Cape Gloucester, left a memory with Sergeant Carl Fulgenzi of his regiment. The Colonel growled to every man as he handed out the medals: "You stick with me, old man, and you'll get plenty of these things."

On one of these days there was a Bronze Star for Puller, given for the action on Guadalcanal in which he was wounded. He told officers in the privacy of his tent: "They recommended me for a Silver Star for that action, and back in Corps Headquarters at Noumea some jerk reduced it to a Bronze Star. What right have those people got to put their cotton-picking hands into things like that? They didn't see the action, and have no way on earth to judge. Wouldn't you think they could see what it does to morale? I can stand it. I've got enough damned medals. But what it does to the young kids is inexcusable."

In the same ceremony Frank Sheppard, now a first lieutenant, pinned on Puller a Purple Heart for the seven wounds of Guadalcanal.

In several of his daily letters to his wife Lewis wrote of his happiness at having direct word of her and Virginia Mac—from Colonel Taylor Selden, who had just come out from the States to be chief of staff to Rupertus in the next landing operation.

> . . . He said that you and our daughter were lovely and the most attractive ladies that he had ever met. He did not have to tell me that about you, Dear. . . .

He wrote her of an offer by Rupertus to send him home by Christmas:

> The time will pass and then we will be completely happy. We will have a lovely home wherever I am stationed. You and Virginia Mac will make it so. . . .
> The war news is fine, and I pray that the good God will give us victory and lasting peace in the very near future. . . . Please do not worry about my health or safety, as there is absolutely no need to. I am fine with the single exception of my longing for you.

He heard from his old friend of boot camp days, Tom Pullen, their first exchange in almost a generation, and wrote in reply:

> . . . I have served on foreign stations over eighteen years and am near to being a foreigner. When this war is finally won, I will be more than satisfied to retire and sit on the front porch of our home in Middlesex County, Virginia. I trust that our leaders will be able to arrange a lasting peace. . . . There is a great deal of hard work ahead of us here.

In the late summer there was a letter from his younger brother Sam, whom he had not seen for years. Sam was on Guadalcanal, the executive officer of the Fourth Marines and a lieutenant colonel; his outfit was training for the re-taking of Guam.

Puller questioned an aviation sergeant who flew a Cub and when he found that the over-water distance to Guadalcanal was only fifty miles got three days' leave and had the sergeant fly him to the big island.

Sam and Lewis had three days together—their last. Most of the time was spent in searching for the sites of the battles Lewis had fought there in '42, for already the jungle had retaken so many of the clearings as to make the spots almost beyond recognition. The old line of his battalion on the perimeter was easiest to find, for there were still curling strands of rusting wire and the brothers stepped on many Japanese skeletons.

The silence stunned Lewis. "I can't realize that this is the spot," he said. "I've never thought of those times without hearing again all that noise, that seemed as if it would never end. It's so quiet now that it's all unreal."

They talked late at night in Sam's tent, ranging over the days of their boyhood, their hunting and fishing, and fights with village boys, to the actions of the war, and the invasions both of them faced. In his last glimpse of Sam, Lewis thought: "Lord, he's almost white-haired. We're getting old."

Puller returned to Pavuvu to find a new stir in the camps. The Allied landings in France were expanding; the new B-29's had begun to bomb Tokyo; Saipan had fallen. Whole fleets of cargo ships had brought the First Division new equipment to Pavuvu and there was word of an independent role for the Marines in a new operation. General MacArthur would follow his own southern course in island-hopping, but the Corps would stab into the Central Pacific. Puller could hardly conceive of the scope of the new Marine Corps, which he had known as a force of a mere 19,000 in his prewar days: There were now five divisions and a brigade in the Pacific and another division training in California—well over 100,000 men.

In late July, on the same day Franklin Roosevelt and Harry Truman were nominated for the coming elections back home, Marines landed on Guam. A few days afterward

Lewis got the news: Lieutenant Colonel Sam Puller had been killed, shot through the heart by a machine gunner's bullet. His intimates noticed a new reserve in the Colonel in these days, but it was not long before still another false report was added to the growing Puller legend: Marines whispered that Lewis, when he got word of Sam's death, had said grimly: "Those who live by the sword must die by the sword."

The loss of Sam had in fact touched Lewis deeply; he covered it with silence and a hurried turning to other topics when officers spoke of his brother's death.

On Pavuvu the Division intensified its work and sweated at war games on the beaches and in the palm groves. There was a new watchword: Peleliu, the next target.

One evening General Rupertus stopped by Puller's tent for a quiet talk, and when it was over the division commander said: "Lewie, you should make general on Peleliu. It's tailored for you. Your performance of duty should bring you another Navy Cross, and a brigadier's star, too."

XIII

WRITTEN IN BLOOD

BOB HOPE and his company made a brief stop in Pavuvu in August, to the roaring approval of the troops who had been so long from home. Puller heard men talking of it in a chow line:

"Man, what a show! One of them every day and we could fight the damned war."

"Yeah, but I wish I'd stayed in my sack, and never gone near it."

"You gone nuts?"

"Oh, them girls! Until I saw 'em prancing out there, I'd clean forgotten there was such a thing as an American woman. Now I could swim back home."

Puller wrote his wife of the incident that night:

> I did not go to the show, but if I had seen the performers I wouldn't have been affected like this. I have not forgotten that you are waiting for me and I haven't been content since I left you at the Washington airport. . . .

He finished reading a new volume of Douglas Freeman's *Lee's Lieutenants,* which she had sent for his birthday, and sent it back home. His leg began to trouble him from the big shrapnel wound on Guadalcanal, and he limped slightly but made no mention of it in his letters.

> I hate to cause you any worry or anxiety. The time of our separation is drawing to a close, so have no fear. I am confident that I will return to you by Christmas. I am checking off the days to our happiness. . . . You may rest assured that I will take every precaution, if necessary.

By now the time was growing short. Navy amphibious experts and staff officers from Pearl Harbor went in and out of Pavuvu, laboring over the plans for an assault in the Palau Group which would soften the enemy for the retaking of the Philippines. The plans often mentioned Tarawa, a swift, costly operation fought late the preceding year. Officers often displayed aerial photographs of the chief target in the Palaus, Peleliu.

Infantry officers saw at a glance that the problem was not that of Tarawa; rather than a flat sandy island, Peleliu was a jumble of coral crags. Documents captured on Saipan indicated that 10,000 crack Japanese troops defended Peleliu, among them units of the never-defeated Manchurian Imperial Guards—whose mention stirred Puller's memory.

Puller went with scores of other officers to briefing sessions, to be told of the strategic picture, and to see the maps and pictures. From these sessions the infantry commanders went back to their practice landings and assaults. On one of these exercises General Rupertus broke an ankle scrambling from a boat.

The strategy had a grand simplicity: Seizure of bases on three of the Palau islands would neutralize 25,000 Japanese in the northern end of the group and lessen the threat of 100,000 more on Truk and other nearby islands. This would offer air bases within 600 miles of the Philippines and cover the rear of a drive on those islands.

When the staff planners got down to cases the task seemed more demanding. Peleliu on the maps was in the shape of a great lobster claw, an airfield at its base and two pincers thrust to the northeast. The Division was to land on the west coast, take the airfield, drive the enemy against the sea and cut him in two.

The assault plan: Three regiments abreast, Puller's First Marines on the left, the Fifth in center, and Seventh on the right. In reserve was only one battalion, from the Seventh Regiment. The Army's 81st ("Wildcat") Division could be called up within eight hours, if needed.

The first glance was enough for every Marine officer of experience: The First Marines faced the gravest danger and their role would be crucial. They would land on a narrow beach west of the airfield, then turn northeast along the larger pincer in a dangerous maneuver which would be imperiled by enemy fire from coral ridges 200 feet high. The First must pull itself together in a shallow staging area to

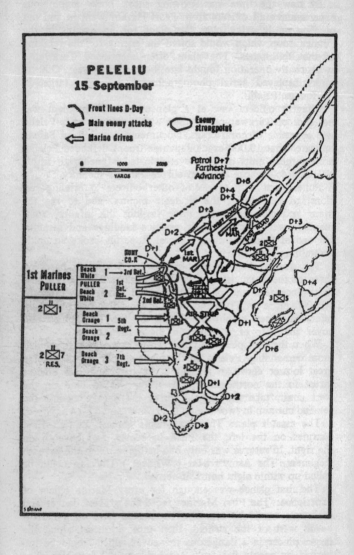

PELELIU
15 September

Front lines D-Day
Main enemy attacks
Marine drives

Enemy
strongpoint

0   1000   2000
YARDS

Patrol D+7
Farthest
Advance

1st Marines
PULLER

2 ⊠ 1

2 ⊠ 7
R.E.S.

Beach White 1   3rd Bat.
PULLER
Beach White 2   1st Bat.
Res.
              2nd Bat.
Beach Orange 1   5th
                 Regt.
Beach Orange 2
Beach Orange 3   7th Regt.

HUNT
CO. K

1st
MAR

AIR STRIP

assault the jagged hills which were interspersed with over-grown ravines. More ominously, a rocky promontory at the waterline would cut off the First from the Fifth Marines.

Puller never forgot these planning days: "I told General Rupertus that though we might have 27,000 men at Peleliu, no more than 10,000 infantry would have to do all the fighting, and that the specialists on ships and beaches could not be counted on.

"They thought my fears were groundless, but I had my say. I didn't like landing operations in the face of a pre-pared enemy, anyway. There didn't seem to be an alternative, the way higher command had planned. But I pointed out the differences between Tarawa and the photographs of this Peleliu. I told them they were going to need a replacement infantry regiment. I knew the Japs, and I knew they would be ready and would fight to the death. We ended up with an explanation of how the fire of ships and bombing by planes would clear the way. I was still apprehensive. I told them we would pay."

Optimism reigned through the Division. When practices were done on Pavuvu, Oliver Smith was sent to find a site comparable to Peleliu for a final rehearsal. He settled on Cape Esperance, on Guadalcanal, after having been denied more likely spots by the Australian government on the ground that native populations should not be uprooted from their islands.

For several days the troops practiced landings on Cape Esperance and Koli Point. There were no coral ridges and there was no reef to defend the beach but the work went on, and assault elements trained together smoothly.

General Rupertus was optimistic; he spoke of taking Peleliu in two days, besting the record at Tarawa. There was a mass briefing in an outdoor movie theater, where many officers spoke, among them Puller. A combat corre-spondent, George McMillan, was struck by Puller's brief words; the Colonel exuded confidence to the men, but in tribute to them as veterans, gave them a grim picture of the cost of coming battle.

The last scene on Guadalcanal remained long in Puller's memory:

"After the other briefings, I was called to the command ship with the other regimental commanders, Hanneken and Harris, and Colonel Harrison, of the artillery. Selden, the chief of staff, and Oliver Smith, the assistant division commander, were already there, and then Rupertus came in and told us:

" 'You have your orders. I will not be ashore on D-day, and may not be there on D Plus One. It depends on the course of the action. But I want you to understand now that there will be no change in the orders, regardless.

" 'Even if General Smith attempts to change my plans or orders, you regimental commanders will refuse to obey.

" 'Do you understand, General Smith?' 'Yes, sir.' 'You, Harrison . . . Puller, Hanneken, Harris?' He asked us all in turn, and we all said that we understood.

"When we went out, I remember saying to Smith that it looked bad."

But in early September, when the big fleet left for the Palaus to follow the bombardment ships there was but a single somber note: Aboard one of the vessels were stacks of many hundreds of white wooden crosses—far more than a two days' supply.

The slower ships, the LST's, left on September 3, and four days later the rest of the convoy sailed; carrier forces followed. Troops were often on deck, playing cards or working on weapons. Two days from Peleliu there was a report from underwater demolition teams whose men had boldly swum into the shore and inspected Jap defenses. Nothing serious, they said. The way would be cleared.

Puller's mind was not relieved; he had never before felt pessimism at the opening of battle. On shipboard he studied the maps of his sector until he felt that he had committed the terrain and the plan to memory. He did not tell his younger officers of his forebodings, but as he went over the maps he felt them anew.

In his final briefing, when he had called attention to the promontory flanking his position, he had said, "This ridge enfilades my regiment." He was dismayed to see that many of the officers from higher staffs did not understand the term; he explained.

He had stressed the need to cover the area with fire of ships and aerial bombing; he had been promised full support, and yet an admiral, in presenting air plans, had said that his planes would fly at 2000 feet. Puller's reaction was that they would never damage the enemy from such heights. And when the convoy was still two days from its destination a message had come back from the naval bombardment squadron: "At nightfall there were no more targets on Peleliu worthy of fire. All destroyed. Have ordered bombardment to cease. Await arrival of transports."

The skipper of Puller's ship handed the Colonel a copy of the message: "What do you think, Puller?"

"Well, since you've asked my comment on this asinine order, I'll say this: In the next hour, if I know Admiral Nimitz as well as I think I do, you'll intercept an order from Pearl Harbor to that admiral, ordering him to turn over his command to his next senior officer and continue the bombing and shelling for three days as ordered. If we don't keep up the fire, they'll be loaded and waiting for us."

The order never came.

There was no moon. The sky was filled with stars and there was not a trace of cloud. Toward dawn of September 15 the transports had come into position. On the horizon the guns of the fleet spurted fire; for hours the thunder was unbroken, but as gray edged the sky the pace slowed and fire became desultory. The island was invisible. Occasional flares erupted above it in the darkness and drifted from sight.

The troops had breakfast before daylight—steak and eggs again—and when the first of them came to the decks the chain of the Palaus lay in black silhouette across the sea. There was a moderate swell. A breeze sprang up, coming from the island of Peleliu. The guns broke into full cry once more and the final shelling struck the target.

The two assault battalions of the First Marines went aboard the big landing vehicles on the decks. The maws of the ships clanked open and the amphibious tractors were spewed forth, milling as they formed lines, ready to move toward the beach. They were 4000 yards out. Vast flights of planes came over—TBF's and F6F's, wheeling in from all directions. They dived, bombed, and climbed over Peleliu for an hour or more and soon after the first of the bombs fell, a slow, hesitant curtain gathered over the land. It seemed impossible that any living thing could have endured, but at last, as the assault began, a puff of anti-aircraft smoke flowered in the sky and a plane dropped in flames.

Just before 8:30 the first wave started shoreward. Puller

watched for the signal flag to dip from the yardarm of a
control boat in his front. The amtracks foamed away on
broad wakes.

Puller went to the bridge of his ship to thank the skipper
for his treatment of the troops. The commodore of the
flotilla greeted him: "Puller, you won't find anything to stop
you over there. Nothing could have lived through that hammering."

"Well, sir, all I can see is dust. I doubt if you've cleaned
it out. I know they have underground oil dumps, for that
airfield. We haven't seen that blow. I've been boning over
those maps for weeks, and I believe they'll have pillbox
stuff and fortifications like we've never seen before. They've
been at it for years."

The officers talked for a few minutes as the regimental
front formed on the water: twenty-six armored amtracks
were the first line, fanned out to cover the limits of Puller's
sector. The LVT's and DUKW's were six deep behind them.
The last touch was given by small rocketboats which moved
in close and showered their rockets behind the beach. White
phosphorus smoke blew out of the heavier pall, designed
as a smokescreen for the Marines.

"We won't find little log barricades like they had on
Tarawa," Puller said. "We're going to catch some real fire."

As he left the bridge he said:

"You watch me in the third wave and see what happens
to those amtracks at the beach."

"Good luck, Puller. We'll expect you for dinner this evening."

"If we get out of this one, you'll be back in Hawaii
long before we're through the job."

The Colonel had divided his headquarters, in case of dis-
aster, and had only half of his staff in the vehicle with
him, plus a party of thirty-five riflemen and machine gunners. His exec, Lieutenant Colonel Richard (Bunny) Ross,
led the second headquarters group, five or six waves behind.

The amtrack was in the third wave and for a time there
was no sound over the roar of the motors and the reports
of guns flinging shells from the ships—now firing far inland. The vehicle rode clumsily, but sat low in the water.
There were a few pings against the armor plate on the
prow, and the men thought of the long drills Puller had
put them through, learning how to leave the tractor the in-

stant it struck land. The Colonel shouted final orders:

"When we beach, get the hell off here. We'll be a big target."

Ahead of them Japanese mortar shells were plunging into the water in a line before the beach; the geysers were like a ragged curtain. In the distance Puller saw beached vehicles already burning, some of them overturned. Fire grew louder from shore.

The First Marines approached the target area known as the White Beaches, just seaward of the Peleiu airfield. They were to seize and hold the position on the left of the Division. Puller had two battalions abreast, the Second on the right, under Lieutenant Colonel Russell Honsowetz, and the Third on the left, led by Lieutenant Colonel Stephen Sabol. The First Battalion was back of them, as a reserve. Its commander, Major Ray Davis, was to bring it to the beach at 9:45, turn north along the beach and attack toward the airfield.

Puller was a bit apprehensive about the new officers, but he said nothing to his staff. "They're good enough," he told himself, "but they've never been in a fight." He especially admired Davis and Honsowetz and Ross, but he knew that first reactions in combat were unpredictable. "Why the hell can't Headquarters see that the business of rotating out all the good veteran officers after one or two fights is killing us? They could at least leave us fifty per cent of them."

In the ranks below battalion command, however, there were fine fighting veterans left to him, especially the executive officers, three majors: Nikolai Stevenson, Charles H. Brush, Jr., and William McNulty. And at Puller's side in the tractor was one of the most valued of all his veterans, Lieutenant Frank Sheppard.

On the regiment's right, not far down the beach, the Fifth Marines were landing, commanded by Colonel Harold D. Harris.

Above the scrubby growth which still clung to the battered coral crags on shore Puller made out the tops of blockhouses and he told Sheppard: "Some of those things haven't been touched. We'll catch hell, is my guess. One of these days we're going to get caught on an amphibious landing and be driven into the sea."

At 8:30, almost precisely, the vehicle ground on the sand. Puller never forgot the scene:

"I went up and over that side as fast as I could scramble

and ran like hell at least twenty-five yards before I hit the beach, flat down. When I looked back to the amtrack I saw four or five shells hit it all at once. A few men were killed, getting out too slow, but most of them were saved, because they got out before we stopped moving. We lost our communications officer; his leg was blown off and he couldn't be saved. I looked down the beach and saw a mess —every damned amtrack in our wave had been destroyed in the water by the enemy, or shot to pieces the minute it landed."

Enemy fire swept the beach, especially heavily in Puller's sector:

"I tried to get a line set up for defense. The wiremen were there fast, as soon as I was, doing their job without further orders—and we lost several of them in the hot fire. Every platoon leader was trying to form a line of his own, just as I was. Runners were going up and down the beach as we tried to get organized. That big promontory on my left hadn't been touched at all by the ships' guns and planes, and we got a whirlwind of machine gun and anti-tank gun fire."

Puller's Second Battalion drove through a heavy growth of woods, now torn by the shelling and by 9:30 had driven 350 yard ahead, to the edge of the airfield. They tied on to the line of the Fifth Marines. Casualties were reported as heavy, but the trial of the Second had only begun. The new position was faced by an obstacle marked on none of the invasion maps—a sheer coral ridge whose sides were honeycombed with Japanese positions, from foxholes to gigantic dugouts of reinforced steel and concrete, some of them with four levels, each of which could be closed off with steel doors.

For eight hours the regiment endured the most savage fighting of the Pacific war. A gap opened in Puller's line, and despite the hurrying of the last "reserves"—A and B Companies—Japanese clung to their positions. Puller moved his command post inland from the first post, not far from the sea, and just as he left, a shell burst killed half a dozen men. The enemy seemed to be gathering for a counterattack between the ridge and the sea which might roll back the regiment and expose the Division. Puller put every man from headquarters, engineers and communications into the line, but the attack did not come.

By nightfall Puller was 1000 yards from the beach, within sight of the portion of the airfield overrun by his men. He could see from his new dugout the wreckage of half a dozen enemy planes in the open. His wiremen were quick to follow him with the field wire and now put him in touch with General Oliver Smith, the assistant division commander. Headquarters only now learned of the loss of many of Puller's communications experts and their equipment, when their landing boats had been hit in the early morning.

General Smith had come ashore at 11:30 A.M., but though his lines to the Fifth and Seventh Regiments were open, and he talked with Rupertus on the command ship by radio, he could not reach Puller. The field lines to the First Regiment were broken and Smith could not raise Puller by radio. The high command became concerned for the position on the left. A rumor came to Smith that Puller had been calling for corpsmen and reinforcements, but when the phone line was spliced in late afternoon, and he talked with Puller, he had only a calm report:

"We're dug in solid, and we've got the O-1 phase line all right."

Puller made no mention of especially heavy casualties or a need for help. It was estimated that the First Marines had lost 500 men during the day.

The first water had come ashore in oil drums, and was foul. Puller shouted his rage to officers on the ships, bellowing for a new supply.

The Colonel went down the beach with a runner to talk with Colonel Harris and other officers. He overheard a conversation which piqued his curiosity:

"You got your rifles?"

"Yeah, we're okay. We got more than a hundred."

Colonel Harris explained to Puller: "Division wants one hundred Jap rifles from each regiment every day. We'd better get 'em, too."

Puller called the command ship and talked to a staff officer soon after: "What the hell do you guys want with those Jap rifles?"

"We trade 'em to the Navy for food."

"Well, by God, if you get any rifles from me, you're going to divide the food with us."

Puller got turkeys and steaks for his men—but there was at first no time to prepare them.

Companies began calling for salt tablets, for the fierce

heat of the day had taken its toll; Puller asked the headquarters ship for a supply. Many casualties were reported
due to coral cuts, for the sands were full of the knife-
like stone, broken and ground.

Fire decreased in the night, but never stopped entirely.

Puller got reports of individual companies; one from Captain George Hunt's K Company impressed him so strongly
that he made a note to recommend the veterans of New
Britain for a Navy Cross.

K Company held the key to the position on the far left
flank, the last unit of the Third Battalion, and when the
dust cloud had lifted, it faced the fire from the pitted
ridge from which the Japanese enfiladed the whole beach.
Hunt described it:

> The Point, rising thirty feet above the water's edge, was
> of solid, jagged coral, a rocky mass of sharp pinnacles, deep
> crevasses, tremendous boulders. Pillboxes . . . had been dug
> or blasted. . . . Others, with coral and concrete piled
> six feet on top, were constructed above, and spider holes
> were blasted around them for protecting infantry. It sur-
> passed by far anything we had conceived of when we studied
> the aerial photographs.

Hunt had turned this ridge from the land side; his losses
were heavy, and his reserve platoon was quickly thrown in.
For two hours he fought the enemy at short range, until
thirty men—the remnants of the two platoons—took the
point, approaching the pillboxes from their blind sides after
driving out the supporting infantry.

The largest nest, a concrete and steel casemate at the
base of the cliff, had been cleared when a corporal fired a
rifle grenade through a gun port. There was an explosion
and as flames swept the dugout screaming Japanese flew
from the rear, in agony as ammunition in their belts went
off like firecrackers and their clothing blazed. The survivors
were shot down by waiting Marines of Hunt's company.

Now, during the night, Hunt was isolated with eighteen
men on the point, standing off superior enemy forces by
using captured enemy machine guns. For eighteen hours he
was alone with these survivors. Fire from the Japanese in
this sector was so effective that Puller could not push other
units into the front to heal his line. He was forced to
establish a second line in the rear to plug the gap.

Puller reported to the command ship during the night:

Enemy well dug in. Opposition strong. Little damage done by our preliminary fire. A hard fight ahead. Casualties over 20 per cent. I've ordered no man to be evacuated unless from bullet or shell wounds. Request further supply fresh water. Ours still undrinkable; men retching.

On the morning of Saturday, September 16, the regiment joined the Fifth Marines in a fresh attack, but it stalled around the airfield, and the enemy resisted stubbornly all down the line. Puller complained to headquarters of the slow progress of the Fifth, but things were little better elsewhere. Regimental casualties reached almost 1000 by the end of the day. At night, as Puller planned for the next day's attack, ordering the First Battalion to the center of the line, the enemy struck the front.

The Japanese came behind grenades and mortar fire at 10 P.M., about 350 strong, against K and B Companies. Automatic weapons and the new M-1's shattered the attack, but it was 2 A.M. before quiet returned, for a small party of enemy infiltrated lines at the base of Hunt's coral ridge for several hours and there was an occasional flurry of hand-to-hand fighting.

On the third day fighting was even more severe; the Second Battalion plunged across the airfield, passed the administration buildings under a hail of fire from within, took a small settlement known as Asias—and ran into a coral ridge once more. Mountain guns popped in and out of caves above and Japanese observers coolly called down mortar fire on the attacking Marines. Tanks and amphibious tractors joined the fight and many were left flaming. Casualties were again heavy, but the ridge was taken and a salient had now been driven into the Japanese line. Hill 220 was Marine country.

The center of the line halted for an hour or so before a blockhouse, and the 14-inch guns of the battleships were called to level it. A direct hit with an armor-piercing shell killed all the Japanese defenders without a scratch, the result of its terrific blast.

By nightfall the regiment had a foothold on the slopes of the first chain of coral ridges inland of the airfield, but the line on the right lay in the form of a constricted W. Japanese drifted through the irregular front after dark in such numbers as to threaten a break. F Company of the Seventh Marines was brought up from the beach to stop this and attacked until the enemy was cleaned out. Guns from the fleet blasted at the Japanese until dawn.

Puller called Division and talked with Colonel Selden, the chief of staff. He remembered the conversation years later:

"Johnny, half my regiment is gone. I've got to have replacements if I'm to carry out Division orders tomorrow morning."

"You know we have no replacements, Lewie."

"I told you before we came ashore that we should have at least one regiment in reserve. We're not fighting a third of the men we brought in—all these damned specialists you brought."

"Anything wrong with your orders, Lewie?"

"No. I'm ready to go ahead, but you know my casualties are fifty per cent."

"What do you want me to do?"

"Get me some of those seventeen thousand men on the beach."

"You can't have them. They're not trained infantry."

"Give 'em to me, and by nightfall tomorrow they'll be trained infantry."

Puller went out with a runner, stumbling through the night to find the posts of his battalion commanders and pass the order: "We press the attack at eight o'clock in the morning. No change. Full speed. Use every man."

He fell more than once and cut himself on the coral. Sheppard and others left at headquarters noticed that the Colonel was beginning to limp and that his left leg had swollen.

Selden called back: "Puller, you got my orders okay?"

"Yes, you needn't explain further. I just came back from my battalions. We're going to take ground tomorrow without replacements. We're willing to try, but don't forget we're just going to add ten or fifteen per cent to our casualties."

When the sun rose on September 18, 200 of the 473 men in Puller's Third Battalion were headquarters personnel; many front line units had been decimated. Long before noon there were cases of heat prostration; the blazing sun was hotter than ever. Faces and lips were cracked and bleeding; salt pills became scarce again. Puller was optimistic, for they started the attack from high ground, but the crucial days still lay ahead.

Hank Adams came by Puller's command post and found him half clad in filthy, sweat-soaked trousers, with heavy beard on his face: "I'm coming back this afternoon, Colonel. Don't you want me to bring you a fresh uniform?"

"Hell, Hank, I've got no time for that. Every man in the outfit will get clean before I do."

Lieutenant Colonel Lew Walt, now the executive officer of the Fifth Marines, saw Puller at a command conference during the day: "He was absolutely sick over the loss of his men; he thought we were getting them killed for nothing."

The terrain was an ally of the Japanese. Marines did not see its equal in the Pacific fighting: The western peninsula of the island heaved up in a rocky spine, a contorted mass of decayed coral covered with rubble among which crags, gulches and ridges lay in a confusing maze. Enemy mortar shells dropped into the jumble, spraying the attackers with slivers of coral which multiplied the effect of the explosions. Marines were slashed by the flying stone, but they fought their way along the crests, taking bunkers and pillboxes in succession. Toward noon progress became more rapid and large stocks of enemy shells were captured. Enemy artillery observers were found chained to their dugouts in these hills; Jap machine gunners were strapped to their weapons to prevent retreat.

At 6 o'clock Puller moved his command post forward to a revetment on the corner of the airfield and after a half-hour softening from planes and big guns the Marines trotted past the Colonel into the ridges. There were almost immediate calls for more corpsmen, for salt tablets and plasma. By 2 P.M. the Second Battalion reported it was in a desperate situation.

Lieutenant Colonel Honsowetz called Puller:

"I'm afraid we can't go on, Colonel. There's just nobody left here."

"You're there, ain't you, Honsowetz?"

"Sure."

"Okay. Hang on."

A smoke barrage was fired over the battered battalion to hide it from enemy mortar observers, but fire continued to rain into the sector. B Company of the First Battalion was hurried up to support Honsowetz. By 4:30 P.M. it had taken a commanding knoll, with only light casualties—but as they moved on they reached the first slopes of Peleliu's most terrible hill, Bloody Nose Ridge. This was the screen for the central concentration of Japanese power, where the Man-

churian veterans operated big guns and large-caliber
mortars from caves, rolling them in and out to avoid counter-
barrage fire. Night fell with Puller having found the heart of
enemy resistance. He had gained little ground and losses still
mounted. His casualties had reached 1500, excluding those in
the attached units. On his front lines there was only a thin
scattering of the riflemen who had hit the beach with him.

But on the eighteenth the first American plane had landed
and by now Marine Cubs hovered over enemy positions, spot-
ting for the artillery and mortarmen, and the enemy began
to suffer.

Oliver Smith had found Puller's command post:

"My aide and I started from the beach following the wire
line. After proceeding inland some distance I found Lieutenant Colonel Ross. His location would have been well advanced for a regimental command post. Ross, however, told
me that his group was the rear command post, and that
Colonel Puller could be found up ahead. My aide and I continued to follow the wire line, sometimes crawling, and finally
found Colonel Puller and his group in what had been a
small quarry. The Japanese were 150 yards ahead. Lewie was
stripped to the waist, his battered pipe in his mouth, never
bothering to remove the pipe when he was talking. He was
in his element, making his presence felt. His battalion commanders could not possibly have been between him and
the enemy."

Puller explained his attire: "The damned undershirt rotted
away, and I'm trying to get a little fresh air."

Smith went down the line and when he next came seeking Puller, found him in a new post. A sniper opened up
and bullets tore a post overhead. Puller organized a small
party and sent it after the Japanese marksman. Within a few
minutes there were shots from the front; there were no more
bullets from the sniper.

Traffic began to reach Puller's post. Several Navy admirals
came ashore with Marine guides, and stopped by in their tour
of the regimental positions. One morning General Rupertus
came, trailed by a small staff and a *Time* magazine reporter.

The reporter looked carefully about him and from beneath the tin roof under which they baked in the shade saw
the enemy on the exposed ridges ahead. When the group
had been in the dugout about fifteen minutes a mortar shell

dropped nearby, raining coral and steel fragments on the roof. The Division commander and his party went rearward.

September 19 brought gains, but no decrease in casualties. The Third Battalion went forward at 7 A.M. and the men dashed 400 yards before the line was pinned down. From two hills in its center the Second Battalion got withering fire; some units were down to a quarter of their strength, and by 11 A.M. E Company had only a squad of effectives. Puller called up every man left to him. At the end of the day he was in the command post with Frank Sheppard, two runners and a communications man.

A Company of the First Battalion went past them to attack with a total of fifty-six men and Puller saw them cross a ridge under fire. This unit drove forward until it reached a sheer drop of 150 feet on a cliff in the Seventh Regiment front. At the last, with only six men left, the company fell back and went under control of the Seventh.

Bloody Nose Ridge was assailed despite these losses. Portable and self-propelled flamethrowers, bazookas, tanks and every mortar of the Second Battalion led the attack and until the last moment planes seared the hills with napalm. Early in the afternoon, as the units were whittled away, F and G Companies were combined on the field into one and even a squad of men from a War Dog platoon was used as a company replacement. C Company of the battalion worked so far forward that it was cut off during the night. It fought the enemy hand-to-hand until daylight, beating off charges that no survivor could count. As the first light spilled over the ridge the shrunken company beat back the last Japanese attack with stones, ammunition boxes, bare fists and bayonets. Several of the enemy were flung bodily off the cliff and fell shrieking onto the splintered coral below. The fifteen survivors were ordered to withdraw across a swamp and rejoin Puller's line.

The new day brought no respite. A battery of a dozen machine guns, formed to help bolster the front, was manned by cooks, wiremen and quartermaster clerks. Mortars and machine guns fired until barrels were red, but the infantry still could not move against the Japanese. These positions were not to be taken until three weeks later, when they were flanked in a drive from the north.

At the end of the day the regiment reported a total of 1878 men lost since D-day. The fighting went on without a break until September 23, when the First Marines rested in lines without advancing. They beat off several counterattacks and patrols pushed about 1000 yards down the west coast without serious opposition.

The regiment was relieved at 2 P.M. of this day by the 321st Regiment of the 81st Army Division. The new commander took one look at the forward command post Puller had occupied and ordered it moved more than 1000 yards to the rear.

The First Marines went to the beach to be rested and fed while new defensive sectors were planned for the east coast. Puller could hardly walk by now. His left leg was seriously swollen.

In nine days on the line Puller's regiment had eliminated one major blockhouse and 144 defended caves and lesser pillboxes. Division reported that 3942 Japanese had been killed in the regiment's zone. No enemy had been captured. Puller's total casualties of men were 56 per cent—the highest regimental losses in the history of the Corps. The First Battalion had lost 71 per cent; the Second, 56 per cent; the Third, 55 per cent; Headquarters and Weapons Companies, 32 per cent.

General Smith, who walked this terrain after it was finally captured, said: "It seemed impossible that men could have moved forward against the intricate and mutually supporting defenses the Japanese had set up. It can only be explained as a reflection of the determination and aggressive leadership of Colonel Puller."

On September 24, the day he reached the beach, Puller wrote his wife, scratching with a pencil on a sheet of lined paper as he held it on the hood of a jeep:

> Darling: I am well and safe and there is nothing further for you to worry about. . . . God willing I will be with you around the first of December. . . . God is good to us.

Two days later, as he prepared to board ship with his regiment, he wrote her once more:

> . . . I am delighted that you declined to have anything to do with the soliciting of funds for our soldiers; the head of it is probably on the payroll of the fund for some $20,000 a year. In the future please give your work and time to our church. . . .

This operation is practically over and after reorganizing the First and getting it back into shape. I will then only have to await the arrival of my relief. Life with you will then be grand and all that I desire. . . . You are the loveliest woman in the world and you belong to me and I treasure you more than you will ever know. I am the most fortunate of men and will never forget it. . . .

It was October 2 when he went aboard ship with his regiment to sail for Pavuvu; they left the final conquest of Peleliu to the Army and the rest of the First Marine Division.

By now his leg was swollen until his thigh was almost twice its normal size, and the throbbing pain was constant. Doctors hurried him to the ship's sick bay, gave him a local anesthetic, and probed for the shell fragment he had carried since Guadalcanal. The surgeon, a Commander Patterson, went to the bone to fish out a metal slug about an inch long and a quarter of an inch wide. Puller lay for an hour and forty minutes on the operating table.

Six days later, on October 8, he struggled from his bunk despite the cautions of doctors and hobbled about for several minutes. The next day he was able to walk off the ship to the old camp at Pavuvu, and thereafter improved rapidly.

In the mail awaiting him in the rest camp was a letter from Dr. Edward Smith, of the Guadalcanal campaign, who was now in the States. Puller's reply:

The Peleliu expedition is over and we made the grade, with the help of God and a few Marines and corpsmen; the fight was costly but worth the price in order to get to Tokyo some day. May God rest the souls of our dead and make life less bitter for our maimed and crippled. The officers and men of this regiment were splendid and never hesitated to attack, regardless of enemy opposition.

I believe that our home front is now beginning to realize what a tremendous fight we have ahead of us in the war with the Japanese; we not only have to fight them in hundreds of islands but we will have to fight them on the continent of Asia as well.

Young Marines who met Puller on the island were still impressed. Private John Loomis, a recruit from California, was walking a guard post at Puller's tent one afternoon when the

Colonel beckoned. Loomis was a Puller man from that moment:

"I was scared; I'd never talked to a colonel before. He asked me my name and where I was from, and asked me to sit down. He asked how I was getting along, and then told me about his home down South. I think he wanted to talk to somebody."

Soon afterward, when Loomis was waiting in a long line before a tiny PX in a coconut grove, patiently enduring delays to buy paper and soap, Puller fell in at the end of the line.

A new second lieutenant strode up, shouldered his way through the line, shoved aside two men at its head and demanded service. Puller seized him by a shoulder, spun the young man about, and to the delight of Loomis and other enlisted men said sternly: "Now get to the end of the line where you belong."

About a week or more after he had returned to Pavuvu, Puller was surprised to see General Rupertus enter his tent, livid with rage. The commander had a copy of *Time* magazine in his hand, and pointed to an article about Puller entitled "Man of War." There was a picture of Lewis and a story about the visit of Rupertus and the reporter to the command post on Peleliu. Puller scanned the story as Rupertus stood there:

> "In front of Bloody Nose Ridge on Peleliu a Marine colonel fretted under his command post—a piece of tin under a poncho which shaded him from the sun. He worried the end of a frazzled cigarette, surveyed the field before him with hard, bloodshot eyes. . . .
>
> "The field telephone buzzed. The colonel listened and growled into it: 'We're still going but some of my companies are damned small.' A Jap mortar opened up and the men around the colonel flattened out. The C.O. himself did not change position. He stuck out his chest and spat: 'The bastards.'"

The article ended with a review of Puller's career.

Rupertus spoke coldly: "Puller, you've got the best publicity bureau in the Marine Corps."

"General, I had nothing at all to do with that, and you know it better than anyone else. I saw that reporter maybe ten minutes, and you were there with me all that time. He was making the rounds with you for several days. I don't know what you're talking about."

Rupertus turned away.

Puller carefully pasted the article in the back of his tattered copy of Henderson's *Stonewall Jackson*.

The article also drew attention in the States. Virginia Puller was so distressed by it that she wrote their old friend of China station days, Admiral Thomas Hart:

> I have just red an article in *Time* about Lewis and it made me so unhappy. I don't understand why the press wants to publish such a terrible description of a man deep in the throes of battle. . . . I wonder if you think the article as dreadful, in spots, as I. Poor dear, he has been in the field so long that few know his fine gentle side. . . .

The Admiral replied vigorously:

> I think that article is splendid. . . . There are a few phrases in it which none of us particularly care for, but what the article in general says makes me particularly proud. . . . You *must* have a feeling of entire pride that your husband should be so written up in a publication of such wide circulation. . . .
>
> You are away off the track, Virginia. . . . In the Pacific we are engaged in a no-quarter war which is not of our choosing. We fight an enemy that yields only when exterminated. We must win the war and we must go on with more and more of just what evidently horrifies you. . . .
>
> Now your husband is one of those few who have stood out as superlative in that war in the Pacific. We must thank the Lord that we have a few like him. . . .
>
> Your husband is coming back. I can imagine nothing worse for him, when he returns, than a realization that you look upon his past accomplishments with anything other than pride.
>
> Despite what he has been through, you will not find him changed insofar as you are concerned. This other side of him is what he carries to the office, so to speak, and has no part in your daily lives together. Please do your best, Virginia, to effect such mental adjustment as is needed.

Puller went to a happy reunion in Saluda, Virginia, but left some mournful Marines behind on Pavuvu. John Loomis saw the change immediately.

Puller hadn't believed in pads for the cots—but they now appeared. He had insisted upon equal food for officers and men and ate in the same mess hall as his enlisted men. There was no officers' club. All that was changed, and enlisted men were put back in their places. Loomis noted that morale dropped almost as soon as the Old Man left the island.

PULLER became restless after a few days in Saluda and proposed a trip to New York. Virginia was astonished:

"Don't you realize how things are there? You couldn't buy a hotel room with the crown jewels. We'd never get into a show. How would we even get there?"

"Don't you trust me any more?"

He carried off the holiday as if there were no war and no ration cards, shortages or queues of waiting civilians. They went to New York by train and when they reached the city were picked up by an escort who had been alerted by Marine Corps Headquarters. He was Diggory Venn, now a lieutenant, a young Englishman Puller had known on Guadalcanal and New Guinea as a combat correspondent.

Venn had made a futile effort to find a room for the Colonel and his wife—but when he squired the Pullers into the Hotel Commodore, and the room clerk saw the spread of ribbons on the Colonel's chest and the grim, atabrine-yellowed face, he quickly held out a registration card: "Yes, sir, Colonel! We'll always find a place for you. The law says three days, but we'll see what we can do, if you want to stay longer."

Somehow, Venn found tickets for shows for four or five days. The Pullers crowded into *Oklahoma!* and at Mrs. Puller's insistence saw *The Voice of the Turtle*, which starred her childhood friend Margaret Sullavan. She sent a note backstage and they obeyed the summons to the star's dressing room for an intimate talk, but declined an invitation to dinner, to be alone on the town.

There were interviews with several magazines and newspapers, with Venn as escort, and after a whirl of a few days the Pullers returned home.

In January, 1945, Puller was sent back to the Marine base in North Carolina at New River, now known as Camp Lejeune, where he commanded the Infantry Training Regiment, with 12,000 men to prepare for battle.

Mrs. Puller and Virginia Mac were with him again, he had a free hand with training and he was as content as he could be in wartime when he was denied a place in combat with his troops. His training methods were almost exactly those he had dinned into the First Battalion, Seventh Marines in the months when he was preparing them for Guadalcanal.

His commander, Brigadier General Alfred H. Noble, gave Puller good fitness reports: "One of our outstanding combat officers. A thoroughgoing Marine who can be relied upon to use good judgment. . . . Brought training to maximum efficiency. Highly regarded as a troop leader."

This was the result of Puller's abilities, for Noble opposed the Colonel's training program at many turns.

Puller's table of organization gave him plenty of officers and noncoms, but General Noble seldom allowed him more than half of these. Puller never forgot it: "Noble had them in school all the time. He thought that was more important than duty in the field. So, just two or three days before the battalions were about to ship out for the Pacific, Noble had them filled up with officers and noncoms who had been in school, but not in the field. Most of them lacked combat experience. They hit Okinawa without field training, too.

"One of these green officers, a second lieutenant, landed on the beach at Iwo Jima and was ordered to take his platoon to the front line. He ran them through a gap, or marched them crooked, the result of inexperience, and ran them into the Japs. The whole outfit was killed.

"The sad part was that all the officers and noncoms he took for his schools had just finished schools at Quantico, and they got the same thing again at Lejeune."

Still, there were signs that Puller was making himself felt. More than one front-line officer in the Pacific said: "I can always tell when we get a Puller-trained Marine. He's ready to go."

Near the end of his duty at Lejeune, just as the war in the Pacific was coming to an end, Puller became a father once more—this time of twins, a boy and a girl. For several days the base was covered with a smoke screen in the wake of his distribution of cigars.

There were signs that the outside world had not forgotten Puller. In December, 1945, there was a letter from Marine gunner Charles R. Jackson, who had served under him in the old Second Battalion, Fourth Marines, in Shanghai and had been captured by the Japanese in the Philippines:

> I am back from the living dead, being released on the 13th of September. . . .
>
> I have heard of your distinguished war record with great pleasure. When we were prisoners in those dark and dreary days we used to speculate: "If Chesty Puller doesn't get killed, he will surely make Major General."
>
> To the sorrow of your old men of Shanghai the prediction did not come true, and we are all terribly disappointed that you are only a colonel. I can truthfully speak for all of your old men—that we never, never forgot the best Marine officer we ever had the privilege of serving under.
>
> When the men were released, their first question was: "How is Chesty Puller?" Your well-nigh incredible career is the admiration of us all.

If Puller suspected that he had not been promoted as rapidly as his record warranted, or that he had enemies around Headquarters, he gave no sign. He still expressed himself vigorously on every issue of importance to the Corps, and did not hesitate to write to the commandant, now General Vandegrift, when the Corps cut adrift hundreds of its best combat officers.

With the war's end, the Corps began to require college degrees for its officers and thus cut off many fine commanders of platoons and companies who had distinguished themselves in action. Puller wrote to Vandegrift:

"The former enlisted men who became officers and proved their worth in combat should be sent to college to get degrees. If we don't do this, thousands of your new officers will be in without combat experience—and you'll never know, until war actually comes, whether or not they are fit for combat."

He got no satisfaction and no copy of the letter found its way into Puller's file at Headquarters; he followed up the argument with Vandegrift in person, but had no effect upon the policy.

It was not the only time Puller found Headquarters deaf

to his voice of experience. With the defeat of Japan, the Marine Corps sent all its war dogs to Camp Lejeune and Puller was ordered to have them "detrained" for return to their owners—but only those thought to be safe for use in civilian life; others were to be destroyed. Puller had his men demobilize the hundreds of dogs gathered there; Marines discouraged them in their attacks on strangers and beat them when they persisted. The men made pets of the animals with such success that only twenty had to be destroyed.

General Vandegrift notified Puller that the Corps would maintain no War Dog corps in peacetime and asked him for a recommendation on the training and use of the dogs in the next war. Puller complied.

The best breed for war, he wrote, was the American version of the German Shepherd, intelligent, courageous, stable and easily trained. Boxers were also good. The Doberman Pinscher was to be avoided:

"On Peleliu, more than half of the dogs assigned to my regiment were Dobermans. They proved too highly bred to stand artillery fire and turned against their handlers at crucial moments. Some men were badly torn by these dogs and we were forced to destroy all of them. They are grand dogs, intelligent and efficient under most conditions, but they cannot bear artillery and mortar fire. I recommend that this breed be dropped from the war dog program for the future."

Within a week or so Puller had a telephone call from Chicago, a woman obviously excited, who announced herself as president of a national Doberman society:

"Colonel, I have seen your outrageous report—an insult to all Dobermans and those who love and know them. No true American could write such a thing! I demand that you retract every word, this very night."

"Madam, I was under orders from the Commandant to outline a program for the wars of the future—something which might endanger the safety of our country if it weren't accurate. This is an important matter, and there is nothing personal about any breed of dog, so far as I'm concerned. I *like* Dobermans; they simply won't do for the job they've been assigned to."

"How far is it from Chicago to that Camp—Lejeune or whatever you call it?"

"We're in North Carolina. A long way. But I can save you the trip, if you're thinking of that. I'll never retract that report, because it's based on the best information from competent men and officers."

"I'll be there within twenty-four hours."

On schedule, a long black limousine with a chauffeur and footman and the leader of American Dobermans drew up before Puller's office and for some time they warmly debated the matter of the Dobermans as war dogs. When Puller continued adamant the woman left him with a final word ringing in his ears: "I'll see that you do retract that report! I'm going to Washington this instant."

Within a few days, to Puller's surprise, someone at Headquarters returned his report on the war dogs, asking that he make changes in his recommendations. He scratched on the back of the document his refusal to do so, saying that he had made the report at the request of the Commandant and that it had been made to the best of his ability. He heard no more of the matter.

Puller told his aides: "I knew we had many minorities in our country, and that some were powerful indeed—but not until now did I realize that the damned Doberman Pinschers had organized, and were ready to take over at any moment."

In June, 1946, Puller was called to Washington for three days. He expected orders to a new post, but the personnel office could tell him nothing of his future. When he went to the office of General Vandegrift, an aide gave him ominous news:

"Colonel, you've been ordered to Reserve duty. In New Orleans. It's a big district, you know, and very important to the Corps."

Puller was not misled. He realized what it meant to be shunted to Reserve duty, into a side pocket; many a Marine career had ended in that way. He went in to General Vandegrift when he was called; the Commandant was the officer who had first recommended Puller for a Marine commission in the Haiti days of 1921. Vangegrift greeted him warmly:

"I imagine you don't like your next assignment."

"No, sir. I do not."

"I suppose you'd like to be given a regiment."

"I would."

"Why should you be?"

"I think I've demonstrated that I'm fully qualified."

The Commandant reddened; Puller never forgot his reply: "Puller, the war's over, and I'm trying to get two permanent divisions in the Corps, and three hundred colonels. It's up to me to qualify these three-hundred colonels as regimental commanders."

Puller laughed, and Vandegrift's mouth grew firm, but he asked the Colonel to speak up:

"Sir, if you can keep two divisions, you'll have eight regiments. You'll never be able to train three hundred colonels with that setup. They'd never really qualify in peacetime, anyway. No one will ever know their abilities until they've been under fire."

Puller left Washington with his friendship with his old friend Vandegrift unstrained, but he realized that somewhere in the vast and growing retinue at Headquarters were officers who did not wish him well. He heard these men spoken of in these days as the Young Turks now rising in the Corps, and Puller sometimes expressed himself to Mrs. Puller or officers with whom he was intimate:

"One of the inevitable problems with the Marine Corps or any other military service is that staff officers take over the minute a war is ended. The combat people run things when the chips are down and the country's life is at stake—but when the guns stop, nobody's got a use for a combat man.

"The staff officers are like rats; they stream out of hiding and take over. It's true. Just watch what happens to paperwork. God, in peacetime they put out enough to sink a small-size nation into the sea—and when war breaks, most of it just naturally stops. That's the way they do everything. There must always be staff people, of course, or we'd never get anything done—but if we don't stop this empire-building of the staff, somebody's going to come along and lick us one of these days. We'll be so knotted in red tape that we can't move."

Puller and his family went off to New Orleans in July, 1946, and though the Colonel was sometimes pessimistic, and once or twice spoke to his wife about "turning in my suit," he threw himself into the new job and managed to find consolations.

Vandegrift was soon smiling over reports from New Orleans. Puller built his district until he had doubled the number of reservists, wangled barracks and training areas for them—and in his two-year tour reached a peak of six battalions and in addition some 8000 unattached men, a record for the country. He soon commanded a quarter of the organized Marine Reserves in the nation.

The building of this new morale in the district began with his arrival. The newspapers spotted him instantly and the local *Times-Picayune* displayed him in color on its Sunday magazine cover, with a striking quotation:

"These days it looks like time for America to get realistic instead of starry-eyed. Whoever they are, whether they have atomic bombs and rockets or not, we can lick 'em if America gets hard, and American fighting men are trained to march 30 miles a day with a pack, and hit whatever they shoot at with any weapon they're trained to use. Just as long as Americans have the will to fight, we'll be all right."

That helped to draw a tide of recruits which never dwindled so long as Puller was in command.

In January, 1947, in his request for future duty assignments, he asked for a post with the Second Division in the Mediterranean, and reminded Headquarters: "I served in the *Gendarmerie d'Haiti* during 1919-23 and the *Guardia Nacional de Nicaragua* in 1928-33. I believe that I am well qualified for guerrilla warfare or any other type of warfare that might develop in that area."

The family life of the Pullers was quiet, as usual. Virginia Mac, the oldest child, went to dancing school and the Colonel went to her recital, where he drew attention by climbing over the knees of other spectators when his daughter had left the stage. He went out to puff at his pipe and returned only for her finale.

Once there was a call from Virginia Mac's swimming teacher, to say that the child had injured her head in a fall at the pool. Puller paced the floor as they waited for her arrival, but told his mournful wife: "Don't worry, dear. Puller heads are mighty tough." He accurately forecast a minor injury.

There was an occasional laugh for the Colonel. Once Marine Headquarters sent a team of three colonels who had been transferred from aviation to infantry, to inspect Puller's district. One of the officers confessed that they were green and hardly knew how to begin. The Colonel smiled disarmingly. "I imagine you have some kind of forms to fill out, don't you?"

"Yes."

"Well, I'll make it easy for you. Don't worry."

He summoned his sergeant major and muttered: "Fill out these damned things and make 'em look good—but not too good. I'll take these birds over to the bar, and they'll pick 'em up about five o'clock."

The inspection went as Puller had planned; the officers left happily, work done, and Puller's district was rendered a model of perfection, in reports which would go into his record.

In July, 1948, Puller was moved once more—and this time he felt certain that he was nearing the end of his Corps career, for he was sent to command Marine barracks in Pearl Harbor. Barracks duty was even more deadly than Reserve duty and to be sentenced to it after performing so well in New Orleans was a clear signal that all was not well. Puller did not need to be reminded that he had the most distinguished record of any living Marine colonel, and the wound rankled.

His chief concern was for the Corps itself. He told his wife: "It's the Young Turks again. They're making room for young officers who've never served as platoon, company or battalion commanders by pushing out all the older and experienced officers. The law said that we could serve to age sixty-four, and they had that reduced to sixty-two. Even that wasn't enough and they put across Selection Boards to rule that, in peacetime, one officer may be rated as better than another in his grade. They've even violated all Navy tradition by having the Secretary of the Navy declare that nobody can be selected for promotion unless he's had staff duty. One of these days we'll pay for this; I hope it won't be disastrous. If war comes, we'll have officers leading troops who've never commanded so much as a platoon in combat."

He packed his family and they sailed on July 29, on the *General J. C. Breckinridge* from San Francisco.

The Pullers were settled in the finest of their service homes, a large, well-staffed house behind a hibiscus hedge, complete with a post swimming pool. While Mrs. Puller settled happily to the raising of her children, the Colonel gave the outpost a shakedown.

The machine guns, he noted, were only a bit more ready than they had been when he had first served at Pearl Harbor, twenty-three years before. This time they had plentiful equipment, but no one was training gunners; he put men to work immediately and soon the weapons were hammering away on the firing ranges.

His command consisted of 620 Marines and 250 Civil Service policemen, but he inspected the islands as if he had been sent to attend to national security. He saw that there were no fortifications except for the gunsites of the Coast Artillery—and this time the guns were out of place, dismounted and rolled aside to rust.

He found morale among his enlisted men low, and soon detected one reason. There were clubs for officers and for staff and top noncommissioned officers but the lower ranks of sergeants, corporals and privates had no place to go in leisure hours. They were finding recreation by going into Honolulu, often getting into trouble and overstaying their leave. Puller enlisted the help of wives and men, set up three new clubs, and cut absenteeism by 50 per cent.

In March of 1949 the Pearl Harbor commander, Rear Admiral S. S. Murray, gave Puller a rank of "Outstanding" in his fitness report, adding: "An outstanding, capable Marine officer, of high personal military character. Strongly recommended for promotion. Annual inspection found marked improvement in the past year under his command."

Late in the year the threat of war in Korea rose; this was nowhere clearer than in the pages of the Korean press in Hawaii, which served many thousands of readers. Puller found a good source of information in one Wong, who had the shoe shop concession in the Marine barracks, an intelligent man of means and education.

"Wong, things seem to be in a mess in Korea."

"Colonel, it can be no other way, since your people have divided Korea so. We are like the North and South in your own Civil War. Instead of cutting our country in two in that way, if you had cut us into East and West, so that each half could have some industries to keep the people alive, maybe we would have no trouble. As it is now, they will fight."

"Wong, if I had my way, you'd be the chief advisor on Asiatic affairs for our State Department, instead of a barracks shoemaker."

Other experts on Korea were less convincing to Puller. A U. S. Army general who had armed and trained the South Korean armies stopped in Hawaii on his way back home, and in a newspaper interview declared: "The army of South Korea is the finest in the history of Asia. It can move anywhere in the region, virtually unopposed. No previous Asiatic army can be compared with it, even that of Genghis Khan."

Reports of border incidents in Korea continued, however, and some two months after the visiting general had made his reassuring statement, a North Korean force drove a South Korean battalion many miles into its own country in utter defeat. An enterprising American reporter hired a small plane and flew up to interview the defeated commander, whose words struck home with Puller:

"My men are brave enough, and know their job. What else can you expect of us but retreat? We have carbines from America—that is all. Will these light guns stand up against good Russian rifles, and mortars and machine guns and even tanks? We were not made ready."

Puller was sickened by the familiar sign of the unpreparedness of America and her allies, but was not surprised.

Rear Admiral C. H. McMorris, the new commander at Pearl Harbor, made a fitness report on Puller in June, 1950, even more resounding than the one filed a year earlier: "An outstanding Marine officer in every respect who can be relied upon to do a fine job in any circumstances. I never knew a finer or more able officer and I know many. Immediate promotion is urged."

Puller's private reaction: "Unless we have a war right away, I'll never make general." He had requested, for his next duty, service with the Second Division in the U.S., or at the Corps Schools or Parris Island.

On June 25, 1950, North Korean troops poured across the 38th Parallel in strength and war had returned. President Truman announced that the nation was not at war, but ships, planes and men were in motion, and in the gathering of "a fire brigade," a token force of Marines was sent to the front to aid American Army forces. The United Nations buzzed briefly before taking action; Puller recognized all the signs. He immediately asked for a modification of his orders and said urgently to Headquarters:

"Attention is invited to the fact that I served as an officer in Haiti and Nicaragua, and in the Pacific Theater for eight years prior to the Japanese attack on Pearl Harbor. This experience will prove of value in an assignment to combat duty in Korea."

This was not enough, and he went to the cable office and at his own expense sent appeals to the Commandant, the Assistant Commandant, and the commander of the First Marine Division, begging for assignment to Korea. The cables cost him nineteen dollars.

In the days of waiting he saw that the South Korean battalion commander who was an early victim of the Communist attack had been tragically prophetic; the North Koreans were still cutting their way at will through large forces of South Koreans and brushing aside with almost the same ease the first American forces to be thrown against them. It appeared that the Communists were rolling toward complete victory.

In July, at last, Puller's orders came; he called Virginia from his office. It was late Saturday afternoon:

"Can we leave for home tomorrow?"

"Have you gone mad?"

"No, I'm sending a driver for you and the children now, to get your shots."

"Lewis, you know we can't possibly get this house cleared, the furniture ready, and the children off in such time."

"My orders are for Camp Pendleton, California, dear, and the matter is fairly urgent. A small war."

"Well, we'll try. I'll call the McMorrises and tell them we can't come to the party tonight."

"No. We'll go anyway. It may be a long time before we're out on another one together."

Mrs. Puller retained a memory of that night: "We had a wonderful time, a big crowd of Navy and Marine people, and Lewis was the life of the party. Did the hula, even, and brought down the house. No one would ever have guessed that he had orders to go immediately—and that he knew the kind of thing that was waiting for him in Korea."

Admiral McMorris asked Mrs. Puller privately if she wanted the orders held up for a few days until the family was ready—but they went off by plane on Monday morning.

The Corps would allow him transportation for the family only to Camp Pendleton, his new post, and he would have to pay their fare cross-country to Virginia himself. He told a friend: "This damned war has already cost me $1019, and I'm not even in an outfit—much less on the scene."

XV

WAR ON A SHOESTRING

PULLER arrived in Southern California in the heat of late July and found the San Diego area a bedlam. Marine Reservists thronged in from every corner of the nation; thousands of vehicles stored since World War II were being overhauled and driven to port; trains bore regulars from the East Coast. Unattached officers came from everywhere, without a call, volunteers for war. The First Marine Division was being created almost from scratch.

Puller went to the office of his division commander, the white-haired, soft-voiced Oliver P. Smith, with whom his friendship went back to student days at Fort Benning. He found even the calm Smith a bit unstrung:

"Lewie, you've got what you want. The old First Marines again. But I don't know if you can do it. You've got to activate your regiment and begin loading in about ten days, by our orders. What do you think?"

"Has your staff made plans for me?"

"Only to put you in Area 17, and we can move you to Tent Camp 2 later."

"It would take two days for the shift. If you'll approve it I'll meet the Quartermaster at the tent camp in half an hour."

"Go to it."

It was not hard to see, from Smith's reports and the wall maps, the urgency of affairs in the bustling camp. The struggle for Korea seemed almost over. The Eighth Army had reeled back to the south and east and now defended itself against rising North Korean pressure from a perimeter around the port of Pusan. Marines already sent there seemed unlikely to change the course of the war.

General Smith knew only that General MacArthur desperately wanted the First Marine Division; he did not yet know where it was headed.

Puller soon walked the familiar old tenting area with a Quartermaster colonel; the place was a shambles. Nothing had been kept up since the end of the war, all was weedgrown; even the stoves had been cannibalized to keep other areas. Puller asked the supply officer to send him all possible equipment and before nightfall things began to move.

When Puller went back to headquarters Smith hailed him happily: "Good news, Lewie. They're sending you three battalions of the Second Marines from Lejeune, already up to peacetime strength. You'll need only forty or fifty per cent reserves to fill up."

By the next morning, when the tent camp area had become a sea of newly risen canvas, the news was even better. Smith told Puller: "The Commandant is hand-picking your team, Lewie. He's sending you two thousand post and station men. There'll be almost no Reservists in the First Marines."

As they streamed in, Puller found that more than 90 per cent of the officers and about 80 per cent of the enlisted men from the posts and stations were veterans of World War II. When the trainloads of regulars from Lejeune came in they had the look of well-drilled youngsters in fighting trim, though most were postwar recruits. Puller and a small staff fed the new arrivals into tents and made up outfits with a mixture of regulars and those from scattered posts.

There was little chance to improve the raw material he was given and Puller fought a losing battle for equipment. Strangely, dogtags were the hardest item to find in the rush to prepare for shipping to Korea and the men wore no identification until they reached Japan. Most training was limited to the rifle range.

The three battalion commanders who had come from Camp Lejeune reported their weapons were fair—but no new ones had been issued as they left camp. "We'll see," Puller said. "I'll meet you on the range in the morning at daybreak."

The rifles and automatic weapons were in poor condition and marksmanship with them was impossible. With the aid of an expert gunner, Puller checked every weapon in the regiment and discarded 67 per cent of all rifles as unfit for use. New ones hurried down from the supply base at Barstow, in allegedly perfect condition, were also poor and Puller ordered 37 per cent of these surveyed out.

Puller wasted little time cursing the civilians who had stored these weapons at the end of World War II, supposedly in condition for use in the next emergency: "Hell, they didn't even take the trouble to separate the broken ones from the good ones, and jammed 'em all into cosmoline without looking at them. What a way to run a country!"

Somehow, almost every man was supplied with a good weapon and fired twenty-five rounds with it under Puller's eye. The commander spent most of his waking hours on the range, driving to see that firepower was provided, and that it would be accurate.

He was not long in making himself known to the rank and file, though he moved unobtrusively. Lieutenant George Chambers, a veteran platoon leader in B. Company of the First Battalion, noted that Puller habitually wore old utilities as he worked and that passing privates thought he was only a gunnery sergeant: "Hi, Gunny!" Puller only grinned and waved; other colonels might have put men under arrest for less.

Lieutenant Lew Devine, a rifle platoon commander in Fox Company, was just out of Annapolis when he reported to Pendleton, nattily uniformed and sternly military. Devine reported in an old Quonset hut shed. As he talked with the captain on duty he noticed a man seated on the floor, chewing on a pipe. The collar of his utilities was turned up and the lieutenant could see no insignia.

"I tried to brush him off when he spoke to me," Devine said. "I thought maybe he was some old character hanging on, the way he was telling the Captain how we'd kick hell out of the North Koreans when we got there. I thought maybe he was even someone they had to sweep up. I gave him a sharp reply about something, but he took no offense. Fortunately, he turned his head and I saw the eagles on his collar and I knew who he was in a flash. I had heard hundreds of tales about Puller, and he was a legend to me long before, in World War II.

"His greatest touch was his earthiness, his ability to make the men feel he was one of them. They'd literally have gone off to Moscow with him."

The same appeal to the troops brought Puller one of the most faithful and capable companions of his career—Sergeant Orville Jones.

Jones was an Okinawa veteran of World War II, a big, slow-moving blond from Bremen, Indiana, who had been an unlicensed driver of steel trucks in the Midwest throughout his teens; he had torn down and reassembled his first old Ford at fifteen. He was a nine-year man in the Corps when he met Puller.

A Quartermaster man searched the camp for a man of combat experience as Puller's driver—but he must be man who could read and make maps, and could judge distances. Jones resisted: "Tell him you couldn't find a soul in this regiment. I know that old man from what they said in the war. You go with him and you'll get killed off. He likes to go right on up there."

That night Jones went to the improvised beer hall in his area and stood in the long line waiting to be served. He also caught his first glimpse of Puller in the flesh. The Colonel entered and sat at the bar. "Who's in charge here?" he asked. A corporal indicated a lieutenant, who thrust his head through a door:

"Last night you ran out of beer, Lieutenant?"

"Yes, sir. I'm afraid we did."

"And what you served was warm?"

"Yes, sir."

"It won't happen again, Lieutenant. You understand me?"

"I sure do, sir."

"Maybe you don't. These boys are going to war, and some of them won't be coming back. They're working like hell all day and half the night to get ready, most of 'em at least sixteen hours straight. What they do with their off hours is their own business, and if they want a couple of beers, Lieutenant, they're going to get 'em."

Jones made an instant decision to sign up as the Old Man's driver, and the next day, after he had been accepted, went back to the beer hall: "I mean they laid in the suds. That next night you could hardly walk for the cans tossed in the gutters of company streets, and men sat around on the hills, drinking their beers after chow. Work never stopped, and morale was humming."

Puller enlisted the help of Jones in finding another important recruit—a "shotgun," or bodyguard, to ride in the jeep with them in Korea. Jones found him quickly: Jan Bodey, a San Francisco iceman in civilian life who had spent years in the Corps, and had gone out after World War II, the result of a San Diego street fight in which he had allegedly tied two sailors together by their arms. He was now back as a Frisco Reservist, and was reputed to be the strongest man in the Marines, as well as an expert with small arms.

The Colonel found an old friend, Major W. C. Reeves, whom he had known in Nicaragua; this old-timer came in with the regulars from Lejeune, and was soon Puller's adjutant. Most of the officers around Puller were new to him: Lieutenant Colonels Robert Rickert, his executive officer, and the battalion commanders, Thomas L. Ridge, Allan Sutter, and Jack Hawkins.

Old and new, they seemed to blend into one happy team, as Puller saw them, from the moment the First Marines were told that they were shipping out for Korea: "I never saw a more contented bunch of men when they got the word, and knew this was it. All friction faded overnight, and with a real objective all were happy. There were no absences—and, as usual when war comes, some of the best fighting people came out of the brig. For the last few days we were organizing, the only missing people I had were those who had been hurt in traffic accidents."

There was no time for combat loading; the ammunition, supplies, vehicles and weapons went on the ships at San Diego piecemeal as they arrived. There was a shortage of stevedores, as well. The Division did not go out in convoy, but had been moving a ship or two at a time until August 8, when loading began on the fleet of nineteen vessels which was to bear Puller's First Regiment and others. Loading was complete by August 22, but a blown boiler delayed them further and they finally cleared the States on September 1. Puller still did not know their destination.

The ships were so jammed with equipment that there was limited room for training or exercises, but some officers gathered their companies on deck hatches for lectures in night patrol, guerrilla fighting, and weapons drill. Lieutenant Joe Fisher of I Company, a Massachusetts boy who had been seasoned at Iwo Jima, specialized in map reading and bayonet fighting practice with his men. Fisher was an impressive figure, six feet two inches tall and a muscular 235 pounds.

There was an effort at an exercise program and Puller did some stationary running with the men to keep in trim. He once saw half a dozen Marines chipping paint off a deck, assigned to the task by some Navy officer. He dismissed them: "Throw those chippers over the side and go about your business. Let the Navy paint the damned ship. You're going to fight this war."

Almost as soon as they left port Puller and other officers were bending over maps of Korea, speculating as to their landing place. Several fingers jabbed at the port of Inchon on the west coast as the obvious target for an amphibious strike. "It'll be there," Puller said, "providing the Eighth Army can hold on until we get in."

There was no "official" news of their goal until they had docked in Japan, at Kobe, and Puller's sergeants returned from the bordellos to report that the news was all over town: Inchon.

On some ships staff officers were locked up with the plans in the hectic process of untangling the details involved in history's greatest amphibious operation. General MacArthur's staff in Tokyo had begun the work on Operation Chromite, as the expedition was known, but the work went on almost around the world.

Behind Puller's First Marines the Seventh Marines of Colonel Homer Litzenberg were on the way; some units were being taken from the Atlantic Fleet through the Panama Canal and even from the Mediterranean. General Smith and Division officers were flying to Japan. A third regiment, the Fifth, under Lieutenant Colonel Ray Murray, was to be pulled from the Pusan perimeter and fed into the convoy as it moved toward Inchon.

The target itself was fantastic, once planners got down to the facts behind the charts. MacArthur, known for much of his career as an "enemy" of the Marine Corps, had insisted, against all opposition, that the Division could end the war in Korea with this one blow and that it would be relatively inexpensive. He planned to remove the pressure from Pusan, cut off the North Korean armies, destroy them, and restore peace. The troops would be home by Christmas.

MacArthur clung to the plan but Marines were not optimistic. Inchon was a city of 250,000 population. Its

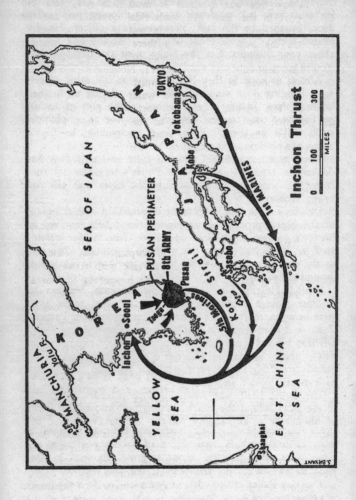

Inchon Thrust

"beaches" were in truth sea walls and jetties which screened factories, warehouses, salt evaporation pans, and marshy lowlands. Its harbor was one of the world's most treacherous and at low tide was a series of mud flats and reefs. No other port in the East had such tidal conditions, for the average rise and fall of the tide was twenty-nine feet.

Within the next few months there were three possible landing dates with tide high enough to float the larger landing ships: September 15, October 11, November 3. The first date was chosen and the hour must be at peak tide, at 5:30 P.M. Within six hours the water would fall to only six feet. The channels into the port were so narrow and devious that the standby ships of the fleet must be thirty miles away when the landing craft hit the beaches.

Some of Puller's officers were so deep in these plans when they docked at Kobe that they were not aware of a typhoon which swept over, damaging several ships, snapping a dozen hawsers and ruining much equipment. During and after this storm the ships had to be unloaded and reloaded, ready for combat. This required more ships; several rusty landing craft which the Japanese had used for fishing and coastal traffic were called into service.

Puller hailed a passing medical corpsman and went to a nearby Army hospital. "I want to talk with some of the casualties. I've got to find out what's happening in Korea."

He went up in an elevator with an Army doctor who seemed on the point of tears. "Go into the wards and see those kids and you'll soon know more than you want about Korea. Take a look at all the self-inflicted wounds we've got—and those kids are so green they don't even realize how obvious it was, just from the powder burns."

Puller walked down many rows of beds, talking with men, many of them frightened and broken, and heard their tales of Korea. Puller was sobered, but did not despair. He told some younger officers that night: "There's nothing wrong with American kids. Their leadership has just gone all to hell. There's a whole hospital full of babies, you might say. They were never given a chance to grow into men. It won't be that way with our Marines, I'll tell you that."

One day Puller talked with an Army corporal on the docks, a youngster just back from Korea who had a word of advice: "Colonel, keep them Marine leggings on your boys. The

North Koreans call Marines the Crazy Yellowlegs, and they never attack 'em except by accident or ignorance."

Puller inspected the troops in a nearby training camp and gave only one order: "Put the leggings back on the men. We wouldn't want to disappoint anybody over there. Maybe we can throw some business to the Army."

They left Kobe on September 12, heading across the Yellow Sea. Four of their old landing craft broke down and they waited, wallowing, as weather reports warned of another approaching typhoon. By the following night the Navy had the engines going again and the convoy moved on; the typhoon did not strike but there was much seasickness aboard the small craft.

The convoy grew larger as it approached Inchon—four carriers, two of them large, two cruisers, twenty-five destroyers and many smaller craft. For two days in advance the Navy pasted the key to Inchon defenses, the fortified island of Wolmi-do, and to confuse the enemy, planes and ships also struck nearby ports. Thus, on September 14, the armada neared its goal, the Marine and Navy command still dubious of a landing in the heart of an industrial city where the defense had every advantage—including that of the "best-known secret in the Orient," the destination of the assault. Yet more and more officers were won by the commander's assurance, which rang in a much-quoted Mac-Arthurism from a strategy conference: "We shall land at Inchon and I shall crush them."

In Puller's ship, as in others, there was hurried preparation to the last moment. Briefing sessions were endless, as teams of officers came in to get the latest word. Puller's reaction was unique. When the briefing officers were through —having shown a number of aerial photographs of Inchon harbor and its defenses and spoken ominously of casualties to come—the Colonel himself ended each session: "Don't pay any attention to that kind of stuff. They might have guns in any of those spots he pointed out, but you can't see 'em on the pictures, and I'll bet they don't have 'em. I think the ships and planes will clear 'em up pretty well. You can prepare for a successful landing, and tell that to your troops."

Privately, Puller had reservations: "Here we are, about to try the biggest stunt of its kind, with a total of three hundred colonels in the Marine Corps to draw from—and two of our four assault regiments are commanded by lieutenant colonels; and seven of our twelve battalions are led by majors; good men, but we need experience here, if ever we did. The trouble is, we have so many officers on staff duty, there are not enough to go around for the fighting units."

He said nothing of the sort to young officers who kept crowding in for his final briefing on D-day, until late on September 15, near the time for landing. While the fleet and its planes poured last barrages of shells and rockets into the city Puller spoke to a final group. Among the officers was Second Lieutenant Lyle Worster, of Gardiner, Maine, the assistant intelligence officer of the regiment, who never forgot the forthright little speech from the Colonel, unlike any that was heard in the fleet that day:

"We're the most fortunate of men. Most times, professional soldiers have to wait twenty-five years or more for a war, but here we are, with only five years' wait for this one.

"During that time we've sat on our fat duffs, drawing our pay. Now we're getting a chance to earn it, to show the taxpayers we're worth it. We're going to work at our trade for a little while. We live by the sword, and if necessary we'll be ready to die by the sword. Good luck. I'll see you ashore."

When the company officers had gone Puller explained: "Old man, when you have something to say to officers or men, make it snappy. The fewer words, the better. They won't believe you if you shoot bull. When you face ranks of men and try that, you can hear 'em sigh in despair when you open your mouth, if they sense you're a phony. They can usually look at you and tell. Maybe it doesn't sound like it, but that's an important thing in a Marine's career."

Somehow he found a moment alone to scratch a few lines in pencil to his wife, writing as if it might well be his last letter:

> Sweet:
> I will be unable to write you again for a few days but you, Virginia, Virginia Mac, Martha Leigh and Lewis, will be constantly in my thoughts. May God bless you always and provide for you, giving you much happiness and useful lives. You, my children, must take advantage of all opportunities and develop into good Christians. Much love to all of you.
> I love you, Virginia, I always have and I always will.

Lewis Puller was a little more than fifty-two years old. He was thirty-one years from his baptism of fire in the jungles of Haiti.

XVI

MacARTHUR'S TRIUMPH

BY 5:30 in the afternoon, when the first waves of Marines reached shore, the men of the fleet could no longer see Inchon. Hundreds of boats milled in the outer harbor, in their turn crossing the embarkation line and moving toward land, where they disappeared into a bank of smoke and dust. The guns of the ships had ceased. Firing came most hotly from the north, in the heart of the city, where Murray's Fifth Marines were landing on Red Beach.

Puller went in to his objective at Blue Beach with the third wave, in a twilight hastened by the smoke pall, and climbed a fifteen-foot sea wall on one of the scaling ladders improvised on the ship en route. It occurred to him that the Corps had not used ladders since Chapultepec.

He sat on the wall, briefly watching the enemy in his front; there was scattered fire on the landscape, a region of boggy lowlands with few buildings. Marines were blasting some machine gun nests in the area, but Puller saw few North Korean troops. Major James Treadwell, who had fifty-two amphibious tractors in Puller's command, passed along the beach below the Colonel and drew artillery fire. A few of the armored vehicles halted. Treadwell looked upward and saw the Old Man: "If he can, we can," he yelled to his men; they chugged ahead. When they were in position Treadwell returned to the sea wall.

"It won't amount to much tonight," Puller said. "We took 'em by surprise. Might as well move the CP." There were only two or three men near him, and Treadwell assumed that this was the entire command staff of the regiment at the moment. Puller leapt for the ground below and tumbled on

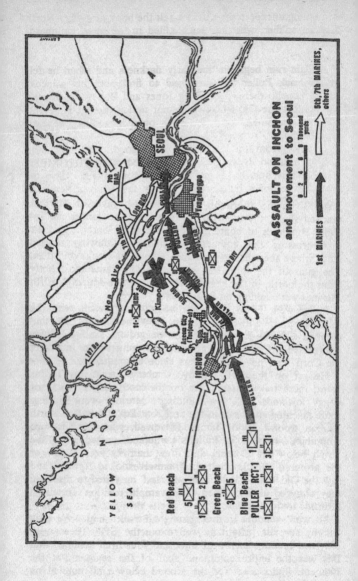

ASSAULT ON INCHON
and movement to Seoul

0 2 4 6 8 Thousand yards

5th, 7th MARINES, others

1st MARINES

YELLOW
SEA

N

Red Beach   5|11   1|5   2|5

Green Beach   3|5

Blue Beach   1|1   2|1   3|1

PULLER   RCT-1

INCHON

Ascom City
(Tongsong-ni)

PULLER

Kimpo

Yongdengpo

SEOUL

HAN RIVER

HAN RIVER

7th DIV

1st DIV

B. BRYANT

something unexpectedly soft. He felt the body of a dead North Korean soldier, who had been killed in the naval bombardment.

A light rain began in the early darkness and when he felt in his pack Puller was surprised to find both his raincoat and a poncho there, packed by Jones and Bodey, on Jones's theory that the Old Man would not notice the extra weight. The new command post was soon open in a ditch, beneath the poncho.

Reports from the battalions were good, but there was some confusion. Naval guns had blocked the only exit from Blue Beach and engineers had had to dynamite a path; hundreds of men had swarmed over the sea wall on nets before the breach was made. The assault had been made by Sutter's Second and Ridge's Third Battalions, which were now going into position on a line which could be defended for the night. It was 2 A.M. before all troops found their outfits and there was much stumbling, clawing, falling and cursing as men moved out in patrols toward the enemy. Puller's casualties had been light and the Division's total for the day was only 20 killed and 170 wounded.

Puller was relieved; he had expected confusion from his unpracticed troops and feared heavy casualties as they crossed the sea wall and the open ground beyond. Puller walked his lines before he slept. He found Hawkins and most of his First Battalion along a railroad about half a mile inland; Sutter's Second held the nearest road intersection and outposts had fanned onto hills commanding the road. Sutter reported one dead and nineteen wounded, and estimated he had killed fifty North Koreans and had captured fifteen. Ridge's battalion had driven deeper, about a mile inland, to take a prominent hill, where one platoon of How Company drove the enemy from their holes, killing and wounding thirty without loss to themselves.

Sergeant Jones was one of the last men ashore. He had loaded the Old Man's jeep on an amphibious tractor which was handled by a green crew. Shells dropped near them in the harbor and the skipper of the amtrack hung back until Jones drew his pistol and spoke quietly in the boy's ear: "You can run all you like when your time comes. But you take me in to that beach or I'll let some daylight into you." He was landed without delay. Jones left the jeep at the base of the sea wall and began his search for Puller.

He went stealthily over the sand, whistling "Dixie," hoping that sentries would recognize him as a Marine. He was halted by the familiar voice of a gunnery sergeant, gave the password, and went forward. He found Puller crouched in his gully under the poncho.

The Colonel peered out at Jones: "Old man, how the hell did you know it was going to rain?" A few days later when an officer proposed that Puller set up a weather information service Jones heard the Old Man growl: "Hell fire! Whenever I want to know about the weather, I'll just ask Jones."

Puller came upon Jan Bodey on one of his rounds; the bodyguard was digging furiously on a hillside. "What the devil you doing, Bo?"

"Fixing the Colonel's hole, sir."

"Oh hell, Bo. Just knock off the rocks. Don't bother about me. This isn't the first time I've soldiered."

He handed a folded American flag to Bodey: "You keep this, old man, and take good care of it, or else. We're going to fly it over Seoul."

Puller passed the night on this ridge, an eminence covered with young pines planted by Japanese in a reforestation project.

Major Treadwell had a night call from one of his outposts, Warrant Officer Harold Sobel, an old Navy pilot who had joined the Marine amtracks. Sobel called by radio:

"Major, I'm being gassed."

"You can't be. There's no gas around."

"Oh, I am! I know what I'm smelling." After a few desperate exchanges Sobel went off the air, and returned later in great relief: "Major, it's okay. It's not gas. It's garlic. I backed over a patch coming in to this old house. Smells like hell, but I'm okay."

Puller was awake at 3:30 A.M., calling the battalion commanders and making plans for attack at dawn. Orville Jones appeared with a miraculous breakfast: poached eggs on toast served on the lid of a cartridge case, the eggs liberated from villagers and the bread filched from the Navy. Puller grinned: "My God, old man, how'd you turn up this stuff out here?"

"Colonel, we're just sorry there's no Virginia ham and grits."

The jeep began its combat career before daylight. Jones

drove the Colonel down the ridges to a road on the front where a gap lay between the First and Fifth Marines. The first unit to reach the crucial road junction was a fire team from Company A, First Battalion, led by Corporal John R. Petree, a North Carolinian. This party approached the roadway warily, expecting the enemy—but when they emerged from the brush Petree saw a jeep: Puller was studying the gray mist with his field glasses (the old survivors from Haiti). Jones and Bodey sat in the front seat; Bodey was surrounded by a small arsenal, a shotgun, an M-1, a BAR and a .45. The country was unbelievably dusty, but somehow, though he was never seen to shine them, Bodey's weapons gleamed.

Contact was made with the Fifth at 6:30 A.M. when a company from Murray's command came to the junction. The trap was now closed on North Koreans in the Inchon pocket. The mopping-up was already under way when Puller left this spot; a regiment of South Korean Marines was working through the city, house by house, flushing the enemy.

Not long after 7:30 the assistant division commander, General Eddie Craig, an old friend from Nicaragua, found Puller near the front. Craig had checked the link between the regiments, then sought Lewie: "He was having a cup of coffee and things at his CP looked very calm and collected for the first morning after a landing."

By 9 A.M. Puller had driven 4000 yards inland against machine gun and mortar fire. To the north, beyond their view, there was more serious fighting; a sortie of six Russian-made tanks into the outskirts of Inchon had brought down Marine Corsairs with napalm and bombs to scatter the supporting infantry and finish off the tanks.

Puller's swift drive hurried adjoining forces in an effort to keep pace. Captain Ray Stiles of Ridge's Battalion saw that the secret was not only in Puller's incisive orders: "He gave us pride in some way I can't describe. All of us had heard hundreds of stories about him, and today, though we couldn't actually *see* him doing great things, he kept building up our morale higher and higher, just by being there.

"When we were moving up, two companies from the adjoining battalions marched abreast and got a little mixed. One of the kids yelled: 'What outfit you with, Mac?' 'The Fifth Marines. How about you?' 'I got it better. I'm in Puller's.'

"The troops in the First thought of the Old Man before they thought of the regimental number."

The attack moved toward Kimpo airport on the road to Seoul, the captive South Korean capital, and resistance grew as the afternoon wore on. The enemy used the ridge country to advantage, forcing Puller to press all the harder. Major Treadwell reported about 3:30 P.M.

"Colonel, I'll have to take the amtracks back for servicing."

"Can't be done. We'll fight until dark."

"We can't go on like this, sir. They're falling out for fuel and repairs. They'll have to go back sooner or later. I don't want to work on 'em after dark."

"Nothing doing. No tanks or tractors attached to me ever go to the rear."

"What do you want me to do?"

"Get your service men up here and start to work."

"I never heard of that before, Colonel."

"A little something I thought up on the spur of the moment, Major. Just for this war."

It did not strike Puller as absurd that a Marine hailed him at the roadside late in the day with a copy of the *Reader's Digest* fresh from the States, indicating an article by Alexander de Seversky on the future of air power. "Shove it down my pack for me, old man," Puller asked. The Colonel read the article in the night, a prediction that even aircraft carriers were doomed, that sea power was outmoded, and that only long-range bombing could defend America.

"I wish that bird could be out here tonight," Puller told Rickert. "I'd like to see him check the air power we had overhead today—every damned bit of it off the carrier decks out there in the pond. This is going to be a great war for the experts."

By the end of September 16 the assault phase of the landing was over and the two regiments had reached the Force Beachhead Line marked so vividly on command maps. Puller had gone far beyond in some areas, for his outposts were three miles inland. The drive for Seoul would open in the morning. The capital was seventeen miles away.

The Colonel had an introduction to one of Bodey's myriad talents during the afternoon. They were speeding along the highway when a tire blew out, caused by a shell fragment. Puller stepped to the roadside for a look across the valley and before he turned back the tire had been changed. The giant Bodey simply held up a corner of the jeep while Jones slipped on the spare wheel.

By September 17, D Plus Two, General MacArthur was impatient to go ashore from the command ship, *Mount McKinley*. He saw that his blow to cut Korea in two had taken the enemy by surprise and that chances of ending the war were good. The commander had an intimation that this might be known to history as the most dazzlingly successful of all amphibious strikes, the crowning achievement of his career. He had been in that mood from the early moments of D-day when he radioed Vice Admiral Arthur D. Struble, the task force commander, after the first good news from shore:

> The Navy and Marines have never shone more brightly than this morning.
> MacArthur.

By now, as he knew, planes were dropping his leaflets some two hundred miles to the southeast, among Red troops at the Pusan perimeter:

UNITED NATIONS FORCES HAVE LANDED AT INCHON

Officers and men of North Korea, powerful UN forces have landed at Inchon and are advancing rapidly. You can see from this map how hopeless your situation has become. Your supply lines cannot reach you, nor can you withdraw to the north. The odds against you are tremendous. Fifty-three of the fifty-nine countries in the UN are opposing you. You are outnumbered in equipment, manpower and firepower. Surrender or die. Come over to the UN side and you will get good food and prompt medical care.

Planes buzzed shoreward on their regular schedule over the harbor: Eight F4U's went in from the carriers every ninety minutes, giving close air support to the Marines. And every ninety minutes other flights of eight more Corsairs and four AD's went over, giving deep support by bombing oncoming enemy troops, highways and railroads.

Major General E. K. Wright of MacArthur's staff noticed the commander's interest when messages came from Puller's First Marines, for the Colonel was one of his favorite field officers of World War II. MacArthur gave orders to take him ashore.

"Nothing would do," Wright said, "but that he immediately visit Chesty Puller."

A message that General MacArthur was on his way went to Puller; the commander wanted to give Chesty a Silver Star. The Colonel sent his reply while enemy fire was bursting on his ridge:

"Signal them that we're fighting our way for every foot of ground. I can't leave here. If he wants to decorate, he'll have to come up here."

After the entourage made other stops, General Wright led MacArthur to a ruined house at a roadside. Wires led in and out, but Puller was not there. Marines pointed ahead, toward the fighting.

It was the adjutant, Major Reeves, who first saw the distinguished visitors. He looked down from the hill to see a long string of jeeps, six or eight of them, and shouted to Puller: "General MacArthur's coming."

"How do you know?"

"Who the hell else in Korea could have enough jeeps for a funeral, and have a light-colonel dog-trotting out in front?"

Puller was atop a cruelly high ridge, but the seventy-year-old commander made it, puffing a bit, trailed by most of his staff and some reporters. He shook hands with Puller and studied the terrain. Puller had his hands in the pockets of wrinkled fatigues; he sucked at a pipe. A folded map in a hip pocket seemed to be his entire paraphernalia of command.

"We thought we'd find you back in the CP," someone said.

Puller patted his map. "This is my CP," he said.

MacArthur turned abruptly to Puller: "Colonel, your regiment is performing splendidly and I am gratified to present you with the Silver Star." He fished in his pocket for the medal, but found he had none. "Make a note of that," MacArthur told reporters. Puller turned back to the east, pointing.

"Thanks very much for the Star, General. Now if you want to know where those sons of bitches are, they're right over the next ridge."

Percy Wood of the Chicago *Tribune*, who was taking notes, reflected that he had never seen such a cool customer as the disheveled Marine colonel.

MacArthur and his staff watched shells burst on the town of Yongdong-po two or three miles away; Seoul lay beyond.

"How long do you think you'll need to get into Seoul, Colonel?" MacArthur asked.

"No more than three or four days, General."

"How are you so sure, Puller?"

"Every prisoner we take says there's only cadets left down there. We'll roll 'em up."

"Don't forget what the cadets of Virginia Military Institute did at the battle of New Market."

"General, these aren't V.M.I. cadets—and those V.M.I. boys weren't fighting Marines, either."

MacArthur laughed. "The Marine conspiracy is complete. But I wish they would come out and fight. It would make things easier for you."

"We'll make it. If they're dug in, we can use napalm and have no trouble. It's nothing to what I hit at Peleliu. There I lost sixty-two per cent of my men and seventy-four per cent of the officers."

"I landed at Moratai the day you got to Peleliu," the commander said. "I picked the Moratai date for that reason, to go in under your wing. That got us a six-hundred-and-fifty-mile jump in the war. I believe I was the first Army man to give all my ground forces to the Navy to handle. I trusted them to land me, cover and guard me for a month. They did. The Navy never failed me."

Puller guided the party for a couple of hours as they wound toward the front lines. At one stop MacArthur turned to him as if he had forgotten: "Colonel, I want your regiment to have an Army Presidential Unit Citation, a symbol of my respect for these troops with you. They're magnificent."

The procession passed the scene of the day's big fight, an encounter with half a dozen enemy tanks which were now smoking wrecks, some of them still blazing inside.

Puller explained that these tanks had been killed with the 3.5-inch bazooka, which the Army claimed it could not do. "It's just a matter of having the kind of men who can get in there close enough to knock out these caviar cans. One of my finest boys was killed here today—got two tanks and was after a third."

MacArthur expressed his sorrow and looked at the tanks with interest. He joked of the Army-Marine rivalry. "I know the Marines are good," he said, "but just how you got the enemy to fake a fire fight just so the commander could see this, I don't know."

The Corps seemed to be winning an ally.

In the next days when MacArthur's staff officers and correspondents came for jeep rides on the front Puller took Jones aside and whispered: "Take 'em up and get 'em shot at. Let 'em see what this is all about."

Jones tried valiantly, but at the first sign of firing, his guests shouted for him to halt. Jones had a load of reporters in the jeep one morning when bullets kicked up a dust at the roadside. There was a chorus: "Stop!"

"Nothing but spent bullets," Jones said. "Couldn't do more than sting you."

"Ain't you afraid, Jones?"

"Nah. All you guys sitting on that side are shielding me. They'd never drill me."

The reporters leapt for the ditch.

The afternoon of September 18 was busy for Puller—and for Oliver Smith, whose division headquarters were now ashore. On the trail of MacArthur came Major General Frank Lowe, a hardy Maine man on a top-secret mission as "personal spy" for President Truman. The Marines were impressed at first glance: Lowe arrived with a "Task Force"—an Army jeep with a 50-caliber machine gun mounted between its seats, complete with a driver and gunner. Lowe and Puller got on well from the start, for the sixty-six-year-old National Guard veteran of two wars did not stand in awe of the Army and observed combat with a knowing eye. Oliver Smith had warned Puller of his coming: "The President has sent Lowe for a personal report. Be careful, but show him all the interesting sights you can."

Within a day or two Lowe was telling correspondents: "When things get rough I feel safe only when I'm with the Marines. Greatest fighting men I've ever seen, anywhere."

He was regarded with suspicion for some days, however, since President Truman had attacked the Corps shortly before the Inchon landing and had branded it as "nothing but a police force." In response, many of the Division's vehicles were painted crudely: "Truman's Police," and tanks bore the legend "MP."

There was another call late in the day from General Smith: "Brigadier General James Gavin has come with a team from Washington to observe close air support. He's on his way up."

"Fine," Puller said. "He couldn't come at a better time. We'll start hitting hard in the morning as soon as the mist is off the valleys. He'll see a show."

Although Gavin does not recall it, this is Puller's memory of the incident:

"General Gavin came to our CP, on the reverse side of a ridge from the enemy, and with the staff and our tactical air man I briefed him on the situation. The Reds were dug in on a parallel ridge about fifteen hundred yards away, and in the valley between. At dawn Marine planes came in, close behind the infantry, bombing and strafing the enemy while two artillery battalions fired support.

"The planes came in so low that they were blown upwards fifty feet or more by bomb blasts. General Gavin said, 'Can I believe my eyes?' We called off the air, lifted the artillery to the opposite ridge and the infantry went ahead. We took the positions with light casualties.

"General Gavin told me, 'This close support of yours must be given first priority. I never dreamed air could be used like this. When I get to Washington I'll see that your Marine system is adopted. But there's one thing I'm afraid I can't put over—having these air people on the ground with your troops.'

"I explained that this was the secret of the whole business, that the Corps had proved after years of work that the only way to make the system effective was to have air liaison on the ground radioing to the fliers, men who understood the language of fliers, and men they trusted. When General Gavin left us he was most enthusiastic. He said he would do his best to see to it that our ideas were adopted, but I heard no more about it."

General Lowe, who spent the night near Puller, explained his mission to the Colonel: "The President wants me to tell him what I see, honestly and without pulling punches. He doesn't want long documents, just the real dope. I'm going to do my best. I don't want any publicity, either, because he wants me to work anonymously."

He showed a small card mounted in plastic, announcing him as the President's personal emissary and asking the cooperation of all hands. Lowe handed Puller a letter.

"Here's a report to the President. I'd like you to look it over."

"I shouldn't be reading a dispatch like that, not to the President."

"It's all right. The President and I understand each other. I want to get your ideas."

Puller read the letter—a paean of praise for the Marines as the finest troops in the world, who had saved the war on almost every occasion they had fought. There was plentiful credit for the First Regiment and a report to Mr. Truman of what captured North Korean officers had said: "We cannot make our men stand and fight those men who wear canvas leggings, even if we threaten to shoot them."

Puller said he could add nothing to such a report, but made an offer: "You don't want to send it like that to the White House—penciled on ruled paper. Why not try to have it typed at the rear?"

"No. The President knows me well. He's a good scout, and he doesn't stand on ceremony."

After sundown on September 18, after a day of rapid advance by his men, Puller rode toward the front in the jeep, which Jones drove in the dark with the other vehicles on the road. There was still heavy firing to the north, the aftermath of a day's hard work by Murray's Fifth Marines, who had seized Kimpo Airfield, the finest in the Orient.

As they hurried by a line of infantry they passed a truck with its lights on. Puller stopped Jones, jumped out and charged the offending driver. "What the devil are those lights about, old man?" He did not wait for action, but knocked out the headlamps with the butt of his .45.

Heavy mortar fire fell in Sutter's Second Battalion position along the road to Seoul at night, killing two and wounding three men. At about 6 A.M. Puller, now solely responsible for the highway, attacked, since Murray had detoured around the airfield. By 9 o'clock Ridge's battalion had passed the small town of Sosa, after a lively tank fight which broke a stubborn North Korean stand. Ridge held his objective on a commanding hill by 11:30. Sutter had hard going; the road was heavily mined and some tanks lost their treads.

The dangers did not keep Puller from the roads. In the afternoon as Jones and Bodey sped along the highway, with the Old Man snoozing in the back seat from lack of sleep the night before, Jones spotted the deadly finger of a buried mine in the rut ahead. He wrenched the wheel sharply.

Puller jerked awake: "Damn, Jones, you trying to kill me?"

Jones stopped. Some excited Korean women came to the roadside, pointing to the mine, and gestured, signaling an explosion. Puller grinned. "Must have missed it at least an inch, Jones."

Jones and Bodey had already settled into a routine. They stayed in the command post area when Puller worked or slept there and even at night their communication system worked perfectly. Puller gave a shrill whistle and Jones or Bodey replied with a curious "Whoooooooeeee" reminiscent of the Rebel Yell. Marines who heard it for the first time were awed: "My God, that ain't no way to talk to a colonel!" But understanding between the three was complete.

In the push toward Seoul, when Puller was driving the swifter phase of the attack, Jones saw a man the troops never knew:

"The Colonel was always far away in his mind. He'd look at you and tell you what to do that day and you could tell he was thinking out something else. His whole eye wasn't with you. It would come out now and then as we rode along, from little things he would say to us. He'd been putting himself in the enemy's shoes, figuring out what he'd do if he were a Korean commander. He knew just where every gun emplacement ought to be, too, I mean. He would talk about that.

"Sometimes he would be in his seat, nodding, like asleep and then stir and tell me and Bodey: 'Never underestimate the enemy, boys. If you don't figure him to have as much sense as you've got you'll have trouble.' Sometimes he would talk about his wife and children; he never forgot 'em."

In Jones's eyes Puller was unerring in dealing with enlisted men or administering justice.

On one of the fiery days of the drive toward Seoul a popular chaplain, Father Keating, captured five North Korean soldiers and herded them along as prisoners. He hailed a passing Marine jeep driven by a Private Wolff: "Son, take these prisoners off my hands. Get them to the rear before they're hurt."

"I can't, Father. I'm running ammo into the edge of town, and they're getting low. I can't stop to do it."

"Private, this is an order. Take them over."

Wolff looked rearward at the burning city. "You mean they're mine now? Under my responsibility?"

"Yes."

Wolff pulled up a light machine gun and sprayed the group, killing all five. The outraged Keating went to Puller and demanded action. The Colonel listened carefully, ordered Wolff arrested, and the priest went away content that he had done his duty.

Ten minutes later Puller asked an aide: "What outfit was it that lost all those boys last night?"

"Barrow's company, sir."

"All right. Give that boy Wolff a BAR and send him up there."

Jones took the story to his cronies as an example of military justice at its best; it spread through the outfit to become part of the Puller legend.

The First Marines ran into harder fighting on September 19, on a day when one battalion—Hawkins's—made an eleven-mile trip by truck in a realignment. (The Fifth Marines had already crossed the deep Han River.) It was after dark before Puller's advance company got to Hill 118, a dominant ridge near the river, but at last Captain Bob Barrow's men dug in on the slopes, ready to meet the expected enemy reaction. At daylight, a counterattack which hit Barrow's lines was driven off and the enemy retreated to nearby hills, which were then taken by Marines in bloody frontal attacks.

At the same time Sutter's men beat off their second tank attack in two days, with grenades, rockets and bayonets. The day passed with Puller seizing, bit by bit, the commanding high ground for the final assault on Yongdong-po. The Seventh Marines landed in support at Inchon that day and the First Division was complete. General Smith sent Litzenberg with the Seventh to the north, on the upper flank of the Fifth. The plan was now for Murray to strike down the far side of the Han River, open a crossing for Puller at Yongdong-po, and join a twin assault on Seoul itself.

Sutter's battalion first probed into the industrial suburb and lost many men in a confusing jumble of dikes, warehouses and dwellings. Aided by planes and artillery and a bold charge of Bob Barrow's company, they broke the enemy. Barrow was cut off during the night but halted several fierce counterattacks and when dawn came Yongdong-po was taken.

By nightfall of September 23, Puller was ready to cross the Han and join Murray, who was fighting bitterly in the hills northeast of Seoul. Ahead of the First, just beyond the river, was a maze of pillboxes whose guns had been carefully set with overlapping fire zones. The terrain was perfect for defense, an old training camp built by the Japanese before World War II. The North Koreans were dug in for their last stand. Marine Headquarters knew that the winning of the city would be costly, but the newly formed X Corps, commanded by General Edward M. Almond, was optimistic, and predicted that the enemy would flee.

In the seven days since D-day there had been 1148 Marine casualties, 145 of these killed; 20 more died of wounds and 5 were missing.

Puller's regiment crossed the Han at a spot where he was not expected and the enemy was unprepared. Palisades towered over the stream; on the far side was a narrow beach which could accommodate no more than two landing craft at once. It was an unpromising crossing, but it worked like a charm for Puller.

By 7:45 A.M. Sutter's men were crossing; they drove rapidly 400 yards beyond the river under sniper fire from pillboxes. A few rounds of artillery burst near the CP which Reeves had set up for Puller on a slope; two men were wounded. Puller behaved as if the crossing had been planned a year earlier. He disregarded a squabble between Jim Treadwell and headquarters as to whether LVT's or DUKW's should be used, turned his lead battalion over to Treadwell and watched the ferrying.

Major Reeves approached Puller with a Silver Star sent by MacArthur. Puller turned back to the river. "Send it to my son for me, old man." He did not mention the medal again.

By now, across the river, Sutter had turned east toward Seoul, approaching ridges which guarded the city. Puller crossed and found Jack Hawkins on the far shore with his men at rest.

"What the hell are you doing, Hawkins?"

"I'm in reserve, sir."

"Well you won't be in it long. Get in the attack."

"Sir, we can't pass Sutter. He's moving fast. Are you going to stop him so I can get out front?"

"Hell, no. I had trouble enough getting 'em started."

"By the book they should halt and then we pass through them."

"We're using no book here today, Hawkins. I'll give 'em the word to cease fire when you pass. We can't give the enemy time to catch his breath. Take up double time."

Hawkins's men trotted out to obey the unprecedented order, through the ranks of the lead battalion. When Bob Barrow's company came onto the heels of Easy Company of Sutter's battalion, Captain Carter ran back: "What the hell's going on?"

"This constitutes a passage of lines, friend, Puller style."

"My God, I don't even get time to get 'em out of the way?"

"Not today. On to Seoul."

The first such passage of lines in military history was soon complete; to observers it seemed a mad race for the commanding hills ahead, where the enemy waited in confusion. The advance pushed so rapidly that Barrow's company literally ran to the top of Hill 79 and raised a U.S. flag over a schoolhouse—though they were not yet in the city proper.

Captain Bob Wray, of Hawkins's C Company, was amused by the sight of this flag-raising, for, as he saw it, the schoolhouse ground had been taken by his second platoon and the conquerors lay on their hill, watching, as Barrow's men put up their flag and had their photograph made.

When Wray reflected upon the pell-mell charge he was surprised to discover the lesson Puller had taught: "We thought that Puller just wanted to impress General Lowe with the fast drive. The passage of lines was not really formal, just knots of men driving across the landscape so fast that the enemy didn't have a chance to get organized before our lines were whipping through them.

"This scared the company commanders at first, when we were told to just take over and bang in there. But Puller knew the value of that shock to the enemy and that all the niggling around with flanks and keeping fancy formations would have cost him lives. We barreled on, and it worked to perfection."

Puller was not content with the quick thrust by his infantry to the screening hills. He had been promised tanks which were still held by Murray. A runner from the Fifth Marines had reached Puller at the riverside with a message from Murray that he was heavily engaged and could not spare the tanks.

"I'm busy right this minute, old man," Puller said. "But don't you move a muscle. As soon as I can leave these troops you're going to guide me to your CP and we'll find out something about those tanks."

A few minutes later the young Marine led Puller to Murray's sector, and after a brief, heated exchange the Colonel had made clear his claim to the tanks.

"I can't advance," Murray said.

"Have you tried the bayonet?"

"No. We're deep in the hills, fighting like hell."

"Then use it, and follow the First Marines into Seoul."

The tanks soon joined the First and the push picked up speed. There was rivalry between the two regiments which would continue until Seoul had fallen.

The forward elements were pushed so fast from Puller's roving headquarters that communications men in the front lines began defending themselves against the driving Colonel. Puller laughed when news of their device came to him: Infantrymen held rifle barrels against their walkie-talkie radios and scraped them to garble the Colonel's rasping voice as he called commands. He could grin in memory of his own trials at Guadalcanal and Cape Gloucester, when he had told his communications sergeants: "Cut off that damned radio. We know what we're doing, and those headquarters birds will never figure it out."

On the morning of September 25, Puller's line of attack lay directly into the heart of Seoul, through its main streets. At sunrise he got two platoons of Pershing tanks to help him—though the big vehicles fell into a fight just after crossing the Han and were in trouble until a flame thrower came up to demoralize the enemy. The count: 15 enemy dead and 131 prisoners, all in twenty minutes.

On this day General MacArthur announced that the city of Seoul had been secured—an announcement which later brought a wry rejoinder from Oliver Smith: "The following day we had 185 battle casualties; the next day, 183. It wasn't secure for us."

The Marines still faced their major battle for the capital of South Korea, and the hottest of it fell to Puller's First.

When Captain Bruce F. Williams, the tank commander, reported to Puller with an effusive story of his victory by the river, the Colonel spoke without removing the pipe from his mouth: "I'm not interested in your sea stories, young man. You're forty-five minutes late. Get your unit into position. We've got fish to try."

The day of September 25 netted Puller only 2000 yards into the city's edge, even with the aid of air strikes and artillery. Along a rail embankment and from rooftops and houses the enemy fought fanatically.

Puller watched from a hillside as artillery shells burst among the houses. He had a sad note in his voice as he muttered to Reeves: "They'll remember us for a thousand years for this, and hate our guts."

A reporter, H. D. Quigg of United Press, found Puller in this spot:

"The colonel was sitting in a turnip and onion patch atop a high hill. Swallows fluttered and dipped over thatched and corrugated tin roofs of a shabby collection of huts on the side of the hill below us. A little boy exercised on crude parallel bars. A little girl in a red skirt and white blouse watched him. The roar of artillery and bombing and strafing planes was all about.

"'The North Koreans,' Puller said in his deep drawling voice, 'are defending the city in such a way as to force us to destroy it. There's a billion dollars' worth of publicity in it for them.'

"Puller picked a blade of grass and nodded toward a plastered, stone-walled house with a sewer-pipe chimney and an adjoining stable from which came the neighing of a horse.

"'I hate to see people in a shack like that get hurt,' he said. 'The same family probably has been living for generations in that same dump.'"

A few minutes later, Quigg met a young Marine officer who talked about Puller: "I've never seen a guy like him. I'd follow him to hell—and it looks like I'm going to have to."

As much as Puller regretted the destruction of Seoul, there was no other way.

General Almond's staff urged a bypassing of the city, but General Smith realized that the determined enemy would defend Seoul house by house, yard by yard, and insisted that the drive be pressed to destroy the defenders. X Corps clung to its story that North Koreans were fleeing Seoul, a report originated by an airman who had seen civilian refugees on the roads. At the end of the day Almond ordered the Marines to press on to catch the "retreating" enemy. Even then advance Marine elements were under flank fire and commanders realized that a night attack through a strange city, against well-prepared enemy positions, could be suicidal. There was no revision of orders. The attack was on.

Smith warned Puller and Murray personally: "Move deliberately and concentrate on streets you can identify in the dark. I'll get you a fifteen-minute artillery barrage."

Lieutenant Colonel Ridge was in Puller's front, holding a roadblock in a street when the attack order came. His line consisted of two rifle squads, a heavy machine gun section, a rocket squad and a few men from a platoon of 75 millimeter recoilless guns. The command post for the block was in the cellar of a nearby house. In the darkness Ridge sent an eight-man patrol through mine fields, with three native guides, to make contact with the nearest Fifth Marine post.

Corporal Charles Collins led this patrol, which ran into an enemy battalion gathering for a counter-attack down the street, a force so strong that it seemed certain to wipe out the roadblock. Collins sent his men back under fire, covered them with his M-1, hid in a house, and reappeared the next morning in Korean dress.

The battle boiled past him. At 1:45, when Puller was supposed to jump off, there was a fresh Marine artillery barrage, since the first had not satisfied Colonel Puller. Just as this second barrage fell the North Korean battalion charged the roadblock—supported by Russian-made tanks. The tanks caused numerous Marine casualties, but the new salvos of shells tore the enemy attack with perfect timing. When the big guns had been roaring for almost two hours the roadblock commander was told that they could fire no more; the tubes were on the point of burning out. The North Koreans returned to the attack just at that moment.

Three tanks and some infantry appeared around a curve and blasted the outpost at short range; a few rounds from 155's scattered them, but within a few minutes the sally was repeated. This fighting continued through the night and losses were high on both sides. At 5:30 the Marine rifle companies were running out of shells, and jeeps and trailers crowded the streets, carrying in ammunition.

The fire of artillery and mortars had set a record for the Korean war; the four battalions of artillery had fired all shells at hand and had depleted a nearby Army dump. The

4.2 mortars had fired 326 rounds, and the big 81's, 650 rounds. The .50-caliber machine guns had used 120 boxes, or 30,000 rounds.

In the first light the wreckage before Puller's lines was spectacular. That section of Seoul was blasted to rubble, including ruins of three of the big T-34 Russian tanks and one T-70, several anti-tank guns, and the bodies of 250 enemy troops. Ridge's men were pulled back from the scene to repair their weapons, for most of the barrels were burned out.

Reporters found Puller at his command post in early morning and questioned him about the "fleeing enemy."

"All I know about a fleeing enemy is that there's two or three hundred lying out there that won't be fleeing anywhere. They're dead. Some fleeing they were doing last night, too."

The night's battle had put Lieutenant Joe Fisher's Item Company to the test. The burly veteran who had been a sergeant and platoon leader on Iwo Jima was one of Puller's favorites, of whom he often said: "One of the best company commanders who ever lived. Equal to any assignment. As long as I'm around he'll lead Item Company."

Fisher dug in for the night on an isolated hill in the city's factory district, overlooking the roadblock, which was on his left flank. From midnight to dawn he beat off waves of attacks.

Fisher called for artillery at the same time other front-line commanders asked for help, but between barrages the North Koreans swept up Fisher's hill in banzai charges, urged by a shrill-voiced commander in their rear. Item Company's weapons, including machine guns, fired at top speed and bodies piled up below them. Toward the end, when attacks weakened, the fight turned into a turkey shoot and Fisher's men slaughtered the enemy. They were glad to see the sun rise. Fisher never forgot that daybreak:

"I looked down the hill behind me and saw a man hurrying up toward our position. I could see that he wasn't lugging ammunition and thought it must be an important message too hot for radio. Then I saw that it was Colonel Puller's runner—and he had brought us a bottle of Black and White Scotch. My God, were we glad to see that! We passed it down to the platoon with the most casualties and they rationed it out to those who needed it most. We knew then that the Old Man was thinking of us—and in fact never forgot us."

At 9 A.M. on September 26 the First and Fifth Marines began the slow, hard drive into the heart of the city. In the Fifth's sector Murray's vanguard entered Seoul from a rugged spur where it had fought in the night. Puller's route was down the streets, the chief of them a main thoroughfare where streetcar tracks were laid. The enemy fought at every intersection, from roadblocks of sand-filled rice bags, most of these defended by anti-tank guns. Snipers worked from houses, high and low. Captain Bob Wray of C Company said: "Our kids were green at the start, because they'd never had street fighting, but by the end of the first block they were veterans. They learned to cover each other and watch the windows and doors of houses and to handle the intersections." This company, supported by tanks, drove to the railroad station in Seoul, where there was a fierce fight.

Puller's orders went out to the company commanders: "Keep the men moving. All the buildings and rooftops are full of Reds. Leave the snipers if they're beyond your reach. Let the Korean Marines mop up behind you. Circle to the side streets when you have trouble at the barricades. The important thing is to keep moving."

Just behind the front rank of infantry during the hours of storming the city, Puller walked with Jan Bodey. Orville Jones had the jeep a few yards to their rear. Jones weaved back and forth in the column; Puller was beside the lead tank.

Jones watched a grenade fly from a house; it landed eight or ten yards behind Puller, but the Old Man did not so much as turn around when it exploded. Jones got a flying fragment in a tire and halted to fix the flat. He was some time in catching up with the Old Man and Bodey.

Puller was astounded by Korean civilians in the street, hundreds who stood on the walks with calm disregard of flying bullets and bursting shells, among them children five or six years old who played soldier with wooden guns.

Bob Wray watched David Duncan, the news photographer, squatting in the street, casually taking pictures. An old man came to the door of his home, held the door ajar and swept the threshold and walk without taking notice of the battle.

Puller had a sudden thought: "These Oriental civilians

are tougher than our people. What it will be like when America is invaded, God knows."

An International News Service reporter was near Puller when bullets kicked up dust at the Colonel's feet and wounded an enlisted man a few yards away. "The damned snipers," Puller said. "They're a nuisance, but that's about all. We can't waste time sending patrols after them, or we'd stop the advance. It would cost us more. I've told 'em to drive on and let the ROK's mop it up. They'll do it better anyway. They're the only ones who can tell the cowboys from the Indians."

Puller came upon Marines dug in around a barricade, taking cover from fire down the street. He walked among them with the pipe stub in his mouth: "Get up, boys. Get up and go. That's the quickest way to get it over. If you're going to get it, you can get it in the holes, too." The line moved on.

Joe Fisher saw Puller in the street: "He was going along where the fire was heaviest, just like he was back in Pendleton and as if he didn't know there was a fight within miles. I couldn't express how much good it did me and my troops to see him steady like that, just puffing that pipe. It made us feel like we could do no less than he did. If there has ever been another one like him in the Marine Corps I never saw him in my day."

Corporal John Blazer saw Puller several times in the day's fighting: "Whenever he saw a Marine walking away from the front, whether for ammo or to an aid station or whatnot, Puller would frown at him with a hard, unfriendly stare. When he saw one of us going toward the front, for any reason, he'd wave and smile and call, 'How you doin', old man?'"

Lieutenant Lew Devine of Fox Company met Puller at midday, when they were near Kung Hua Noon Circle, where North Korean resistance pinned down two companies and stalled the advance. The area was a litter of stones, fallen and burned timbers, bricks, enemy dead and ruined anti-tank gun mounts. Black smoke boiled in the streets and cut visibility. A chaplain, Otto Sporrer, went by with a team he had organized, carrying wounded on metal shutters ripped from buildings.

Devine had been slightly wounded two days earlier and corpsmen had slit his jacket; he now wore the blouse of a dead sergeant. Puller watched Devine and his rifle platoon take a barricade and swarm over enemy bodies to the front. The Colonel caught up with them.

Devine treasured a memory of it: "Puller put his arm around my shoulders and said, 'Great work, Sergeant.' But Rickert, his exec, had come up by then and told him I was a lieutenant, not a sergeant. Puller's face changed, and he spat and said, 'Lieutenant!' and went off. I believed, as most of the second lieutenants did, that Puller preferred sergeants to us, but the junior officers were strong for him, just the same."

Bill Ferrigno, the veteran who was field sergeant major, had a glimpse of the Colonel: "It was like going through hell, passing down that Seoul street. And who should we pass in the middle of it but Chesty? It was so hot that I thought the grenades and ammunition we carried would explode. The flames almost met over our heads from the burning houses, but the Colonel didn't seem in the least concerned. It gave us an extra push."

X Corps headquarters announced that most of the city was under control, but there was even harder fighting ahead. After a short night's rest Puller's advance drove on, using lessons of the previous day with telling effect.

Barricades grew larger as they advanced and the infantry worked out a pattern with the engineers: Riflemen crawled to windows and rooftops and alleyways and drove defenders behind the barricade; engineers ran into the streets, located mines and shouted, "Fire in the hole!" Troops took cover as explosions rocked the street. Then tanks came in. The enemy broke from the roadblock to flee wildly down the street—only to fall before the machine guns and heavier tank weapons. The troops spent about forty-five minutes on each barricade in the process. Enemy fire was so heavy that the tanks were swept clean; all radio antennae, phone boxes and periscope heads were shot away. In front of this fiery assault the Corsairs worked, coming down just over the rooftops to sear the enemy with napalm and bombs. In the end the North Koreans were terrorized and the advance picked up speed.

Before 11 A.M. Sutter's battalion raised an American flag over the French consulate and at 3:37 P.M. one fluttered over the U. S. consulate. Murray's men fought their way toward Changdok Palace in these hours and the flag-raising race was on in earnest. Credit for the official victory went to Puller's men, led by Bill Ferrigno, who put up a flag over Ambassador Muccio's residence.

Ferrigno and Easy Company of the Second Battalion were first at the American Embassy, tramping through tons of official papers which Red looters had tossed to the floors. A jeep arrived from regiment with a flag and orders that the oldest man should raise it. Ferrigno was the senior, at forty-four, but gave the job to Platoon Sergeant Fichter, who had been in the midst of the fighting, and Old Glory soon fluttered over the damaged residence. A few Korean onlookers cheered; the troops moved ahead.

There were complaints from X Corps headquarters, as well as from Murray's Fifth Marines. An officer from Almond's headquarters growled: "Ever since that flag-raising picture at Iwo Jima, I'm convinced that a Marine had rather carry a flag than a weapon."

"Not a bad idea," Puller said. "A man with a flag in his pack and the desire to put it on an enemy strongpoint isn't likely to bug out."

Puller made headquarters for the night in Duk Soo Palace, which was battered but usable. Some of the staff urged the Colonel to move to the nearby Banto Hotel; he went to inspect it. Puller walked the empty corridors with Major Reeves and halted at the sound of voices, flung open a door and saw two of his Marine privates drinking beer. American beer.

"Where the devil did you get that?"

One of the young men tugged at a bell pull. "Rang for it, Colonel. First-chop service. We'll fetch you some."

Officers found the hotel cellar intact, stocked with fine British and American whiskies. The amiable Korean clerk on duty grinningly accepted any chits which the Marines would sign and the potables were lugged out by the case.

Puller left the place ruefully: "We can't have our CP here. The Army will be in here by tomorrow, and they'd run us out." Twelve hours made him a prophet; the hotel became X Corps headquarters.

Puller returned to Duk Soo for the night. Jones and Bodey carried the blankets of the Colonel and General Lowe into a shrine, a portion of the palace, where Lowe slept on the floor and Puller on an old sofa which was too short for him. He curled up, but in the morning found that he had pushed both ends off the sofa.

There were official visitors in the morning. A helicopter brought Admiral Won Yil Sohn of the South Korean Navy, whom Puller had met before the war. Oliver Smith also arrived, and not long afterward General Clifton B. Cates, the Marine Corps Commandant, out on a tour of inspection.

Puller explained to Cates his plan to sell his new friend Lowe on an expansion of the Marine Corps to three divisions, but neither Smith nor Cates shared Puller's enthusiasm. "It might be too big and unwieldy, Lewis," Cates said. It would be little more than a year before Puller saw his dream of a bigger Corps come true—though without the proper shipping to move troops in an emergency.

Puller had come to trust Lowe completely and no longer regarded him as a spy; he tried to have "Task Force Lowe" decorated by the Corps, but Lowe protested that he must remain anonymous, and that an honor from the force he was praising so highly in his reports to President Truman might cause embarrassment.

One morning Lowe and Puller sat together in a cemetery as troops moved past them in a road.

"My Lord, Puller, look at those sergeants of yours!"

"Well, what's wrong with 'em?"

"Nothing, man. They should all be lieutenants in the Eighth Army, right this minute."

"Don't start your proselyting around me, or I'll take you behind the hill and have you knocked off, where the Army would never find you."

Lowe laughed.

A few minutes later they overheard two of Puller's runners gossiping:

"The first atomic bomb the Russians drop will hit the White House, and the next one will get the Pentagon."

"Like hell they will! Them Russians know what's causing all this confusion out here. They wouldn't dare touch them places."

Seoul was hardly secure, but on September 29 General MacArthur led President Syngman Rhee and a herd of newly arrived staff and flag officers from Tokyo to the Capitol for a ceremony restoring the city to the Republic of South Korea.

Original plans had been much grander, but General Smith had sternly rejected requests for bands and honor guards from his Marines on the ground that the men were still fighting and could not be spared. MacArthur reduced the honor guard and imported Army men from Tokyo for the purpose.

At 11:45 A.M. the historic occasion opened with a procession through rubbled streets to the assembly hall in the Capitol. Smoke still rose from the cellars of the building and from the skylight dome overhead slivers of broken glass fell now and then upon the celebrities.

Suddenly, about mid-morning, the streets had filled with big staff cars, all Army—spotless Buicks and Chevrolets brought in from Japan. These made Puller's jeep seem more battle-worn than ever. Still, the Old Man was one of the four Marines summoned to the festivities, and Jones made ready. Puller had argued in vain with Oliver Smith that he should be excused from the ceremony, since his job was not restoring governments. He also grumbled over the order that he must wear his battle helmet, when he had come all through the fighting in his wrinkled cap.

Puller literally had to fight his way into the ceremony. Before they left Duk Soo Palace the Colonel came upon Bodey, who was sloshing suds over his head and chest from a helmet half full of water. "What's going on, Bo? Don't tell me you've taken to bathing."

"Colonel, I've got to get ready for the shindig."

"What shindig?"

"Yours. Ours. The MacArthur party, Colonel."

"Knock it off, Bo. If you get cleaned up you can't go with us. People will think we haven't been working."

Bodey lumbered across the Palace yard after them, grinning as he pulled on his jacket. Puller deliberately postponed his own sprucing up, though he had not shaved since the landing and his utilities were rumpled and dirty. They crawled into the jeep.

Bodey was in the rear seat, drinking from a quart of liberated Korean beer and nibbling from a bag of peanuts. They were halted at the gate of the Government House compound by a natty Army MP officer, a major. Puller looked mildly at the MP, inspecting his gleaming black boots and white shoe laces. His jaw tightened when he saw that the laces had been ripped from silk parachutes; he remembered the shortage of chutes in the drive on Seoul, when supplies had been needed.

"Sorry, Colonel," the MP said. "Only staff cars allowed in the compound."

Puller took the pipe from his mouth: "Major, I left my staff car in Japan a month ago, when they told us there was a war going on here."

"I was told cars only, sir."

"This is our real estate, Major. My boys took this damned place."

"Orders, Colonel. I'm sorry. I can't let you pass."

Puller stood, clinging to the windshield. "I don't give a damn what your orders are, old man. My orders are to go in there, and I'm going. Now get out of the way."

"Not today, Colonel."

"Listen, Major, if you wanted to throw your weight around you should have been here when you could get your nose bloody, while the First Marines were coming through these streets."

"My orders, sir. You cannot enter here."

"Run over him, Jones!"

Jones gunned the motor so abruptly that Puller was flung back into the seat and Bodey sloshed himself with suds and nuts. The MP major scampered out of their path, taking refuge on a patio. He shouted after them: "I'll see you when you get out of there!"

Puller entered the Capitol. MacArthur and Rhee were already there, with some UN officials and Ambassador Muccio; most of those present were staff officers from Tokyo, all in fresh uniforms. There was only a little clutch of the Marines who had fought the campaign: Smith, Craig, Murray and Puller.

Around the walls was a ring of spit-and-polish Army MP's, also from Tokyo—the honor guard. Eddie Craig muttered to Puller: "It looks like they'd have the decency to give some of the honor to men who captured the damned place."

Puller retained vivid memories of the few minutes there:

"General MacArthur prayed and talked for half an hour, so fervently that you couldn't tell one from the other. All the time, tears as big as buckshot came down his cheeks, evenly spaced, like soldiers at drill. He talked about our struggle there and the people of Korea, but the only promise he made that stuck in my mind was his promise to reunite North and South Korea.

"I watched Syngman Rhee closely and talked with him a little. A very tough old man, a fighter. He had fought the Japanese for thirty or forty years, trying to save his country. His fingers are ruined, all broken and gnarled where the Japs tortured him by putting his hands through clothes wringers. He fought the Communists just as hard, too—and why America, ten years after the Korean war, turned him out after a few yells from students, probably Communist-inspired, is more than I can see. Suppose he did gain a million dollars or so? How many millions did we waste in Korea? And how many Americans have been in rackets out there?"

When Puller emerged from the building the MP major was not in sight, and it was perhaps as well. The Colonel was fuming: "They never said a damned word about the Marine Corps. Not one. Can you imagine that? Who the hell do they think carried this whole fight?"

One of the most demanding operations in Marine history had ended—all but the first two days of it spent in a role that traditionally belonged to the Army. The Division had sustained 2430 casualties, 414 of them dead. Of this total, 1064 had been in the last five days, in the streets of Seoul and its outskirts. Murray's Fifth Marines had the worst of it, with 1038 casualties, 177 dead. Puller had a total of 787, with 92 dead. Litzenberg: 368 total, 72 dead.

The enemy's losses in fifteen days were 4792 prisoners and over 13,000 total casualties; vast stores of weapons and supplies had been captured, much of it U. S. Army issue.

In the afternoon of the day of liberation, Jones appeared at Duk Soo with the jeep piled so high with rice bags that it was like a rolling haystack.

"What you got there, old man?" Puller asked.

"Money, Colonel. Billions. We're rich."

"Son, don't you know it ain't worth a dime? That's Korean. They declared it worthless, to start all over again."

"Maybe some of 'em don't know it yet."

"Get rid of it, and let's get a bath. Find us a bath house, and make sure they've got plenty of hot water and soap."

The bath house was dominated by an enormous hollowed stone under which a fire blazed; the water steamed. They soaked and scrubbed for a long time, and when they dressed, Puller opened his wallet for the first time since leaving the ship at Inchon. He had only ten-dollar bills.

"I can't give that bird this much money, Jones. You got money?"

Jones fished out a million-wan note.

"Hell, don't you have something smaller?"

"What difference is it, Colonel? I saved a few of the biggest bills, anyway. I junked the rest, like you said."

The Korean was beside himself with joy as he bowed them out, overcome by his new riches.

The Division rested for a few days after the capture of Seoul, but on September 30 General Smith was ordered to plan a landing on the opposite coast, at Wonsan, so that he could cut across country to the North Korean capital of Pyongyang and effectively end all resistance. He was given no details as to the shipping, but was told that he would have only four days for loading and getting to sea. The target date for Wonsan was October 15.

There was more talk of being home for Christmas, or even Thanksgiving—though there were already disquieting rumors of Chinese troops moving along the borders of North Korea.

As the First Marines rested in camp near Seoul, Puller improved his acquaintance with Jan Bodey and Orville Jones.

Bodey, who was slow to anger, had been bedeviled by a young radio operator in Puller's headquarters who had ambitions as a practical joker. The boy disregarded Bodey's warnings and continued to pester him. One morning as Bodey lay asleep in the sun near Puller's tent the young radioman crept up a slope toward him and reaching with a slender twig tickled Bodey's ribs. Jones was watching idly.

Bodey struck like a rattlesnake. Jones could hardly believe his eyes: "He carried his .45 in a holster on his left chest, and he snapped it out of there with his right hand and in one motion pulled that thing into cock, sighted on the kid's helmet and fired. I've never seen another man who could do that with one hand, give him half an hour."

The bullet zinged off the kid's helmet and the radioman dropped as if dead.

Puller came from his tent: "What in hell's going on, Bo?"

"Your radio kid, Colonel. I shot him."

"In God's name! What for?"

"He aggravated me."

Puller peered at the boy's body, over which Jones was crouching, took a long look at Bodey, shook his head and disappeared into the tent. Within a few minutes Jones had the boy out of his faint, much sobered, and with a throbbing head.

Puller would not tolerate drunkenness, but he once came upon Bodey, lying prone in the CP area, looking suspiciously as if he'd had a few beers, at least. The California giant was blowing his mustaches in great snores. Jones expected the Colonel to explode, but he only said mildly: "Put a rock under his head, Jones, so he won't strangle. We can't afford to lose a good shotgun. Corps commanders are easier to find."

On October 6 the Division was moved by trucks back to the west coast, near Inchon. Puller's letters to his wife revealed the changing times, and his state of mind:

> Everything is quiet and I now have little to do except get my reports prepared and submitted. I wish I had a flair for writing, as then I am certain this regiment would get the credit due them when the history of this operation is finally written. Now everyone knows, but in a few years what is written will govern. Rest assured that I will do a better job of getting the facts in my reports than I did in the past war. I will also claim everything due the regiment.
>
> Many times I have regretted that my English education was cut short during the first war. Please do your best to impress on our children the necessity of taking advantage of every opportunity . . . in this hard old world of ours.
>
> I am getting more homesick now for you and our children and pray that we will soon be reunited.
>
> It appears that the Division will not be employed further unless the other crowd again bogs down. Then we will be shoved into it in a hurry. It is funny how so many persons have regained their courage since the 15th of September. . . .
>
> When we will be reunited I do not know, but Russia and Red China appear to be keeping out of Korea and if this continues our Army should not have too much trouble in winding up the Korean war and releasing the First Marine Division. . . .
>
> I was in excellent shape for the entire operation, even better than I thought I would be; as you know I had not been taking much physical exercise during the past four years. The answer is that you took good care of me, Virginia, you deserve all the credit.

On October 10 Puller went with Homer Litzenberg and Ray Murray to dine at the headquarters of General Almond at X Corps. Lewis was staggered by the display of luxury and wrote his wife in detail:

> The Army staffs live better than ours. An excellent salad with fresh lettuce, tomatoes, celery, spring onions with good

mayonnaise; soup; roast beef, mashed potatoes, biscuits, butter; apple pie, coffee. Drinks, of any kind, before the meal, which was served in courses.

He wrote of the fine china and linen and silver and white-uniformed soldiers who waited on the table. After dinner Puller fell into a conversation with the operations officer:

"How big is your staff, General?"

"Well over three thousand."

Puller wrote of it to Virginia:

> Imagine! Enough men to form an additional infantry regiment! If we become involved with Russia, our Army must change its ways and in a hurry, or else we will go down in defeat. This is not my way of fighting a battle, and if I had authority I would change such things in less than 24 hours. Our country and our leaders had better wake up, and that in a hurry. May God protect us if we do not!
>
> Before this meal, for 26 days I had food out of a can, almost entirely. If you wanted it hot you had to build a fire under the can. I will always remember my dead and cripples and those of other units either buried or evacuated. . . .

From the time of the landing at Inchon the order had been that no dead Marines were to be buried; the bodies were lashed in ponchos and saved for the appropriate time and place. When they returned to Inchon the First Division held a funeral for its dead at the outskirts of the city; loading of the ships was under way at the docks.

Puller took two of his battalions to the cemetery for the ceremony and was standing in front of them as the bugles pealed and a flag was raised. He heard men growling in the ranks behind him. He did not turn:

"You guys keep quiet."

The sound subsided, but when it was over they besieged him, pointing: "Look there, Colonel. Look at that damned rag they're flying up there—that United Nations thing. Hell, there's hardly a man lying out here but what's a Marine! How the hell they get that way, that United Nations crap?"

Puller went to General Smith:

"I can control my men, but tonight, after they get out in town and get some liquor, I can't swear you won't have trouble. I'm serious about this. They feel keenly about that damned United Nations flag over our cemetery."

Smith took the problem to General Almond. Before sunset the UN flag had been replaced by the American flag, and the Marines were content.

On October 15, from aboard the USS *Noble*, ready to sail for a port unknown to him, Puller wrote his wife again:

> A month ago today we landed and I am thankful that those days are past. . . .

He replied to an expression of concern in one of her letters over a newspaper story:

> I assure you, Virginia, that I never in my life have ever made a statement that "I like to fight." Rest assured that I do not *now*. I just want you.

He asked whether five-year-old Lewis had received the Silver Star, or a North Korean bugle he had sent by an officer. The Division convoy left Inchon the next day, bound for the east coast—and a new war in North Korea.

XVII

THE HORDES OF CHINA

KOREA had become a martial race track. After the Marine stroke from Inchon to Seoul, the Eighth Army had popped out of its little perimeter at Pusan in the southeast and begun the chase of fleeing North Koreans. While the conquerors of Inchon-Seoul were at sea, circling the peninsula to fall upon the port of Wonsan, there was heavy northbound traffic on land.

Gossip swept the ships almost as spectacularly as the attacks of dysentery which laid low thousands of men. No one could foretell the next move in this strangest of wars: There were rumors that the Division would sail for home now that the war had ended—and others that it would invade China. General MacArthur's visit to newly fallen Pyongyang, the North Korean capital, lent weight to his prediction of an early peace; President Truman appeared in Toyko. All was optimism.

Puller behaved as if the war might never end. Before they left Inchon he had spoken with General Almond: "You'd better see to it that we get winter clothing before long, General. I've lived with that northern climate. We'll freeze."

"Oh, it'll be there. We will see that you're properly clad."

"Make sure the supply people don't delay. It's impossible for a stranger to understand. One day it's summer, and the next that Arctic wind hits you, and like turning over your hand you have ice, and temperatures start dropping toward zero."

"When the time comes, Puller, we'll take care of it."

Lieutenant Lew Devine saw the Colonel on deck one day

after Puller had come from the barber with a shaven skull. Devine laughed, and the Colonel laughed too.

"It's the only time I ever got away with laughing at a superior officer," Devine said. "He had dignity and common sense enough to realize he looked funny, and he didn't chew me out, as any other officer would have."

Devine did not realize that Puller was following one of his strict orders—that all troops should keep scalps cut short to avoid the menace of lice. Sergeant Jones overheard the Colonel upbraiding a company commander who ordered that there would be no more shaven heads.

When an Army health team visited his troops to lecture on the threat of disease from lice and other pests, Puller introduced them: "I want you to pay close attention and do as they say. I know how to write your parents and tell 'em you've been killed in battle for your country—but damned if I can write and say you were done in by a buggering louse."

The troops howled with laughter.

There was not quite unanimous appreciation for Puller on the trip. Captain Bill Hopkins, of Roanoke, Virginia, had just come from the States to command headquarters company of Jack Hawkins's First Battalion, and what he first heard about their commander from Hawkins was not reassuring: "Why, when we had our big attack across the river outside Seoul, and I asked Puller which way to go, he just told me, 'Straight ahead, dammit, Hawkins!' How do you like that?"

Hopkins was receptive to such tales, for he had been so chilled by Puller legends before leaving home that he told his wife on parting: "I've landed in Puller's outfit, and I might as well throw in the sponge."

The young Virginian enjoyed Hawkins's stories of his own World War II experiences, when he escaped from a Japanese prison camp after capture at Corregidor, but he noted that Hawkins was "nervous." Hopkins looked forward to a meeting with Puller.

The Division thought it would never go ashore. Dysentery spread until it affected almost every man on the foul ships. When the convoy reached Wonsan it was found that some 2000 mines had been sown in the harbor and the ships turned south—setting off fresh rumors of a return home. For almost ten days they steamed back and forth off the coast until, on October 25, the harbor was cleared and they entered Wonsan. Bob Hope and Marilyn Maxwell and an entertainment troupe had landed ahead of them—for the ROK army had taken the city some days before, and busy air traffic moved overhead. The Marines debarked with relief from the voyage they called Operation Yo-Yo.

Puller went ashore in one of Major Treadwell's landing craft to be met by a broadly grinning Oliver Smith: "Congratulations, Lewie! You've made it. Your board has selected you for Brigadier."

Puller wagged his head. "By God, if it hadn't been for this war, I'd never have got that star." There was a mild celebration ashore that night for the new general-to-be.

Back in the States, Mrs. Puller had the news before her husband, for Corps Headquarters had called from Washington. She had immediately driven the six miles to the nearby school in Urbanna, Virginia, where Virginia Mac was in the sixth grade and excitedly called her daughter outside to impart the news that her father was to become a general.

The child's manner was disappointingly calm: "Well, Mother, I'm really not too surprised. Didn't we always know he would?"

On October 26 the Division was split into small segments by the high command. Oliver Smith was dismayed; he sensed danger in the planned drive through North Korea to the Yalu River, despite the "Home By Christmas" spirit in the streets of Wonsan. His protests were in vain: Litzenberg's Seventh was sent northward by way of Hamhung toward Chosin Reservoir and the Yalu; Murray's Fifth would follow; Puller's First would remain behind, itself divided into isolated battalions. Hawkins was sent to Kojo, a small town on the coast thirty-nine miles below Wonsan; Ridge was sent inland into hilly country at Majon-ni, twenty-nine miles away. Puller remained in Wonsan with Sutter's battalion.

The Division would soon be spread over an unfamiliar territory of three hundred miles from north to south and sixty miles east to west.

Litzenberg was one who took little stock in General Mac-Arthur's announcement: "The war is very definitely coming to an end shortly." On his way north the regimental commander told his officers: "If there is anyone here who expects an easy walk to the Yalu, erase it from your mind now. We're going to have to fight. It's most important that we win our first one when we meet the Chinese."

Puller agreed, though he made no pronouncements; he probably had more knowledge of the Chinese troops than anyone in the command. Just now he was concerned with defending the Division's rear.

Captain Hopkins got his first glimpse of Puller in action during the day: "He called in Hawkins and his Quartermaster officer and went over every single item with Hawkins, equipment, ammunition, geography, transport. He had more concern for supply than any officer I'd known. I'll never forget his final words to Hawkins:

"He said, 'There's not a damned thing down there at Kojo. Besides, if they do hit you, you're strong enough to knock hell out of 'em.' "

When the battalion was on its train, rattling along behind an antique engine, with the riflemen in gondola cars, Hawkins told his staff: "How about that? Puller says there's nothing down there, and in the next breath says if they *do* hit you, you can knock 'em. We've got to watch our step."

The train passed through several tunnels where the enemy might have trapped them but all was peaceful on the route to Kojo, which they found to be a beautiful, unspoiled resort town overlooking white beaches and a bay. The battalion passed a quiet night in a perimeter near the village, relieved a ROK unit the next morning, and watched its allies pull out on a train, overcrowded with women, children, pigs and chickens. The First Battalion was now alone except for some ships in the bay—even the supply dump it was ordered to guard had gone, consumed by the ROK's and their families.

Hawkins laid his positions with care, since defense of the low-lying spot was difficult. Captain Wes Noren's B Company blocked the approach from the south, the men strung along a series of rice paddies. To the west there were other companies—C under Captain Bob Wray, and A under Captain Bob Barrow. As the men dug their holes, Hawkins looked with some concern at columns of refugees passing nearby; he herded them into an area on the northeast of the village for the night. North Korean soldiers in civilian dress, or their spies, took note of the Marine foxholes on the ridges and waited for darkness.

The night was cold and quite dark and there was a fifty per cent watch, with half the men alert and others zipped into their sleeping bags. Without warning a shower of grenades struck the first platoon of B Company in the south, followed by a charge. A fury of firing did not stop the unseen enemy; many Marines were bayoneted in their sleeping bags. The attack struck both ends of the B Company line.

Lieutenant George Chambers of B Company, who had an adjoining position with his platoon, got a warning by radio: "We've been overrun, and the rest of us are pulling back to battalion area." The command post was almost three miles away.

Before 1 A.M. Captain Noren called Chambers from his southern line: "They're about to push me out, and I've got Hawkins's okay to pull back. When I get to the road, I'll signal you, and you bring up the rear."

"Okay. Will do."

As Chambers took his men across the railroad in this movement he was literally doused with fire from rifles, machine guns and grenades. Chambers thought for a time they were also under mortar fire, but things happened too fast for analysis:

"They gave us a banzai rush and it was hand-to-hand there in places. We fought 'em off, but the rearguard was scattered. We spent the night in the rice paddy there, and the water froze over on us. We called in ship's gunfire on the village because we figured the Red troops were in there."

Fighting was sporadic through the night. Hawkins had put in early calls for help to Puller in Wonsan. Captain Hopkins thought these calls "a little excited," and Puller thought he detected the danger of panic.

The Colonel remembered the night: "Hawkins was burning up the air with calls for support, and of course Almond got them at Corps, and then Smith at Division, so Almond jumped Smith and Smith jumped me. I got my spare battalion ready to move."

By daylight at Kojo, Hawkins was taking all precautions. He had reports from each company by now; the bodies of the Marines in sleeping bags had been found. Hawkins felt that they had been hit by a very strong North Korean force. Later in the day he ordered artillery to fire on a small boat in the bay and some ROK troops were hit. Captain Hopkins, who had a machine gun outfit in position, retained a vivid memory of the morning: "There were refugees coming from Kojo, and I was ordered to get them with the guns, since there might be Red troops among them. I told my men to fire over their heads. We did hit a couple, and they called for doctors. We sent some medics. That shooting has never gone out of my mind."

Hopkins also remembered his battalion commander's urgent orders, given often that morning: "All right, now. We've got to hold to the death. Don't give up a foot of ground, whatever happens." Officers around headquarters became increasingly tense as the morning wore on, though the enemy was not now within view. .

In Wonsan, Puller put his men aboard two trains. As they left he told his officers and senior noncoms: "Keep it from the men, but we may have trouble getting down there. This damned line is so rickety that it may not hold up the train; we've got some bridges to cross and some tunnels where they could hit us. We'll hope for the best."

Sergeant Major Ferrigno held his breath on the ride: "We went, barely creeping, over the trestle which trembled under us. It was the deepest ravine I can remember in my life, but the men were as unconcerned as if they were at home. They didn't know a thing."

Corporal Harvey Owens of Fox Company, a Minnesota Sioux who had won a Silver Star at Yongdong-po, needed no officer to explain the peril to him: "It was the tunnels that worried me; we dragged through those long, dark holes on open flat cars, and I knew damned well the Reds could blow us to hell any minute they wanted to. They just didn't think of it."

Puller found it all quiet in Kojo; he prowled around the position with little comment, but morale soared from the moment of his appearance. Hopkins overheard him talking with the men of a mortar platoon: "Can you boys shoot those things?"

"Colonel, you know it."

"Got enough ammo?"

"Yes, sir."

"Well, by God, tonight we're going to make some Communist fannies roll. You be ready."

He climbed the hill to the inaccessible CP of Hawkins, puffing a bit. Captain Hopkins was impressed by the resulting change in the atmosphere:

"Puller was relaxed as he could be. He had no orders about holding to the death. All he said was, 'Well, if they come back tonight, we'll get our share.' Neither Hawkins nor any of the rest of us got nervous while Puller was there. He settled us down."

There was no doubt that there had been trouble, for there

were twenty-three bodies, forty-seven wounded and thirty missing, though all but four of the latter turned up. Puller concluded that a northbound enemy outfit had found Hawkins's battalion in its path and brushed against it in retreat.

The Colonel spent two or three days in Kojo. He supplemented his field rations with the aid of Jones and Bodey, who found the cellars of burned Kojo filled with a harvested crop of Irish potatoes—most of them roasted to a turn. Bodey also boiled a liberated chicken in his helmet and despite the dire warnings of staff officers that Korean pork was unfit for consumption the two foragers roasted a pig. Bodey scoffed at critics: "Whaddya mean, it's no good? Five minutes ago he was running down the road. A good, healthy pig."

The two battalions returned to Wonsan by sea and camped around the airfield for a few days. Hawkins was ordered back to the States and was succeeded by Lieutenant Colonel Donald M. Schmuck. The regiment prepared to join the movement to the Yalu.

General Lemuel H. Shepherd, Jr., now commander of the Fleet Marine Force, Pacific, visited the front and made a trip to see Puller.

"Congratulations, Lewie," he said. "I know you'll make a fine general officer."

The Colonel became involved in a minor matter of discipline. One of his Marines, alone on the roadside, tried to hitch a ride with an Army MP who passed in a jeep and when the soldier increased his speed without stopping, showering him with mud, the Marine fired a shot over the MP's head. The boy was arrested by an officer and three MP's from Corps Headquarters, sentenced to sixty days' restriction, and his papers came to Puller. The Colonel scratched on the document: "This man can't be guilty. In the opinion of the undersigned, if he'd fired at the MP, he'd have hit him." General Smith advised against this endorsement: "You can't do that, Lewie."

Puller's reply: "Hell I can't. I signed it, didn't I?"

Puller wrote home daily. He sent Virginia Mac a five-dollar check for her good school marks, adding some parental admonitions:

I am very proud of my family and I expect you to do

well, plus, in everything you undertake. The difference between success and failure in this life of ours is mostly hard
work, so you must constantly work to try to improve yourself.

To his wife:

I am tops physically. I passed both my physical examination for promotion and the annual one. I am sorry you
seem to have gotten the idea that things were not going to my
liking. I will be more careful how I write you. I know that
higher echelon decisions are none of my business and I only
mention them to you.

He sent her some native carvings and enclosed the old
sweater he had worn from Inchon to Seoul, saying that it had
shrunk after a washing, and might now fit their daughter.
He added:

There are constant rumors about the return of this Division, but I will believe it when I see the order. If I am
promoted soon that may result in my being ordered
home. . . .

On November 8, when he heard from her that she was
worried over gloomy newspaper accounts, he wrote:

Damn this and all wars. . . . I hope and pray that now
the elections are over, President Truman will call out the
National Guard. The first Roosevelt said it was a good policy
to speak softly and carry a big stick. Since the last war we
have only had a big mouth and no stick. . . .

On November 10, the Marine Corps's birthday, Puller
used a captured North Korean sword to slice a 100-pound
cake prepared by his bakers, an enormous confection trimmed
with radishes and jelly in lieu of candles. He also delivered
a brief speech. He read an article from the manual as required by regulations, thrust it into his pocket and shouted
to his troops:

"Now that's complied with, and I want to tell you something straight. Just do one thing for me—write your people
back home and tell 'em there's one hell of a damned war on
out here, and that the raggedy-tailed North Koreans have
been whipping a lot of so-called good American troops, and

may do it again. Tell 'em there's no secret weapon for our country but to get hard, to get in there and fight.

"I want you to make 'em understand: Our country won't go on forever, if we stay as soft as we are now. There won't be any America—because some foreign soldiery will invade us and take our women and breed a hardier race."

He wrote his wife afterward:

> Today is the Corps' birthday—175 years of age. How I wish you and I could celebrate 175 years of married life and have our precious children and their children and grand-children with us. . . .
>
> The situation has improved in the last several days, but as I have often told you, only a terrible defeat will change our present system, which is leading us to disaster. . . . An Army Division commander sent twelve of his officers over to my place with a request that I conduct an evening school for them. By the time they left it was midnight and I was quite sleepy. . . .

A new test of Puller's men was at hand. Lieutenant Colonel Thomas Ridge had led his battalion along the hairpin turns of a mountain road to Majon-ni on October 28, his mission to block the road junction against Red troops moving north. They found the place an insignificant village perched among hills so rugged that the scene might have been the Swiss Alps. Majon-ni was twenty-nine miles from Wonsan. It now became the western outpost of a territory of 15,000 square miles under Division control. For some days the battalion screened refugees passing the town, put some North Korean soldiers into a prison stockade, and prepared defenses. Puller sent a couple of road convoys with supplies, but these were ambushed and several men were killed and wounded in each.

There were frequent attacks on the perimeter and in one long night fight the line was broken; it was restored the next morning. Sergeant Major Ferrigno, when he went out on a relief party with Easy Company, found things hot: "In fifteen seconds we had about forty casualties, a number of them dead. We made a quick recovery and really cleaned house, but of course the dead don't come back. My boys came to me with five rascals in full uniform under their white robes and two of these were North Korean sergeants who had left two of my sergeants dead on the road. So a little decision was made." The captives were shot.

The battalion ended its defense of the place with 1400

prisoners taken, 525 enemy dead, and an unknown number wounded. Ridge's losses were 20 dead and 45 wounded.

The arrival of Army support now made possible a Marine concentration to the north; some of the 7th Infantry Division came ashore under Major General David G. Barr, with the 3rd Army Division just behind. The push to the Yalu began in earnest. Headquarters in Tokyo scoffed, but Marines reported Chinese prisoners in stockades as early as November 1, and ROK troops reported the Chinese armies had crossed the Yalu on October 16.

General Smith had left Puller behind in Wonsan, at Corps Headquarters: "I want you to attend the briefings and let me know what goes on. I must know the state of their minds." Smith went to join Litzenberg and Murray in their exposed positions around the Chosin Reservoir, amid some of the most rugged country in the Orient. Freezing weather had arrived as he left.

Puller retained a colorful memory of his adventure as a Marine spy in X Corps Headquarters:

"One morning before Thanksgiving I went to a briefing. General Almond gave us the word for the day, then said he had a plane waiting for him, that he hoped to get back in the early afternoon—but that if he did not, he wanted the staff to care for some visitors from Tokyo, General C. A. Willoughby and some of his people.

"I knew Willoughby was MacArthur's intelligence chief, so the next morning I asked General Clark Ruffner, our Corps Chief of Staff, what had happened.

"Ruffner told me: 'Well, when Willoughby asked Almond how things were, and Almond told him about the Seventh Regiment fighting Chinese Reds, and said that both sides had casualties, Willoughby said: 'That's another goddam Marine Corps lie.'

"So Almond led him out to the prisoner of war stockade and showed him about eighty Chinese sent down by the Seventh. Willoughby left us without so much as a word, and got back on his plane."

Every night, at midnight, the Korean "situation map" was sent out from Tokyo, with detailed positions of the forces. The night before, Puller noted, the map showed only UN and North Korean forces—and no Chinese. But this night, abruptly, it was revealed that "about half a million Chinese troops" were scattered over the map, some of them as far as 100 miles south of the Yalu.

Puller told his staff: "Now that's the fastest damned troop movement in the history of the world, gentlemen. You'll never see another such. And don't forget this lesson: Tokyo wouldn't admit we had Chinese fighting us even after the Eighth Army was in flight, because some damned staff officers hundreds of miles away willed it to be so. You can't will anything in war."

After the Marines had taken Seoul, the Eighth Army of the United Nations forces had driven through the capital, moving rapidly northward along the Korean west coast. To meet them, Chinese Communist armies had marched 1800 miles northward since mid-August. The Chinese strategist, Chu Teh, at first concentrated against the Eighth Army position in the northwestern hills, but when the Marines landed, he hurriedly switched much of his power to meet and overwhelm them in the Chosin Reservoir region. The Chinese drove between the Marines and the Eighth Army, and maneuvered into a position from which they could attack each force at will.

Litzenberg's Seventh Marines had been first of Smith's Division to meet the Chinese—and destroyed the 124th CCF Division. That was only the beginning, for ten Chinese divisions, more than a hundred thousand men, were moving to meet the Marine thrust.

Puller was in Hungnam when the survivors of a tragedy of Army unpreparedness swarmed back from the interior: "An all-Negro artillery battalion, sent to the front, was delivered by a Negro transport battalion to its place in the front lines. On the way back, by night, the transport men were ambushed by six North Koreans, and the four hundred truckers ran without a fight, leaving the vehicles standing with lights burning and motors on. The Reds burned the trucks and hiked up the road into the rear of the artillery battalion, which they sprayed with fire and scattered. The Reds took all guns. I saw many of the broken men who came back. It was a terrible day for our arms."

The Colonel made a personal check of supplies before they took the road northward. Lieutenant Joe Fisher of Item Company reported his men short two parkas and within a few hours a runner brought two of the heavy jackets. One of these bore the name, "L. B. Puller," and the other that of Rickert, his exec.

Major Don Ezell, walking through the regimental area, saw another young Marine with a parka bearing Puller's name. Ezell stopped him:

"What're you doing with that parka, son?"

"Colonel Puller gave it to me."

"Yeah?"

"Sure did. He took it right off when he passed me, and said by God I needed it more than he did. He wouldn't have it no other way."

"Okay, Marine."

"Yeah, and you know what he said? He said that if he got cold, he could go to the warming tent."

When officers asked him how he would guard against the cold the Colonel said, his pipe chattering in his teeth: "Hell, I can always find something, old man."

He found a great deal, in the end, for when the regiment got into trucks for the trip to the Chosin Reservoir Puller wore: A suit of cotton underwear, woolen underwear over that, then a wool sweater, and shirt. A pair of green wool trousers, one pair of windbreaker trousers, a fleecy woolen vest, and over all, fleece-lined trousers and coat. "How the hell I'm going to walk is a mystery," he told Jones, "but by God, I won't freeze."

Puller got into the jeep with Jones, Bodey and a radio operator. They were in close contact with elements of the long column as it crept up the snowy passes. When they went over the first crest Puller shivered anew: "Holy smoke! That damned wind came right out of the heart of Manchuria. I believe Genghis Khan was right—nobody can win a winter campaign in the land of the Mongols."

They passed through Schmuck's battalion, which was dug in at the foot of the highest hill on the road. Near the pass at this peak they saw the bodies of Chinese soldiers, victims of a fight with the Seventh Marines. Puller climbed from the jeep to inspect them and pointed to their packs. Jones held up a square of dirty white cloth and a straw mat.

"They're a hell of a lot smarter than we are in the field," Puller said. "They cover themselves with that cloth when there's snow, and a plane comes over. They can hide a whole damned division from us, right along this road. They use the straw on open ground. It's too sensible an idea for

American forces—and too cheap, so we'll never have advantage of it."

The jeep made it up the final slopes in style, and they arrived in the rugged little plateau at Koto-ri at 2 P.M., just as it began to snow. Puller stepped out into the raw wind, shaking, and Jones fished under the hood to remove a can of C-ration beans he had wired to the manifold. He handed it to the Colonel, smoking hot. Puller was incredulous: "Old man, how the hell did you keep hot chow, the way we came?"

Puller shook so violently from the cold that he ate no more than a bean or two at each spoonful. Jones and Bodey worked fast to erect the Colonel's blackout tent. They laid canvas on the frozen ground, placed logs around the sides and poured water at the edges, instantly sealing the canvas to the ground and making the tent airtight. They installed a potbellied, oil-burning stove, which was soon red-hot. Puller and Rickert lived alone in this tent, with Jones and Bodey sleeping some ten feet away. Several times each night Jones or Bodey crept out to see that there was still oil in the Colonel's tank.

The camp was noisy all night, for the motors of the vehicles had to be run twenty minutes of each hour to prevent freezing. Jones had thoughtfully put diesel oil into the crankcase of the jeep, so that he had to warm the motor only every other hour.

There were many days of twenty-five below zero on this plateau; the Marines at first suffered shock from the cold, and for a few days many men were handicapped by a low rate of respiration. Canteens must be carried inside clothing and every man was ordered to keep a spare pair of socks inside his uniform, next to his skin. Only dry rations could be used, since the frozen wet portions caused intestinal distress. Within ten days most riflemen in the mountains lost fifteen to twenty pounds, though they were already hardened by weeks of hard fighting. Gunners used hair oil on their weapons and wiped them lightly; artillery fired more slowly in the extreme cold and ranges were shortened. Complaints about the Shoe-Pac boot were numerous; frostbite became common. A new Navy boot, using the principle of the vapor barrier, was hurried from the States; it prevented frozen feet, but Puller said wryly: "It's fine, except for one thing. You can't march in it."

The warming tents were filled with men seeking relief from the cold on the lines; it was estimated that a man lost two percent of his efficiency for every degree the thermometer fell below zero.

By November 27, after long delay, the Division pulled more closely together. Ridge's battalion of Puller's regiment defended Hagaru-ri, some four miles north of Puller's at Koto-ri. Murray and Litzenberg held Yudam-ni, about six miles northwest of Hagaru. Puller was left in Koto-ri with only Allan Sutter's battalion. Schmuck was down the hill at the foot of the pass, defending the rear at Chinhung-ni.

On his second day at Koto-ri Puller saw his first live Chinese enemy—an officer who stood 800 to 1000 yards away on one of the towering hills over the perimeter. The Red was studying the Marine position through glasses. Puller called Lieutenant Colonel Merritt Adelman of the 11th Artillery.

"You see that bird? I want you to blow his head off."

Adelman went to a 105, bore-sighted the weapon and fired. To the astonishment of the little group he made a direct hit on a tree near the Chinese officer; the tree and the man disappeared. Chinese troops moved in on them in force during the afternoon and night, from every side, but one outfit did not make it. Puller discovered an enemy column on pack mules moving through a gorge, an artillery train. When the animals descended into the pass he called in Marine planes; the Corsairs burned the enemy train with napalm, and no survivors emerged from the gorge.

The Chinese broke through the perimeter briefly that night in a penetration along the unfinished railroad track which ran through the area. Puller's tent was torn by a few bullets.

Sergeant Major Ferrigno had seen the last relay of his troops finish chow just before nightfall: "Hurry and clear the area, men," he said. "It'll be dark in five minutes, and I want you to be ready." The railroad tracks in this area were raised five or six feet above ground level; when Ferrigno's Easy Company men crossed the tracks they were caught in volleys of rifle fire. A platoon of white-robed Chinese had come over the snow undetected into the heart of the company area. Ferrigno remembered it: "They all died in the same spot as though they'd been stacked like cordwood. Except for seven or eight they were all in one pile. They hung on to one another and just rushed madly at us. We had three dead and six wounded, mostly by bayonets. Half of these Commies were armed with beautiful Thompson submachine guns. I never knew why they didn't push the attack, with the hills so full of Commies, but I guess they saw what happened to that platoon and hung back."

Puller's tent was some 800 yards away, but he soon appeared to inspect the scene and returned early the next morning. "Fine work, boys," he said, as he inspected the enemy dead. Many of the Chinese were found to have frozen hands and feet, already turning black. Morphine was found on some of the bodies and the story spread that all enemy troops were doped. Suicidal attacks could be expected.

A prisoner told Marines the enemy had lost 400 men in this night attack. Before the fighting was over Puller had word that a truck convoy had been ambushed on the road from the south, just three miles away; rescue was impossible. From hills on every side of the perimeter, Chinese fire was heavy during the day. The enemy blew a tunnel and bridge on the railroad below the Koto-ri position, cutting the line to Hamhung and the Marine base on the sea. For two days Puller called in heavy air strikes upon concentrations of Chinese in the surrounding hills.

Things were even worse in the two positions to the north of Puller. At least six Chinese divisions had been identified in the area where Murray and Litzenberg fought; on November 26 these two posts lost 95 dead and 543 wounded in night-long attacks. Hagaru was preparing to fight for its life. An offensive launched by the Fifth Marines was called off after the day's grim news from the west: The Eighth Army had collapsed, one wing of it was torn to pieces and the Chinese were slashing deep into the lines. The Marines must now defend themselves against an enemy free to approach from any direction through the frozen mountains.

The night of November 27 tested the men at Yudam-ni, when three Chinese divisions fell upon two Marine regiments. The enemy cut the road to Hagaru and sent their assault battalions in quilted uniforms and sneakers into the Marine lines with disregard for casualties. The first waves were driven off with great losses, but others were thrown in through that night and the next. To the dismay of the Chinese commanders, not even envelopment of Marine command posts slowed the tempo of the fighting and the Americans staged vicious counterattacks even when many platoons had been reduced to the size of squads. There were not enough tents for Marine wounded and the less seriously hurt were piled outside, close together for warmth, covered with straw and tarpaulins, as doctors worked over the more than five hundred casualties.

Lieutenant Colonel Ridge was short one company at Hagaru on November 29 when the Chinese made their major effort to exterminate the force in his four-mile perimeter. The valley was crowded like a circus village with a variety of small units and Korean troops mixed with the battalion, but there were too few riflemen to hold the line; one sector was almost unmanned when the enemy struck just after dark. A blaring of bugles, the fiery flowers of trip flares and land mines and the flowing threads of tracers opened the night—and the roar did not cease until dawn.

General Smith was a guest for the night, and at the height of things, when Communist soldiers were prowling through the perimeter, looting instead of pressing home attacks, bullets rattled through his quarters. In the end the understrength battalion, aided by two artillery battalions, beat off a full Red division; one of the attacking regiments had ninety per cent losses.

By morning the defeat of the Reds was clear from the snow-covered piles of dead before Item Company (Captain Joe Fisher) and How Company (Captain Clarence Corley). Puller's favorite, the giant Fisher, had helped assure victory by using shaped charges to blow up the deep-frozen earth, so that men could build sandbagged positions from which their heavy weapons slaughtered the Chinese.

As it was, the battalion barely escaped and only a hand-to-hand fight in pre-dawn darkness had cleared the center of the camp. One artillery battalion fired 1200 rounds in the night; two mortar companies shot more than 3200 rounds between them; machine guns had fired almost incessantly. By daylight, planes came in with napalm to help restore the line and save the position.

It now became clear that the three Marine positions in the Chosin area were surrounded, and during the day Smith learned that Ridge's missing company could not get through from Koto-ri to Hagaru-ri. He ordered Puller to open the way.

Puller's reaction to the dread news was given to newspaper men who flew in to Koto-ri: "We've been looking for the enemy for several days now. We've finally found them.

We're surrounded. That simplifies our problem of getting to these people and killing them."

To Schmuck, southward down the road, he announced in a radio conversation: "We have contact on all four sides."

The newspapers in the States were black with headlines. The Division was "Trapped." Families of Marines besieged Washington headquarters. In Saluda, Virginia, Lewis Puller, Jr., who was now five, heard a radio commentator speak of the entrapment. His prayers that night betrayed his misunderstanding: "And dear God, please let my Father out of that rabbit trap."

Dr. Douglas Freeman, who learned of the incident, repeated it in a Richmond broadcast, and the Pullers had word of it for weeks.

In the midst of the ominous situation Puller wrote his wife:

> I did not get an opportunity to write you yesterday until quite late, and by then my gasoline lamp wasn't working so well and I put your letter off. . . . You were never out of my mind during the entire day.
>
> The only thing I want for Christmas is your continued love, Virginia, and that for ever and ever. Please do not send me anything. If you insist, send me a cheap pipe but get it as near the size I have drawn on this page as possible. Please don't get a longer one than this rough drawing, as the stem will either break off or I will lose it as it falls from my pocket.

On December 1 Puller wrote again from his cold tent:

> I understand that the news back home is to the effect that the First Marine Division is cut off, surrounded by the Chinese. This is *not* so, although the situation has not been good since the Chinese crossed the border. I am terribly sorry that this news has been published on account of the worry it has caused you and the families of other Marines here, but perhaps in the long run it may accomplish the awakening of our people as to the state of affairs and our lack of a military machine.
>
> I want the people of the United States to wake up but I surely do hate for this to mean more worry and anxiety for you. . . . I just hate our leaders who got us into this mess and the far worse mess that may be the consequence of the first decision. The whole affair seems to have developed due to gross ignorance and I pray that God will in-

tervene to straighten it out before it is too late. Now don't worry and don't believe all the stories you read in the newspapers. . . .

On the same day an army truck convoy into Koto-ri had been shot to pieces in a Chinese ambush. Survivors who reached the perimeter told Puller that some vehicles had been burned on the road. The Colonel sent a patrol to check for wounded; from this patrol a sergeant brought Puller a letter from his wife: "Colonel, I found this on top of a pile of thousands, thrown out in the snow, lots of 'em burned."

Puller prepared to open the road to Hagaru with "Task Force Drysdale," a British Commando unit of Royal Marines under Lieutenant Douglas Drysdale, accompanied by Captain Carl Sitter's company of Ridge's battalion, and a company from the 31st Army Regiment, which had come in. The road had been blocked in several places, two bridges were out, and the Chinese swarmed on heights overlooking the route.

Drysdale went out jauntily, planning to work the hills with his Royal Marines and Sitter's company in leapfrogging style, while the Army company kept to the road. Orville Jones listened as Puller talked with the column by radio in the first moments of its trek: "I see your men charging up the crests after those birds. Keep 'em down. You'll find all the Reds you want before you're through. Push on."

The party met bitter opposition and within a few minutes had fourteen casualties; in three hours and a half they moved only two miles, with eight more to go. Puller sent tanks as support and men came down from the hills to walk with them. They fought through roadblocks and around a blown bridge, but at dusk, in a narrow defile, met an ambush and took serious casualties. By radio, Puller, Oliver Smith and Drysdale agreed that the unit must push on to Hagaru, whatever the cost. The Royal Marines finally reached the Hagaru perimeter at 1:30 A.M., with 90 of its 255 men casualties; Sitter had 63; only 70 of the 210 Army men made it. A truck column sent behind this ill-fated party was virtually destroyed after a night-long fight and parley with the Chinese, who captured all the trucks and most of the men.

The survivors of this party were crucial to the defense of Hagaru; their added firepower helped turn back another massive Chinese attack. The companies of Sitter and Joe

Fisher killed the enemy in droves and by the next dawn their lines, though bent, still held.

Puller's perimeter was under almost constant Red fire, but for several days the Chinese did not press heavy attacks upon him; they were held at bay by superior firepower and the skill of Marine artillerymen.

A new airstrip was opened at Koto-ri, since the old one exposed helicopter pilots, the wounded and incoming commanders to enemy rifle fire. Newspaper correspondents turned up frequently despite Puller's effort to ban nonessential visitors. One reporter appeared without a parka:

"Colonel, I'm freezing. Can you help me? My paper will gladly pay you for a jacket."

Puller got the man a parka from the sick bay, a worn one marked with bloodstains. "I hope you didn't take it from one of your men, sir," the reporter said.

"You're damned right I didn't. I don't give a damn if you freeze, if it means keeping them going. The boy that had that parka will never need it again."

The reporter paled; Puller thought the man was going to retch.

Marguerite Higgins of the New York *Herald Tribune* appeared from a helicopter, after having been chased from Hagaru. Puller frowned. "Get her out of here," he told officers. "Never know what will hit us next—and I won't have a pretty American girl around with all these men about, anyway."

Puller was hospitable, and invited her to a warming tent and a drink, but soon sent her to the safety of the rear. Jones took her to the airfield in the jeep:

"I couldn't use the road, because it was full of troops moving. I drove her down the railroad tracks. I passed a big four-holer at the track-side, with lots of men sitting in there, exposed, but I didn't see anything embarrassing. Miss Higgins never said a word, but General Smith's aide chewed me out, and told me I should have known better than to drive her by a latrine. I just told him that was the only way to get her out, if he wanted her out."

The perimeter at Koto-ri was supplied by air after the enemy closed in. The first air drop came without warning from low clouds and the chutes tumbled cases and cartons across the mountains for three or four miles. Heavy shell boxes landed in the tent area and several Marines were killed or injured.

Puller was quickly on the radio, barking his anger at the Air Force pilot who circled somewhere above.

"We can't help it," the aviator's voice said. "We're tired of flying through these mountains in this cold, getting shot up, can't see where we're going. It's the best we can do."

"You're under arrest," Puller said. "Fly back to your commanding officer and report. My letter will follow."

The next drop was on target within a two-block area and thereafter the fliers worked heroically to keep alive the Division.

A battered and half-frozen Army outfit came to safety in the perimeter at the height of Communist attacks; Puller assigned it a position for camp and ordered its men fed. The commander of the newcomers said that all his survivors had come with him and Marine roadblocks were ordered to fire on anything moving in the snowy weather. Lieutenant Worster soon got a call from an outpost:

"Sir, we've got movement in front, and I don't think it's Chinese."

"Can't be ours. All the Army is in."

"Okay, but something funny is going on. I'll watch 'em."

Through the night and the next day the Army stragglers came in, frostbitten, wounded and exhausted; Worster was incensed that their officers did not get outside the barrier to guide them in: "They stayed in the warming tents, drinking coffee and talking about the big fight they'd had. I couldn't get 'em out to help. Puller finally ran 'em out to bring in their men."

Puller sent a rescue party to get the stalled survivors off the road; most of them had been held back by sniper fire from Chinese on ridges but made it to the perimeter under Marine direction.

It was one of these Army men whose encounter with Puller furnished the Corps a new legend. When the Army commander was shown his position he asked the direction of the line of retreat. Puller called his artillerymen, gave them the exact Army position and the quiet order: "If they start to pull back from that line, even one foot, I want you to open fire on them."

Puller turned to the Army officer: "Does that answer your question? We're here to fight, and nothing else."

The high command now ordered the Division to pull back from the Reservoir country to the sea; it was to fight its way by stages to Hungnam, where it would board ships for South Korea. The first task was to bring the northernmost units into Puller's area at Koto-ri. On December 1 the trek began and for four days the men of Murray and Litzenberg fought against the greatest odds the Corps had faced, blasting their way over the frozen road into Hagaru-ri. They brought with them 1500 casualties, a third of them frostbitten and frozen; the rear units had been 79 hours in covering the 14 miles, under almost constant attack. Fleets of planes evacuated more than 4000 casualties from Hagaru. More than five hundred replacements were flown in and ammunition, fuel and food were dropped. The Air Force offered to evacuate every man from Hagaru and was stunned when General Smith replied: "We're going to break out over the road. We'll need every able-bodied man for the fight. We intend to leave behind no equipment we can salvage."

As Smith prepared the men for the southward march, intelligence reported that two new Communist divisions had come to cut them off—a total of nine in the area. General Almond flew in from X Corps headquarters on December 4 and decorated several officers, including Army Distinguished Service Crosses for Smith, Litzenberg and Murray.

The movement south from Hagaru began on December 6.

General Almond turned up in Koto-ri and went straight to Puller's tent: "God, Colonel! What weather you keep. Haven't you got a drink?"

Puller produced a half-filled bottle and the Corps commander took a drink. They joked about Puller's warning about the Arctic weather, in the days at Inchon. Almond shouted: "What about this stab in the back by Red China, Puller?"

"I think it's the luckiest thing that could have happened."

"What the hell do you mean?"

"If they hadn't hit us here, we'd be all the hell the way up there on the Yalu, lots colder than this. You'd have no supply dumps built up. With the fool equipment, food and clothing we've got, your Corps would literally have frozen to death. As it is, all we've got to do is run downhill to the sea, get under the ships' guns and hold there all winter. When spring comes, we can get reinforcement and strike back up here as far as we want to."

Almond had come to decorate Puller's men, too. There

was a shortage of medals and when he pinned an Army Distinguished Service Cross on Puller he snatched it off, pinned it to the blouse of an Army officer with the same words of congratulation and then snatched it back. "Yours will be sent up on the next flight," he told the Army officer. He returned the medal to Puller.

There were three Silver Stars for enlisted men and three for officers. Puller told Almond that Rickert, his exec, deserved a Star and Almond borrowed one for him from one of the men, promising delivery of a substitute.

Puller's officers thronged about Almond's aide, burdening him with letters to be carried out—and many gave him money and other valuables. They did not expect to survive the battle down the hill to the sea.

Puller's letters to his wife in these hectic days reflected neither peril nor hardship:

December 2: "The situation shows a marked improvement. . . . Do not pay too much attention to the news. . . . Please write me that you have hired a cook. Yes, I am getting plenty of food and have good warm clothing. Good night and kiss our children for me."

December 3: "When I think of all the worry I am causing you, and of the times that I haven't been as nice to you as I should have been, I am more than disgusted with myself. . . . I will send a check for $100. Please go to Richmond and buy yourself a Christmas present. I wish it was enough for a mink coat."

December 4: "Conditions have improved today, and with the help of God, my outfit will be back on the beach about day after tomorrow. The leadership, especially that of the higher command during this operation, has not been of top grade, especially in determining an estimate of the situation and the capabilities of the enemy. In spite of all this our Division will hold, with the help of the Almighty, and I will return home safely. . . .

"What do our people think? What are they doing? Do they realize what they have been led into? What do they intend to do in order to get out of this mess? . . . Kiss our children for me and tell them that I will come home as soon as we put the bad people in the brig."

On the night of December 7, the bulk of the Division was in Puller's perimeter after the 38-hour battle from Hagaru.

The cost: 103 dead, 506 wounded, 7 missing. But now the force of 10,000 and its 1000 vehicles was at Koto-ri. The perimeter could hardly contain them all.

Puller was ready for them, despite the burdens of handling the 4000 men already on the site, and he had hot food and warming tents ready as the men came in from the north. Planning was almost complete for the march south the next morning. Eight sections of a steel bridge, each weighing 2500 pounds, were dropped by the Air Force during the day and huge trucks were ready to move them into place below Funichilin Pass, where a concrete bridge over an abyss had been blown. The bridge must be repaired before the column could clear for the south.

There was Chinese fire from the surrounding hills day and night, but no more of the suicidal attacks, for the massed mortars, recoilless rifles and a battery of the 11th Artillery rained death on every enemy concentration as it formed.

The Colonel had no contempt for the enemy. One of his reports was a tacit warning that the Chinese should not be underestimated: "CCF troops are well-trained and led, get as close as possible for grenade use, covered by automatic fire. Infiltration is excellent. Under fire they crawl from one position to another, displaying no reluctance to engage in close hand-to-hand combat."

His men were not awed by the enemy, however. One tank was painted with the legend: "14 More Shooting Days Until Christmas."

Puller wrote his wife:

> Tonight the entire Division is together. . . . This concentration means that we are now in better shape than we have been since launching on the East Coast. Our losses from battle, and from frozen feet, face and hands have been heavy. . . . I hear that our commander has recommended to Mr. Truman that all U. N. forces be withdrawn from this country. I pray that it will be approved. No thought should be given to saving face, as our country has already lots its head, and as a consequence has no face left to save.
>
> Today has been a success not only in getting our Division concentrated, but also in getting your dear letters of seven days in November. How thankful I have been today.

After supper the Colonel disappeared. Only Sergeant Jones knew where he was: "The Old Man would sneak off with Bodey and go up into the lines, climbing right up those damned straight-up hills, all ice and rock, going from hole to hole for half the night. He would go to every man he could find in a foxhole and say 'How you doing, old man? Where's your field of fire? Who's on your flank? Getting enough chow?' On the way back he would check the warming tents to see if there had been casualties, and how the men were doing."

On one of these subzero nights Puller found Sergeant Bob Cornely, a veteran who had been with him on Guadalcanal. In the privacy of a snow bank the Colonel produced a miracle—a drink of Old Grand-Dad. Cornely said: "It was like something from heaven, not just a drink of tanglefoot. You can't know what that did for a freezing man who'd been up there for six hours without relief, watching, watching. I never saw the Old Man drink, but he knew when a little nip would save a fellow from going mad or becoming a casualty."

Sergeant Jones and Bodey found a moment of relief even in these days. A pompous colonel of the command who spent much time issuing imperious commands in the spit-and-polish tradition was a burden to Jones and Bodey, who scorned his directive that every man must carry a weapon every waking moment, even to the best-protected privies.

One day they saw this colonel walking below them on a trail, hands in pockets, without his helmet. Jones bawled from the tent: "All right there, Marine! Hands out of the pockets! Assume correct posture. And don't let me catch you without battle gear on your head again!"

The colonel marched off like a mechanical man. Jones savored the moment: "Lookit him! He wants to turn around so bad he can taste it, because he suspects it might be us—but he's scared to, because it might be the Old Man yelling at him."

There was furious work on the runway of the Koto-ri air strip, but it could not yet receive large planes; airmen came in dangerously, flying old torpedo bombers to which they were unaccustomed. On December 7 they took out eighty casualties, six or eight at a time. The planes were brought to the ground by signal flags. On the next day a snowstorm broke, just as the column wound southward and a Marine transport hovered overhead, waiting its chance. There was literally no visibility, but during a brief lull in the storm the plane dropped down and took out nineteen more casualties. It left in the howling snowstorm, the last plane to leave for twenty-four hours. By now only two hundred casualties were left in Puller's perimeter for evacuation.

Early on December 8 the Marines began clearing the ridges on either side of the road south but the going was slow and the trucks bearing the bridge sections made little progress. A funeral service for 117 Marines in a common grave brought the day to an end in the perimeter. It was a scene that lived in Puller's memory—the burial of frozen bodies by a tank battalion which crushed them under the frozen ground.

A Marine photographer took movies of this burial. Puller said, "How I wish our people could have seen the sight—to see just what happened to us in Korea!" He later heard that Army censorship in Washington kept the film from the public.

The southern march was preceded by an attack from the lower end of the road. General Smith organized Task Force Dog, led by Puller's old schoolmate from Fort Benning, Brigadier General Armistead D. Mead, assistant commander of the 3rd Army Division. This force fought through Red roadblocks from Hamhung north to Chinhung-ni, where Lieutenant Colonel Donald Schmuck had Puller's First Battalion. The Army took Schmuck's post and the First went north toward Koto-ri, to clear the way for the Division.

Schmuck's men left at 3:30 A.M. in a snowstorm, Bob Wray's C Company in advance; the way was over almost impassable crags, to reach the rear of a hill which dominated the escape road. Chinese were dug in on the face of this towering hill, covering the road with fire for well over half a mile—but Schmuck had found that they were all facing north, waiting for the escape.

Wray remembered it: "It was rough work, just getting there. We had nothing but some old Jap maps to guide us, and I overran my first objective in the storm. To then, not a shot had been fired. Others, especially Bob Barrow's company, had to fight like hell all day, but it was 3:30 in the afternoon before we opened."

In the end the Chinese were cleaned off the hill, with Barrow's men closing in a hand-to-hand attack which demoralized the enemy. Grenades finished the action the following morning. Within two or three hours after the hillside was taken, the head of the Division column appeared.

It was a near thing at the blasted bridge below the pass, for the enemy had been dynamiting even the ruins. In two hours and a half the engineers had the new bridge sections in place and traffic moving—but one of the first vehicles, an earth-moving machine, wrecked it, and the sections had to be stretched out. There were only two and a half inches to spare for big trucks, but these scraped through and the advance wound down the mountain.

There were signs that the enemy was suffering much more than the Marines. Prisoners were taken in greater numbers and some told stories of whole battalions being wiped out, frozen to death after having been run through the valleys parallel to the American route of escape.

Puller wrote his wife on December 9—a brief message sent down to a radio center:

> With the help of the good God we are making it. I will come home for my precious wife and children. Love to all the family. Kiss our children. I love you, Virginia, I always have and will. May God keep you always.

On this day the rest of the Division was rapidly clearing Koto-ri, and on the next, Puller was left alone. He was now the rearguard. He was ordered to destroy equipment and vehicles and to abandon the rest. He fumed: "To hell with that! I'm going to take out everything I came in with, if it'll still move. More—I'll bring all this stuff the Army abandoned." He gave orders to take out every removable vehicle and was astonished to find many at the roadsides with their keys in the switches, left there by the Army.

The press of civilians worried him most of all as he prepared to lead the First Marines down to the sea: "I had to fire over their heads almost every day for a week or more. There were a few times, I'm sorry to say, when I had to fire right into them, and killed a number. It was gruesome, but I knew what would happen if we let them in on us—it would be the end of our outfit. The Chinese troops had got among them in disguise, and were just waiting to knock us off."

At the end, on December 10, the First abandoned Koto-ri, the rifle companies leapfrogging down the icy road to provide cover. The reconnaissance company was last to leave, and Puller was with them to the final few minutes. He watched the vast cloud of smoke ride from the plateau as the abandoned ammunition went off, glanced at the huddled mass of civilians at the barrier, and prepared for the road.

Orville Jones was ready with the jeep. Across the bumper lay the stiffened body of a tank commander, a recent casualty. Two other bodies were strapped on the rear and top. Three or four wounded huddled in the rear. Jones made a search for other bodies in the perimeter.

"Just make sure they're Marine," Puller said. "Take our own people."

When the jeep was loaded Jones rolled off. Puller left at 3 P.M., walking. It was slow going to the pass, where he arrived at 5 o'clock. Reeves saw him there; the Colonel waited with others until the road was cleared of an obstruction.

Jones found Puller at this point and stripped the boots off his feet. "They were beginning to freeze," the sergeant said. "The felt ripped like tearing cloth when I pulled 'em from him. He made no complaint then or later. I put him in the jeep, and the heater did a little to bring life back into him. He kept getting out of the jeep, despite all I could do. He walked most of the way down."

Puller was issuing orders to the moment he left the pass. He was harshly insistent to his commander at the rear, where a tank column covered the tail of the division: "Whatever happens and whatever you think of it, don't let the civilians come in on you from the perimeter. Keep 'em clear. If they get close, you'll get hurt. Watch it." He had the officer repeat the order to him.

From the start of the downward march there had been Korean refugees. Lieutenant Colonel John Partridge recalled: "There was artillery fire; there was the crunching of the many feet and vehicles on the crisp snow. There were many North Korean refugees on one side of the column and Marines walking on the other side. Every once in a while there would be a baby wailing. There were cattle on the road. . . . It was as eerie as anything I've ever experienced."

But when Puller's First went down there was the order: No civilians.

Lieutenant Worster had one last glimpse of Puller at the pass, before he went down for the last time: "I went downhill once and came back, and when I got up, there was Puller. There were several blazing fires, built in defiance of the Chinese who were strung all around, on the hills. It was freeze without a fire or take a chance on being shot by the Reds. They didn't shoot. I think they were being frozen themselves, and they'd been kept out there in the hills by our planes, which literally shadowed that road all day.

"I huddled over a fire in a crowd on the pass and felt

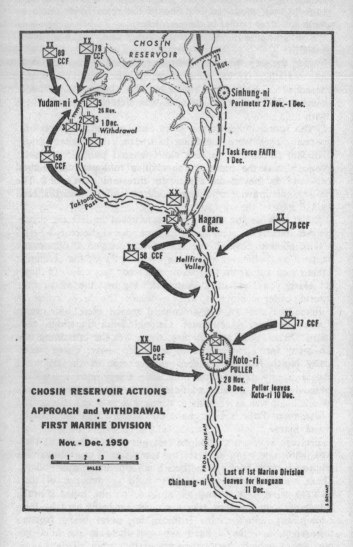

CHOSIN RESERVOIR

RESERVOIR

Sinhung-ni
Perimeter 27 Nov.-1 Dec.

27 Nov.

XX 89 CCF

XX 79 CCF

Yudam-ni

1 5
26 Nov.

2 7
3 7
1 Dec.
Withdrawal

7

Task Force FAITH
1 Dec.

XX 59 CCF

Taktong Pass

XX 1

3 XX 1 Hagaru
6 Dec.

XX 76 CCF

XX 58 CCF

Hellfire
Valley

XX 77 CCF

XX 60 CCF

1
2 Koto-ri
PULLER

28 Nov.
8 Dec. Puller leaves
Koto-ri 10 Dec.

CHOSIN RESERVOIR ACTIONS
•
APPROACH and WITHDRAWAL
FIRST MARINE DIVISION

Nov. - Dec. 1950

0 1 2 3 4 5
MILES

FROM WONSAN

Chinhung-ni

Last of 1st Marine Division
leaves for Hungnam
11 Dec.

S. BRYANT

someone shove beside me—there were two Chinese soldiers, half dead with cold, their canvas shoes broken and the frozen flesh hanging out, trying to get warm and save themselves. We let 'em warm, and sent 'em down the hill as prisoners."

Before the end of the column reached the pass, coming from Koto-ri, Puller had word of a tragedy: The tankmen at the rear had been attacked when the civilian press approached them, Chinese soldiers had tossed grenades under the treads of tanks, and three of the vehicles had been lost, with their crews.

The rear had been covered by twenty-eight men in the reconnaissance platoon of Lieutenant Ernest Hargett, a former All-Marine football star. He had ten tanks to cover; his chief concern was the press of the civilian refugees, who surged as close as they dared under the threatening weapons. The pace was a crawl, for tanks skidded on icy curves and labored with lights burning. At 1 A.M. the ninth tank from the rear had a brake freeze; the tail of the column was left behind, alone. They were 2000 yards from the repaired bridge.

The Korean civilians milled uncertainly. From the mass came five Chinese soldiers. "We want to surrender," one of them said.

Hargett went to meet them for a parley, covered by Corporal George Amyotte with a BAR. The first Chinaman stepped aside and the four behind opened with hidden burp guns and grenades. Hargett cracked one skull with his carbine butt, but was felled by a grenade. Amyotte killed the rest and after a wild fight on the road the platoon retreated. The platoon hammered on a closed tank, trying to get the crew to open and aid them, but there was no answer. Chinese tossed grenades, one of which exploded on Amyotte's back but left him unscathed, thanks to his body armor. The rearguard party found the next seven tanks abandoned, with hatches open. The wounded Hargett led his twenty-four survivors out with the aid of a corporal, C. P. Lett, who operated a tank for the first time in his life. The bridge was blown behind them and they were safe.

The Fifth and Seventh Marines had now passed through Puller's ranks, and the First was the rearguard for the entire Division, responsible for covering the withdrawal down the frozen loops of the road. Puller started down, and hundreds of men saw him, for he thought that his job had only begun. He shouted to every passing unit to cheer the men, yelling until he was hoarse: "Don't forget that you're First Marines! Not all the Communists in hell can overrun you."

He rode part of the way in the jeep, but walked with the troops for miles, and could not be persuaded to leave them until he was sure that they had escaped the trap the Chinese had attempted to close on the road.

At the southernmost Division outpost, Chinhung-ni, the column supposed that the danger zone ended, but the Chinese circled the Army unit there and cut the road leading south. Colonel Ed Snedeker had been sent by headquarters to make the road safe, but despite his efforts the enemy attacked a convoy at Sudong, firing on trucks with grenades and burp guns, killing and wounding twenty-one; ten vehicles were lost.

Sutter's battalion walked the entire route from Koto-ri to Majon-dong, 22 miles, in 20 hours, despite enemy attacks, icy roads, and heavy uniforms and packs. At a bit after noon on December 11, the last of the Division climbed on trucks at Chinhung-ni, and rolled to the sea a Hungnam. By midnight the last of them were safe in the beach perimeter.

News photographers met them, shouting, with a thought for the people back home: "Wave and look happy!" The Marines obliged.

XVIII

END OF A NIGHTMARE

SHIPS almost literally rubbed gunwales in the Hungnam harbor—a vast fleet gathered from every corner of the Orient to carry out the forces from North Korea. Marines were first to begin loading.

Puller wrote his wife on December 13, a date which he circled as their anniversary:

> Darling:
> With the help of the Almighty and no other unit or person, my Regiment is on the beach at Hungnam and will be aboard ship before the day is over. I am thankful to the good God for all his blessings.
> Love to all. Kiss our dear children for me. God bless you all.

Reporters found him. "Remember," the Colonel told them, "whatever you write, this was no retreat. All that happened was that we found more Chinese behind us than in front of us, so we about-faced and attacked."

The press at home depicted the Reservoir campaign as one of the great military actions of history. *Time* magazine said: "The running fight . . . 40 miles by air but 60 miles over the icy, twisting, mountainous road was a battle unparalleled in U. S. military history. It had some of the aspects of Bataan, some of Anzio, some of Dunkirk, some of Valley Forge, some of the 'Retreat of the 10,000' as described in Xenophon's *Anabasis*. . . . It was defeat—the worst defeat the United States ever suffered."

Returning Marines were astonished to find this spirit in the air. Puller pointed out that they could spend the winter under the big guns and planes of the fleet if they wished. He also grumbled to his officers: "We should be ashamed of the leadership that forced us to pull out. We never should have undertaken that campaign in winter in the first place— but now that we're here we should stick. There's nothing to hinder us."

Marine casualties for the campaign, from October 26 to December 15, were 718 dead, 3508 wounded, 192 missing. Communist losses, their accuracy supported by captured documents: 25,000 dead, 12,500 wounded.

Morale among Marines in the perimeter was as high as if they were fresh from triumph. Father Kevin Keaney, a Division chaplain, sketched them:

> You cannot exaggerate about the Marines. They are convinced to the point of arrogance, that they are the most ferocious fighters on earth—and the amusing thing about it is that they are. . . . You should see the group that is about me as I write—dirty, bearded, their clothing food-spattered and filthy—they look like the castoffs of creation, yet they have a sense of loyalty, generosity, even piety greater than any men I have ever known.
>
> These rugged men have the simple piety of children. You can't help loving them, in spite of their language and their loose sense of private property. Don't ever feel sorry for a priest in the Marines. The last eight weeks have been the happiest and most contented of my life.

General Oliver Smith wrote of Puller's role in the saga: "During the Reservoir operation I was never concerned about the security of Koto-ri. When he was told to hold Koto-ri, Lewie never questioned whether or not he had enough men to hold it; he simply made up his mind to hold it. His very presence reassured men; and he circulated constantly. The men knew Colonel Puller's reputation, that he had emerged with credit from many critical situations, and here he was in the flesh exuding confidence."

There was a funeral in a hastily made cemetery at Hungnam for men who had died on the way down from the Reservoir or had been carried on the vehicles from Koto-ri. At the end of the ceremony Puller left a group of officers and walked down the line of Marines who had formed the firing squad to thank them for their services. He was the one officer who remembered that this was voluntary duty—and to feel that the men should have some credit for their performance.

Loading was difficult despite the shipping which crowded the harbor; there were more than 100,000 men to be carried away, including U. S. Army and ROK troops. In addition there were more than 100,000 Korean refugees, four times the number expected. One freighter designed for twelve passengers and her crew took on 14,000 Koreans; five babies were born aboard on the short trip to the south of the peninsula.

On December 14 Puller was aboard his transport, the *General Collins.* He got ten hours sleep and had all the fresh beef, eggs and fresh frozen milk that he could eat. He had a shave and haircut and two showers and, as he wrote his wife: "I am now normal again, that is physically. Not even a cold." He found several of his wife's letters waiting at the beach, and read them over and over.

Reeves noted that the Colonel played poker all night with officers and men and that the game lasted so long that the skipper complained to Puller at dawn: "Colonel, you'll have to let my officers get to bed. They can't stand their watches, they're so sleepy." It was less than forty-eight hours after Puller had returned from the Reservoir campaign.

The ship was thronged like all others in the harbor, with four men for each bunk. Marines lay on every gangway and corridor and took turns in the bunks. Lieutenant Stiles remembered: "The Colonel wouldn't allow them to be disturbed while they slept, and things were mighty quiet on that ship." Puller also declined to use a bunk until men of his staff had taken their turns at sleeping.

The Marines had gone south by the time of the big explosion of supplies at Hungnam, "the black blossom" that lived in so many memories: Two cruisers, seven destroyers, three rocket-firing ships and the battleship *Missouri* blasted the Korean hills behind the perimeter as the last men boarded the ships, cutting off any possible enemy sortie. More than 34,000 shells and 12,800 rockets were fired, in addition to the *Missouri*'s 16-inch shells, a barrage much greater than that of the landings at Inchon. The mountains of supplies on the beach were detonated at last—and to add to the explosion were 400 tons of frozen dynamite and 500 thousand-pound bombs. The blowup literally shook the earth and sea.

Little that had been left behind belonged to the Marines —and literally nothing to the First Regiment. Puller wrote his wife:

> I am aboard ship with 5000 enlisted men, nearly 500 officers, my guns, rolling stock, arms and tentage, and sailing south, thanks to the good God. I left nothing for the enemy except planted land mines that will damage him and slow his progress. I brought out all my wounded and most of my dead. We were ordered to retreat and did so. This regiment was the rear-guard of our Division. . . .
>
> My prayer now is that our leaders, knowing that we have no war machine, will evacuate Korea completely, have a thorough house-cleaning, and then build a real war machine before becoming involved in another war. May God give us wisdom and common sense!
>
> Today I heard about the cold weather on our East Coast. If you and our precious children haven't warm clothing, please purchase it immediately. I trust that the oil stove has been installed in your room and I am distressed that I didn't get one for you, Sweetheart, last fall.

The Division settled in Masan in South Korea, out of the combat zone, but it appeared that it would soon be back in the fight, since the Eighth Army was retreating in the northwest. In late December, with the coming of General Matthew B. Ridgway to command, the Marines took heart. The new chief had the look of a fighter and his first orders promised better days: The U.N. forces would cease their retreat at the 37th Parallel, digging in to prepare for a future offensive.

Puller had his first glimpse of Ridgway when the new commander summoned his field officers for a briefing, and took an instant liking to the former paratrooper: "Lord, I wish they'd left him there long enough to do the job. I have a feeling we wouldn't have taken a licking in Korea with Ridgway to lead us."

Ridgway also liked Puller:

"I had, of course, known of his reputation for intrepid battlefield leadership and indomitable spirit, and, as I first saw that rugged face and looked him in the eyes, I knew that here was another one of 'The Old Breed' on whom a commander could utterly depend."

Puller remembered their first brief talk:

"General Ridgway asked me about the quality of the Chinese troops.

"I told him they were damned good. He looked as if he didn't believe me, and I told him, 'Up there in those hills are the Chinese. They're commanded by an officer who's been fighting since 1911, almost without a break. Who've we got with that kind of experience? We spent just those five months of World War I in action—and in the last war very few of our officers were in more than two big fights.'

" 'But they have no staff school, or war college,' Ridgway said. I told him that was just the point, that warfare couldn't be learned in schools alone, the way we're trying to do it in America, and that the Chinese approach might be far superior—especially since they had the help of combat-trained Russian officers."

Ridgway seemed to enjoy Puller and his Marines. Sergeant Jones was sent in the jeep to bring the commander to Puller's headquarters on visits.

"The first time I went," Jones said, "I took our beat-up old jeep beside some slick Army staff cars, all attended by colonels and majors, also waiting. Ridgway passed them all and came to me. He asked me if I were Sergeant Jones and hopped in and we took off. The Army stared after us.

"When he came the next time Ridgway recognized me at first glance, called me by name and walked out with me."

Jones also witnessed Ridgway in an act which struck him as "just like Colonel Puller":

Ridgway and Puller were at a roadside one day as troops went toward the front. A heavily laden radioman, a private, struggled by and became stuck fast in the muck. His bootlaces came loose and he shouted for help. Ridgway stepped toward him.

"Thanks, pal," the youngster said, as the general stooped to tie the lace, then gasped as he saw the stars on his shoulders. He looked back, open-mouthed, until he had passed from sight.

There were frequent Army visitors while the Division was in the South. Jones noticed that the Army officers who came to see Puller were always on their best behavior:

"When they were around the Old Man, even the Army guys who were seniors—generals and all—would stand at attention and hold it. They were scared to death of him. Bodey and I thought it was funny as hell, but we could understand how he made them feel."

There were miracles at Puller's headquarters on Christmas Eve. A Virginia ham came for the Colonel from Henry Heming, his companion of World War II. The same mail produced a fruit cake, sent by "Nick the Greek," a restaurateur in Quantico who had been a friend for thirty years. An aviator who dropped by the First Regiment left two bottles of whisky with Puller. The Colonel had a dozen loaves of bread and a carving knife brought from the mess; the staff of seven or or eight officers feasted.

A ten-foot fir stood in front of Puller's tent, decorated by the men with a star and some ornaments sent over from Japan. Toy birds perched in its branches. Puller went to Episcopal service and Communion on Christmas Day and joined the Division's senior officers for an eggnog party at General Smith's quarters in the afternoon.

The Navy shipped in a feast for the Division: Turkey, cranberry sauce, sweet potatoes, fruit cake, apples, nuts and beer.

Puller did not forget the men. He wrote his wife:

> I have just returned to my tent after visiting my three battalions, headquarters company, heavy weapons company and attached units. The officers and men are putting up a good front with what we have and their spirit is fine considering that this is Christmas and what they have been through. The American people should be proud of, at least, their Marines.

The units had organized choruses and sang carols for the Colonel and his staff—some of them in Latin. They made Puller homesick.

A letter from Mrs. Puller arrived a day or two after Christmas. He replied:

> I hate to think of all the worry that I have caused you, Sweetheart. Maybe I would not have permitted you to have married me, if I had known all this was coming on! I would have at least hesitated. I meant to give you only happiness and believed that I could. Never fear. This too will pass, and with the help of God I will come home for you and our precious children before too long. That will be a glorious day and I will never want to have you or them out of my sight again. I must have known (I did know) that this separation was ahead of us and that accounts for my reluctance to *ever* leave our home even to go to see a moving-picture or out to dinner. . . .
>
> How thankful I am to have your true, fine and great love, Dear, and I value it more than life. It is right for people

to love deeply, as that is the only way for lasting love.

The weather was still bitter in the new camp, and only after persuasion by Rickert and other staff officers, abetted by Jones and Bodey, did Puller agree to try the new field shower.

Jones drove the officers to the tents on the bank of a frozen river. Pipes had been thrust through the ice to draw water from the river and a gasoline burner produced piping hot water for the shower. The operating crew was a group of Negro Marines.

Jones and Bodey showered first, without incident. Puller and Rickert stepped under the shower heads and soaped themselves in streams of hot water. Jones never forgot the sight:

"They were so soapy you couldn't tell which was which, and the Old Man was ready to enjoy himself. He'd quit shaking for the first time since we went up to the Reservoir, I believe.

"Those colored boys were so anxious to do everything just right, and please the Old Man, that something was bound to go wrong. One of them picked up what he thought was a can of gasoline and dumped it into the heater—it turned out to be cold water and the heater went out like a light. Ice water came down on Rickert and the Old Man.

"I never thought men could turn blue so fast. They yelled bloody murder and the Old Man was hollering for 'em to turn hot air in the tent. It was some ruckus, I mean. The Old Man chewed Rickert and told him not to propose another shower as long as they were in Korea. Rickert rushed outside and began eating up the Marines and told them by God he'd send them up to the front lines—to get shot the next day—but of course he never did it. It was quite a time."

For many weeks after the return from the north Puller was besieged by transport officers of the 7th Army Division who tried to reclaim trucks he had brought down the mountain road. He refused: "Sure I've got your trucks. And you know how I got 'em. You ran away and left 'em. If you want to get them back, just write General Ridgway and explain to him how I got them."

Bodey and Jones had an adventure with fellow Marines while the regiment was in this camp. The adjoining headquarters of a Marine colonel, in contrast to Puller's lightly defended area, was aglow with searchlights, a fortress behind concertinas of barbed wire, with many guards, tanks and dug-in guns. The jeep was sent there on an errand one night, after taking an Army colonel to his quarters.

A sentry halted them, peering at Bodey and his lapful of weapons: "Are them guns loaded?"

"Certainly. What the hell you think?"

"Then you must unload them before entering the area. Colonel's order."

"Okay, fella," Bodey said. He emptied his M-1 skyward. The sentry scurried for cover. Jones whirled the jeep and they fled.

An officer soon trailed Jones. "Did you shoot up our area tonight, by chance?"

"I don't know what you mean, Lieutenant."

"You went downtown tonight, didn't you?"

"Yes sir. Took the Colonel down. . . ."

The officer stiffened. "You had the Colonel with you?"

"Yes, sir."

The lieutenant retreated. Jones muttered to Bodey: "No need to tell 'em *which* Colonel. Bo, you ever see anybody could scare 'em like our Old Man?"

Puller was impatient to be at the enemy. From January 15 onward he flew with pilots in a tiny observation plane, buzzing over the hills around Andong, Pohang and Yong-chon, spying out the Chinese. They were often fired on, but Puller's battle luck held, and there were no hits. His missions were so daring and talked of so breathlessly by returning pilots that he was awarded an Air Medal for the daily flights in the last half of the month—and soon after he won two gold stars for the Air Medal, for more of the low hops over the heads of the enemy.

Oliver Smith told Headquarters in Puller's fitness reports: "This officer can always be depended upon in combat. He gives his best without question and without stint. He should be given a different type of duty in the Fleet Marine Force. . . . A vigorous, aggressive officer who pursues his objective without deviation. A splendid leader of men who inspires complete confidence on the part of his subordinates . . . he participated in hazardous low altitude flights over enemy-held territory in an unarmed aircraft. As a result of his flights he obtained tactical information which was valuable to the Division and contributed materially to its success."

Smith recommended Puller for a Navy Cross for his work in the Reservoir campaign—his fifth, and a Marine Corps record.

Puller's letters to his wife revealed his usual concern for his family in the midst of campaigning:

> Please tell Lewis that I will finally come home and teach him how to shoot and many other things that boys and men must know. . . . Tell him to be patient and the swords and a helmet I sent him will arrive. . . . Tell him to change his bait in the rabbit trap every few days—a piece of apple, lettuce, carrot, celery, and turnip, and that he must not go near the trap or touch it except to change bait or when the door is sprung; also he must keep the dog away from it. . . .
>
> The mail service has been excellent out here, and in my opinion this is all that the Air Force has accomplished during the war. . . .
>
> I haven't minded the hardships here but the killing and crippling of the young men is awful. Due to the weather our wounded die; blood plasma freezes before it can be administered. . . .
>
> I realize that this war is far harder on you than it has been on me and I am sorry to have caused you all the worry and pain. . . .
>
> I will never be able to understand the difference between our enlisted men and young officers and those of the Army. There appears to be no example of leadership in the latter organization. No pride and nothing to look up to. The truth is unknown.
>
> . . . I wish the world was different, especially our country, but I'm afraid that I cannot do anything about changing the world or our country. I can only pray and trust that God will give us leaders who are wise.
>
> Please rest assured that I am not volunteering for any assignment that will separate us or keep us separated. I want to return to you. . . .
>
> The Pentagon is largely responsible for this mess out here—they were given the money to provide and train an Army. When I entered the service, the regulations stated that the object of all military training is "success in battle." This short sentence has been rewritten on three pages and I defy anyone to read it over three or more times and then explain what the object of military training is. Even the Pentagon has not the slightest idea why they are commanding

the forces of the United States. In fact, out here, we wonder if we are a part of the United States. . . .

I will not influence my son as to choosing a profession. It will be up to him. I will not even recommend the service. I have had to stand with my mouth closed on too many occasions and then carry out orders from too many half-wits. . . .

I am greatly distressed to hear that Martha Leigh's tonsils are acting up and that she is in bed. We must get them out in May and we will. God willing, I will be home to help you. . . .

Puller was finally promoted to Brigadier General on January 24, the rank to date from the first of the year. He was called to Division Headquarters to get his stars, but flew back to his regiment, where Master Sergeant Joe Guiliano, his old gunnery sergeant, directed a surprise ceremony for the new general. Guiliano had made an enormous star of cardboard and aluminum foil to pin on Puller's shoulder. A photographer was standing by. Guiliano had found the regiment's smallest man, a tiny musician, and had Puller stand on a stone so that the Marine had to tiptoe to reach his shoulder. Puller appeared as a giant in the photograph.

The attached artillery battery fired an eleven-gun salute. Puller growled happily: "What the hell do you want to waste ammunition on me for?"

But when, a few minutes after the firing, a return salvo came from the enemy he grinned: "Maybe you didn't waste it, after all."

An honor guard was drawn up and Puller left a cluster of officers to speak to old friends among the enlisted men. Corporal Bob Pratt was surprised when the General slapped him on the back and roared: "How're things, old man? Your chow good enough these days?"

The General made a brief speech: "All the credit for this star belongs to the noncoms, junior officers, and enlisted men," he said. "You all know that. I've tried to do my duty, but we'd never get anywhere except for you fellows in the ranks. This is a great regiment, and it's going to hurt me to have to leave you. I'll never forget you."

To these men of Task Force Puller he also issued a formal memorandum:

In compliance with orders I am, today, leaving this command for assignment as Assistant Division Commander. It is not without misgivings and a certain reluctance that I carry out these orders. All of you, officers and men alike, realize, I am sure, what the 1st Marine Regiment has meant to me. . . .

I ask one thing more of you—give my successor the same full measure of cooperation and willingness you have always given me, and the 1st Marines will be worthy of the name it has already won.

I first commanded you on New Britain, later on the bloody hills of Peleliu, and it has been my honor to command you in Korea where, by your deeds, you captured the city of Seoul and successfully covered the withdrawal of our Division from the Chosin Reservoir area.

I shall look to your future movements and shall expect to hear and see still greater deeds and higher reputation won on the field of battle.

Colonel Sutter took over the regiment when Puller left to become assistant commander of the Division under Oliver Smith. It was not hard for Smith to see where Puller's heart lay: "He at first found the atmosphere somewhat rarefied. He had always before been in direct command of troops and now all he could do was visit the units and observe. For a while he took every opportunity to observe his old regiment. He soon adjusted himself to his new duties and became a very effective Assistant Division Commander."

Puller and Smith worked well together. Smith's detached, but relentless, methods of making war combined with Puller's drive to make the Division highly effective. Smith understood Puller and only occasionally tried to restrain him.

Once the staff of the Division dined with the X Corps staff after a Chinese attack which had driven U. S. Army and ROK units from their fronts, leaving the Marines with both flanks exposed. A Corps staff officer spoke to Puller: "Didn't you fellows know that all units were ordered to withdraw in face of strong enemy pressure?"

"I knew of no such order," Puller said. "It took this Division fourteen hundred casualties and eleven days of hard fighting to reach that position. If I'd known we were going to withdraw the first time the Chinese turned and yelled 'Boo' at us I'd never have moved an inch. If I were commanding I wouldn't be looking for units to pull back—I'd be forcing those people who pulled back to fight their way into position."

In the silence which fell around the table Smith gave

Puller a warning boot on the shin and the exchange was ended.

One day General Craig flew into Puller's area by helicopter and complained: "Lewie, you'd better have that electric cable taken down from your airfield—we damned near hit it coming in. Somebody's going to wreck on it."

Puller nodded agreement, but the wire remained in place. A few days later Puller was flying into the field himself, with Captain Harold McCray as pilot of his helicopter, when they struck the cable. They hung for a moment, swinging like a pendulum until the wire snapped and the ship fluttered almost twenty feet to the ground; there was a rending crash. Troops ran to the spot.

Puller was flung forward, smashing through the plexiglas nose. He got to his feet, brushing at himself. Orville Jones plucked a jagged piece of plexiglas from the General's neck and said in awe: "My God, look! He never even bled!"

The 'copter was standing on its nose, a wreck; the engine had spilled out, sheared in two. The pilot was still up in the ship, frozen tightly to the stick. Puller peered up at him: "Turn loose, old man, and fall down here with me!"

Jones gathered hundreds of shotgun shells the General had been carrying, now scattered over the field. Puller and McCray left the wreck without injury.

On a spring night in 1951 Puller led his men northward into Central Korea in a drive against the Communists the Corps called Operation Puller. The General rode at the head of his convoy in the jeep, Jones driving and Bodey riding shotgun. For many miles they left a great column of dust behind them.

It was an impressive sight to Jones: "We looked like a tribe of gypsies instead of Marines. We were supposed to have everything snugged down under taut canvas, but almost every vehicle was piled with chairs or tables, or wooden panels from Korean huts or native A-frames, for carrying packs. The men wanted to make themselves comfortable in camp.

"It was against regulations but lots of the men wore big straw Papa-san hats. God knows what the people thought of us. We were barreling along like that when we came up behind an Army convoy."

The Marines were slowed to a crawl. The Army vehicles

moved up a few miles, then halted. There was half an hour's wait and the process was repeated. Puller growled his impatience but for a time endured the delay; regulations forbade the passage of another convoy in attack.

"They're pussyfooting!" the General said. "They're sending out scouts to be sure the way's clear, then going on, then stopping everything again. Dammitall, Jones, pull around 'em!"

"Yessir!" Jones lurched the jeep around the Army trucks on the narrow road, and behind them, somehow squeezing by, came the whole column of Marine vehicles. An Army jeep bore down on them from the front, headlights burning.

An Army colonel yelled: "What the hell you doing, passing a convoy? Don't you know regulations?"

Puller stood up: "Next time you open your mouth, open your eyes, and see who you're talking to."

Jones saw the officer's face sag as he recognized Puller.

"Yes, sir," the Army colonel said.

"And now, get outta my way, we're coming through," Puller said.

The colonel turned his jeep sharply off the road, plunging it over a six-foot embankment to escape the Marine's wrath. Jones gunned the jeep ahead into open country. The outfit pushed on without a halt, near full speed.

"With any luck," Puller said happily, "we'll run into a Red roadblock." He hefted the new Thompson submachine gun an Army admirer had given him.

They sped along the narrow road. The Old Man fell asleep and Jones, as usual, reached behind him with his left arm to catch the dozing General on left-hand turns. He slept all the way into Andong, where some Army units were already camped; many officers made headquarters in old buildings on a knoll, but Puller led Jones and Bodey outside. They pitched his tent on a hillside.

Oliver Smith left the Division on February 24, temporarily assigned to command the IX Corps, whose chief, General Bryant E. Moore, had died of a heart attack. Puller became commander of the First Marine Division. He was grieved by the death of Moore, his old companion of Guadalcanal; Moore had incessantly told the story in Korea: "Puller's the man who gave me my baptism of fire, there when we fought for Henderson Field, and I've been grateful to him ever since."

As he took over the Division Puller said only: "It's the greatest honor to command the greatest division." He had one opportunity to fight it in battle, and he made the most of it.

Weeks before, Puller had been in Corps Headquarters when an order came from Tokyo, directing that the body of the commander of the Dutch Brigade be recovered from the town of Hoengsang. The village was a road junction from which the 2nd Army Division had been driven by the enemy.

Now, when he was ordered to retake Hoengsang with his Marines, Puller determined to make his attack as nearly perfect as possible. He put two infantry regiments abreast, to advance through the rolling country toward the town, and called for air attacks the next morning. He told his staff: "I don't believe there's more than a handful of Communists in there. They can't hold us."

His Division was at 80 per cent strength, about 15,000 men—but at first he did not plan to throw all of it into action. He rose long before dawn on March 1, having slept little, and went to a galley where cooks worked in a school building. He put a frying pan on the edge of a stove, cooked six frozen eggs, gulped them and took off in a helicopter.

He told his regimental officers: "I don't give a damn what orders I gave last night. I won't let half the Division sit here. Get the other infantry regiment and the tanks going in a sweep to the right. Start fast."

The planes and artillery hit the town—but it was not enough for Puller. "Look at that," he growled. "We ought to have twice as many planes in here. The trouble is, not even a five-star general of any other service can give an order to an Air Force corporal out here."

All the same, the attack moved without a hitch. The infantrymen in the center poured along the road the four or five miles into Hoengsang; the Communist troops, when they saw the tanks and infantrymen on the flank, bolted from their positions and fled. The Division used only half a day in driving forward and occupying the place. Puller divided his time between the jeep in the central road, with Jones, and the helicopter.

Victory was complete and casualties were light, but Puller was not content: "If the country hadn't been so open, they'd never have seen the flank attack, and we'd have cut 'em off and annihilated 'em."

On the route he saw a sickening landscape:

"We passed an American battalion of artillery—105's ambushed and cut to bits by the Reds. They'd shot up the first and last vehicle and made mincemeat of the rest. About a third of those dead boys—and I counted 530-odd—were white Americans, a third Negro Americans, and a third South Korean. Most of the dead were on the guns, or vehicles, or very near them, cut down without a chance. They had fought hardly at all; the Reds had worked so fast that few shots were fired from our weapons. The interior vehicles and guns were so jammed on the narrow road, with rice paddies on either side, that they could not be turned around.

"I allowed no reporters or photographers to see that place. It was a disgrace to American arms. And this was not the only such incident. If I saw one shot-up American battalion in Korea I saw fifty, and I mean fifty. All were Army units."

Sergeant Jones left the jeep and walked over the scene: "I found dead boys in hiding everywhere. They had crawled into haystacks, under bridges, or into bushes and the Reds found them and shot them in the back of the head. It was pathetic. There had been a paymaster with them, with a full chest. That valley was covered with ten- and twenty-dollar bills and when the Marines came along, boy, there were some rich men that night."

After three weeks at Hoengsang, the First Marine Division was ordered to pull back. "Another damned retrograde movement," Puller called it, "caused by the withdrawal of Army troops hit by the Reds—they broke and ran, so instead of making them claw their way back, they pulled us back another ten or fifteen miles.

"We began to take prisoners who told us that the order was out among the Communist troops: 'Do not attack the First Marine Division. Leave the Yellowlegs alone. Strike the American Army.'"

Marines were soon ordered to discard their distinctive khaki leggings.

Not long afterward Marines sang a ribald song about the defeat of the 2nd Army Division, which they called "Bugout Boogie," and Puller once overheard them. Jones feared an explosion, but the General's expression did not change. Jones thought he must have been distracted and did not hear it at all.

A few days later, out of a clear sky, Puller barked at Bodey: "Bo, sing me a chorus of that 'Bugout Boogie' "—and laughed with the enlisted men at the irreverent ditty.

During Puller's brief command of the Division he had a run-in with Headquarters over the touchy matter of close air support for Marine infantrymen. Puller carried a memory of it:

"One day General Richard C. Partridge, the senior air officer in Korea, came in to our little field. He got out of his plane and his first words to me were, 'I came up to see what all this damned bellyaching from the Marines was about. How about this close air support?'

"I asked him into my office and told our tactical air people to get General Partridge's headquarters by radio—they were back at Taegu. The men tried for fifteen minutes and couldn't raise an answer. Then I asked them to try by telephone. No answer.

"General Partridge was losing his temper. He said, 'What the hell you trying to pull on me, Puller?' I told him this was what we went through every day, when we wanted air support. I asked him to look over some of our log books and note the elapsed time between our calls for air and the arrival of planes. He found that they took from one to five days to get there.

"Then I tried to explain about air power from the viewpoint of a fighting man on the ground, and that air targets were usually targets of opportunity, so far as we were concerned, and that if they weren't hit within a short time, these targets disappeared.

"Partridge went out of there without saying goodbye, though he had been drinking Marine coffee and smoking Marine cigarettes. I guess we just didn't see eye to eye."

Puller's life as division commander in Korea was cut short after ten days. Oliver Smith came back from the Corps command when a replacement was hurried from the States. Puller agreed with other veterans: "You can bet the Army wasn't about to leave a Marine in command of anything as big as a corps. Not on your life."

Puller's health had been poor for some days, but he declined to take note of his fever and weariness, as if he would rout this enemy by will power alone. Jones and Bodey saw that he was dragging and pleaded with him to see Commander Johnson, the Division Surgeon. They were surprised when the General submitted to examination. The doctor was quick: "You've got pneumonia, man. You'll have to go to bed."

"Out of the question," Puller said. "I've got work to do here."

They compromised. Puller stayed on his feet but had to submit to penicillin shots three times daily for at least four days. Jones was assigned to shadow him and when the hour for the shot arrived, was to bring in the doctor, much as if directing artillery fire. When he was finally caught, Puller docilely bared his buttocks to the needle, then went on with his work.

The tactical situation in Korea was changing, but hardly for the better. The Eighth Army had moved up toward the 38th Parallel, with the aid of a Marine drive, but despite the lack of Communist air power, progress was slow and the long line across the peninsula was often broken. There were many routs of individual units.

One day a retreat streamed past Puller's flank along a river bank in the trail of an Army unit which had pulled back under Chinese attack. The movement was led by a battalion of self-propelled guns under a young Army colonel. Jones witnessed his meeting with Puller:

"The Old Man told him to turn and fight and he could stop the Reds, who now came across the river. The colonel said he had tried, but couldn't stop 'em. The Old Man said, 'It's just because they haven't shown you how to use the guns. They're fine guns. They'll stop anything.'

"He asked the colonel if he didn't have muzzle blast shells, and found that he did. He told him to load it, and turn his guns on that attack. The Army crews began firing and made mincemeat of those Chinese. The Old Man had lined up the guns for him.

"That colonel couldn't get over it. He kept saying, 'General, I didn't lose a gun. I never saw such shooting, and we blew the Reds to pieces.' The Old Man just said, 'Colonel, you stay with me and you'll never lose a gun.' He nodded to me and Bodey. 'At least you'll never lose one as long as I've got my fire team here with me.'

"He never put on airs, that Old Man of ours, but he taught more people to fight in Korea than any school that ever was."

Before dawn one morning a runner woke Puller with word that the Chinese had broken the front of a ROK division on his flank. Puller went to his field phone and called the command post of a front-line Korea battalion.

"How many Chinese in the attack?" he asked.

"Oh, many, many, many."

Puller called the ROK division headquarters, asked the same question, and got the same answer. In disgust, he called the Marine officer with the ROK's: "How many Chinese you got, Lieutenant?"

"A whole goddam peapot full, Colonel."

"Thank God somebody up there can count," Puller said.

Puller witnessed some bad moments for the First Cavalry while he was on the line: "One night they were overrun by Chinese horse cavalry. They had dug in tanks to use as guns, and after dark the Chinese came in, galloping fast, and overran them. The First Cavalry broke, and the Chinese sabered them, hundreds of them, from horseback. My God, how could commentators tell people back home that the Eighth Army is the greatest army in American history?"

On one of his forays from headquarters Puller made a deep reconnaissance to the rear of the Division by jeep; he had already probed the country in their front. Just after dawn, when he was ten miles from the front, he and Jones met an Army general, also in a jeep.

"What are you doing out here?" the Army man asked.

"Hell. I'm reconning the rear. Afraid you guys will bug out again."

"Come on with me. We'll see the commander of the Turkish Brigade. He's a riot and he'll be full of the fight they had the other night. We'll wait until he's had a few drinks under his belt, and then he'll warm up."

They were welcomed at headquarters of the Turks and had a drink or two with their general, who described his defeat of the Chinese:

"Ahh. I can see the Chinese, he advances in formation. What you call it? Approach marching. He has on the uniforms white, for the ground with snow. I say to my children, who see them as they coming, 'Wait, my children.'

"The Chinese he is 1700 meters away, and now 1600 meters, and now 1500, and still I caution my children, 'Lie there in the snow, and fix bayonets. Do not move.' Then the Chinese he is 1200 meters away, and 900, 600, 300—100 meters. Then I say to my children: 'Allah is about to bless us, rise up and slay.' And the bayonets of my children ran red with the blood of the infidels."

Puller and the Army general laughed their appreciation, but Puller rose: "We'd better get on, General. He's had about five drinks now, and he's soon going to realize that we're infidels, too."

On his next visit to the Turkish general, Puller saw three Koreans crucified on poles before headquarters, one hanging head down. The Turk explained: "My children are poor, my country is poor, and supplies they are always stolen. When we catch thieves, we put them to death. It is the only way we can halt the thieves. It is most effective. I commend it to you."

Puller admired the brave Turks: "The best troops in Korea, by all odds—except for our Marines. They fought like demons. I wish our people had more of their spirit."

The General also defended his South Korean allies: "Now they're beginning to say the ROK's are no good, and that they always run. But they can be good. We've proved that. Don't forget those 3000 South Korean soldiers—just ordinary soldiers—that the Fifth Marines trained aboard ship on the way to Inchon. They made them into South Korean Marines.

"The way they handled them in combat made all the difference. U. S. Marine officers and noncommissioned officers assigned to each unit lived with the troops, up on the front line. When they got into fights these officers used weapons to help stand off the enemy. So the South Korean Marines never broke.

"But the ROK's who've broken so often are Army-trained. It's not because the Army is evil or cowardly—they get the same kinds of American boys we get, by and large. The difference is in their attitude and training. Army officers assigned to ROK units didn't live with the troops up front, but stayed in the rear in some kind of staff headquarters. When attacks came there was nobody around to steady the ROK's—and the officers in the rear headquarters were usually the first to run. Who could expect anything but a retreat?"

Puller then and afterward stood by his scathing denunciation of U. S. Army training: "There was not a U. S. Army or a ROK division in Korea, in my time, whose officers did not go to the rear and report that they were driven, and had to be re-equipped. Now, I consider that a scandal and absolute proof that we have been wasting money on our military machine—and that we haven't one to this day, in 1962. What we are lacking, despite all our talk about fancy weapons systems, is the fundamental spirit that alone can produce great armed services."

Puller was still a lure to men and officers. Sergeant Jones noticed that in a lull a crowd gathered about the General, men trying to get him started on his battle tales. The sergeant said: "The Old Man was too smart for that. He wouldn't let 'em bunch up enough to start drawing fire. He would always walk away, leave the officers and talk to enlisted men down the line. Good for morale, too."

Puller's reputation grew among the men, but Sergeant Jones noted that the Old Man was regarded as a man-eater:

"They would ask Bodey and me over and over how the hell we kept our stripes. They thought he chewed on people all the time, and when there was a fight, recklessly exposed his people—and of course we knew better. It was hard to convince guys who had heard so much about him, but really didn't know him. When you got close to him you found he had a heart as big as all outdoors."

Puller, Jones and Bodey worked together as a team even now that the Old Man had become a general and assistant division commander; Bodey had gone off briefly to join a front-line unit but soon reappeared as the shotgun.

Many passers-by brought gifts of whisky to the Old Man and Bodey and Jones kept a close watch upon it. Some went under Puller's cot where he could make sure of its fate, but when there was a large stock, brought by an unusual traffic of aviators, reporters and staff people from rear areas, some of the bottles were entrusted to Jones and Bodey for safekeeping. They learned that he never forgot a bottle, despite the fact that he was forever sending presents of whisky to men on the front, wherever it was needed.

A high-ranking officer once sent him two bottles of I. W. Harper and after a decent interval—during which later arrivals had been called for by the General—Jones and Bodey thought it was safe to sample this fine stock. They drank one of the bottles of Harper.

Soon after Puller got his Brigadier General's star he called for a bottle of the Harper. Jones took it in smiling—but when that was gone and Puller called for the second bottle, Jones mumbled: "That's all there is, General."

Puller genially cursed the sergeant.

"That other bottle must have got broken, General," Jones said.

Puller was not deceived: "You bastards might at least have asked me."

He never mentioned the incident again.

Once when Jones and Bodey wanted beer for a party among their friends, Jones told his gang: "I'm going up and ask the Old Man for some. He's got a couple cases, and I bet he'll give me one."

Other sergeants were aghast: "Hell, man, you don't go asking generals for a case of beer."

Jones came back with his case, grinning over a broken Corps tradition.

Jones and Bodey still cared for Puller as in the days after Inchon. Jones said: "The Old Man could tell whether it was Bodey or me came into his tent to get him up in the mornings. He said I would stomp and kick the cot and say, 'General, it's almost noon.' But Bodey would sneak in easy like a cat and shake him as if he were a baby. We tried to look after him and he looked after us."

In mid-March Puller was told that the original officers of the Division would be sent home in late May. Puller was almost fifty-three. He had been in the forefront of one of the most strenuous campaigns of his career; he had walked much of the time over punishing terrain, temperatures ranging from 120 degrees in the streets of Seoul to 25 degrees below zero in the Reservoir region. His weight was almost unchanged, and he had become harder in the process of outmarching men half his age, many of whom had lost from thirty to forty pounds during the Reservoir campaign. He had decided notions about the reasons for that—and for almost every other phase of American failure in Korea:

"Our men lost weight on K-rations. We were better fed than in World War II, everyone says, but most of my boys lost too much weight. I think it's because we had no beef. I believe that we got into trouble when the Midwest farm lobby put the services on pork in World War II—and let the British have the whole supply of Argentine corned beef."

As to the handling of American troops:

"We can't hope to win future wars—and we got the hell beat out of us in Korea—unless we have discipline. It is going to take some brutality to get it.

"I am alarmed to see that we've abandoned the Articles of War and the Articles for the Government of the Navy under which we grew great, and have only this so-called Uniform Code of Military Justice. This is an abortion. It weakens our services at the bottom."

Puller made no secret of his belief that the Communists had seriously defeated UN forces, or of his discontent with the state of affairs. He expressed himself freely to officers:

"It's a good thing I'm leaving, the way things are going. They'd have me under arrest in a couple days. Can you imagine the things they're doing now—it takes ten days to get permission from Tokyo, by God, to send out a platoon-sized patrol! Tokyo finally was forced to get permission from Washington in order to move a battalion.

"Now what's all this talk about wanting to extend the bomb line a thousand miles up into Manchuria, too? We haven't scratched things here on the tiny land mass in Korea. They've got more miles of railroad running now than when our bombers began work, and more engines and cars on the tracks."

He was equally positive in his criticism of United Nations ground strategy:

"They're going to wear us out, trying to hold a rigid line from coast to coast. It can't be done that way. We've got about 280,000 men of our own, and 10,000 British, and some 1000-man brigades of French, Dutch and Turks. Our whole trouble has been trying to hold that long line. If it had been mine to handle, I'd have formed them all up in column of divisions and marched for the heart of the enemy strength. We'd have wiped them out.

"Western armies, especially American, worry far too much about their flanks. The British retreated hundreds of miles on the Malay Peninsula in World War II, though they outnumbered the attacking Japanese, because they were too sensitive about their flanks. The Japs put a squad in the rear of a battalion of British, and forced them to retreat. It's about what we've seen in Korea. No one should retreat automatically, when they have as many men as the enemy.

"If we have a conventional war with Russia we'll find out that we have plenty to learn—and lots of courage to gain."

In May, when his departure was near, Puller sent Jones south a few days early to catch a ship: "I'm going to command the Third Brigade, at Camp Pendleton, and I want you to drive for me there. I'm flying, and you'll get in soon after I do. Good luck, old man. I'm sorry we couldn't have had a better war together."

His last days in Korea were frustrating to Puller, who found things suddenly different. He wrote his wife:

> Now age has probably changed me, and the Corps has changed, too, due, I suppose, to man being what he is today. I never thought this change could or would happen. Maybe I have been wrong from the beginning.

If Puller was losing confidence in himself in the strange new times of American defeat he quickly recovered—but he was not misled by talk of a drawn battle against the Chinese Communists: "Stalemate, hell! We've lost the first war in our history, and it's time someone told the American people the truth about it. The Reds whipped the devil out of us, pure and simple."

Before he left Korea Puller was made aware of the Eighth Army order governing all officers and men going back to the States: There would be no criticism of the American role in Korea, of allies or other services. Returning veterans were expected to watch their words.

Puller determined to obey the order. Almost as soon as the plane took off he made a list in his notebook: "Topics I will not discuss with the press."

XIX

ARE THESE AMERICANS?

A PACK of reporters waiting for Puller at San Francisco got unexpected headline copy. The General held himself in check; there was not a word of profanity in his forceful message. He did not so much as mention the Army by name, though he did have a word or so for the Air Force. He gave the writers a grim, candid picture of the Korean war:

"What the American people want to do is fight a war without getting hurt. You can't do that any more than you can go into a barroom brawl without getting hurt.

"Unless the American people are willing to send their sons out to fight an aggressor, there's just not going to be any United States. A bunch of foreign soldiers will take over.

"Air power can't live up to its billing out there. Somebody—not so much the aviators as the aircraft manufacturers—has sold the American people a bill of goods as to what air power can do. From what I've seen, one bomb will hit a section of railroad track and one hundred bombs will miss, some of them by miles. The enemy puts coolies on the track with picks and shovels and in twenty-four hours they're rolling again. The answer is infantry.

"Our officer corps have had far too much schooling and far too little combat experience. They can't learn war like that.

"Push-button war is as far off as in the days of Julius Caesar. The rifle, hand grenade and bayonet are still the most important weapons. We're going to lose the next war if we don't get back to them. . . . Why, half our infantry out there is still armed with carbines, against the enemy with their fine Russian rifles."

He then turned to the training of Marines, which he would soon be conducting at Camp Pendleton:

"We've got to get 'em tougher to survive. Throw all these girls out of camp. Get rid of the ice cream and candy. Get some pride in 'em—that's what we need now most of all, pride."

A reporter piped up: "What do you think of the protest of the Women's Christian Temperance Union over sending free beer to the troops?"

"It's news to me," Puller said. "But if a few cans of beer or a snort of whisky will make men fight better, it might not be a bad idea. At least it's better than ice cream and all this soft training."

He said farewell and boarded a plane for the East. More reporters awaited him when he touched down at Chicago. He was quizzed on his remarks in California, and gave swift replies. He expanded on the theme: "There's too damned much recreation in military training. We should have only one purpose—to fight and win. They're not being taught that now. You can bet that Marines don't get ice cream."

Would he change Marine training methods?

"I'll train my new men as Marines have always been trained. I want 'em to be able to march twenty miles, the last five at double time, and then be ready to fight."

He was off again, this time for Washington. Reporters who surrounded him at the airport in the capital were calling questions even as he kissed Mrs. Puller and Virginia Mac, who had come to meet him.

He was pumped for details about the Air Force role in Korea and came out with his theories: "The Air Force does not understand close air support, does not believe in it and has never practiced it. I do not mean to criticize any service, but I'm just stating what I saw in action. All these boys in all services are good American boys. Only their training is different."

He left for Saluda with his wife and daughter; and when he got home the telephone was buzzing. As more reporters pressed pointed questions and he sensed that the story was growing beyond recognition, Puller complained that he was being misquoted and his remarks distorted. He was astonished to see the headlines the following day:

MARINE GENERAL WANTS BEER & WHISKY FOR TROOPS

ICE CREAM GI'S LAMBASTED BY PULLER

MARINE GENERAL BLASTS AIR FORCE

The furor was reaching across the nation.

Puller turned to other affairs: His younger daughter Martha Leigh, one of the five-year-old twins, had a tonsillectomy in a Richmond hospital. The General carried the child in his arms down a corridor to the operating room, then handed her, wailing, to an orderly. He turned to his wife: "She'll never forgive me, Virginia. This is worse than Peleliu."

Martha Leigh recovered quickly, and Mrs. Puller was soon treated to an amusing sight: "I came upon my husband in her room one day, sitting on the floor happily cutting paper dolls for Martha Leigh, smoking his pipe—just a few days out of Korea. And not long after he turned to little Lewis, trying to teach him to march. He had him thumping around the house going 'Hup! Hup! Hun! Hoo! Hree! Hour!' I wish some of the people around the country who think he's such an old iron man could have seen him then."

There was a brief round of parties for the General in Virginia—one of them in the home of a cousin, Lewis Catlett Williams of Richmond. There was a crowd of forty or fifty for cocktails, and into the midst of this well-dressed throng marched a remarkable band, about twenty strong.

They were the Ampthill Guards, a neighborhood military company of little boys from eight to ten years old, armed with a variety of weapons from wooden guns to BB rifles and a .22. Their spokesman, in the most gaudy of their homemade uniforms, stepped forward:

"We thought General Puller would want to inspect us."

Their faces fell when they saw that the hero from Korea was in civilian dress, but they presented Puller with a flag made from a bedsheet emblazoned with a crude Marine Corps emblem and their own company name. Puller saluted and walked down the file, solemnly inspecting their arms. He took the name of their captain, and later sent him a sword.

One of the dinner guests that evening was the dean of Civil War historians, and biographer of Lee and Washington, Dr.

Douglas S. Freeman. Puller talked intimately of Freeman's work, since he had practically worn out a set of *Lee's Lieutenants* during World War II, and in the course of an animated conversation Freeman led him into the library for a private talk.

"Why don't you write a history of the Korean war, Dr. Freeman?"

"General, the true history of a war cannot be written for at least eighty-five years afterward."

"Where would you go to find out the truth about the war in Korea, eighty-five years from now?"

"Why, to the archives of the United States—to the official records."

Puller grinned wryly. "That's exactly where you'd never find the truth, Doctor. The truth about battle, by its very nature, can't get into the records—and the truth about Korea has yet to come out anywhere."

After a month's leave in Virginia the Pullers reported to Camp Pendleton, where the Third Brigade was preparing for overseas. There were echoes from the "beer and whisky" incident daily, but not until Puller settled in his new post did he get the full impact. He was shocked by the deluge of vicious letters awaiting him, and the insulting telephone calls which came in salvos. He would grumble to Orville Jones or officers of the staff: "What the hell kind of people have we got in this country? I believe they'd rather have their sons killed in war, for lack of training, than have them made into men. You'd think I was one of the enemy. Look at this."

One letter opened:

> You yellow-livered bastard. I'll bet my last nickel you're a fat-headed command post soldier who never heard a shot fired. . . . I challenge you to fight me in a duel, if you have the guts.

Puller was stung to reply:

> I accept your offer. I specify sawed-off double-barreled shotguns at ten paces as the weapons. You may specify the place—any place between San Diego and Richmond. I will meet you.

There was no reply.
Another letter opened: "Dear Sir: You beast!"

A Texas college president began a campaign to have Puller drummed out of the Corps.

Though Jones and aides kept many of these letters from the General, their impact was strong enough; Puller never understood the public reaction and particularly that of people who said that they preferred Russian rule to such a regime as Puller proposed in the armed forces. Within a few days tempers cooled a bit, and a more serious phase of the incident began, with letters from organized groups couched in a vein of injured restraint. A typical one went to an Alabama Congressman from the woman chairman of the Spiritual Life Committee of Birmingham, Alabama, protesting "the diet of beer and whisky General Puller has proposed":

We understand he is shortly to take over the 3rd Marine Brigade at Camp Pendleton, California, where any number of young men from this area are sent from time to time. In the light of the new draft law, placing the age of draftees at 18, believing firmly in temperance in all things, abhorring the evils of alcohol and its effects upon humanity and knowing that it has never made a good soldier . . . we hereby petition you to use every ounce of influence that you possess to keep Brigadier General Puller from inaugurating his BEER & WHISKY campaign in the U. S. military training camps.

Marine Corps Headquarters, worried over the attack on one of its most distinguished officers, fired back.

. . . General Puller did *not* advocate giving our troops whisky and beer, and if he did the Commandant most certainly would reprimand him for such a gross misrepresentation of Marine Corps moral standards. . . .

We regret this unfortunate application made in the press, but we are firm in our defense of him and of his later statement in which he denied ever having advocated beer and whisky for our troops. And General Puller would fight such a proposal vehemently, for he is a moral and temperate man. . . .

No one need fear that General Puller will encourage his troops to drink alcoholic beverages, for believe me, the contrary is true. However, to reassure you I offer an official statement that the Marine Corps today, as it always has in times past, regards intoxication as an offense punishable by court martial and we will never encourage such offenses by issuing our men whisky.

There was a letter from the public information office of the Corps, signed by Brigadier General J. C. McQueen:

> It may surprise you to learn that General Puller is a devout church member who would never permit, let alone advocate, intemperance among his troops. The suggestion that he would change an American boy into a booze-hound is a source of deep distress to him, because he and Mrs. Puller are raising their own children in the finest tradition of Christian living. As for his courage, for three decades his name has inspired Marines from Nicaragua to Wonsan; his valor has made him beloved among the enlisted men of the Corps, and we all share a tremendous pride in his leadership.

There also was a scattering of letters of impassioned defense from old Marines in newspapers across the country.

The minority for the defense was led by an old Puller student. Gregory (Pappy) Boyington, the World War II ace who had once been decorated by Harry Truman with the Medal of Honor, presumed on that acquaintance to write to the President about Puller and the "beer and whisky" furor:

> I am enclosing a newspaper clipping and I would like to take the liberty of explaining the life of the greatest soldier of any service that has existed. I had the honor and pleasure of serving under General Puller when he was a Captain in the Marine Corps. I never served under General Puller in combat; however, I know his record from A to Z. I would like better than anything in the world to have you look into his record.
>
> General Puller is entitled to the Congressional Medal of Honor more than any living person in the United States. He has been awarded five Navy Crosses and numerous smaller honors. . . . He has had at least ten men that I know of serving beside him that have received the Congressional Medal of Honor. I know to be a fact that because of professional jealousy in the higher echelon this truly great and courageous man has not been given his just deserts.
>
> Believe me, I want nothing for myself. If my friend can be recognized I will have the one and only wish that I shall ever ask from a President, Congressman or Representative as long as I live. . . . I pray to God that something may be done for General Puller while he is still living.

When the President's office passed this to Marine Headquarters there was an official reply that records revealed no recommendation for the Medal of Honor for Puller—but the Corps sent a list of his decorations and copies of citations for the Navy Crosses. There the matter dropped.

On his first tour of inspection of Pendleton, Puller found that the Brigade had no enlisted men's club. He summoned the officer in charge: "This is Wednesday. By Friday there will be a slop chute open for the men of this brigade, with a free beer party the first night."

The club opened Friday night somewhat disastrously. Two companies of celebrating Marines staged a free-for-all with such enthusiasm that twenty went to the hospital. The incident shook their regimental commander, who was fresh from Washington headquarters duty and unaccustomed to troop command. Puller calmed him: "If I were in Company A and you were in B, and you told me B was better, I'd punch you in the nose. That's what happened. It'll wash out. When you handle this thing don't forget that I make out your fitness report."

Soon afterward Puller gave the troops a 72-hour pass, and when they came straggling in on Monday morning sent them on a twenty-mile hike, with orders that no one should ride. Sergeant Jones drove the General out to check results about mid-morning:

"The Old Man came up on the colonel in a jeep, and man, did he blow. He asked him if he didn't hear the order that all would walk, and then sent the driver back to camp with that jeep. He told the colonel he needed conditioning worse than anyone else.

"That night, we rode way up in the hills and found the colonel soaking his raw feet in a helmet—but after a few months that man was down to a good, hard hundred and eighty pounds. When Puller left the post, the colonel told him he'd done more for him than anyone else in the Marine Corps. He said he felt better than he ever had."

The General seldom took his eye from the troops and once when he and Jones entered a post exchange and encountered long lines of waiting men Puller asked: "What's all this about, Jones?"

"They're getting breakfast, sir."

"Why don't they get it at the regular hour? Hell, it's eight o'clock."

"They don't get up for breakfast, General. They turn over

for thirty more winks when the bugle blows, and wait until it's time to go to work, then they come in here later and take their coffee break."

"Any idea how I can fix that?"

"Yes, sir. March 'em to chow."

The revival of the old-fashioned system began the next day.

One morning Jones entered the office to find the Old Man angrily tearing a government booklet into ribbons and flinging them into a waste can. "Look at this, Jones," he said. "A guidebook for liars—they want every officer back from Korea to toe the mark, and carefully avoid saying anything that would frighten the taxpayers. Anything but the truth. Dammitall, I'll never lie to 'em. Why, twenty years ago, they'd have put you in the brig for proposing something like that to an officer."

When anyone asked about the fitness of the Third Brigade, Puller responded characteristically. Jones overheard him reply to a question one day: "We're in perfect shape. I could take it to China today, burn Peking, and be out in ten days." Jones winked at the duty sergeant: "He could do it, too, boy."

Many youngsters of the Third Brigade, who were being formed into a new division, had never seen Puller but had heard hundreds of legends about him. Hundreds were introduced on a day when the General inspected a field transport outfit during a training exercise.

Puller went down the ranks and halted before a platoon leader: "Have the men drop their packs, remove boots and socks and make changes to those in their packs."

The young Marines stared, for most of them had not obeyed his order to carry extra footgear—an item they never afterward forgot.

"All right," Puller said. "You march in what you have, under my orders. If you brought boots and socks, good. If you brought socks but no boots, you march in sock feet. If you brought neither, you'll go barefoot."

They marched back to barracks over rough, rocky roads. The lesson struck home.

Mrs. Oliver Smith called Mrs. Puller on the morning of February 2, 1952.

"Virginia, I know Lewis probably hasn't said a word of it,

but my husband is pinning his fifth Navy Cross on Lewis today—I thought you'd like to be there."

"Heavens, no! Not a word. Thank you. We'll be there."

Mrs. Puller rushed to the drill field ceremony with her mother in tow and watched with the troops as General Smith awarded medals, including Puller's Navy Cross.

As he pinned on the gold star for his fifth Cross, Smith said: "Lewis, you ought to be getting the Medal of Honor for this—like they do with the Air Medal, win five, and get the next highest."

The fifth Cross was for heroism at the Reservoir, holding together the rear guard. The citation summoned up memories: "Fighting continuously in sub-zero weather against a vastly outnumbering hostile force . . . although the area was frequently covered by grazing machine gun fire and intense artillery and mortar fire, he coolly moved among his troops to insure their correct tactical deployment. . . . During the attack from Koto-ri to Hungnam, he expertly utilized his regiment as the division rear guard, repelling two fierce enemy assaults which severely threatened the security of the unit, and personally supervised the care and prompt evacuation of all casualties."

Puller grinned when he came off the parade ground and an officer hailed him: "What's this one for, Lewie?"

"I guess I got on the mailing list," he said.

The star was added to the collection of the "most decorated Marine" in history and Sergeant Jones complained, with some reason, that his hardest job was the care of the General's fifty-odd decorations. The sergeant was forever changing, arranging or repairing these, since regulations required that they be in apple-pie order. Changing of uniforms damaged clasps and ribbons; Jones kept a maintenance kit with needles, thread and soldering tools.

In the summer of 1951 there was a spirited reunion of veterans of the First Marine Division in Philadelphia, where Puller was the star of the show. The crowd drowned out speakers at a banquet program with chants of: "We want Puller! We want Puller!" and was quieted only when the master of ceremonies waved the General to the podium. Puller spoke for about two minutes, and after a brief bedlam of applause the Marines quieted for other speakers.

The climax of the reunion was a street parade led by

Puller, which he brought to an end by bellowing from the head of the column without breaking step:

"Fall out! Follow me!"

He strode into a bar, followed by more than fifty men and ordered the stunned bartender to serve the crowd. The General paid the bill.

Puller once opened a package from Korea—the last souvenir from that campaign: It was his copy of Henderson's *Stonewall Jackson,* dirty and worn on every page, with much of the text underlined, and Jackson's mottoes copied in margins and on flyleaves in Puller's hand. The firm resolve of Stonewall, "Never take counsel of your fears," was written large on the pages. At the end of the book Puller had listed the casualties of his battalion at Guadalcanal and a list of its decorations. The covers of the book were held on with bicycle tape, but a Marine officer who had found it in Puller's vacated van in Korea knew that it was priceless to the General.

With more than one hundred officers from other services, Puller was ordered to Sandia Air Force Base, New Mexico, for a briefing on atomic warfare. The Government made an elaborate security check on him before he was allowed to join the group.

Puller met an admiral at the base who spoke with some pride of the vast amounts of money spent on the project:

"General, do you know that it cost the Government three thousand dollars to clear you before you're allowed to set foot here?"

"That applies to all of us who came in?"

"Absolutely."

"Well, I'm a general officer of the Marine Corps, and I've been in service more than thirty years. Why was all this necessary? You'd think that by the time they promoted me to general that they'd have made all necessary investigation years ago. It looks to me as if they check the wrong people, and pass up the right ones."

The First Division reunion of 1952, in Washington, all but dissolved in anarchy at its banquet session while the Commandant, General Lemuel Shepherd, was speaking. Puller, still only a brigadier, was not scheduled to speak, but was within view of the rowdy veterans. A chorus began:

"Siddown, Shepherd! Give us Puller. We want Chesty!"

Within a moment it was beyond control. MP's came in and dragged about fifty men from the room; Colonel Henry Heming, Puller's World War II paymaster, bailed them out of jail.

The ballroom continued to resound to shouts of "We want Puller!" until Shepherd could no longer be heard. The Commandant cut short his talk, and Puller spoke briefly.

Lewis was acutely embarrassed; when the session was over and he passed a cool, silent Shepherd in a corridor, he had a twinge of alarm.

In the summer of 1952, as the Korean War neared an end, Puller was moved from Camp Pendleton to the amphibious training center at Coronado, California, where he had command of the Troop Training Unit. He was restless at first and missed being with his brigade in the field, but General Shepherd calmed him with an explanation that the post was vital to the Corps as the heart of the amphibious warfare program.

Puller's fitness reports in these days were glowing tributes: "A highly qualified troop leader, loyal, honest and firm in his convictions . . . I would very much like to have him with me in the field at any time. . . . An officer of strong and firm military character and the very highest personal integrity . . . on the field of battle he would have no superior in leadership. His administration of his present command has left nothing to be desired. . . . We need more officers of the Puller stamp in our armed services, and I very emphatically recommend him for promotion to Major General at the earliest opportunity."

Brigadier General J. C. Miller, Jr., who served with him at Coronado, found Puller a good administrative officer, though impatient with paper-shuffling. "He would often call Washington direct on some problem—a thing that would have scared most Marine officers to death. He got things done."

One of Puller's chief interests in these months was the building of a Marine Corps for Chiang Kai-shek on Formosa. Miller was in charge of the training of this allied force, but Puller watched every move and made constant suggestions. He insisted that the training be on an individual basis and that every man be taught the use of every weapon, to climb landing nets, get into small boats at sea, and learn all tricks of the amphibious trade. He was intent upon perfection in the creation of the world's second largest Marine Corps.

Twice a year Puller flew to Formosa to inspect the work of Taiwan's Marines at first hand. He frequently saw Chiang Kai-shek, who once invited Puller to an intimate luncheon meeting. Chiang used an interpreter:

"The Generalissimo hopes that the General Puller has given thought to his problem of invading the Chinese mainland."

"I have," Puller said. "Say to him that he must first have plenty of bullets and beans."

The interpreter hesitated over "beans," but Chiang soon understood.

"It matters little where he lands, since the coast is so long," Puller said. "Just pick a spot where the population would be friendly. Then all he has to do is drive on at full strength. There's plenty of room to maneuver."

Chiang grinned his approval.

"But the most important of all," Puller said, "tell him that he must put to death every Communist bastard he meets. There can be no quarter."

Chiang's eyes filled.

"Tell General Puller," he said, "that I used to have generals like that myself. But no more. No more."

The old man brightened and added: "I think I know why my generals are not brave like that nowadays—it is because they were trained at your Leavenworth."

Puller laughed. "You're right. They teach little war in that place."

The friendship between Chiang and Puller lasted for years. The Generalissimo does not forget the retired Marine General at Christmas; he sends boxes of fine teas to the family in Saluda, Virginia.

Puller made two visits to the Korean forces while he was at Coronado and was depressed by what he saw: "My God, the men had shoes shined and pants pressed, and irons in every tent to keep them looking trim. It looks to me as if we've settled back to an occupation force out here—and that's never been worth a tinker's dam."

In August, 1953, Puller took examinations for Major General and passed; the board which chose the new group of officers of the rank approved him unanimously.

Near the end of his stay at Coronado, in 1954, Puller inadvertently stirred up another hornet's nest, this time inside the Navy Department. He wrote the Secretary of Navy, pointing out that the two great training bases of the Marine Corps, Camp Pendleton in California and Camp Lejeune in North Carolina, were of limited use. Pendleton, he reminded, could not be used for realistic landing games, since a well-used highway cut between the sea and the camp. Camp Lejeune was similarly handicapped by the Inland Waterway.

Puller proposed that the U.S. take advantage of the Bryan-Chamorro Treaty of 1914 under which Marines might establish a training base in Nicaragua. He suggested the Bay of Fonseca as a perfect spot, for there an entire corps could practice landing at once, rather than splitting into divisions on each coast. "Not since World War II," he reminded, "has a Marine officer been able to handle a corps."

The letter was returned from Washington "for consideration." An admiral told Puller privately: "In all my tour of duty in Washington, yours was the only sensible suggestion that crossed my desk. You're the only one around who even knew there was such a treaty with Nicaragua. You embarrassed some of the big boys."

A Navy team investigated the Bay of Fonseca and found the waters and beaches to be ideal, but the matter went no further. Though the plan was approved by General Franklin A. Hart, commander of the Fleet Marine Force, Pacific, and by the Navy's Pacific Commander, Admiral Radford, it did not get approval of the Marine Corps Commandant.

Puller later thought: "This was the beginning of the end for me in the Marine Corps. They just couldn't admit to Congress and the public that we'd wasted all that money and time on inadequate training bases."

Puller's time on the Pacific Coast was short. In July, 1954, he was sent to Camp Lejeune to lead the Second Division, his first major peacetime troop command. He took over the division on a searing hot day when men toppled from the ranks and were taken away in ambulances waiting in the rear. Puller fretted at the arrangements, for instead of walking down the ranks as he preferred, he was obliged to ride in a brass-railed jeep with the outgoing commander, darting back and forth across the parade ground.

When he took the microphone to call his welcome to the Second Division Puller said: "It gives me great pleasure to assume command of the First Marine Division." He corrected himself when there was laughter from the ranks, but the men understood that he had spent his career with the First. They seemed to like him from the start.

Sergeant Orville Jones, who was still with him as driver, saw that Puller had not lost his touch with the men. One rain-swept morning when the troops were in the pine woods on maneuvers Puller rode out in a staff car with a colonel. Jones drove them. Puller rolled down his rear window when they neared a marching column so that he could see the men. A raucous and anonymous voice called:

"Yeah, we're getting wet, Chesty, ya ol' bastard! Ya satisfied?"

The colonel shook with rage. "Stop!" he shouted. "Stop, Jones! I'll get the name of that sonofabitch if it's the last thing I do."

Jones glanced into the mirror. Puller's expression had not changed.

"Drive on, Jones," the General said. "If it had been me out there, and the C.O. had come by in a staff car, I'd have said the same damned thing."

One of Puller's first discoveries on the base was that there were staggering numbers of court-martials. He called in his sergeant major for an explanation:

"Well, sir. It's the beer. They don't allow beer in the enlisted men's clubs at noon, and the men have been stepping across the street to the civilian beer joints. The MP's pick 'em up."

Puller solved the problem within seconds: "Tell the clubs to serve beer at noon and let me hear no more of this foolishness. You just make sure we have no drunkenness. We've got more to do than hold courts." The problem of absenteeism disappeared.

The new General also canceled orders requiring Marines to wear dress uniforms to baseball games and other sporting events, ending more gripes and discomfort.

Puller was now just past his fifty-sixth birthday, but was evidently in good physical condition. One of his privates, Robert Dutro, long remembered an August day when Puller walked out two miles from headquarters to inspect his unit, and looked at every rifle of every Marine in the ranks. "Colonel's came puffing up in his rear, trying to catch him," Dutro said. "He walked 'em down."

The date was August 26, 1954. Puller inspected more than 800 men of a battalion being sent overseas during the hottest part of the day and in the evening went on a stag party with the mayor of the nearby town of Jacksonville and a few friends. He was out late. The next morning he began inspection of stores in base warehouses, and was not content until he had crawled up ladders in the concrete-and-steel buildings to see that supplies were ready for overseas shipment in case of war. He left the warehouse area just before noon and returned to his office.

He walked across the room toward his desk and bumped into a lounge chair. He retreated—and struck the chair again. The third time he stumbled Puller kicked the chair from his path and sat at the desk. He signed a stack of mail, and when Brigadier General Ed Snedeker, his Assistant Division Commander, entered the room, Puller was ready for lunch.

Snedeker noticed that he was pale and tense, but sensed nothing more until they were seated at the mess table. Puller attempted to snuff out a cigarette in an ashtray and ground it into the table instead. Snedeker saw that he had difficulty getting food to his mouth.

Puller turned to his aide, Captain Marc Moore: "Marc, I feel sick."

Moore called a car. At the nearby dispensary a young officer greeted them: "All the senior doctors are out, sir. They'll be back at one o'clock. I suggest you go to the hospital."

The doctor at the base hospital took quick stock of the General's condition: Difficulty in vision, intense vertigo, clearing quickly. Fully conscious. Difficulty in releasing an object grasped with the left hand. Blood pressure 150/100, pulse rate 88, respiration 20. He gave Puller an injection of sodium phenobarbital: "Shortly afterward lapsed into an unresponsive state, threshing wildly about. This was controlled with sedation."

The General went under an oxygen tent.

Snedeker called Virginia Puller: "Brace yourself. We've taken Lewis to the hospital, and they can't say just what's wrong. He looks pretty sick."

Doctors and officers found Mrs. Puller less excited than they had expected. She insisted that he have doctors around the clock and not be left to nurses or corpsmen. She slept in a nearby room. At 2 A.M. a doctor entered to tell her the General was noticeably better, but a chaplain who came told her to prepare to lose her husband.

"Oh, no," she said. "You don't know him. He's not about to die. I know he'll pull through."

Orville Jones stayed all night in the hospital, waiting for a glimpse of the Old Man. When someone entered the door Puller caught sight of the sergeant and beckoned: "Jones, what happened to me? I crack up out there?"

"No, sir. Just too much heat. The sun got you. That inspection would've killed most officers."

"Jones, you're the best doctor in this hospital."

His doctors seemed puzzled that Puller regained consciousness that morning and that his reactions returned quickly to normal. After the third day he complained only of a morning headache, which disappeared after breakfast. Puller carried on a lively campaign to obtain tobacco, and begged a nurse: "How about bringing me a pipe or at least a cigar?"

"General, nobody smokes in this hospital, anywhere, except in the nurses' quarters."

"Hell, that's fine. I'd like that. Let's go."

The original diagnosis had been ominous: "A mild stroke, followed by more severe recurrence in the hospital. Cerebral vascular thrombosis." But as Puller recovered, with no signs of paralysis, all doctors attending him came to the conclusion that he was fit for duty. The diagnosis was changed: "Hypertensive cardiovascular disease (benign)." In lay language, the doctors told Puller, he had high blood pressure, but if he took care of himself, he was fit for any duty. He took a brief sick leave.

In November he passed his annual physical by a board of three Navy doctors who reported: "There is no residual of his thrombosis. The left field defect has completely disappeared. The Board is further of the opinion that the benign hypertensive cardiovascular disease is mild in character and is not disabling. There is absolutely no complication. . . . The Board is of the opinion that he is fit . . . to perform the duties of his rank at sea and in the field and recommends that he be returned to a duty status."

Puller was elated.

There had been many cheering messages. One came from Rear Admiral Arleigh Burke, now commanding Cruiser Division Six of the Atlantic Fleet:

> Dear Chesty:
> I should like to add my good wishes for your early recovery. . . . The United States, the Marine Corps, and the

Navy owe a great deal to you, who have exemplified over and over again in many battles those tenacious, hard-fighting qualities which are so essential to any military force, and particularly to our men. I will never forget the feeling of pride when you and your troops took Seoul, and the splendid example of the hard-fighting Marines which you led so magnificently. It isn't often that I get sentimental, but I would like you to know that your brand of leadership is the brand that the United States needs badly. . . . Take it easy. Best regards,

Arleigh

There was another from Oliver Smith, now commander of the Fleet Marine Force, Atlantic, who knew Puller so intimately:

I am very happy to know that you have come through your ordeal in fine shape. I am sure you will obey injunctions of the doctors to take it easy for a while. The Division, as you well know, is in good hands and you will not have to concern yourself with the Lantflex-1-55 exercise.

You may not realize it, but all hands in the Marine Corps were pulling for your rapid recovery. You occupy in their affections a place which no other officer does. You have every reason to be proud of and grateful for the respect and affection you have earned.

There were hundreds of such messages. One of his mates from Fort Benning, Class of 1932. Major General C. T. (Buck) Lanham, of the Armed Forces Staff College, wrote:

In common with everyone else who has known and admired you, and indeed marveled at you, I have long entertained the conviction that you were immortal. . . . Ever since those grand days we shared at Benning I have looked on you as a legendary character. All that has happened since has confirmed my original conviction. . . . If there is anything that you would like, from reading material to rubbing whiskey, give me a ring. . . ,

Brigadier General J. S. (Buzz) Letcher, of Nicaraguan days, wrote:

You are the most distinguished officer of the Marine Corps and your distinction comes from being the greatest combat officer that the Corps ever produced. You epitomize what the Marine Corps stands for in the hearts of the American people . . . you are its greatest fighter. . . .

A retired major general, Bill Scheyer, now living in California, sounded a warning:

> Perhaps I shouldn't say this, but anyone who has been through what you have, will probably be threatened with retirement. If you are, remember that there is a bright side to retirement. I have been happier since my retirement than I can remember. . . . Have you ever thought that "the most decorated man" in the Marine Corps could write the story of his life. . . . Your story would be an inspiration to every American boy. . . .
>
> Take it easy. A lot of people have failed in their attempts to kill Puller. Make sure that you don't do it yourself. . . .

Puller relaxed. His trouble, he was persuaded, had been sunstroke. He dutifully took the pills doctors prescribed and went about the training of the Second Division.

On a late November day not long after the good news from his annual physical, Puller was jolted by a penciled note from General Ridgely, the personnel officer in Corps Headquarters. General Shepherd had asked, before flying to the Orient, that Puller come to Bethesda, Maryland, Naval Hospital for a further check of his condition. Admiral H. L. Pugh, chief of the Bureau of Medicine, had agreed to this.

Puller telephoned Ridgely in anger. "I'm ready to come up today," he said.

"You can't do that. It'll take two weeks to get ready for the tests."

"I'll be there then. What the hell kind of an outfit are you running up there, that it takes all this time?"

Puller was apprehensive, but did not suspect the worst. He never forgot his visit to Bethesda.

"Almost the first person I saw there was Admiral Pugh, rolling in a wheelchair—he'd had a heart attack. We'd been enlisted men together back in World War I days. He asked me what the hell I was doing in the hospital and I told him he'd ordered me there—or Marine Corps Headquarters said that he had. He said he'd done no such thing, and when I showed him Ridgely's note he said it was not true. He said he hadn't even talked to General Shepherd about it—but that he had talked with Ridgely and General Pate.

"I could see then what the game was—they were going to retire me, despite all the doctors had said back at Lejeune. They had pulled me up to Washington to get rid of me. I didn't mind retiring all that much, but the way they did it made me sore. I'd had all the service and honors I needed or wanted; I'd come all the way from private to major general. But I was boiling mad about this thing. I saw lots of officers around Washington in poorer condition than I was, but that wasn't going to matter."

He remained in the hospital in Bethesda for about two weeks. After many consultations, the doctors found him unfit for duty. He wrote his wife daily from his room on the sixteenth floor:

> Please do not worry. We must take things as they come in this life. There doesn't seem much that we can do to change events.

He wrote of a visit from the commander of the hospital which produced a surprise from Headquarters:

> He brought me up a copy of a modification to my orders. My orders read to report here for a physical examination and not retirement. The modification will send me before a retirement board. Nice people at Headquarters. We now know beyond a doubt what I suspected all along!

General Shepherd phoned with an invitation to dinner, but Puller declined. He attended a conference of Marine generals and appeared at a reception given by Shepherd. He wrote Virginia of this, enclosing a newspaper clipping which mentioned him, saying: "I am glad that when they wrote of my ribbons they mentioned the five Navy Crosses."

He also wrote briefly of the problem of his retirement:

> I spent the morning and early afternoon at the second day of Marine Headquarters conference and talked privately with Shepherd. I went over the whole question again exactly as I did in my talks with you, many times, and his reply was, "It is out of my hands and entirely up to the doctors." So that is it. Again he remained mute when I asked if he had talked with Admiral Pugh. I hope they will soon send me home to you and happiness.

Just before his return home he wrote:

My retirement board will meet on the 10th of August. We may count on going to the retired list anytime between 10th August and 1st September. Marine Corps Headquarters has decided and that is the end of me in the Corps. I am all right in all respects except that I did have that accident on the 27 of last August. My blood pressure is now 140 over 80. And there are no aftereffects of the accident. The doctors say that if I take care of myself and get plenty of rest, I can expect to reach an old age. I will live only for you and our precious children and my requirements will be your great love, a little food, and a daily can of tobacco.

Puller never changed his opinion that there had been a conspiracy of sorts within Corps Headquarters to shunt him aside, though he mellowed a bit in later years. He took advantage of every appeal, and retained Colonel Paul D. Sherman as his counsel to appear before boards of the Corps.

Toward the end, in September, 1955, Colonel Sherman filed a statement:

Each board in the complicated system of retirement proceedings has arrived at a different conclusion in this case. One board, the Physical Review Council, has expressed two different conclusions. . . . Furthermore, medical officers, Marine officers and a Naval officer have made diagnoses differing radically from that established by the doctors at the Naval hospitals who examined the evaluee while he was a patient. All of the former have arrived at separate diagnoses without examining the patient. . . .

If General Puller, with all his professional qualifications, has only the minimum of disability—less than many officers now on active duty, and equal, even, to that of one member of the Board before which his case was appealed—then there is no doubt that he should be given special consideration and his value to the service weighed against that of others who are currently being retained on active duty. . . . Not only justice to a distinguished officer, but plain humanity requires that his desires be deferred to in the matter of retaining him on the rolls of the Marine Corps.

. . . It would be improper and unconscionable to use the very minimum of disability found by the Physical Review Council . . . for eliminating this fine officer from his profession.

It was in vain. The findings of the Bethesda doctors prevailed and Corps Headquarters did not intervene to give Puller further duty which would have retained him as a morale-builder. Oliver Smith thought he should have been kept as commander of a recruit depot. General Frank Lowe, the Army agent for President Truman in Korea, thought Puller's retirement was not in order and was a grave disservice to the Corps and to the country.

Headquarters had two sharp notes of inquiry from U. S. Senators—John F. Kennedy of Massachusetts and Herbert H. Lehman of New York, who wanted the reasons behind the departure of the fighting symbol of the Corps. Staff officers replied with a résumé of official facts in the case.

The letters between Shepherd and Puller were unfailingly polite in tone. Shepherd had written:

> I am most distressed. . . . I have personally discussed your case with Admiral Pugh, Admiral Hogan, Captain Tayloe and other medical officers. These officers are unanimous in their opinion that they do not consider you physically capable to perform the strenuous duties of a commander in the field, nor to sustain for any period of time the mental strain of a great responsibility. . . .
>
> I have made inquiry as to whether I have the authority to disapprove the entire proceedings and order you to full duty. This, I am informed, is outside the scope of my authority.
>
> I fully realize, Lewis, how crushed you and Virginia are at the findings of the Board of Medical Survey. I can assure you of my personal as well as official distress that your illustrious career in the Marine Corps should come to a close at this time. You have served your country with great distinction over a period of many years, including two wars and Korea. Your name is legend as a troop leader and professional soldier and will go down through generations of Marines yet to be born. Frankly, Lewis, you and Virginia must face up to the facts in this case. . . .
>
> Lest there be the slightest shadow of a doubt in this matter, I wish to make it perfectly clear that neither I personally nor any officer in this Headquarters was responsible for your being brought to Bethesda for further examination. . . .
>
> Although I deeply regret to do so, in view of the recommendation contained therein, I cannot leave you in command of the Second Division.

General Shepherd revived the old post of deputy commander of the base at Camp Lejeune and offered it to Puller for five months. He ended with a note of warmth:

This has been a difficult letter for me to write, Lewis, as I know how hard it will be for you to live any other life than that of an active Marine officer. You must realize, however, as I am beginning to do, with only eleven months more of active duty before I retire, that there comes a time when all old soldiers must pass on their swords to those we have been training to take our place. I confess it's a tough bullet to chew, but I am confident you will face it with the same courage you have demonstrated so many times on the battlefield.

Puller went back to Camp Lejeune to serve as deputy commander until October, 1955, but there was little or nothing for him to do. His office was moved from the bustling quarters he had once occupied to a small room far down the hall, beyond a barber shop and supply rooms. He was so lonesome that an old acquaintance on the base, Sergeant Major Robert Norrish, who had been on Puller's winning drill team of 1925, was once asked to visit the General, if he had nothing important to do.

The base newspaper conducted a contest to name a new baseball field, and though the vast majority of Marines seemed to be voting for Puller, a Marine baseball player won the honor instead—and still the Corps had accorded Puller no honor beyond those he wore on his chest.

There was little ceremony at his passing from the service. Headquarters sent down a special Cravat to be given to Puller as he was awarded the third star of a Lieutenant General, a rank he would reach as he retired. Washington also asked if Puller would like to have *Life* magazine send down for a story, as it had offered to do. Puller declined. The troops were away on maneuvers and the base was empty: "I knew it wouldn't look like anything. I didn't want a fuss, anyway."

A day or so before he went out, there was a party in the noncommissioned officers' club on the base. Puller had declined an offer from the officers' club, but could not turn down the enlisted men. It began as an intimate party, but when Puller arrived he found a crowd of more than five thousand who had come to say goodbye. Twenty pigs were barbecued and there was feasting and drinking until late in the night. The General made one of his short, brusque talks when they shouted for him, and as Sergeant Orville Jones remembered it, he said only:

"Men, I'd rather be toting a rifle in a rear rank than

going out now as Lieutenant General. . . . Now, if you're
Marine, you're all Marine. You'll put the Corps above your
family, your country, even God and all else in some cases.
You stick to your Corps. God bless you."

The day came on October 31, 1955. The place was the
office of General Russ Jordahl, the acting commanding officer
of the base and a companion of Basic School days.

The crowd was small: General Jordahl; Captain Marc
Moore, the aide; Sergeant Orville Jones; Sergeant Major Bob
Norrish; an officer from the post information office; and a
latecomer, a civilian newspaper man.

Puller had broken tradition to the last. It was an unwritten
regulation that the senior Marine officer on the post would
pin Puller's third star on his shoulder as he retired—but
Puller had called for Bob Norrish, the senior noncom, and
the oldest man available who had served with him.

"Okay," Puller said. "Let's get it over with."

Norrish pinned the stars on the shoulders in silence. A
photographer's flash bulb crackled and it was over.

Puller stood at attention, eyes straight ahead. He smiled.
"I hate like hell to go." Someone handed him a three-star
flag, he shook hands around and went out.

The reporter who followed him got a formal statement: "In
having Sergeant Major Norrish attach my third star at my
retirement, I wanted to show my great admiration and appreciation to the enlisted men and junior officers of the Marine Corps. I fully realize that without the help of the enlisted men I'd never have risen from a private to lieutenant
general.

"I've commanded everything from a squad to a division
and without the help of men and junior officers, these units
would never have gone forward and achieved their objective,
regardless of almost certain death.

"My only regret is that as things now are I won't be
present for the next war.

"I also want to express my regret at the deaths of many
hundreds of Marines and the crippling and maiming of other
hundreds who followed me blindly into battle. Again I would
like to thank all Marines for their feelings toward me."

There was a flurry of protest from the public, chiefly
from old Marines. The magazine *Esquire* published a biting

article, "Waste of an Old War Horse," deploring the retirement of the Corps's living legend.

Puller had still more letters from officers in the Corps. General Shepherd wrote:

> The glorious history of our Corps has been forever illuminated by your illustrious achievements. Time will not dim the record of your burning devotion to duty, or the brilliance of your leadership. . . . Marines who served with you in battle were inspired to seek victory and honor at all costs. Marines shall always be inspired by that tradition which honors the name Puller as a symbol of fighting courage.

There was one from Oliver Smith:

> My association with you has meant much to me over the years. Your example of devotion to duty is a legend in the Marine Corps. Your methods have always been honest, direct and forthright. There is no indirection or deviousness in your character. You have acted with singleness of purpose guided by your highest sense of right. These are the traits of character I have admired, in which I am joined by your host of friends.

Lieutenant General Eddie Craig, who had served with Puller from Nicaragua to Korea, wrote from retirement in California in a different vein, expressing the feelings of men of the Corps:

> It's a damn shame that they would not let you continue on as you and your many friends would like you to do. So many have been nursed along on active duty regardless of their condition, while you, who are really OK and capable of performing your duty, are forced to retire. It is all hard to understand. However, the way some things go in the service today one feels just as well off on the retired list.

Lewis Puller went home to Virginia. It was just thirty-seven years, four months and two days since he had boarded the train for South Carolina to exchange the uniform of a V.M.I. cadet for that of a Marine Corps boot. He was fifty-seven years old, five years under the mandatory retirement age.

GREAT elms arched over the streets of little Saluda, a Confederate monument dwarfed the tiny brick courthouse, and on every side farmlands rolled gently toward the tidal Virginia rivers. Each morning, almost without fail, General Puller strode from the white cottage he had bought for his family and went down the unpaved walks of the town as vigorously as if he still led a jungle patrol. He became one of the familiar sights of village life as he walked, often with a retired naval commander at his side; the two made terse conversation as they paced along under a pall of smoke from Puller's pipe.

The walking pair seldom made it to the courthouse and back without an interruption.

The isolated village is on the south bank of the Rappahannock, about an hour east of Richmond, but the house was on U. S. Highway 17 and it seemed to Mrs. Puller that the Marine Corps, past and present, used the road like migratory bird flocks.

Old Marines from Puller's past came in a stream that did not dwindle over the next half dozen years—privates, corporals, top sergeants and officers to the rank of general. They often spotted the familiar figure in its erect stride and braked their automobiles, leaping out to shout: "Chesty Puller!" In the midst of their roaring talk the commander excused himself and the Marines lost themselves in Guadalcanal, the hills of Nicaragua, or the Korean frosts. More often than not they ended in the Puller dining room, where Mrs. Puller served oysters fresh from the Rappahannock or Virginia ham and batter bread. Hundreds of these visitors had never before seen Puller in the flesh, but were drawn by the legend.

One afternoon in hunting season Mrs. Puller saw the General and their eleven-year-old son Lewis turn into the drive earlier than usual. The General scrambled from the car as if it were afire and dashed for the door like a boy. He flung open the door, shouting:

"Lewis got a deer. His first deer! Going to be a great shot!"

"I declare, Lewis, you're more excited right now than when you got the fifth Navy Cross."

"Virginia, do you understand? It's not every day that an eleven-year-old boy kills a deer. I'll bet Daniel Boone wasn't much younger."

Virginia Mac made her debut at a famous nearby resort hotel on the Rappahannock, Tides Inn, and Puller took her on his arm down the stairs as she was presented to Tidewater Virginia society. On one Marine base a newspaper photograph went on a bulletin board with the caption: "Beauty & The Beast."

He read scores of new military books as they appeared, especially those on World War II or Korea or the American Civil War, but he was not quite always the soldier. He more than once told his wife: "If I had my life to live over, I'd like to be an engineer, and get a chance to build something, rather than having to wreck things."

She reassured him: "Don't forget that you've been defending the country most of your life, dear, so that building could go on."

Much correspondence went unanswered, including invitations to appear on radio and television, and to make public speeches. There was one from Nebraska State Teachers College, which sought him as commencement speaker.

Puller's reaction to paper work was what it had been on fighting fronts: "Hell, I had the world's best filing system. Like U. S. Grant. One pocket for In and one pocket for Out. Couldn't beat it. Never kept any papers, and never missed 'em."

Dozens of photographs of the General were sent for his autograph and even these often waited many months for signature and mailing. A typical one came from Captain Alfred Croft, Jr., a Marine who served briefly under Puller in his last command, but never knew him personally:

Like all Marines who love their Corps and revere its highest traditions, I have long respected and admired you. . . .

As a company commander in your division, I once did something for a man about which a Warrant Officer later said, "Captain, that's just the sort of thing General Puller would have done." I have always considered that sentence the highest compliment I have ever received as a Marine officer.

The enclosed photograph is habitually displayed in our home. I send it to you, along with a return envelope, in the hope that you will do me the great honor of signing it as a memento of the greatest Marine of our age.

We miss you, General. Your name is invariably mentioned during every conversation in which the finest traditions of the Marine Corps are discussed. I know that the entire Corps joins me in the hope that your spirit will continue to permeate our ranks and that God will continue to bless you, Mrs. Puller and your entire family.

There were echoes of the General's troubles with the Corps command and its doctors, for many of his old men and officers continued the fight for him even when it had become hopeless. From his law office in North Carolina James Hayes, once a captain on Guadalcanal, sent the First Marine Division Association a resolution, its *whereases* made eloquent by his wartime memories. The document cited Puller's career, his value to the service and his fifty-three decorations, and ended:

It is believed that his loss would be felt by Marines on active duty and Marines of civilian status throughout this nation to a degree not justifiable by any administrative or medical consideration;

Now, therefore, be it resolved that the Directors of the First Marine Division Association be recorded as respectfully petitioning the U. S. Marine Corps to do for this great hero as has been done for other great heroes of the past, to retain General Puller on active duty for an indefinite period of time.

It went for naught. The Association declared itself neutral in this "political issue" and the resolution failed of adoption.

Active duty of another sort was not far away.

On the dimly moonlit night of April 8, 1956, a platoon of Marine recruits at Parris Island, South Carolina, was marched into a tidal arm of Broad River by a thirty-one-year-old veteran drill instructor, Staff Sergeant Matthew C. McKeon. Six recruits drowned. The Commandant, General Randolph McCall Pate, immediately relieved the commanding officer of the recruit depot and told Congress that McKeon would be punished "to the full extent allowed by our Uniform Code of Military Justice." There was a nationwide outcry from the press, pulpit and scores of civic organizations.

Matthew McKeon came from Worcester, Massachusetts, one child of a large Catholic family. In the Navy in World War II he had served on the redoubtable carrier *Essex*, and as a Marine, for fourteen months in the Korean war. He was the father of two children and his wife expected a third within a few weeks. He was strong, trim, alert, with a good record and marks of "outstanding"; his intelligence was high and there was no trace of emotional disturbance. Survivors of his Platoon 71 said that he was patient through the process of training.

On the day of the tragedy McKeon had a few drinks of vodka, no one knew just how many—three or four, he recalled. Some of his platoon had been "goofing off" and engaging in unsoldierly roughhousing. After two or three such incidents during the day McKeon determined on a night march in the swamps—the same march he had been taken on in his own recruit days. The platoon's bad morale, its "bad habits" and inability to shoot would reflect on his record.

After dark, in a jocular, singing mood, the column of seventy-five recruits followed McKeon to the marshes. There was a good deal of catcalling from the ranks as McKeon led them once across the channel known as Ribbon Creek, slogging onto higher ground of a marsh, then back again.

Just before they entered the stream McKeon called to his men: "Anyone who can't swim is going to drown. Those who can swim will be eaten by the sharks."

The sergeant playfully touched one of the first waders under water with a stick and shouted: "Shark!"

The sergeant did not order the file into the creek, but merely plunged in; the men followed. On the second crossing there were cries for help in the rear, where the shorter men marched. McKeon swam back to help and dragged one man to safety. As he passed the group on a second trip one of the Negroes in the platoon jumped on his back in panic, seizing him by the neck; the two went down together, and

McKeon fought off his assailant. He did not see him again.

At this moment the tide in Ribbon Creek was at its peak, over seven feet deep at this crossing.

McKeon led the survivors toward the main camp to count heads, but before they had moved a hundred yards an officer arrived. McKeon was put under arrest.

General Pate not only promised Congress that "justice" would be done. In the next weeks he issued a bewildering salvo of statements, defending Marine Corps discipline in one breath and attacking it in the next. A court of inquiry descended upon Parris Island. McKeon became a national *cause célèbre*, assailed by prohibitionists as a brutal drunkard, as a symbol of a military tyranny which must be destroyed, as a racist, bigot and ne'er-do-well. There were cries for harsh punishment—even for execution.

In the heat of July, after long delays, the public phase of the drama unfolded with a court-martial whose unchallenged ringmaster was a flamboyant New York attorney, Emile Zola Berman. This tiny, thin-voiced "lawyer's lawyer" had been trained in the labyrinth of New York City's courts, with time out for World War II service in Air Force intelligence. He had taken the case for no fee, declaring that, like Zola, he must see justice done—not only to Matthew McKeon, but to the Marine Corps as well. The nation's security might rest on the integrity of its system of discipline.

There was no doubt that McKeon's brother-in-law, the New York lawyer, Thomas P. Costello, enlisted Berman's aid; it seemed that no lesser skill could save Matt McKeon.

Berman opened with a shrewd double-edged statement to the press: "I thought the Marine Corps was using this boy to cover its own responsibility."

The next move, as yet secret, was to call General Puller from retirement.

The first call came from Costello in New York:

"General, McKeon needs help that only you can give. Are you willing to testify for him?"

"I don't know McKeon, but he's not what interests me. If what I read in the papers is true, it's the Marine Corps that needs help. I'll do anything I can for the Corps. What is it you want?"

"We want you to talk about Marine training and tradition—that's all. Nothing about McKeon. They know your record and what you stand for. You can work out the details with Berman."

"All right. If the Secretary of the Navy orders me to active duty to testify, I'll do it. I don't see how I can refuse."

Mrs. Puller protested: "Lewis, for heaven's sake, stay out of this mess. We've had so much trouble and controversy in our career. Can't we have a little peace for a change?"

"Dear, I'm not picking a fight. I don't give a damn about the Drill Instructor himself. The important thing is the Marine Corps. If we let 'em, they'll tear it to pieces. Headquarters won't speak up. It's my duty to do it."

Marines had been writing Puller from many parts of the country since the opening of the case. Hank Adams, his Guadalcanal companion, had called from California to express concern for the future of the Corps. "They're going to give us the works over the loss of these six unfortunate boys," he said, "but I notice the Air Force has killed a hundred and sixteen men in the past month, from published notes of crashes, and not one word has been said in protest."

The courtroom was the auditorium of the depot schoolhouse, where the temperature was 104 degrees. It was August 2, the thirteenth day of the McKeon trial. Berman and his adversary, Major Charles B. Sevier, had sifted through every detail of the case. A parade of witnesses had been heard. The defendant himself had spent many hours on the stand. The Corps's training routine had been probed until it seemed that there was nothing to be added. Fifty or more reporters had filed their reams of copy. Public opinion was still firmly against McKeon and the Parris Island system, though the evidence had been inconclusive to this point. The sergeant was likely to pay dearly.

The Commandant, General Pate, had already appeared. He had been urbane and witty, tossing off jokes with Berman —but had skirted the point at issue. When asked his opinion of McKeon's guilt he had reversed his earlier stand in halting terms:

> There's no final say as to what an individual would do under all circumstances. . . . It's evident this drill sergeant did drink some vodka and I assume that it was against the regulations—the conditions under which he did it. I don't

know. I think maybe I would take a stripe away from him for a thing like that. It's a fairly serious thing. . . .

As to the remaining part of it—it's a little fuzzy and hazy to me just what transpired. But I suspect I would probably have transferred him away for stupidity. . . . I would probably have written in his Service Record Book that under no conditions would this sergeant ever drill recruits again. I think I would let it go at that. That's not a final answer, I know.

Nobody in the crowded courtroom failed to sense the difference when Puller appeared. The New York *Times* chronicled his entrance:

> A living legend came back to Parris Island today. He is Lieutenant General Lewis B. (Chesty) Puller, retired, the most decorated and revered of living Marines. . . .
>
> The appearance of the stubby, tenacious man with the face of an English bulldog and the chest of a pouter pigeon brought the largest crowd yet to the schoolhouse. . . .
>
> Ramrod-straight, his uniform blouse ablaze with ribbons, the general sat in the witness chair and testified in a drill-field voice.

Berman used the General like a master showman:

"The defense desires to call to the stand Lieutenant General Puller."

Colonel E. L. Hutchinson, the court president, called solemnly: "The court will please rise." As the crowd got to its feet General Puller approached the witness stand. Berman gave him a dignified introduction to the law officer and each of the members of the court. Puller sat down.

"Now," he said, "if I don't talk loud, somebody back there sound off and I'll talk louder." He began a testimony of fifty minutes:

Sevier: Sir, do you know the accused?

Puller: No, I don't know him except by his pictures in the newspapers and what I've read about him.

Berman took over and questioned the General about his career as a Marine.

Berman: How long were you in Korea?

A: About nine months.

Q: Were you in combat?

A: Yeah.

Q: Were you decorated?

A: Yeah.

Q: Without going into your other decorations, isn't it true that you have received five Navy Crosses?

A: Correct. (Berman asked Puller to point out the decoration.)

Berman asked his opinion of the Marine Corps's mission.

A: The definition of military training is success in battle. In my opinion that is the only objective of military training. It wouldn't make any sense to have a military organization on the backs of the American taxpayers with any other definition. I've believed that ever since I've been a Marine.

Q: What is the most important element of that training?

A: I'll quote Napoleon. He stated that the most important thing in military training is discipline. Without discipline an army becomes a mob.

Q: Now, then, in that context, can you tell us whether you have an opinion, based again on your experience, as to whether or not the training in discipline is for all situations confined to lesson plans, or syllabi or training regulations?

A: No. The training of a basic Marine is conducted almost entirely outside—in the field, on the drill ground, on the rifle range—that kind of work. The Marine gets an idea of how the Marine Corps is run during this training, but his training is outside work.

Q: Can you tell us, General, of the things you learned here as a recruit?

A: Well, the main thing—that I have remembered all my life—is the definition of *esprit de corps*. Now my definition —the definition I was taught, that I've always believed in —is that *esprit de corps* means love for one's military legion, in my case the United States Marine Corps. I also learned that this loyalty to one's Corps travels both ways, up and down.

Q: Now, General, I want you to assume that what is the evidence in this case is a fact. That on a Sunday evening a drill instructor took a platoon that was undisciplined and lacked spirit and on whom he'd tried other methods of discipline. And that for purposes of teaching discipline and instilling morale he took that platoon into a marsh or creek —all the way in front of his troops—would you consider that oppression?

A: In my opinion it is not.

Q: Can you state an opinion as to whether leading troops is a good practice?

A: Any kind of commander or leader is not worth his salt if he does not lead his troops under all conditions.

Berman reviewed the story of the tragic march into the creek and asked Puller a longer question on the same point.

A: In my opinion the reason American troops made out so poorly in the Korean war was mostly due to lack of night training. And if we are going to win the next war I say that from now on fifty percent of the training should be devoted to night training.

Q: So, in your opinion, was this act of this drill instructor in leading his troops, under those conditions and for that purpose, good or bad military practice?

A: Good.

Sevier took over for cross-examination:

Q: It takes some training for the leader in night work?

A: Well, we take it for granted that when a leader has been made a leader by higher headquarters the man is qualified.

Q: And if you were taking untrained troops into a hazardous situation, would you make some reconnaissance or take some precautions for their safety?

A: Oh, yes. I would take safety precautions.

Q: Do you believe that night training should be the initial training that any raw recruit should receive?

A: Well, the trouble is that not enough night training is prescribed. . . . And I know that in anything that I have ever commanded I got most of the glory and I got all of the blame. I have willingly taken the blame. I would train my troops as I thought—as I knew they should be trained —regardless of a directive.

Q: . . . I lead these recruits into waters over their heads and I lose six of those men by drowning. Would you say that some action should be taken against me?

A: I would say that this night march was and is a deplorable accident.

Q: Would you take any action against me if I were the one who did that, if you were my Commanding Officer, sir?

A: Since I have been retired there was an accident similar to this down off the Florida Keys. It concerned the American Army. A soldier, acting as coxswain of a landing craft, took his landing craft around and outside the breakwater. The landing craft filled and sank. Seventeen soldiers were drowned. It hardly made the newspapers. As far as I know, there was no Court of Inquiry. As far as I know there was no court-martial—or any kind of disciplinary action. I think, from what I read in the papers yesterday of the testimony of General Pate before this court, that he agrees and regrets that this man was ever ordered tried by general court-martial.

Puller was excused. Court recessed for half an hour—and when he returned, Berman astounded the prosecution by resting his case, though thirty-three defense witnesses stood by. He also added a final touch:

"Mr. President and Mr. Law Officer: I have never seen a Marine Corps review. I understand that General Puller will conduct a review tomorrow at eight-thirty. I should hate to leave here and not have seen a review."

"Very well," Colonel Hutchinson said. "We will adjourn until nine-thirty tomorrow morning."

Puller went into the noncoms' club that night with Berman, two Marine generals and other officers; the big crowd stood, shouting until he spoke:

"I've talked enough for today. This will be my last request. Do your duty and the Marine Corps will be as great as it has always been for another thousand years." The applause was deafening.

After the next morning's review Puller left for Virginia. Behind him Berman and Sevier went through long final arguments, but it was all over. Puller had turned the tide, inside the courtroom and out. McKeon was acquitted on charges of manslaughter and oppression of troops; he was found guilty of negligent homicide and drinking. His first sentence was stiff enough: a bad-conduct discharge, nine months at hard labor with the rank of private and a $270 fine. Later, when it was reviewed, the sentence was lightened and McKeon served but a few weeks.

For weeks there were telegrams and letters that came to Puller by the hundred, almost all of them praising his testimony.

Lieutenant General Edward M. Almond, the Korean Corps Commander, now retired, telegraphed from Alabama:

> Your testimony was magnificent. Discipline is indispensable.
> Are you thawed out after Koto-ri?

From Oregon his old Parris Island mate, H. W. Shoemaker, broke a silence of more than a generation to wire:

Congratulations on . . . your defense of Marine training methods. Keep up the good work. Your 1918 Parris Island Drill Commander.

His heavy weapons specialist from Guadalcanal and Cape Gloucester, Joe Buckley, wired from Massachusetts:

Having known you for over 30 years I knew you wouldn't let the Marine Corps down.

Most of the messages came from strangers:
From Wellsville, New York:

I am deeply moved by your testimony. You are truly a wonderful man. I am proud of you.

From Philadelphia:

Thank you for affirming for all of us past, present and future the indispensable qualities of a leader, general officer and Marine.

From a recruit at Parris Island:

As long as our country has leaders of nobility and genius such as yours it will stand like Gibraltar, never to fear an enemy outside our borders. The only people we have to fear are the civilians who protest against their sons being treated like men when they go through boot camp. When you stood up for the Corps Marines rejoiced throughout the world that you did not fail them. You will never be forgotten by the men of the Corps.

Puller was not forgotten in Saluda. Big-city newspapers called him in moments of crisis, as when Marines were landed in Lebanon. A graduate student at Indiana University, in a study of brainwashed American troops in Korea, sent Puller a list of more than 100 questions.

The General replied:

"I never studied psychology. I had only one year of college, and always thought I would go back, but enlisted instead. I think the Marine Corps is the best place to learn the art of war. I am therefore not qualified to speak on psychology. But I can tell you this much:

"I commanded the First Marine Regiment in Korea—and not one of my men turned in their suits to the Communists.

So far as I know not a single man of the regiment became a prisoner of war. And if you'll investigate you will find that almost none of the turncoats among American prisoners in Korea were Marines. You will have to look to other services to find those. I say proper training is the answer, and always will be."

Puller was occasionally caught up in the affairs of his community, sometimes with explosive results. He fought one engagement with the Parent-Teacher Association and put it to rout.

Mrs. Puller went regularly to meetings of the Middlesex County P.T.A. group, but Lewis had never been. One evening, at her insistence, he ventured forth to a special occasion.

A panel of local experts dealt with the decline of the nation as expressed in the rising tide of juvenile delinquency. The consensus was that the country was going to hell in a handbucket.

In the end, the experts proposed that the county's parents band together and stage two parties each week, on school nights, since the plight of the younger generation was the fault of parents. Someone then made the tactical error of calling for questions. General Puller stood, and his intended mildness of tone, as usual, came forth in a brazen roar:

"I want you people to know something—as long as we can get some decent leadership in our country, our youth of today will be better men than their fathers or grandfathers. I saw enough in Korea to make me sure of that. Our forefathers at Valley Forge have been mentioned here tonight, as they often are. Well, I can tell you that Valley Forge was something like a picnic compared to what your young Americans went through at the Chosin Reservoir, and they came out of it fine. It never was anything like twenty-five below zero at Valley Forge, either.

"I admit we don't seem to have proper leadership at the top, but there's nothing wrong with kids today. This two parties a week sounds like foolishness to me. My wife and I follow the ideas my mother used on her kids, making them study each night after supper, and when they report that they have mastered their lessons, quizzing them. That's how my brother and I were handled, and the method got my older daughter on the dean's list at Smith College, and my son on the headmaster's list at Christchurch School, and helps my younger daughter make out well in public school, thanks to her mother. I find that a great deal of what I learned in public school came through my mother.

"Our children don't need to be coddled, and they shouldn't be condemned. Above all, for heaven's sake, let your sons alone and let them grow up to be men."

He sat down to an abrupt burst of applause, and when the meeting adjourned many people pressed around to shake hands and clap him on the back. The scheme for biweekly youth parties was abandoned.

Puller's oldest child, Virginia Mac, by now a tall, handsome brunette, was a Smith College sophomore. Even in distant New England she was never far from the facts of her father's fame.

For weeks she had mysterious calls from Columbia University boys she had never met, all seeking dates. The solution came from a classmate after a succession of such calls:

"They all study military tactics at Columbia, and their professor, who's nuts about your father, has promised A's to any of them who can get a date with Chesty Puller's daughter."

On a weekend visit to New Haven, when she arrived at the station with about five minutes to make a fifteen-minute run to Branford College to meet her date, Virginia Mac got a taxi and made a plea for speed. The cab careened down the street. The driver grinned.

"Wildest ride I've been on since Korea," he said. "Out there with the Marines."

"Maybe you know my father. He was a Marine."

"Yeah? Who's that?"

"Lewis Puller."

"My God! You mean Chesty?" She thought he would run off the road, staring at her in the mirror—and then that he would jump into the back seat and embrace her.

"How the hell did Chesty ever have a daughter like you? How you like that—Chesty's little girl! Why, that's the greatest fighting man ever pulled on a boot." He continued his soliloquy to her destination, and when he stopped, carried in the bags over her protest, and would accept no tip, and no fare: "Not on your life. I've been waiting all this time to do a favor for Chesty Puller, and I'm going to do it, whatever you say."

Late one night as Puller smoked at home, listening to

the radio, he heard a broadcast from London—the comment of General Gruenther as he turned over command of NATO forces in Europe to General Norstad. The retiring commander painted a grim future, if America and her allies did not strengthen the force. Puller was startled to hear Gruenther predict that the Russian Army, if it attacked, would reach the Channel ports within ten days.

It was near midnight, but Puller could not sleep. He tuned other stations, hoping for more news, but there was none. He slept little, trying to wait up for the morning newspaper from Richmond—but when his copy was tossed on his porch by the delivery boy, the general found nothing about the NATO story. He concluded that the development had been too late for the newspaper, and that he could read of it in the afternoon. He never found it, and thereafter, when stray Marines stopped by to pay their respects, Puller had new words of warning:

"It looks like somebody's trying to keep the truth from the American people. I never could find a newspaper with Gruenther's warning. I've been reading all I could get my hands on about our forces in Europe. Why, do you realize we have as many dependents over there as we have fighting men—maybe more? Children and wives and grandmothers! What a drain on the American taxpayer that is, and what it must be doing to our state of readiness. You know what my guess is? When the Reds attack, our army in Europe will surrender. We just don't sound ready to me. Couldn't possibly be, under that setup."

Visiting officers found him full of striking opinions on the condition of American defenses:

"I'm afraid we haven't recognized the most important lesson from Korea. The Communists have developed a totally new kind of warfare, a warfare of whole peoples; and under that, no modern nation can be conquered. We saw something like that in China when Japan was nibbling away at the mainland. The Japanese controlled only a square yard where a soldier stood, and nothing beyond. In Korea, the Reds improved on that.

"This is a total warfare, yet small in scope, and it's designed to neutralize our big nuclear weapons. Look at Vietnam. The French outnumbered the Communists two to one, yet they were massacred. If we don't design some way to meet this, they'll whip us in the end. Don't forget that

regular armies have never fared well in irregular warfare
—and that lesson was old when Rome fell.

"Suppose a war comes when both sides lay aside nuclear
weapons out of mutual fear. Are we ready to meet the
Reds in conventional warfare? It looks like we're not, to me.
For one thing, we don't have such a simple thing as a
combat boot for subzero weather. I saw that in Korea—
and that's the one reason I see why we can't fight Russia
on her home grounds.

"One Chief of Staff provides enough red tape, and Joint
Chiefs make strategy and policy that much more of a committee decision. It's hard enough to fight at a long distance
from the high command without putting up with these Joint
Chiefs. Before we can make any sense out of our military
problem we'll have to abandon the Joint Chiefs of Staff.
We lost our only war under them, in Korea. I'm violently
opposed to losing wars, and anyone who has studied the
German history of World War II, with their big staffs trying
to handle troops in distant Russia, will understand.

"Americans had better wake up, fast. It might be possible
to bomb our country into submission, unless we have strong
leaders. How many of us have stopped to analyze Red
China's state of mind, for one thing? She thinks she can
lick us—naturally so, since we surrendered in Korea, when
we didn't use the nuclear weapons we had, and had all our
air power concentrated over a little peninsula without opposition. Of course China thinks she can take us on, and is
positive that Russia could defeat us."

Only Marine visitors heard these comments until one
week in the summer of 1960, when his old friend, General
E. W. Snedeker, finally effected a reconciliation between
Puller and the First Marine Division Association. The Old
Man came out of hiding, and after four years went to a
reunion. It was like old times.

A spotlight from the balcony stabbed through the smoky
ballroom to pick out the figures of generals of the Corps
as they were introduced, one by one.

There was a hum of voices that had not stilled; on two
vast floors more than two thousand Marine combat veterans
and their wives watched the parade at the head table.
Washington's Sheraton-Park Hotel had never seen such a
reunion. All records for bar sales had been broken on the
first day.

"General David Shoup, Commandant of the Corps!"

There was a shout for the soldierly commander, a hero of the Tarawa landing, which for the moment seemed not so long ago.

Two former Commandants rose in turn: Thomas Holcomb and Lemuel Shepherd. The crowd applauded and continued when others stood—the veteran K. E. Rockey, now retired, and Phil Berkeley, commander of the Second Division. The master of ceremonies was himself a famous old Marine, General Julian Smith, as erect in his seventies as in the days of World War I.

Quiet fell on the crowded banquet hall.

General Smith blinked against the spotlight and turned to the blackness at the far end of the table. "I now give you Chesty. . . ."

There was a roar which drowned the speaker's voice and shook the walls. The spotlight swung to the last place at the table to reveal Puller in a linen suit, waving a hand and flashing his broad, crooked grin. As the clamor increased he marched to the microphone in a bobbing circle of light.

General Smith shouted through the tempest of sound: "I see you all know Chesty Puller."

Men in the crowd danced among the tables, whirled each other about, and pounded their neighbors on the backs. Some climbed on chairs, shouting wordlessly, tears streaming on their cheeks. Others hammered the tables with cutlery, or embraced women who were staring incredulously at Puller.

The men broke into chants: "We want Chesty! We want Puller!" They called for a speech, but it was almost five minutes before the howling ceased.

Puller faced them with a wry smile that looked as if it had been wrung from him by force. When quiet returned he grasped the microphone and called in an astonishingly penetrating voice:

"MARINES!"

Pandemonium broke out once more, as if he had shouted some secret watchword whose implications were known only to these men. Half the crowd was still on its feet a moment later when Puller could be heard again:

"If you believe the newspapers and radio and television, our country is in a hell of a shape!

"I don't believe it. So long as we've got the First Marine Division, we'll be okay."

The crowd shouted him into silence again.

"We'll keep 'em all straightened out—including the Russians."

Puller went on to the end of the briefest speech of the evening despite roars which greeted almost every word:

"One of the greatest men I ever heard of was a flat-foot—Commodore Stephen Decatur. And he said, 'My country, may she always be right—but my country, right or wrong.'

"Conduct yourselves accordingly and we won't have a damned thing to fear from anybody."

He marched back to his place so rapidly that the spotlight lost him, and in the revived thunder of applause General Smith shouted once more: "Chesty, you won't have to do it all alone. The Second Division is ready, too."

Few people heard him. The shouts died away, but as the chandeliers glowed overhead and the spotlight disappeared, hundreds pressed toward Puller's end of the table. Within fifteen minutes the other generals and their wives had gone.

For two hours Puller was held in his seat by a queue of men, women and children who sought autographs. They kept him there, scribbling his signature on cards, envelopes, scraps of paper, menus and programs until it seemed impossible that he could go on. Still scores of others waited among the tables, patiently awaiting their turns to climb the steps and bend over the retired general.

Their stories were much alike. Middle-aged men said: "I want this for my boy, sir. I can't go home without it. You're all he ever talks about. I told him what we went through, out there on Cape Gloucester, and how you led us all the way." Puller would write out the boy's name and a brief message.

"General, you don't know me, but I got hit beside you there on Guadalcanal, on the big night at the perimeter." Others spoke of China and Latin American wars and Korea and Peleliu and New Guinea. Puller assured all that he had vivid memories of them, until the line finally came to its end. He was the last of the banquet crowd to leave the ballroom; the orchestra had gone, and waiters had borne away the debris of the dinner.

It was near midnight, June 25, 1960. Within a few minutes he would become sixty-two years old.

He was tired when he got home to Saluda and that evening Virginia Puller found him pensive and distracted. They sat on a screened porch, looking out into the Virginia dusk lit by fireflies.

"Lewis, is there anything you'd wish for, now that it's all over?"

"Well, I'd like to do it all over again. The whole thing." She sighed.

"And more than that—more than anything—I'd like to see once again the face of every Marine I've ever served with."

The decorations of General L. B. Puller:

Navy Cross w/4 stars
Army Distinguished Service Cross
Silver Star
Legion of Merit w/1 star
Bronze Star
Air Medal w/2 stars
Purple Heart
Presidential Unit Citation w/5 stars
Good Conduct Medal w/1 star
World War I Victory Medal w/1 star
Haitian Campaign Medal
Nicaraguan Campaign Medal
Marine Corps Expeditionary Medal w/1 star
China Service Medal
American Defense Medal w/1 star
American Campaign Medal
Asiatic-Pacific Campaign Medal w/4 stars
World War II Victory Medal
National Defense Service Medal
Korean Service Medal w/5 stars
United Nations Service Medal
Haitian Military Medal
Nicaraguan Presidential Medal of Merit w/1 star
Nicaraguan Cross of Valor
Korean Presidential Unit Citation
Korean Ulghi Medal w/1 palm
Chinese Cloud and Banner

BOOKS BEHIND THE LINES:

The side of war you will never read about in the history books

"HITLER'S WAR"

From the German point of view and secret Nazi documents never before revealed to the public, here is the whole gigantic drama of the most crucial days of World War II. Bantam now presents the books that individually capture the major personalities and events of the war.

Bantam Book Catalog

Here's your up-to-the-minute listing of every book currently available from Bantam.

This easy-to-use catalog is divided into categories and contains over 1400 titles by your favorite authors.

So don't delay—take advantage of this special opportunity to increase your reading pleasure.

Just send us your name and address and 25¢ (to help defray postage and handling costs).